The civilian population
and the Warsaw Uprising of 1944

The civilian population and the Warsaw Uprising of 1944

JOANNA K.M. HANSON

CAMBRIDGE UNIVERSITY PRESS

Cambridge

London   New York   New Rochelle
Melbourne   Sydney

Published by the Press Syndicate of the University of Cambridge
The Pitt Building, Trumpington Street, Cambridge CB2 1RP
32 East 57th Street, New York, NY 10022, USA
296 Beaconsfield Parade, Middle Park, Melbourne 3206, Australia

First published 1982

Printed in the United States of America

Library of Congress catalogue card number: 81-15545

British Library cataloguing in publication data

Hanson, Joanna K.M.
The civilian population and the Warsaw Uprising of 1944.
1. Warsaw – History – Uprising of 1944
I. Title
940.53′438′4   D765.2.W3
ISBN 0 521 23421 2

Contents

Illustrations

Tables

For Włodek

Acknowledgements

This book is based on my dissertation prepared for a Doctor of Philosophy degree awarded by the University of London in 1978.

I am extremely grateful to the following persons in Poland for their help and advice in preparing this work: Prof. A. Gieysztor of the University of Warsaw, Prof. C. Madajczyk, Prof. M. Drozdowski, Doc. E. Duraczyński, Dr A. Janowski, Dr T. Strzembosz, Dr T. Szarota, Dr S. Lewandowska of the Institute of History of the Polish Academy of Sciences, Doc. A. Garlicki of the University of Warsaw, Doc. E. Serwański, of the Instytut Zachodni in Poznań, Dr Z. Zawadzka, Doc. M. Turlejska, and the late Col. K. Pluta-Czachowski and Maj. F. Majorkiewicz. My special thanks go to Mr W. Bartoszewski.

Likewise in London the following persons provided me with great help and valuable suggestions: Mrs R. Oppman, MA, of the Gen. Sikorski Historical Institute, and Mrs H. Czarnocka, of the Polish Underground Study Trust, and Dr J. Garliński.

I am especially indebted to Dr J. Ciechanowski and Dr N. Davies not only for their advice but also for their pertinent and scholarly criticism. Above all, however, without the support, encouragement and help received from my husband in many ways, both academic and non-academic, this work would never have gone further than draft stage.

Finally I would like to state that the contents and conclusions contained in this work are purely the responsibility of its author.

J.K.M.H.

Abbreviations

AK	Armia Krajowa (Home Army)
AL	Armia Ludowa (People's Army). The Polish Communist underground army founded on 1 January 1944 and responsible to the KRN
B.Ch.	Bataliony Chłopskie (Peasant Battalions). Underground military organisation formed by SL
BIP	Biuro Informacji i Propagandy (Information and Propaganda Bureau)
GRP	Główna Rada Polityczna (Chief Political Council)
KRM	Krajowa Rada Ministrów (National Council of Ministers)
KRN	Krajowa Rada Narodowa (National Council of Poland)
KRP	Krajowa Reprezentacja Polityczna (National Political Representation)
KWC	Kierownictwo Walki Cywilnej (Directorate of Civilian Resistance)
KWP	Kierownictwo Walki Podziemnej (Directorate of Underground Struggle)
OPL	Obrona Przeciwlotnicza (Anti Air Attack Defence)
PAL	Polska Armia Ludowa (Polish People's Army)
PCK	Polski Czerwony Krzyż (Polish Red Cross)
PKB	Państwowy Korpus Bezpieczeństwa (State Security Corps)
PKO	Polski Komitet Opiekuńczy (Polish Committee for Social Care)
PKP	Polityczny Komitet Porozumiewawczy (Political Advisory Committee)
PKWN	Polski Komitet Wyzwolenia Narodowego (Polish Committee of National Liberation)
PPR	Polska Partia Robotnicza (Polish Workers Party)
PPS	Polska Partia Socjalistyczna (Polish Socialist Party)
PWPW	Państwowa Wytwórnia Papierów Wartościowych (mint)
RGO	Rada Główna Opiekuńcza (Main Council for Social Care)

ROM	Rada Opiekuńcza Miejska (Municipal Council for Social Care)
RJN	Rada Jedności Narodowej (Council of National Unity)
SL	Stronnictwo Ludowe (Peasant Party)
SN	Stronnictwo Narodowe (National Democrats)
SP	Stronnictwo Pracy (Labour Party)
SKSS	Stołeczny Komitet Samopomocy Społecznej (Warsaw Committee for Social Care)
SZP	Służba Zwycięstwu Polski (Victory for Poland Service)
WSM	Warszawska Spółdzielnia Mieszkaniowa (Warsaw Housing Co-operative)
WSS	Wojskowy Sąd Specjalny (Special Military Court)
WSS	Wojskowa Służba Społeczna (Military Community Service)
ZPP	Związek Patriotów Polskich (Union of Polish Patriots)
ZWZ	Związek Walki Zbrojnej (Union of Armed Struggle)

Introduction

> Today a battle is going on in Warsaw that I think is very difficult for the British nation to understand. It is a battle that is being carried on as much by the civilian population as by the AK . . . It is total warfare. Every street in the city has been a battlefield for the last twenty four days. The enemy mine-throwers, artillery and aircraft are taking a heavy toll of human life. The damage to property is incalculable. Normal life in the city is of course at a complete standstill . . .[1]

The statement above was written by a British airman, John Ward, who acted as the *Times* correspondent in Warsaw during the Uprising. But reports such as this increased the difficulty which the British had in understanding the situation in the city, and this misunderstanding as to the nature of the Warsaw Uprising has continued ever since. Ward was right in saying, 'It is a battle that is being carried on as much by the civilian population as by the AK . . . It is total warfare', but in spite of this every street was not a battlefield nor was 'normal life' in the town at a complete standstill.

It is too easy to consider any battle to be a purely military affair. Furthermore, when a battle involving heavy bombardment and street fighting is taking place in a confined urban area, e.g. the Warsaw Uprising, the Battle of Stalingrad, or the siege of the Palestinian refugee camp Tel-el-Zaatar, it is hard to imagine that any kind of life, other than sheltering from the fighting, can exist. But when a battle goes on for over two months, as it did in Warsaw in 1944, some kind of life and organisation has to evolve. The Warsaw Uprising was not, from the civilian population's point of view, just a question of sitting in cellars and shelters, sheltering from bombs and attack, not just a long trail of crimes committed against the civilian population.

The Second World War was total war on the largest scale ever experienced in the history of mankind. It is probably true to say that the situation that existed in Warsaw during the Uprising was without precedence. The city cut off from the rest of the country and the world fought the German Army in a lone and desperate fight. Streets and houses formed front lines and battlefields. Warsaw's inhabitants suddenly had to adapt themselves to life in an insurgent city. The Uprising, which was supposed to last at the most seven days, lasted nine times that long. It is the aim of this work to show the type of life which evolved in these conditions, the organisation of insurgent Warsaw, how morale and public opinion developed and crystallised during those two months and what long term effects the experiences of the Uprising had on the Varsovians. Furthermore it is intended to demonstrate how the attitudes and presence of the civilian population during the Uprising gave the battle a specific character apart from its military one.

Although a great deal has been published on the Warsaw Uprising, no special study has been made of the civilian population during it. Most attention has been paid to the military aspects[2] and to the political problems,[3] as well as to the problem of the German treatment of the Poles. Two collections of documents have been published with valuable information on the civilian population,[4] but no attempt has yet been made to try and analyse this information. Thus, there is a gap in the historiography of the Uprising.[5]

This study does not deal with every district of insurgent Warsaw but only with the larger ones, which give as full a picture as possible. It only discusses areas held by the insurgents and not those parts of Warsaw controlled by the Germans or right bank Warsaw. It is an attempt to see the Uprising as it was seen by the civilian population, and is not a study of the political and military problems of the time. These are only mentioned where their explanation is necessary for a further understanding of the text. It is impossible to understand the reaction of the civilians to the Uprising without a considerable understanding of the preceding years of German occupation. It is for this reason that an extensive chapter has been devoted exclusively to that period as it forms an indispensable part of the whole work.

The topic is not an easy one to study, as many documents were destroyed or lost during the Uprising and other archival sources held in Poland are not always available for research. The archives in Poland hold a considerable number of memoirs, protocols and eyewitness reports. These have mostly been written over the last thirty years, only a very small percentage of them actually being written during or immediately after the Uprising. Not all are accessible to researchers, and original documents held in these archives are rarely obtainable. Collections of newspapers published during the Uprising are available. The present author was able to read certain selected files of the papers of the Delegatura Rządu (Government Delegacy) in Warsaw. A few important documents have been published, and other unpublished materials, especially military reports, were made available from private collections. Other details were filled in from documents held in the Polish archives in London. There are few German documents dealing with the civilian population.

Thus it has not always been easy to collect materials for this study nor is it always possible to double check certain facts. Problems created by the availability of materials are further aggravated by the emotive nature of the subject. The experience of the Uprising was for most of the survivors a very vivid and poignant one. For this reason contemporary memoirs, written or oral, must be treated with great caution.

The nature of the Uprising itself presents a further obstacle. It is often difficult to talk about the general morale and attitude of the civilian population, because Warsaw did not fight as a total unit but as isolated districts cut off from each other, where various and varying factors were influential in creating different and conflicting results. Two adjacent houses in the same street could be representative of totally different attitudes. An example of this can be seen in the following situation on ul. Śniadeckich 8 and Nowogrodzka 47/49 on 5 September 1944. There were one hundred and fifty people living in the first house, the majority of whom had lost their homes in the bombing and fires. There was very little food, even the RGO (Main Council for Social Care) having ceased to issue meals, and the inhabitants received no lunch and only a little soup for breakfast and coffee for supper. There was no bread. But in the other house there were only sixty people and food was in such abundance that they did not bother to pick up their sugar rations.[6] The difference in morale in those two houses is not difficult to imagine. Thus it will be necessary to distinguish factors influencing the short term as well as the long term morale.

The 'civilian population' as understood in this study excludes not only those people who were in the Army or attached to it, but also government agents. The latter had an official role to play and therefore cannot be considered as being necessarily representative of public opinion at the time. Members of the BIP (Information and Propaganda Bureau) and WSS (Military Community Service) patrols are likewise excluded, as it was their task to influence the morale of the population in a definite way. The 'civilian population' was the very large group of Varsovians who were caught up in the events of the Uprising, having had no influence on its creation.

I

Warsaw during the Nazi occupation: October 1939 – July 1944

Kiedyś była piękna, bogata, wspaniała,
Teraz tylko kupa gruzów pozostała.
Szpitale zburzone, domy popalone,
Gdzie się mają schronić ludzie poranione.

Lecą bomby z nieba, brak jest ludziom chleba.
Nie tylko od bomby – umrzeć z głodu trzeba.
Gdy biedna Warszawa w gruzach pozostała,
To biedna Warszawa poddać się musiała.

I tak się broniła całe trzy tygodnie,
Jeszcze Pan Bóg na was pomści taką zbrodnię.
Posłuchajcie, ludzie, z nami łaska Boża,
Odbudujem Polskę od morza do morza.[1]

These verses from a song written during the first year of the occupation illustrate the tragic fate that befell Warsaw in September 1939. A bitter comparison is drawn between the former beauty of the capital and its subsequent destruction. Yet in the last line hope is shown that a new Poland will be built. Similar destruction and human suffering on a far greater scale was borne by Warsaw five years later, when the city rose to fight for her independence and the rebuilding of Poland. The fight was to end in defeat and once again Warsaw was forced to capitulate.

In those five years between the siege of Warsaw and the Uprising the whole face, fortune and life of the city and her inhabitants were to undergo total and irreversible changes. The five years of Nazi occupation formed the decisive background to the attitude and behaviour of the inhabitants of Warsaw during the Uprising of August and September 1944.

1.1 The character of Warsaw
and its appearance during the occupation

Pre-war Warsaw was, like all European capitals of the time, a city of great contrasts. The centre of the town around Marszałkowska, al. Jerozolimskie, Nowy Świat and al. Ujazdowskie was elegant, smart and beautiful. Newer districts had evolved outside the city centre and beyond them poorer and shabby districts, whose inhabitants might be living in shacks and wooden houses. The centre of Warsaw was green and intersected with tree lined avenues. The Łazienkowski Park provided calm and beauty for those who had time to stroll, and the central streets were full of fashionable restaurants and cafés, elegant and well dressed crowds, and cars. The cobbled and muddy streets of the suburbs knew no such elegance and along them carts and not cars were driven. The two worlds tended to live apart.

The German Army attacked Poland on 1 September 1939, and on the same day the first bombs fell on Warsaw. The destruction of old Warsaw had started. In a state of siege, the capital held out until 27 September, and its lone struggle, its determination to fight on to the bitter end, united the community in a way which was to be strengthened during the occupation.

The figures given for those killed or injured vary. Drozdowski and Zahorski, put the numbers at 25,000 dead and 20,000 injured.[2] Bartoszewski puts the figure as high as 60,000 killed and injured,[3] whilst Barbara Krajewska puts the number of dead civilians at approximately 15,000.[4] The official figures of the Government Delegate were 40,000 killed during the bombing, including those who were injured or sick and died as a result.[5]

There is also variation in the estimates of the extent of the destruction of Warsaw. Drozdowski and Zahorski write that 10.6% of the buildings were destroyed.[6] Bartoszewski puts forward the figure of 12%.[7] The official figures of the Government Delegate were as follows:[8]

95% of houses damaged by bombs or fire
25% of those unable to be rebuilt or repaired
c. 35% heavily damaged
c. 35% lightly damaged

The German figures quoted were:[9]

10.6% of buildings fully destroyed
41% partly destroyed or heavily damaged
30% suffered damage

Many of the buildings which were destroyed were not repaired but were left by the Germans as a constant reminder to the Polish population of their defeat.[10]

On 28 September the newspaper *Kurier Warszawski* (*Warsaw Courier*) described the destruction of Warsaw as follows:

The damage in Warsaw is colossal. Electricity, plumbing, filters and telephones are out of operation.

All the hospitals have been bombed, and it has been necessary to put many of the injured into field hospitals. None of the permanent hospitals have been left unscathed. The whole of the town centre was damaged during the artillery bombardment on Sunday, and especially as a result of the Monday air-attack.

There is not one historical building or monument which is not totally or seriously damaged. Whole streets have ceased to exist – Nowy Świat and ul. Świętokrzyska. The Castle is totally destroyed, as is the Cathedral of St John, the Church of Bernardynów, the Resursa Obywatelska, the Philharmonia, the Raczyński Palace, the Agricultural and Industrial Museum, Tow [arzystwo] Kred [ytowe] Ziemskie [Society of Landed Credit], the Grand Theatre, Kronenberg Palace, the Ministry of Internal Affairs and many more historical places and houses. The Town Hall, the Ministry of Foreign Affairs, the building of the Chief-of-Staff, the National Museum, and many others have been severely damaged.[11]

As a result of the destruction of Warsaw during and after the Uprising (between August 1944 and January 1945), the extent of its destruction in September 1939 is often forgotten. Later on in the war further damage was also inflicted as a result of Soviet air-raids.[12] The liquidation of the Ghetto brought about the destruction of a further 15% of the living accommodation in the town.[13]

On 1 October 1939 the German Army crossed into Warsaw and the five years of occupation began. Signs of change in the life of the capital were daily apparent in the streets, which soon began to take on a very different appearance to that of pre-war days. The streets were more crowded as a result of the influx of large numbers of people. Carts, bicycles and specially improvised rickshaws became far more commonplace than cars. More cafés were opened as they provided a means of earning a living. Poverty and misery were to be seen everywhere. Most pitiful was the sight of ragged and orphaned children, begging and scavenging in the streets. There was an increase in street trading as everyone tried to earn a living, often by selling their own books, clothes and furniture.

Jozef Retinger, an emissary of Premier Mikołajczyk, wrote after his visit to Warsaw in 1944: 'the aspect of the city amazed me; it had changed so much. The inner courtyards of all the bigger houses and buildings have been turned into vegetable gardens. The grass strips down the centre of the broad avenues have been dug up and made into allotments ... vegetables were everywhere.'[14]

Meanwhile the Nazi authorities were trying to turn Warsaw as far as possible into a German city. Buildings and street names were decorated with German flags and banners, usually carrying a swastika. Polish street names were either totally changed, e.g. al. Niepodległości to Nordsudallee, Most Poniatowski to Neue Brücke, or they were simply translated from Polish into German, e.g. ul. Marszałkowska to Marschallstrasse, and ul. Królewska to Königstrasse.[15] German posters were put up all around the town; they usually carried anti-British, anti-Polish, anti-Jewish and, after June 1941, anti-Soviet slogans, or were aimed at recruiting Poles to go and work for the Third Reich.[16] They were often countered by Polish posters or writings on walls or pavements, work carried out by the Polish Underground.[17] There were continual German patrols by police and gendarmes, the Gestapo and SS. German soldiers were an everyday sight. The capital was for them a transit point, a place to spend leave and a garrison town.[18]

The greatest change in the appearance of Warsaw was brought about by the creation of the Ghetto. The building of it was started at the beginning of April 1940[19] and by November of the same year it was complete.[20] The area of the Ghetto was surrounded by a high wall cutting it off from the rest of the city. The Jews were crowded into the enclosed streets, where they lived in indescribable conditions. Hunger and disease took an ever increasing toll on the lives of the Ghetto inhabitants. The life of the Ghetto ended after the final extinction or transportation of over 400,000 of its inhabitants and the Ghetto Uprising of April 1943. All that was left afterwards was ruins and ashes.

Each of these features of life under German occupation illustrate various aspects of German policy towards the Poles, and the results thereof. They were everyday reminders for the Varsovians of their plight, reminders which sowed the seeds of hate and revenge. Before discussing various German policies in occupied Warsaw and their results, it is necessary to say something about the demography and social structure of the city.

1.2 The population of Warsaw
and its changes during the occupation

A serious study of demographic changes in Warsaw during the occupation is not easy. Figures are not complete, and it is not always possible to establish how they were collected and compiled, or what category of person is represented. The problem is additionally complicated by false papers and registrations, double registrations or failure to register. Here the intention is only to give an outline of the changes.

According to the pre-war figure of the Zarząd Miejski (Municipal Government) the population of Warsaw on 1 August 1939 was 1,407,800, including 380,600 Jews.[21] As a result of the siege of Warsaw this figure fell to 1,250,000 by the end of October.[22] After November numbers began to rise again.

There are three factors which contributed to this rise in population. Firstly, at the beginning of the war there was an inflow of people from the southern and western battle areas. Some of those people stayed in Warsaw and others moved on further east. Prof. Madajczyk quotes 30,000–40,000 leaving for the Soviet Union.[23] Secondly, in September a certain number of Warsaw's inhabitants had either left the capital in search of safer areas or had been part of the evacuation of the government and central authorities. Some of these people returned in October. Thirdly, Poles and Jews forced to flee Polish territories incorporated into the Third Reich as a result of Himmler's order of 30 October 1939 swelled the population of Warsaw. This last factor resulted in an influx of about 40,000 people.[24]

German figures published at the time in the German press put the number on 1 June 1940 at 1,306,950 inhabitants.[25] Rada Główna Opiekuńcza (RGO: Main Council for Social Care) quoted similar figures, which were broken down as follows:[26]

Poles	895,000
Jews	393,500
Reichsdeutsch	2,500
Volksdeutsch	5,500
Ukrainians	5,000
Others	5,000

The opening of the Ghetto in November 1940 brought a new influx of people into the capital. By January 1941, there were 410,000 Jews in the Ghetto and two months later this figure was to reach a peak of 460,000. By October 1942, the number had fallen to 60,000,[27] as a result of the systematic transportation of Jews to concentration and extermination camps, death from disease and hunger and the German reign of terror. After the liquidation of the Ghetto and the Ghetto Uprising of April 1943 several thousand Jews were housed in the labour camp situated in the former Ghetto. By the end of 1942 there were 20,000 Jews hiding outside the Ghetto in Warsaw.[28]

At the end of 1943, the population of Warsaw according to German figures was as follows:[29]

Poles	921,000
Reichsdeutsch	16,078
Volksdeutsch	14,682
Others	2,600
TOTAL	954,360

There are no reliable figures for July 1944. According to the Polski Komitet Opiekuńczy (PKO: Polish Committee for Social Care) the number was 1,100,000 but, as Dr Szarota has said, it is impossible that this number should include just Poles.[30]

It is known that between January and July 1944 at least 5,500 Poles were killed in street executions or by other means.[31] Between February 1944 and the outbreak of the Uprising 5,500 Poles were transported from Warsaw.[32] There was a slight influx of people coming in as a result of the Russian Front approaching from the east, and some people had left the city in order to avoid any conflict that might take place or were away for their summer holidays. But these figures were not large and probably cancel each other out. The number of Poles in Warsaw at the beginning of August 1944 cannot have been much higher than 910,000.

It is difficult to assess how many Poles were living on the Right Bank of Warsaw on 31 July 1944 in the districts of Praga, Saska Kępa, Grochów, Golędzinów, Targówek and Bródno. In 1939 there were about a quarter of a million people living in this part of the city.[33] In May 1940 the number was 196,922.[34] Madajczyk quotes a figure of 140,000 persons living on the Right Bank in January 1945.[35]

The continual fall in the number of inhabitants of Warsaw was due to Nazi racial policy, which resulted in the deaths of between 35,000 and 40,000 Varsovians, who were killed in Warsaw and its environs between November 1939 and July 1944.[36] Others were transported to concentration or labour camps. Living conditions under the occupation forced up the death rate, with people dying from hunger and disease. At the same time the birth rate was falling.[37]

Table 1. *Social structure of Warsaw in 1931*

Social groups	General population	Christians	Jews
All social groups (thousands)	1,172	819	353
All social groups (per cent)	100.0	100.0	100.0
Self employed	25.8	15.9	50.2
bourgeoisie	3.8	2.6	6.5
free professions	1.1	0.7	2.0
lower middle class	20.9	12.6	41.7
White collar workers	16.0	18.3	10.7
Workers	52.3	59.2	35.0
Unspecified groups	5.9	6.6	4.1

1.3 The social structure of the population of Warsaw

Interwar Warsaw was, in spite of being the governmental, financial and cultural centre of Poland, predominantly a working class town. In 1921 the number of workers was 192,900 (i.e. 46.7% of the working population) and in 1938 it was 340,000 (i.e. 53%).[38] By the outbreak of war the lower middle classes (artisans and shopkeepers) made up approximately 25% of the population and white collar workers approximately 16%.[39] The remaining 6% of the population was mainly middle class. Table 1 illustrates more clearly the social structure of the working population of the capital before the war.[40]

In 1939 one and two room flats were the most common type of accommodation, accounting for 67%. Homes with four rooms or more accounted for hardly 16% of the total. According to an analysis in 1931, and the situation is not supposed to have changed to any great extent by 1939, the average number of people living in these homes can be broken down as follows: in a one room flat four people per room; in a two room flat 2.3; in a three room flat 1.7.[41]

A closer but undetailed analysis can be made of each district. The divisions are somewhat arbitrary and are intended to correspond to those which evolved as a result of the fighting during the Uprising. It is interesting to see if during the Uprising the social structure of these districts was reflected in differing morale and attitudes. Due to the fact that the Uprising on the Right Bank fell almost as soon as it started, no analysis of the population there need be made.

The peripheral districts of the city, Wola, Powązki, and Koło, were predominantly working class, with nearly 67% of the inhabitants in this category. The rest was made up mainly of the self employed – lower middle classes, accounting for about 24% of the population.[42] These were very poor areas of Warsaw, and Wola had not long held municipal status.[43] Many of the houses were made of wood and some streets were still unpaved.

Żoliborz expanded considerably in the interwar years and grew into a pleasant suburb of the city. Houses and villas were specially built for officers and civil servants. In 1927 the Warszawska Spółd-zielnia Mieszkaniowa (WSM: Warsaw Housing Co-operative) was building its first flats. Żoliborz had a significant intelligentsia and professional population: 56.4% of the population were white collar workers.[44] No other precise figures are available. Marymont, on the other hand, was predominantly working class (59.3%), but had a 23.6% population of white collar workers.

The Old Town has been described as follows:

In comparison to the type of inhabitant of the eighteenth century who was quite prosperous, mainly craftsmen and poor people were clustered there in the interwar years, and amongst them a considerable number of suspicious types of all kinds.

During the day the streets were peaceful, at night they rang with drunken singing and the clamour of dispute. Even the police appeared there reluctantly.[45]

The population of the Old Town (Stare Miasto, Nowe Miasto, and the area around Świętojerska) was 82.5% working and lower middle classes, craftsmen, shopkeepers and tradesmen. White collar workers constituted only 12.8%. Over half the population was Jewish.[46]

The districts of Muranów and Mirów and the areas around pl. Bankowy and pl. Teatralny presented a great contrast. The well known streets of Muranów and Mirów, and ul. Leszno, pl. Mirowski, ul. Grzybowska and ul. Towarowa, were full of the houses and shops of workers (a high percentage of them belonging to Jews), lower middle class citizens and cottage workers, the latter especially around the streets of Leszno, Wolności, Parysowska, Karmelicka, Gliniana, Dzika and Nalewki.[47] The lower middle classes constituted approximately 43% of the population, and the working classes 39.3%. The same pattern was to be found in the area bordering these streets in the part of Śródmieście between ul. Prosta and al. Jerozolimskie. Pl. Bankowy and pl. Teatralny, being the city areas of Warsaw, had a low proletarian representation but contained more white collar workers and intelligentsia.

Further east in the part of Śródmieście around Krakowskie Przedmieście, Nowy Świat, pl. Małachowskiego and pl. Napoleona, where the Prudential Insurance building stood, up to al. Jerozolimskie, the proletarian emphasis disappeared. In these areas white collar workers and intelligentsia represented a quarter of the population. These were the elegant areas of the neon lights and well dressed crowds. The only individual statistics which are available are for Krakowskie Przedmieście, where the working class represented 51.3% of the population. In other areas it was probably not as high as that and represented nearer 35%. The lower middle classes represented 20–30%, mainly shopkeepers.[48]

The rest of Śródmieście, equally as elegant and visibly wealthy, especially along al. Ujazdowskie where many aristocratic palaces were built on the road to the Belweder, the President's palace, and Wilanów, and the area to the south of al. Jerozolimskie to pl. Zbawiciela, represent very non-working class areas of Warsaw. The inhabitants of these parts were mainly intelligentsia and white collar workers.

To the east of these areas lies Powiśle. Here there was a considerable proletarian population. The inhabitants were working class (42.1%) and white collar workers (31.2%).

Despite their garden suburb character, Mokotów, Czerniaków and Sielce had a high combined total working class population (63.3%). The highest percentage was in Sielce (67.4%). Mokotów had expanded considerably in the interwar years, when parts of it had been divided up into buildings plots,[49] on which villas surrounded by neat gardens were erected. In spite of the amount of space these villas took up they were not representative of the majority of the population. Only about 20% of the inhabitants of Czerniaków in 1931 lived in houses with water and plumbing. In Mokotów the numbers were about 35%, and in Sielce about 7%. In the centre of Śródmieście, however, the figure was 97.2%.[50]

Ochota, another peripheral district, was also mainly proletarian. The working class constituted 71.2% of the population. But it also contained its affluent areas, especially around ul. Filtrowa and ul. Wawelska.

Needless to say during the course of the occupation and especially during the Uprising the social structures of these districts were subject to changes resulting from the influx of refugees from other areas or other German alterations, e.g. German districts and the Ghetto. In spite of this the above analysis forms a basic outline on which to work.

1.4 Nazi attitude and policy towards Warsaw

Wir haben in diesem Land einen Punkt, von dem alles Unheil ausgeht: es ist Warschau. Wenn wir Warschau nicht im Generalgouvernement hätten, dann hätten wir vier Fünftel der Schwierigkeiten nicht, mit denen wir zu kämpfen haben. Warschau ist und bleibt der Punkt, von dem alle Unruhe in dieses Land hineingetragen wird.[51]

Hitler's aim was not to dominate but to destroy Poland.[52] During the Second World War Poland was treated by the Germans as being part of Germany; with the exception of the provinces of Warsaw, Radom, Lublin and Kraków, which formed the Generalgouvernement, the rest of Poland occupied by the Germans in 1939 was incorporated into the Reich and Germanised.[53] After the German attack on Soviet Russia in June 1941, Polish lands in the east likewise fell under German occupation. The district of Galicia, with Lwów, was incorporated into the Generalgouvernement.[54]

Warsaw was stripped of its role as capital, and Kraków became the seat of the Generalgouvernement under Hans Frank, the Governor. Warsaw was reduced to a district centre holding the same rank as the towns of Radom, Lublin, and Lwów.[55]

The Nazi programme in Poland, to annihilate the Polish nation, destroy its culture and reduce the Poles to the level of helots,[56] was gradual and systematic. The policy affected above all the intelligentsia, whom the Germans thus defined: 'The term "Polish intelligentsia" covers primarily Polish priests, teachers (including university lecturers), doctors, dentists, veterinary surgeons, officers, executives, business men, landowners, writers, journalists, plus all the people who have received a higher or secondary education.'[57] Hans Frank wrote in his diary: 'all the representatives of the Polish intelligentsia must be killed. It sounds cruel, but it is the right of life. The Generalgouvernement is the Polish reservoir, the great Polish work camp.'[58]

The Germans had no plans to develop Poland. The axiom of their policy was that 'Polen soll wie eine Kolonie behandelt werden'.[59] Poland formed a source of cheap labour for her occupiers and if that source would not willingly work for the German war machine then it would be forced to. In 1943 Dr Ludwig Fischer, Governor of Warsaw, claimed that the town had become 'ein Rüstungszentrum für das grossdeutsche Reich'.[61] No Pole was to be allowed to rise higher than the level of a factory foreman.[62]

The Nazis realised the importance of Warsaw to the Polish nation; they understood that it was the 'Hochburg des Polentums'.[63] It was for that reason that Warsaw was stripped of her role as capital. She was to have no political, social, or economic significance for the Poles, and no further cultural life was allowed for her native inhabitants. Universities, secondary and high schools were closed, Polish opera and theatre was banned, and only small variety theatre was allowed.[64] The same pattern was repeated in other Polish towns in the Generalgouvernement.

The Germans had planned that the future Warsaw would be 'die neue deutsche Stadt', a German centre of about 130,000 Germans.[65] Any Poles who were left living in Warsaw after the war would be forced to emigrate.[66] The size of this new town was to be one-twentieth the size of that which had previously existed.[67]

These policies and plans resulted in five years of unprecedented terror, destruction and extermination.

1.5 Methods of Nazi terror in Warsaw

Anyone who has not lived through a reign of terror can have no real idea of its implications. They can have no conception of what it means to live in constant fear of arrest, torture, death, transportation or extermination. During the Second World War every nation under Nazi occupation underwent a reign of terror in accordance with Nazi racial policies. It is probably true to say, however, that no other nation suffered more than Poland.

In other European countries such as Holland, Belgium, France, Denmark and Czechoslovakia thousands were arrested and killed for their anti-Nazi and resistance activities, for fighting and defying the occupier. But in Poland people were arrested and killed for being out after curfew hours, or for selling black market goods, such as white bread, meat, and vegetables, in order to eke out a living and keep alive. In the capital cities of Paris, Brussels, Prague and others, there was not the fear of being caught in a street round-up, lined up against the wall and shot just because you were there, just because you were Polish. In Warsaw no one was sure when they went to bed that they were going to be allowed to sleep the night out. 'After all, it made no difference whether your papers were in order or not, whether you were guilty or innocent. The German terror was incalculable and the fact of being a Pole a deadly sin in itself – so you left it at that.'[68]

This was the kind of unimaginable fear that the inhabitants of Warsaw lived under for five long years of the occupation. They did not know whether each member of the family who left in the morning would return in the evening. They had to be continually on the alert to avoid falling into the hands of the Gestapo or German gendarmes. But at the same time they had to live, and to live in occupied Warsaw meant taking continual risks.

Nazi policy was to destroy and exploit the Polish nation by dividing it and by using the country and its resources. It aimed at dividing the nation by forcing all Poles of German origin to accept their German nationality and become '*Volksdeutsch*'. Thus they hoped to divide the community into two categories, loyal and disloyal citizens. Refusal to accept German nationality could mean death. The Polish nationals, on the other hand, were to be used as German labour. The aim of this policy was to get the maximum number of workers to go and work in the Third Reich and in the east. The larger towns, especially Warsaw, were to be purged of their 'inflammatory elements', by sending them to work in Germany, in work camps in the Generalgouvernement, or to the east and to the concentration camps. These policies were accompanied by an intensive fight with the Polish Underground.[69]

The main methods of this policy in Warsaw can be summarised as follows:[70]

1. Street round-ups in which men and women were caught as random victims without any charges being made against them and then transported to concentration or forced labour camps.
2. Snap street raids and public street executions.
3. Massive house searches, which usually resulted in transportation to one of the concentration camps or death by execution.
4. Arrests of persons regarded as suspicious or undesirable. These were usually members of clandestine organisations, members of the intelligentsia, pre-war politicians or activists.
5. The general use of torture against anyone, regardless of age or sex, during interrogation.
6. After the autumn of 1941 committal to the penal labour camp of Treblinka and in 1943 and 1944 to the labour camps in Warsaw itself on Gęsia and Litewska (streets which had formerly been part of the Ghetto) for minor offences.
7. The total extermination of virtually all the Warsaw Jews either as a result of the conditions in the Ghetto, at the hands of the Germans in the Ghetto or by systematic extermination in Treblinka or other camps.

[The two groups most affected were the Polish intelligentsia and the Jews.]In the case of the intelligentsia, apart from the physical liquidation which has already been described, the Germans used three other methods to subjugate and annihilate them. The first method was social degradation. By depriving a large part of the intelligentsia of their means of existence the Germans forced them to find other forms of occupation, which usually meant some kind of manual work, or to depend on charity. Secondly, the Germans halted the process of the development of the intelligentsia by closing down Polish universities, higher and secondary schools, and by liquidating any academic and cultural life, as well as by closing down libraries and banning a large number of books. They also started a propaganda campaign directed at the other social groups to create an antipathy towards the representatives of the intelligentsia, who were portrayed as being guilty of the September defeat and as useless and harmful.[71] The problem of the plight of the intelligentsia will be dealt with in full later on.

The history of the fate of the Polish Jews during the Second World War is well known. The building of the Ghetto and its liquidation as well as the transportation of the Jews to the concentration camps made a fearful impression on the Poles. They were under no illusions as to the methods the Germans were using against the Semite population and after 1943 felt that the same fate awaited them.[72]

The methods described above were applied ruthlessly and arbitrarily on a mass scale. The following is a report in one of the clandestine papers in Warsaw of Christmas 1943:

Christmas in the capital was spent in the shadow of German gendarmes, SS, and police activity. On Christmas Day street chases and searches took on a mass character, nearly all the streets of Śródmieście being blocked and guarded.

On Christmas Eve in various parts of the town, including ul. Złota, the gendarmes carried out a general blockade of the houses, taking away people who had met together to spend *Wigilia* [the Polish Christmas Eve celebration].[73]

1.6 The course of Nazi terror in Warsaw

It is possible to see a pattern in the Nazi extermination policy in Warsaw. This pattern has been broken down into seven phases.[74]

On 27 December 1939 the first mass execution of Poles took place in Wawer, a suburb of Warsaw. The executions were in retaliation for the murder of two German NCOs in a bar by two local criminals. The 107 people shot were all presumably innocent of the crime. 'Dragged out of their beds, none of them had the slightest idea of what had happened in the restaurant . . . All of them were charged with actions not of their doing . . . Their only offence was that they happened to be in the area covered by the raid.'[75] The significance of the Wawer atrocity was that it was the first time collective responsibility had been applied and from that moment people realised 'that under German occupation one could die for nothing'.[76]

The first phase of the terror lasted from the beginning of the war until May 1940. It was mainly characterised by a series of preventative arrests, whose targets were predominantly drawn from the intelligentsia. These arrests were followed by secret mass executions in Warsaw, in the Parliament Gardens or the surrounding areas of Warsaw, e.g. Palmiry and Kampinos forests. Approximately 1,200 people were executed in those early months.

The second phase lasted until the autumn of 1940. A new wave of terror was inaugurated which resulted in the first of the full scale transportations to Sachsenhausen and Auschwitz. Further secret mass executions were carried out in the Palmiry Forest. However, due to the work and infiltration of the Polish Underground, news of these so-called secret mass executions spread quickly. In these transportations approximately 5,000 people were sent to camps, and approximately 850 died in the executions.

The third phase was longer, lasting about two years from the autumn of 1940 to September 1942. It was characterised by further executions in the woods surrounding the capital. Approximately 8,500 people were shot during these two years, whilst simultaneously transportations left for concentration camps and the first trainloads of women were sent from Warsaw to Ravensbrück. About 6,000 people were transported. The end of this period also saw the transportation of more than 310,000 Jews from the Ghetto.

The fourth phase lasting from October 1942 to May 1943 saw further developments. The terror was now extended to the working class of Warsaw who, up until then, in comparison to the intelligentsia, had not been specifically persecuted. This development was probably due to the formation in 1942 of the PPR, the Polish Workers Party, and the German setbacks on the eastern front especially during the winter of 1942–3. Street hunts and round-ups were begun again to find labour for the Third Reich. Men and women were transported to concentration camps, and for the first time to that of Majdanek, Lublin. The most horrific development was the introduction of public executions by hanging. At the same time mass executions in the environs of Warsaw continued. This phase ended with the four week Ghetto Uprising.

The fifth phase, between the months of May and October 1943, saw a decline in the number of transportations to concentration camps. But the mass execution of prisoners, who had usually been imprisoned on the basis of trumped up charges or none at all, did not diminish. These executions were carried out secretly in the ruins of the old Ghetto. Between October 1942 and October 1943 over 11,000 Poles were executed; 13,000 were sent to concentration camps.

The sixth phase from October 1943 to February 1944 saw what is claimed to be the bloodiest chapter in the history of Warsaw. It was characterised by street executions, which were performed almost daily, claiming between 270 and 300 victims a week.

The last phase began in February 1944, and ended with the outbreak of the Warsaw Uprising on 1 August 1944. Street executions on the same scale as the five previous months were not repeated but there were many more secret mass executions in the Ghetto. Between October 1943 and the end of July 1944, nearly 8,500 people were executed. Transportations to concentration camps were increased and between February and 1 August 1944 about 5,500 people were transported.

Up until the outbreak of the Uprising approximately 40,000 of the inhabitants of Warsaw had been shot or killed by the Nazis. Between 150,000 and 160,000 were sent to work for the Generalgouvernement or the Third Reich. These figures do not include the Jews in the Warsaw Ghetto.

1.7 Living conditions in occupied Warsaw

If life was made intolerable by the pressures of living under constant fear and terror, the day-to-day living conditions created by the Germans provided no respite or compensation. If death was not brought directly by a German bullet or noose, it came indirectly as a result of the conditions created by the Nazi occupier for the Poles. If the Poles were not being terrorised or tortured their lives were being mortified, complicated, hampered and destroyed.

Employment

Employment for the majority of Poles during the occupation was as precarious as life itself. The preconditions necessary to find work were no longer status, education or qualification, but ability, talent, physical and psychological disposition, endurance and in many cases financial means.[77] It is not appropriate here to give a detailed description of the conditions and problems of the occupation, but a general picture of those conditions and what they meant is relevant.

The following German figures show how unemployment rose and then fell at the beginning of the war. The figures cover those registered as unemployed in the district of Warsaw. They must be treated with care, however, and the numbers in reality must have been higher. They probably do not include unemployed Jews, and two-thirds of them represent the unemployed in the city of Warsaw itself.[78]

1939	November	82,751
	December	82,239
1940	January	74,791
	February	66,133
	March	59,444
	April	51,320
	May	35,997
	June	25,575
	July	22,967
	August	23,644
	September	26,314
	October	30,228
	November	34,738
	December	37,525
1941	January	41,976
	February	38,948
	March	35,322
	April	39,426
	May	23,310
	June	17,092
	July	17,381
	August	15,013

The reason for the high rate of unemployment at the beginning is straightforward. The siege of Warsaw and the ensuing occupation resulted in the total stagnation of trade, industry and banking. This was due to the lack of raw materials and coal and to destruction.[79] In

Table 2. *Employment in Warsaw industries, October 1941*

Industry	No. of workers	% of 1939 labour force
Minerals	1,447	35
Metal	33,377	73
Electrical	10,152	77
Chemical	6,858	96
Textile	7,653	70
Paper	3,846	83
Printing	3,818	52
Tanning	1,713	57
Rubber	416	22
Timber	6,071	100
Musical instruments	246	30
Foodstuffs	18,177	134
Clothing	14,832	64
Water, gas and electricity	5,853	100

September 1939, 215 of Warsaw's factories employing 18,098 workers were destroyed.[80] There were not the goods available to be traded, business was hampered by new and impractical regulations, and furthermore it was extremely difficult if not impossible to obtain consumer articles.

Table 2 shows how employment in the industries of Warsaw was affected by the occupation.[81] Unemployment was probably higher amongst the working class. At the end of October 1940, *Biuletyn Informacyjny* reported: 'In Warsaw employment is hardly 20–25% that of the pre-war level of the number of industrial workers. The situation amongst white collar workers and intellectuals is even lower.'[82] Madajczyk, however, quotes the figures in January 1941 for the whole of the district of Warsaw as 37% of the pre-war level in the manufacturing industry and 50–55% in the consumer industry.[83] Because of the closure of Polish universities, high schools, theatres, radio, museums, newspapers, publishers etc., many people were suddenly deprived of employment. Furthermore government workers and white collar workers, with the collapse of the Polish government and administration, were left without any source of income. In March 1940, a report from Poland stated:

The majority of public workers are unemployed and have already virtually exhausted their scarce resources, which they received in the autumn in the form of service compensation or evacuation payment. On the other hand the few public servants who are still working (administration, treasury, schools, judiciary, post, rail and Samorząd) are paid irregularly and badly.[84]

In addition to this there were demobilised officers and soldiers who had not surrendered at the capitulation of Warsaw.[85] Furthermore the ranks of those seeking some form of employment were swelled by those people who previously never had to work but were forced to do so by the conditions during the occupation. Many women, whose husbands had either been killed or taken prisoner, were forced to find some kind of occupation to support their families.[86]

The first two years of the occupation were the worst but after that the employment situation improved. This was due to the growth of the German arms industry in Warsaw, which increased the number of places available for employment.[87] Some of the intelligentsia were able in some form or other to return to their old occupations and gave up manual work.[88] Many were employed in primary schools or the Zarząd Miejski (Municipal Government) – but often these jobs were purely fictitious and a cover-up for some kind of other activity, usually in the Underground.[89] By May 1942, there was a shortage of labour in Warsaw especially in the munitions industry, and in the repair and replacement shops for the Army and the railway. There were 5,000 positions unfilled.[90]

Nazi rule in Warsaw forbade wage rises so wages remained as they had been before the war in spite of the spiralling in the cost of living. Some firms which illegally raised rates of pay later cancelled the rises and returned to the old rates. Taxes were increased. There were strict limitations on changing places of work. No contract could be concluded or dissolved without the permission of the Arbeitsamt (Department of Labour). This covered all kinds of work, public and private, even domestic. The prohibition also included members of the family. There were changes made in the system of social security. The right to claim was abolished and the allocation of relief was at the discretion of the German authorities. Where relief was sought it was at a reduced rate. The Jews had no right to claim.[91]

Since no strikes, Trade Unions or overtime were permitted, workers had no power to improve their positions.[92] Industrial action was, however, taken by a few of Warsaw's workers. In April 1943, the director of the 'Dzwonkowa' factory in Grochów met the strikers' demands after an initial rejection, and the workers received a 50% rise in pay plus control of the kitchen in answer to their claims for set overtime payments and the provision of meals. There was also a

Table 3. *Wage rates for manual and clerical workers (in zloties),*
January 1943

	Poles	Germans
Manual workers over 21 years (per hour)	0.75	3.00
Clerical workers – lowest rates for men (per month)	140.50	1,200.00

successful strike in the Lilpop and Avia factory in Wola, but only after a German had been killed. This probably forced the director to recant.[93] The strongest weapon the Polish worker had was the withdrawal of his labour, absenteeism, pilfering of spare parts to sell, sabotage or working slowly. This 'go-slow' to hamper the occupier and his war effort did not help the individual worker materially, but it was part of the general resistance action. In May 1942, the slogan was 'PPPPP – Polaku! Pracowniku Polski! Pracuj Powoli!' (Pole! Polish worker! Work slowly!).[94]

Employment and work, however, did not ensure enough to live on. Wages were totally insufficient to maintain even a basic standard of living due to the incredibly high costs and prices during the occupation. Rates of pay tended to vary but they were neither high nor sufficient. Germans and Poles were paid at different rates, which according to *Biuletyn Informacyjny* in January 1943 were as shown in table 3.[95]

In 1938 the average cost of feeding a worker's family of four was 61.27 zl. per month; by June 1941 it was 1,568 zl.[96] A worker at that time (in municipal work, public work, small industries and crafts) earned 6–10 zl. daily, which meant 120–300 zl. monthly.[97] But in some cases it was even less. The salaries of white collar workers (postal, shops, social security etc.) varied between 100 and 250 zl.[98] It was impossible to live on such a sum. This can be well illustrated by the following examples of people who seem to have earned more than the average.[99] Ryszard Hładko worked in a building firm: 'For zl. 20 daily I could get a loaf of bread and still two zloties remained for cigarettes. Work was heavy and lasted all day. Nearly until dusk.' A woman who acted as a temporary hostess for Jozef Retinger was a doctor working in a medical institute controlled by Germans, where she earned 450 zl. monthly. She received a further 200 zl. from the Underground for her work for them. Her maid sold meat on the black market and their joint income came to 2,000 zł., but they were only able to eat twice a day. The first meal was breakfast, when they ate vegetable soup which sometimes had some lumps of meat in it.[100]

Tables 4 and 5 show more clearly the real value of wages.[101] How did the Varsovians cope with such a situation? Everyone had usually to find a second source of income to make ends meet. This usually meant a second job, smuggling and blackmarketeering, the selling of private possessions or work in the Underground. Women were driven to prostitution. Smuggling and blackmarketeering in spite of the risks involved were most widespread and practised by people from all walks of life.[102]

Housing

The increase in population and the destruction of buildings in Warsaw in September 1939 resulted in an immediate congestion and shortage of accommodation. 'The increase in the number of inhabitants is visible in the streets and trams; they are always overcrowded. The suburbs of Warsaw are especially thickly populated due to the cheaper accommodation there.'[103] Little repair of damaged houses was carried out.[104] However, in spite of the fact that available accommodation was cut by 25% it was not difficult to find free rooms.[105] German districts were opened in Warsaw and many Poles were forced to vacate their homes.[106] The destruction of the Ghetto in 1943 reduced the number of buildings by a further 15%.[107]

By the end of 1941 about 1,350,000 Varsovians had at their disposal 286,000 flats containing 620,000 rooms. This overall increase in the amount of rooms since the beginning of the war was a result of the practice at the time of dividing up larger rooms into smaller ones. According to *Nowy Kurier Warszawski* on 19 September 1941, only 15% of the inhabitants of Warsaw lived in flats with three or more rooms. At the same time there were some 550 known rooms where twelve or more people lived.[108] In the autumn of 1943 a new law was introduced enforcing new norms for the numbers living in one house. In a three room house with kitchen at least five people were expected to live and in a four room house with kitchen seven people.[109]

It was easy enough to find free rooms during the occupation, since the hiring out of rooms was a lucrative way of earning extra money. Rooms, however, were far from cheap. In March 1940, accommodation in new houses cost 150 zł. monthly.[110] Fischer, in his report of August and September 1942, writes that due to the Soviet air-raids

Table 4. *Wage index of municipal manual workers*

	Pre-war	1939	1940				1941		
		Nov.	Feb.	May	Aug.	Sept.	Feb.	May	Aug.
Nominal	100	97	97	97	97	97	97	97	97
Real	100	40	20	18	26	24	23	11	9

Table 5. *Free market prices in Warsaw*

	1939	1941	1942			1943			1944	
	July	May	Jan.	Apr.	Oct.	Jan.	June	Oct.	Jan.	Mar.
Whole-meal rye bread	100	4,250	2,454	4,222	3,693	3,975	5,164	3,464	4,064	3,853
Wheat flour	100	4,500	3,386	4,843	5,312	6,081	8,306	6,426	6,667	6,204
Beef	100	1,000	1,342	1,906	2,785	3,975	6,181	5,524	6,058	5,920
Pork	100	1,370		2,981	4,994	6,748	9,546	7,960	7,812	8,272
Pork fat	100	2,125	3,410	5,682	9,847	11,245	14,646	13,245	10,839	10,808
Butter	100	1,490		3,526	6,601	6,765	10,610	8,488	7,839	10,023
Milk	100	1,000		2,015	3,474	4,512	5,325	5,185	6,048	6,281
Eggs	100	1,300		2,262	4,275	8,150	5,575	7,538	10,100	7,188
Dried beans	100	4,950		6,824	5,771	6,716	6,943	7,306	8,054	7,356
Potatoes	100	2,500	2,043	2,543	1,736	1,879	2,251	2,179	2,214	2,157
Sugar	100	2,300	3,121	5,562	7,471	7,578	9,911	8,040	7,708	7,075

many people had fled to the surrounding areas of Warsaw, which had sent rents of small unfurnished rooms up to 1,200 zł.[111] In such conditions it was inevitable that rents should run into arrears.[112]

The problem did not end with the obtaining and overcrowding of accommodation. Equally great was the problem of maintaining and heating homes. As a result of the bombing of Warsaw in 1939 very few windows were left intact,[113] and it was difficult to obtain the glass to repair and replace windows. Consequently many people had to put up with substitute card windows. Warsaw is cold in the winter at the best of times, but the winter of 1939–40 was one of the coldest and longest that the capital could remember. The first snow fell in October and the frost came a few days later, lasting several months. In January 1940 the temperature fluctuated between $-20°$ and $-30°$ C.[114] There was a great shortage of coal, and black market prices were beyond the means of most people.[115] In spite of the German prohibition people left Warsaw to go to the woods to collect wood, either for themselves or to sell.[116] People lived in houses with no heating; they stayed in bed all wrapped up in their clothes to keep warm.

Brother and sister lay all day in bed, wrapped up in some kind of quilting or clothes, because the flat was devilishly cold, in spite of the fact that he [their father] traded wood. He had had to sell everything in order to live. In any case, what was the use of lighting a fire when you could see the world outside through the wall?[117]

That was in March 1940. Many houses never saw a fire throughout the occupation in spite of below freezing temperatures, and if they did it was usually only one room that was heated.[118]

In October 1941, *Biuletyn Informacyjny* reported that the shortage of coal was so great that even the electricity works and the tramways did not have the smallest reserve of coal and were working on a day-to-day basis.[119]

Gas and electricity did not always prove to be a reliable substitute for coal. The consumption of these two forms of energy was restricted by the Germans from the beginning of 1941.[120] A letter received in London from Poland described how two or three times a week there was no electricity and candles were used. It was never known beforehand which districts would be affected.[121] In November 1943 there was no electricity at all.[122]

According to Madajczyk, after the autumn of 1942, Poles were only allowed to use electricity two to three hours a day,[123] but a later

Table 6. *Availability of electricity in Polish districts*

	April–Oct. 1943	Oct. 1943–May 1944
Even numbered Polish houses	7.00–11.00 p.m.	5.00–7.00 p.m.
Odd numbered Polish houses	7.00–11.00 p.m.	8.15–11.00 p.m.

plan shows that in 1943 and 1944 it was sometimes longer (table 6). In the German districts there was current all the time, but there were restrictions for industry, offices, restaurants, cinemas etc.[124]

The Varsovians learnt to cope. They read, carried out their secret schooling, amused themselves and conspired together by the light of candles, paraffin and oil lamps.

Food supply

The standard of living became primitive in the extreme. The diet of those who fared the worst consisted exclusively of black bread mixed with sawdust. A plate of cereal a day was considered a luxury. During all of 1942 I never tasted butter or sugar ... we were all hungry nearly all of the time.[125]

Worst of all was with food – not far from our house was a hospital, where we used to go and collect potato peelings, which we ground afterwards and baked on the stove and that was our most usual meal. We went around hungry looking for all kinds of impossible and possible things to eat. The easiest to find was vegetation. Once in the hospital we managed to get hold of mouldy bread, which had already been eaten by mice, but it tasted very good.[126]

These two recollections were written by two very different people. The first comes from Jan Karski, a representative of the intelligentsia and an official in the Polish Underground. The author of the second is Jarosław Ciechanowicz, whose father was killed in September 1939. He and his brother, at that time still children, were looked after by their mother who worked as a cleaner.

A glance at tables 4 and 5 is sufficient to show how difficult the problems of keeping body and soul together must have been during the occupation. Warsaw was the most badly supplied town in the whole country and the cost of living there was higher than anywhere else.[127] But this did not mean that at times prices in the surrounding districts of Warsaw were not higher than in the capital itself.[128]

Governor Fischer acknowledged that the problem of food in the district of Warsaw was a difficult one. He gave the following reasons as being part of the cause of the situation. Firstly, Warsaw had a higher relative consumer population than other districts. Secondly, the districts which had previously supplied Warsaw and formed her hinterland had been included in the Reich. Thirdly, the agricultural areas supplying Warsaw were too small. The fourth reason was the destruction created by the September campaign, and the fact that in their retreat the Russians had taken with them a large amount of cattle, wheat and other foodstuffs.[129]

These reasons were to a great extent valid but Nazi policy did nothing to alleviate or improve the situation. As a result of the prohibition of transporting food from the Reich into the General-gouvernement, the latter was cut off from the previous sources of food. The problem was further aggravated by the swelling of Warsaw's population, control of trade, and the German exploitations to obtain food for their own Army and people.[130]

Proper food rationing was introduced in Warsaw on 15 December 1939, and in February 1940 different allowances were introduced for Jews and Poles. At the beginning of 1942 different quantities were given to children and adults.[131] But rationing did not mean that the goods were always available or could be obtained. Even bread, which according to a Government Delegate Report was rationed *de facto*, was not always issued.[132] There was no consistency in the quantity of the rations. A Pole living in Warsaw during the occupation recorded that in the week beginning 5 May 1942 adults received 350 grammes and children 175 grammes of bread for the week, and the same in the week beginning 13 June, whereas in the week beginning 18 May 300 and 180 grammes respectively were issued.[133]

All other rationed food was often only fiction. Meat was not always issued nor replaced by eggs. Oatmeal and a little fat sometimes appeared, and children were given sweets and biscuits occasionally on holidays. Jam, potatoes and salt were also rationed, but there were no such foods as peas, milk, cheese etc.[134] Potatoes formed the staple part of the Poles' diet during the occupation, and therefore the problems connected with their supply and changes in price were always ones of great concern.

The ration allowances provided for 20–25% of the daily calorific value needed for the human organism, i.e. between 500 and 600 calories daily.[135] According to the Warsaw Chamber of Agriculture the daily ration fluctuated as follows: from February 1940 to May 1941 it was 623–834 calories; in August 1941 it fell to 521 and in September to 418.[136] The first years of the occupation were the worst

Table 7. *Comparison of Polish and German monthly ration cards*

Ration cards	Poles	Germans
Bread (grammes)	4,300	9,000
Flour, barley, macaroni (grammes)	400	2,000
Lard, butter (grammes)	—	2,200
Meat (grammes)	400	4,000
Sugar, sweets (grammes)	200	1,675
Coffee (grammes)	75	250
Marmalade (grammes)	240	800
Eggs	1	12
Beer, wine (bottles)	—	3
Cigarettes	—	280
Cheese, curds (grammes)	—	2,000

and people were literally starving.[137] After the beginning of 1943, however, the situation did improve but only in one quarter of that year did it go over the 1,000 calories mark.[138] The Poles had one of the lowest calorie content of the food rationed to them out of all the occupied and Axis countries in Europe.[139] Table 7, printed in *Biuletyn Informacyjny* on 7 January 1943, shows how the Poles were treated in comparison to the German occupier. The Germans could also buy cold meats, lemons, cream cheeses, soup and fruit on their coupons.[140]

It can be seen that the rations were not enough to keep anyone in good health, and, therefore, the black market was indispensable for making up the deficiencies. It was the black market that bridged the gap between starvation and survival, although the prices were greater than most people could afford. The people who smuggled in goods to sell did so at very great expense because of the high cost of train fares and the bribes that were often involved, and the risks of confiscation, being sent to a concentration camp, arrest, and death.[141] The Germans were always on the look out for smugglers. They would set up road blocks and search trains. In the streets the German police and 'Granatowa' (Polish police under German command) were the fear of the traders. A successful raid by the Germans could result in a quick rise in prices due to shortages, often by as much as 30–50%. But the traders were never daunted and always continued to sell their goods regardless of the risks involved. Many shops sold goods under the counter.[142]

In Nazi Warsaw, lying at the crossroads of east and west, everything had its price for those who could afford it.

Anyone who has money can eat well in Warsaw and to their capacity, which is not possible for example in Berlin. In good Warsaw restaurants there are eight to nine dishes on the menu and several types of pre-war vodka.

In the first-class Berlin restaurants there is only one dish costing three to four marks and there is no alcohol.

But such luxuries were for the very few. Only those people who were involved in trading themselves, or the intelligentsia who had sold their possessions, could afford to supplement their diet on the black market. On the whole life was miserable, and the misery was enough to drive some people to volunteer to go and work in Germany, and thus obtain some morsel and hope of survival.[143] According to doctors' observations the average adult in Warsaw lost 10 kg in weight during the occupation.[144]

The cultivation of allotments helped the inhabitants of the capital to improve their supplies of food, and not only allotments in the strict sense of the term. As in Britain during the Second World War, where parks, squares and every available space were converted for growing vegetables and fruit, 'digging for victory', so it was in Warsaw. Parks and squares, any piece of land, and courtyards were transformed into vegetable patches for growing potatoes, tomatoes and other vegetables.[145]

Charity and self-help provided a certain number of people with aid in feeding themselves, but we shall deal with this later on. What is important to remember here is that the conditions created by the Germans were only sufficient to keep the human body at the lowest level of survival.

Clothing

The clothing situation was no better than that of food and heat. New clothes were in short supply and expensive. Many of the people who lost their homes and belongings during the bombing of Warsaw in 1939 were only left with the clothes they were wearing.[146] The impoverished who had only shoes and clothes necessary for their work, even before the outbreak of the war, faced the impossible problem of trying to replace them. Flour and potatoes were bartered for shoes.[147]

Clothing coupons were virtually unobtainable, and non-existent for woollen clothes and shoes. By the autumn of 1941, prices on the black market were as follows:[148]

Men's woollen suits	zł. 2,000–2,500
Pair of shoes	zł. 600–700

Men's shirts   zł.   60–75
Second hand suit   zł.   400–600

By 1942 a man's shirt cost between zł. 800 and 850, and in the middle of 1943 a man's suit cost anything between zł. 12,000 and 15,000. For women a second hand dress in 1942 cost zł. 180–200.[149]

In 1941, 272,000 pairs of shoes and 17,000 items of clothing, and in 1942, 100,000 pairs of shoes and less than 5,000 items of clothing were issued for sale officially in Warsaw.[150] Józef Retinger bought a pair of shoes whilst he was in Warsaw and relates:

> The day after my arrival I went . . . to buy some shoes. I was given the choice of some twenty pairs, chose one and asked the price. It was zł. 4,250, which I paid without tendering coupons. The salesmen confessed that if I had been a German he would have said that he had no shoes, because he would have been obliged to sell them at the official price which was then zł. 56.[151]

The problem of finding footwear was greater than that of finding clothing. Furthermore the Germans had all the stocks of leather, and there was no rubber to resole and heel shoes. As a result the Poles were driven to wearing wooden clogs – even in the snow.[152] An observer writing in 1942 wrote that nearly everyone seemed to be wearing broken and torn shoes.[153] A great many families had only one pair which they took it in turns to wear.[154] The same boy who had to bake potato peel cakes to have something to eat, also had no shoes to wear: 'in the summer we ran round bare-foot, but in the winter we had to sit in the flat, although when we were able to we wrapped our feet up in rags and went into the streets'.[155]

The self-help and charity organisations distributed clothes in so far as they were able to. Needless to say malnutrition and insufficient clothing could only result in a deterioration of the health of the inhabitants of Warsaw.

Health

Hospitals in the Generalgouvernement were open to the Polish population, but in many of the larger towns some of the hospitals were taken over by the Germans for their own use. Almost all the tuberculosis sanatoria, spas and watering places were taken by the Germans for themselves. There was a shortage of dressings and vaccines.[156] Even if people did go to hospital they could not expect to be well supplied with food. The Germans allowed only a limited amount of

Table 8. *Percentage and causes of death in Warsaw 1939–41*

	Pre-war	1939	1940				1941		
		Nov.	Feb.	May	Aug.	Nov.	Feb.	May	Aug.
Population									
(*thousands*)	1,280	1,270	1,310	1,320			1,360	1,390	1,390
Christians	910	910	920	920			960	960	970
Jews	370	360	390	400			400	430	420
Deaths	10.8	25.0	27.8	23.0	17.0	15.0	21.4	41.0	
Christians	11.2	20.0	25.1	22.0	17.0	15.0	17.7	18.5	
Jews	9.9	40.1	34.3	25.0	15.0	13.0	30.1	90.8	
Causes of death									
Tuberculosis	163	232	353	514	267	294	389	612	
Cancer and tumorous diseases	111	105	117	45	138	118	115	101	
Pneumonia	116	182	263	102	104	165	287	302	
Heart and circulatory organ diseases	252	613	860	616	455	387	601	966	
Severe cases of emaciation	60	175	114	99	80	61	202	1,464	
Hunger							120	1,351	

food into the hospitals, and the rest had to be bought on the free market. The supply of energy was not much better.[157]

Julian Kulski, Director of the Warsaw Municipal Government during the occupation, has written that due to the German fear of epidemics, preventive measures were fairly widespread, especially innoculation. Disinfectant teams worked to avert any possible typhus epidemic. Kulski claims further that hospitals in Warsaw continued their usual activity with certain changes and that the number of beds was not reduced. Henryk Pawłowicz, his Deputy, gives the following figures for the number of beds. Before the war, including private hospitals, there were about 8,000 hospital beds in Warsaw (6,000 in municipal hospitals and 2,000 in private). During the war in 1940–1 there were 6,200 beds, and in 1942–3 6,130. Kulski also maintains that the minimum needs of the health service were fulfilled. Yet the death rate rose sharply as table 8, for the first two years of the occupation, shows.[158]

Why was there such a rise in the death rate, and what were the factors contributing towards it? Firstly, there was the low standard of

living during the occupation, insufficient feeding and the bad and
unhygienic housing conditions. All these lessened resistance to disease. As a result of the shortage of soap, fuel, linen and overcrowded
living conditions, cleanliness was of a low standard. Local authorities
did as much as possible to remedy the situation by opening public
baths and hygiene units.[159] Secondly, medicine was expensive, as was
medical treatment. Few could afford it, and would only go to the
doctor in severe cases.[160] Thirdly, there was a general lack of vaccines
and medicine – a typhus vaccine in 1941 cost zł. 800, which was much
too expensive, and even the doctors did not have any.[161]

The number of cases of typhoid fever, however, were few, fewer
than before the war. This was due to the mass vaccination of
1,200,000 people in the winter of 1939–40, who were re-vaccinated in
the spring of 1940.[162] But by September 1941, there were 3,400 known
cases of typhus in Warsaw, although the number may have been
twice as great, for people were afraid to report it. About 90% of these
cases were to be found amongst the Jews. The attempts by the medical
authorities to improve the situation were hampered by the Germans
who tended to believe a 'cure' would be found by terror.[163]

The number of cases of dysentery increased but there was no
epidemic, even though there were no compulsory vaccines against
dysentery. Similarly there was quite a steep increase in the number of
people suffering from tuberculosis. In October and November 1943,
Fischer wrote that tuberculosis was on the increase and was the cause
of the absence of many teachers from schools. Bad feeding resulted in
a much higher level of rickets amongst children, between 70–90%;
before the war it had never been higher than 30%. Vaccines against
small-pox continued normally.[164]

The level of other infectious diseases, e.g. scarlet fever, diptheria,
cerebrospinal meningitis, measles, erysipelas, whooping cough and
malaria, also increased.[165] There were innoculations available for
scarlet fever, but they were so dangerous that some children, even
Germans, had to have hands amputated as a result of gangrene.[166]
There were no camps for sick children, except for the few organised by
charity, and therefore children had very little opportunity throughout the occupation to leave the towns for the country and fresh air.[167]
Poles were not allowed to use sports facilities to keep fit.[168]

It is not surprising, therefore, that in view of these catastrophic
health conditions the Polish Underground should have shown concern about the destruction of the human physical strength of the
town.

Self-help

It has previously been pointed out that various self-help and charity organisations were often able to alleviate the problems created by conditions in Nazi Warsaw. The activity and role of these organisations will now be explained.

Before the outbreak of the war a self-help care organisation had been planned, which was supposed to fulfil or replace the work usually done by official institutions and organisations. The creation of the Stołeczny Komitet Samopomocy Społecznej (SKSS; Warsaw Committee for Social Care) by Stefan Starzyński on 4 September 1939 was probably the realisation of this. The Germans allowed the SKSS to continue its activity until 31 March 1941. Its work was then taken over by Rada Opiekuńcza Miejska (ROM; Municipal Council for Social Care) in Warsaw, being the Warsaw branch of the Cracovian Rada Główna Opiekuńcza (RGO; Main Council for Social Care). In October 1941, it changed its name to Polski Komitet Opiekuńczy (PKO; Polish Committee for Social Care) and acted as such until the outbreak of the Uprising. These committees and their organisations functioned with the consent of the Germans.[169]

Apart from the work of SKSS and ROM there were other smaller organisations acting unofficially or under SKSS. The Polish Red Cross (PCK) was active but only in the sphere of military hospitals, and looking for lost and killed persons.[170] Some people on their own initiative organised some kind of social service, e.g. a priest called Łysik started kitchens for children without the help of SKSS.[171] Richer families were encouraged to provide hungry children with meals.[172]

The role of these organisations was to try and make up for the deficiencies created by the system imposed on the city by the Nazis. This covered the provision of aid to needy persons in the form of food, clothing, medicine, financial help, care of children, orphans and refugees, care for families of prisoners of war and care for prisoners. Their funds came from German subventions, grants from the Zarząd Miejski (Municipal Government), payments for services, subscriptions and gifts, American aid and other sources.[173]

The most significant work was done by the SKSS in providing food. At the beginning this absorbed over 50% of the total SKSS budget but later took only 30%.[174] Their soup kitchens were divided into five categories: general, self-supporting, autonomous, kitchens for refugees and kitchens for children. They varied in the type of food

Table 9. *Type of persons using soup kitchens, 1941*

Without means of support		3.1%
Without any food		16.7%
Unemployed		70.5%
Retired persons and pensioners		2.6%
With small earnings		7.1%

Breakdown of unemployed category	Families	Persons
Workers	11,320	38,780
White collar workers	1,720	4,830
Self-employed	1,710	4,680
TOTAL	14,750	48,290

and the prices they offered.[175] The 'general' kitchens were opened to anyone in need of food who had qualified for help. The applicant was issued with a ticket which entitled him to daily meals. Soup cost twenty to thirty groszy to begin with but later as much as one złoty. The soup could either be eaten on the premises or taken home. Many of the kitchens were run by nuns.[176] The self-supporting kitchens were run on the basis that the cost of meals covered all running expenses but not administrative expenses. They provided soup and a second course of potatoes, vegetables and a little meat. The ingredients for the soup were received from the organising committee, but those for the second course had to be bought daily. Soup would cost two złoties and the second meal two to five złoties rising yearly.[177]

The autonomous soup kitchens were used to a great extent by out of work and impoverished members of the intelligentsia. Individual kitchens were specially run for journalists, musicians, painters etc. The kitchens were dependent on themselves and their professional organisations and had autonomous administration. Relief received from the SKSS was supplemented with products found by themselves, which usually meant buying on the free market.[178] In May 1941, the SKSS was providing daily the greatest number of lunches of its whole existence, i.e. 133,383 meals. After that the numbers fell and, by June 1944, out of 106,000 who qualified for help only 70,466 were using it. In the Ghetto an even larger role was played by the soup kitchens run by a Jewish self-help organisation.[179] Table 9, based on 1941 figures, shows the type of persons using the kitchens and what type of person was represented by the category unemployed.[180]

Because of the difficulties involved in finding food and because of

Table 10. *Distribution of clothing by relief organisations in Warsaw,*
September 1939 – May 1944

Year	Items of clothing	Pieces of linen	Sheets	Baby clothes	Blankets	Pairs of shoes
Sept. 1939–Dec. 1940	26,867	25,295		540	1,044	9,725
1941	26,132	54,503		520	347	24,446
1942	13,832	35,187	944	1,657		17,573
1943	16,103	17,560	1,294	413		11,972
Jan.–May 1944	4,796	2,346	2,911*	12		3,472

* pallets and paper pillow cases

the high prices⟨the calorific and nourishment value of the soup and the food continually fell⟩ The decline of the average calorific value of meals provided by SKSS during 1941 is shown below:[181]

July 1940	381 calories
December	460 calories
May 1941	259 calories
June	182 calories
July	153 calories
August	164 calories

In 1941 when 25% of the population of Warsaw was forced to use public aid, the relief available was so meagre and its nourishment value so low that some people felt that it was not worth the effort to go and obtain it.[182]

⟨Within the bounds of its ability the SKSS distributed clothing, blankets and linen. This help, however, was never sufficient.⟩Table 10 shows the extent of the work.[183] In October 1943, *Biuletyn Informacyjny* described the clothing problem of the SKSS as catastrophic. There were only summer clothes available which would be of little use during the winter.[184]

In the sphere of health care SKSS provided certain medicaments, medical care and supervision over various institutions, medical control, social work in hospitals, and clinics for children.⟨Patients were provided with coupons which enabled them to get treatment from doctors, dentists and midwives which they would not otherwise have been able to afford.[185] ⟩The committees also issued milk and dried provisions for babies. ⁰Crèches, summer camps and shelters were organised for children.[186] Special care was given to people suffering from tuberculosis, to pregnant women and to children.[187]

During the hard, cold winters of the occupation the soup kitchens provided somewhere for the poor and destitute to sit, talk, and keep warm. In the mornings and evenings in some kitchens tea, coffee and bread was provided. For those who could not pay, amenities were provided free. Common rooms were opened for children and the young so that they could have suitable conditions to study in, or some kind of entertainments would be arranged. Concerts were staged to raise funds. SKSS also helped those out of work to find employment.[188]

It was always stressed, however, that the work of these organisations was only a drop in the ocean in comparison to what was needed. Their work was continually hampered, and there were constant financial problems. Quotas of supplies were not always delivered and if they were, they often fell short of the stipulated amounts, sometimes with the result that kitchens had to be closed. The Germans were continually imposing restrictions and introducing new regulations which obstructed the work of the committees. Their grants were cut and in May 1941 it was made compulsory for those wanting care to register in the Arbeitsamt (Labour Exchange). In July 1941, ROM was forbidden to provide relief in cash – this especially hit the intelligentsia. The Germans also held back aid sent from America. Assurances that certain products would be provided were not always fulfilled.[189] Thus the SKSS was involved in a continual struggle to find the financial and material means to carry on its work. For many of the inhabitants of Warsaw, however, the existence of the committees meant the difference between death and survival and helped to reduce the hardships of those years.

Culture, schooling and leisure

'Polish cultural activity will only be allowed to the extent of serving the most basic of primitive entertainment needs.'[190] This was written by Ludwig Fischer when he was Governor of Warsaw. As we have seen, the aim of the Germans was to destroy the cultural and intellectual life of which Warsaw was the centre.[191] This policy resulted in the closing down of all universities and places of higher education. Libraries were closed and many Polish books were burned. French and English literature was also prohibited and this included dictionaries. Polish books, newspapers, maps and atlases, flags, pictures of leading personalities, Polish national and religious songs were forbidden. The street trade in books was quickly closed down. All

Polish national and classical music was banned, as was the theatre (except variety theatre), opera and many Polish films. Poles were forbidden to own radios, and soon after the beginning of the occupation all radios were supposed to have been handed in. Polish sport was also forbidden.[192] *Next*

At the outset of the occupation many Polish schools were shut down by the Nazis and others had been destroyed. Thus from the start there was a shortage of school buildings to house those remnants of the system that were allowed to exist.[193] Both private and public schools did function, but they were hampered by all the maladies of the occupation; frequently schools were closed owing to lack of fuel, or because of typhus, scarlet fever and tuberculosis.[194] Teaching in the schools was complicated by shortages of textbooks and paper. The situation was so bad that children had virtually to write their own textbooks before they could be taught. The teaching of general and Polish history was forbidden, as was Polish geography. The recommended reading list published for the school year 1940–1 contained mainly nature study books.[195] Many children were not sent to school either because of insufficient clothing, or because their parents knew that schools often became the targets of round-ups and transportation.[196]

Different social groups reacted differently to the problem of whether to send their children to German controlled schools or not. According to a contemporary of those days the people of a higher cultural level chose the danger that schooling entailed rather than let their children go astray. Parents of a lower cultural level, however, preferred their children to go somewhere or do something, and not go hungry, rather than go to school where they would not be fed. It was this latter attitude which resulted in children being used for trading and selling cigarettes, newspapers, sweets etc. in the streets.[197]

The cinemas in Warsaw were of two categories: one showing films for the Germans and the other showing films for the Poles. The films for the Poles were of a propaganda nature supplied by the Germans.[198] The Underground, however, ran a campaign to encourage the Poles to boycott cinemas.[199] From the beginning of 1941 this campaign was accompanied by the slogan 'Tylko świnie siedzą w kinie' (only pigs sit in the cinema) which was painted on walls, doors and in front of cinemas, by a small underground sabotage unit called Wawer.[200] But the Poles did go to the cinemas, probably because it was for many their only outlet from the misery of day-to-day life.[201]

In what other ways did these people fill their leisure hours and get over the restrictions imposed on them? (Amongst the intelligentsia secret plays and concerts were performed in private houses. Poetry evenings, play reading and art discussions were held. People also went to concerts which were permitted in cafés and were often performed by well known actors and entertainers now deprived of a living (A lot of reading was done as a result of the early curfew hours which forced people to be at home) Galsworthy's *Forsyte Saga* was popular – its length may partly account for this. The public library in Warsaw and its branches functioned until September 1942, although many books were removed from circulation. Books were obtained either from libraries, and later when they were closed from private libraries, or from borrowing or buying secretly or other means.[202]

The Germans published a daily newspaper in Polish for the Poles called *Nowy Kurier Warszawski* (New Warsaw Courier). It was supposed to be boycotted, but people bought it because it was for them the only source of information. But many Poles were reading clandestine newspapers published by the Underground. In Warsaw the number of papers published by the Underground was as follows:[203]

1939	18
1940	84
1941	111
1942	146
1943	190
1944	166

Of all the clandestine papers published in the Generalgouvernement half were published in the capital, as all the main resistance groups had their headquarters there.[204]

The community in Warsaw seemed always to be well informed about the general war situation abroad. Their sources of information were the radio (secretly hidden ones), the clandestine press, correspondence from abroad and German propaganda.[205]

Free time was also sacrificed to underground and conspiratorial activity. Because of the German restrictions on Polish schooling and universities, secret classes and lectures took place.[206] Young Poles who had not been able to graduate due to the outbreak of war obtained their degrees from the underground universities or school leavers completed their final school exams. These classes and lectures took place in small groups and in private houses at very great risk. In the hospitals, students were secretly studying for their medical exams.[207] This system was supposed to make up as far as possible for any shortcomings which might result after the war because of educational and cultural deficiencies.[208]

The other conspiratorial activity was the planning and preparation of armed resistance and the rebuilding of the Polish nation.

1.8 The plight of the intelligentsia during the occupation

The majority of the Polish intelligentsia was to be found in Warsaw, which was the most serious intellectual centre of the country.[209] The attitude of the Nazis towards this group has been explained above. Now the consequences of these attitudes will be dealt with.

It is a fact that as a result of Nazi policies the intelligentsia was the most underprivileged social group in Warsaw during the war and was to suffer the greatest losses in human lives.[210] Within the group the heaviest losses were among university and school teachers and clergy. During the occupation approximately every sixth university teacher and every twentieth secondary school teacher lost his life. Amongst the clergy available figures for the Archbishopric of Warsaw show that every eighth priest and every tenth monk died. This does not include those who were killed in prisons or concentration camps or died as a result of hardship during the occupation.[211] If they were not killed the material and physical decline resulting from the pauperisation of the intelligentsia left its own mark.

The Nazi occupation deprived whole social groups of the means of earning a living. Academic, social, cultural and professional workers, writers, journalists and artists were without work. The resources which they may have had were quickly exhausted and many were forced to sell their own personal belongings – books, clothes, furniture, jewellery.[212] Soon the relative value of such goods fell in comparison to the real value of money for buying food, clothing and fuel.[213] This unfavourable trading situation led many of those who had not already found some kind of employment to seek it. Journalists, artists, writers and other members of the intelligentsia had to accept the type of jobs which they were least accustomed to and many of them took up manual work. They entered all kinds of employment: they traded, mended windows, became house painters and repairers, some ran rickshaws or opened reading rooms and lending libraries, others became waiters, or opened cafés and eating houses, some managed to obtain horses and carried rubble and bricks and thereby started to clear up the town. Those who had more funds were able to open shops or kiosks selling cigarettes. The majority, however, were employed in the offices of war-time institutions, e.g. RGO and

Zarząd Miejski, where they were paid very little, but were provided with a reasonable insurance against arrest and a cover for other activities, e.g. underground work.[214]

The situation which lawyers and doctors found themselves in was not so difficult. The Polish politician, Adam Bień, has written that the most important role of the Polish judiciary during the occupation was that it gave legal employment to certain sections of the Polish intelligentsia, and thus enabled them to survive those difficult times.[215] Jan Dobraczyński, the eminent Polish author, acknowledges the help of ROM and the Warsaw magistrate but stresses that it was only a drop in the ocean. Other writers were in a worse situation: 'The majority of writers lived in misery. They were people who did not know how to trade or distil vodka. At the beginning of the occupation the Kasa Przezorności Dziennikarzy i Literatów helped – but it quickly exhausted its possibilities. Writers such as Staff, Irzykowski, Nowaczyński and Bandrowski went hungry.'[216] Artists could find work in variety theatres and musicians in café concerts. Franz Blätter, in his diary of the days he spent in Warsaw during the occupation as a Swiss Red Cross driver, describes such a concert in a café, where he met an artist of the pre-war Polish opera who eked out a living as a dancer.[217] High school and university teachers were found positions in secondary schools, archives, libraries, museums and offices.[218] In a report sent from Poland in 1941 it was written: 'The intelligentsia grow increasingly poorer but are the most politically active and unsubmissive.'[219]

By 1942 the situation had improved, for three reasons. Firstly, the Germans had mobilised all German civil servants and this meant that their jobs were often made available to Poles. Secondly, the Polish Underground State was being built up, and it provided opportunities of paid employment. Thirdly, relief distributed by charity and relief organisations was being felt. Some publishing firms were also arranging contracts, which provided material and moral aid.[220] A small number of people who had originally been forced to undertake some kind of manual work were later able to change, e.g. the Rector of Warsaw University, Professor Włodzimierz Antonowicz, who worked as a stoker in one of the schools at the beginning of the occupation later became a clerk in the Zarząd Miejski.[221] Usually, however, any return to pre-war professions was illegal.[222]

Illegal underground activity was one of the main sources of employment for this social group. They became members of the Underground Army, Armia Krajowa (AK: Home Army) or joined the

Underground government and worked in the Delegatura Rządu. Journalists would write for clandestine papers; university professors, lecturers, and teachers generally would teach in secret universities and schools.[223] Even so underground work usually had to be supplemented by some other form of income. The intelligentsia was also helped by food parcels which came through from such neutral countries as Sweden, Portugal and Spain.[224] It was partly due to the availability of work in the Underground and the activity of social workers that the German aim to destroy and totally demoralise the Polish intelligentsia was not successful.[225]

1.9 The plight of the working class during the occupation

In comparison to the amount of source material available on the intelligentsia during the occupation there is little on the working class. This is particularly true of materials of an autobiographical nature. It was not usual for members of the working classes to write their memoirs and the only one available for Warsaw is that of Kazimierz Szymczak, in a collection of memoirs of Polish workers who lived through the Nazi occupation in various parts of Poland.

The abysmal wages and working conditions prevalent during the occupation have already been described. The result of these conditions was hunger, poverty and unemployment amongst the working classes. In 1941 a report of the Government Delegate stated: 'The working class holds on well and behaves with dignity; hunger increases the potential of their hate.'[226] A meal was sometimes provided at work and Szymczak in 1940 had a job where he earned five złoties a day and received a free lunch.[227] Food allowances were negligible but in one or two 'favoured factories' the following goods were issued to workers, as reported in *Biuletyn Informacyjny* in November 1942:[228]

200 grammes fat
200 grammes sugar and sweets
2 kg flour
4 eggs
10 grammes saccharine

This can be compared to what Szymczak received in April 1940 from a German firm:[229]

1 kg dried potatoes

150 grammes 'stinking' meat

50 grammes beans

20 grammes ersatz tea

At the same time most workers were having to work ten hours daily and no holidays were allowed.[230] The Germans handed out severe punishments and fines for low work yields and late arrival at work. Fines varied from twenty-five to a hundred złoties. Punishment might consist of confinement in a factory cell or transportation to a work camp – or even death.[231]

Transportation was the great fear of the working class. The Germans tried to induce people to volunteer to work in Germany but very few went willingly;[232] the exact numbers are not known. Szymczak considered the idea. In February 1940, when he was out of work, he wrote that in spite of his hunger and being unemployed he would not go and work for the Germans in Germany. By March he wrote that he was waiting for a letter from a friend of his in Germany before deciding whether to go and work there or not: 'if he says all is well for him I'll go'. In June he received the letter in which his friend wrote that all was well, that he had something to eat and slept warmly, but advised him not to go and work in Germany because the work was so hard. Szymczak had by then decided that he would not go because the 'organisation' had told him that going to work in Germany was synonymous with working for the occupier and no good Pole should help prolong the war.[233] However, in February 1943, he did sign up to go and work in Minsk, but once there the conditions were so frightful that he escaped and returned to Warsaw.[234]

A letter written in Poland in May 1942 gives further information about workers escaping from their factories to go and work in Germany as their material situation was so miserable and hopeless.[235]

To supplement their wages many workers stole from their factories and then sold the goods or engaged in smuggling and black-marketeering.[236] Others shirked work to find other means of earning extra money. At times only 30% of the work force turned up; it was normal to work only four days a week.[237] In May 1942, Fischer reported:

Work discipline has slackened further. It has often been confirmed that numerous Poles openly leave their places of work once or twice a week in order to carry out illicit black market purchasing. In one firm recently the workers relinquished their agreed wages and warm midday meal, so that they could go into the country each week.[238]

Szymczak's wife, who worked in the Wedel chocolate factory, used to get sugar cheaply, which Szymczak sold for 'not much', but always a few groszy more.[239]

Many workers were also involved in Underground organisations and work, but they were usually rank and file members and therefore received no financial gain. Leaflets and papers would be secretly distributed at work and workers would in turn contribute to funds.[240]

1.10 The results of German terror and conditions during the occupation

Warsaw managed to survive in spite of the great tragedy that befell her and the hardships that she was forced to undergo during the five years of occupation. German methods and policies produced neither the subjugation nor the collaboration of the population. Nor were the Varsovians passive in the face of Nazi policies which had the opposite effect to that desired. Apart from the obvious consequences resulting from conditions existing during the course of Nazi rule in Warsaw – death, illness and deterioration of health, material loss and destruction, poverty and fear – there were also deeper and more constructive effects.

The Nazi methods produced negative results as far as the Germans were concerned. Where they had hoped to divide, they united. The more vicious the terror became and the more intolerable the conditions, the more the Polish community became strengthened, unified, solidified, and the stronger the desire for revenge grew. 'The German propaganda attempts at possible co-operation between Germans and Poles in fighting Bolshevism have had no echo in the community. They [the Poles] are far from giving up the Eastern territories but even further from the thought of helping the Germans.'[241] Another informant from Poland described how 'The solidarity of Warsaw is incredible. Class and party differences have disappeared. Everyone feels themselves to be Poles above all.'[242]

But this does not mean to say that individuals collaborating with the occupier were not to be found. A certain number of actors broke the boycott, the most notorious being Igor Sym, and some Polish writers wrote for German publications.[243] The selling of Jews to the Germans was also practised by certain members of the community.[244] Collaboration and other such activities considered anti-Polish could result in the liquidation of the offenders by the Underground. Death sentences would be published in the *Biuletyn Informacyjny*.[245] But the picture of unbroken solidarity and a strong desire for revenge was true of the majority of the Varsovians.

[The German attack on Warsaw as the cultural and intellectual centre of Poland led to this position becoming stronger rather than weaker,] because of the leading role Warsaw played in the fight against the occupier. It was not just the political and military centre but also the centre of the underground cultural and intellectual life. This can be seen in the blossoming of the underground publishing and newspaper activity which was carried out there.

In 1943 Governor Frank in a memorial to Hitler admitted that the Nazi policy in Poland had not succeeded in dividing the Polish nation.

The paralysing of schooling and the considerable restriction on cultural activity results with increasing momentum in the strengthening of the Polish national unity under the leadership of the Polish intelligentsia conspiring against the Germans. What had not been possible during the course of Polish history and during the first years of German rule, namely the creation of national unity having a common aim and internally linked in life and death, is at present as a result of German action slowly but surely becoming a reality.[246]

The terror tactics of the Germans thus only served to close the ranks of the community and stiffen resistance, which continued to gain increasing support.[247] Appeals by the Germans to hand over wanted persons to the German police in return for the release of hostages being held met with no response.[248] The Underground was continually operating various actions which included general boycotts in Warsaw, small sabotage and the liquidation of German criminals.[249]

The various boycotts were unanimously supported by the Warsaw population, further proof of its unity. On Sunday, 1 September 1940, on the first anniversary of the outbreak of the war, all German newspapers were boycotted, streets were empty between 2 and 4 p.m. and cafés, restaurants etc. were not frequented, but the churches were full. On 11 November 1941, Polish Independence Day was marked with a street boycott after 8 p.m., and enemy press and local matches were also boycotted.[250] Flowers were always laid on memorials and wall and street paintings appeared displaying pro-Polish and anti-German slogans[251]. These actions were usually carried out by small sabotage units[252]. In Żoliborz on 3 May 1943, on the Polish national holiday, the Polish Underground managed to broadcast on public speakers a Polish national melody, followed by a short speech ending with the Polish national anthem.[253]

In his monthly reports Governor Fischer wrote of the increasing activity of the Polish Underground. It was in operation throughout the occupation but its resistance only became really visible in 1942.[254] By the end of 1942 Fischer reported that after a lull during the summer it had strengthened its activity, and by February 1943 he was complaining about the high rate of losses amongst the Germans as a result of the Underground murders and attacks.[255] This activity continued and strengthened. In December 1943, fifty Germans were shot and in February and March 1944, sixty.[256] Needless to say this provoked strong reprisals on the part of the Germans, who sometimes executed hundreds of Poles for every one German killed.[257]

As in Britain during the Second World War, and the same is probably true of most European countries, war and its hardships brought people together who had previously had no contact; it broke down class barriers and was the precursor of social reform. Only the evacuation of impoverished children from the slums of Britain's large industrial cities brought home the real plight and misery of these people to the conservative, middle class countryside of Britain. In Poland and especially Warsaw, the common fate and plight of all Poles brought them into a special kind of contact which was irreversible. This was especially true of the intelligentsia who as a result of the difficulties suffered during the occupation found a new place and role in changing Polish society. This was not just as a result of the readjustment of thinking stimulated by the conditions of these years but also as a consequence of their close contact with the working classes, *petite bourgeoisie* and peasants. This in turn resulted in a change in attitude of political and social consequence for the future of Poland.[258]

Simultaneously with a growth in national unity and revanchism, however, a certain demoralisation was taking place. This is very difficult to evaluate but no analysis would be complete without recognition of it. An increasing nervousness accompanied the growth of German terror. A report written in March 1942 made the observation that it was apparent that as the occupation continued there was a greater breakdown in morals. This was at its worst amongst the youth. Children stole and Jew-baited, and smuggling, which was practised by people from all walks of life, only contributed to the demoralisation.[259] But the occupation witnessed also a great growth in religion, which provided an escape from the nightmare of life and a safety valve. In many of the homes of Warsaw, in all the districts, altars were built and general prayers arranged in front of them.[260]

The German occupation, in spite of the terror and tragedy which accompanied it, had in general a positive influence on the Polish population of Warsaw. Of course not all conflicts were erased, but the Poles were united in their hate and desire for revenge on their German occupier, and this was to be decisive in the formation of the attitude of the civilian population towards the Warsaw Uprising.

1.11 The Polish question and the development of attitudes and morale before the outbreak of the Warsaw Uprising

The German attack on Poland in 1939 started the outbreak of the Second World War, and two days later Great Britain and France entered the war in accordance with treaty agreements. The news of their entry into the war was greeted with great enthusiasm in Warsaw. People from the most distant districts of Warsaw flocked into the middle of the capital to the British Embassy on Nowy Świat. In front of the Embassy crowds sang the Polish national anthem and cheered. They then moved on to the French Embassy, where similar scenes were repeated.[261] The entry of the British and the French into the war did not bring any immediate advantage for the Poles as far as the fighting was concerned, and a great many Poles were left feeling deceived and bitterly disappointed by the Allies at the end of it.

On 17 September 1939 the Red Army entered Poland's eastern territories, in accordance with the Ribbentrop–Molotow Pact of 23 August 1939, which included a secret protocol carving up Poland between the Soviet Union and Germany, 'all territories East of the River Narew, Vistula and San going to the Soviet Union'. This cruel 'stab in the back' by the Russians opened the chapter of Russo–Polish relations during the Second World War, which can only be described as strongly antagonistic and unaccommodating.[262]

This new eastern border was never accepted by the Poles and the problems resulting therefrom were to dominate Russo–Polish relations, as well as Allied–Polish relations, during the war. The Soviet Union regarded the incorporation of these territories into the Soviet frontiers as 'the will of the people there', in an area which had a large non-Polish population, often in the majority, but included the two Polish towns of Lwów and Wilno.[263]

Poland collapsed at the end of September 1939, a defeated and divided country, occupied by both Germans and Russians. In the Soviet occupied territories Polish state and private property was confiscated, the Polish language ceased to be the official one, churches, convents and monasteries were closed, and men, women and children were deported deep into the Soviet Union.[264] Tsarist policy in the congress Kingdom up to the outbreak of the First World War had left many Poles estranged towards Russia, and the treatment of the Poles under Soviet occupation did nothing to endear the Soviet Union or Communism to them. Many survivors of the two years of Russian occupation did not believe anything could be worse.[265]

The defeat of Poland in September 1939 came as a great shock to the Polish people. They had lived under a government which had continually stressed that Poland was a great power. They had been governed by the Sanacja, who were inculcated by Marshal Piłsudski in the martial virtues of discipline, honour, heroism and sacrifice. The speedy defeat and disintegration of the Polish Army as a fighting force resulted in a crisis of confidence in these ideals, and also a disbelief.[266] It was not until the fall of France in 1940 that the Poles changed their attitude to the cause of their own defeat. Up until then the population was convinced that it was not the German military strength which was responsible for their defeat but the shortcomings of the Sanacja government.[267]

This led to great criticism of the pre-war Polish government. Its members were considered to have been 'not mature' enough for the roles they had to play. Piłsudski, himself, was not blamed, but his successors, who appeared to be totally incompetent, were. One observer maintained that the wide masses of people wanted to see these men punished and brought to trial.[268] Others, however, felt after the initial violent discussions had died down that it was better to wait: 'that only history at some stage will show who is guilty and to what extent'.[269]

On 30 September 1939, whilst the remains of the Polish Army were still resisting the German invader, General Władysław Sikorski established a new Polish government in Paris, the former government having escaped from Warsaw to Rumania where it was interned. Sikorski was a prominent opponent of the Sanacja government and his government was based on the pre-war opposition. The establishment of the Polish Government in Exile signified the continuity of the Polish government and state as well as manifesting the desire to carry on the fight. Polish armed forces were reconstituted in exile and Sikorski combined his office as head of government with that of being Commander in Chief of the Polish Armed Forces.[270] After the fall of

France in June 1940 the Polish government re-established itself in
Great Britain.

This continuity of government was equally important to the Poles
in Poland. It directed the establishment of the Polish military and
civilian Underground and also supported the Polish cause abroad
whilst preparing the organisation of post-war Poland. It represented
a new hope and a change in the form of government.

The majority of the Poles had great confidence in Sikorski and they
accepted him as their war-time leader. In him lay their hope and,
according to one contemporary, his every order was sacrosanct. He
was regarded as the true representative of the nation and his aspira-
tions as being also truly representative of that nation. 'He is for the
Poles what Churchill is to Englishmen and Roosevelt to Americans.'
A legend had started to grow up around him.[271] As to the other
members of the government little was known about them and the
country did not seem to be interested in them.[272] But the government
did enjoy the authority of the people.[273]

The decision of Great Britain to continue fighting alone after the
fall of France renewed and strengthened the faith of the Poles in their
Western ally. It is this profound trust and faith in the Allies which is
characteristic of the attitude of most Poles throughout the occupation. The Poles believed in the victory of good over evil and, therefore,
the majority were sure that the anti-Axis powers would eventually
succeed.[274] Anti-British propaganda, practised by the Germans on a
very wide scale, made no impression.[275]

The German attack on the Soviet Union on 22 June 1941 inevi-
tably brought about a total change in the situation and introduced
new elements. The Poles and the Russians from that moment shared a
common enemy and this created the possibility of re-establishing
Polish–Soviet relations, as well as paving the way for an attempt to
effect a new and lasting understanding between the two states. The
first act in that direction was the signing of the Sikorski–Maisky Pact
in London on 30 July 1941. The Pact marked the re-opening of Polish–
Soviet diplomatic relations and provisions for military co-operation
between the two countries were made. It also contained clauses
arranging for the creation of a Polish Army in the Soviet Union and
an amnesty for all Polish citizens detained in Soviet prisons and
camps. The question of Poland's eastern frontiers, to the disappoint-
ment of the Poles, was not settled.[276] The Russians regarded
their treaty with the Germans as null and void thereafter.[277] The
Sikorski–Maisky Pact was well received in Poland, although it was

never regarded as satisfactory, especially with regard to the eastern frontier.[278]

At about the same time the attitude of the community to the government and its representatives in Poland was loyal but growing critical. There was criticism of the lack of communication between the 'emigration' and Poland. It was felt that the politicians in Poland were deprived of information by the government and were without influence in most important matters concerning the future of Poland.[279]

However, hardly had the ink dried on the pact document when problems arose which led to increasing friction between the two countries. The setting up of the Polish Army was far from easy, and there was a continual problem of supplies. Polish civilian agents working in a welfare capacity were accused of being spies, and questions by the Polish ambassador concerning thousands of missing Polish officers were not receiving satisfactory answers from the Soviet Union.[280] Sikorski visited Stalin in December 1941, a visit which, although apparently successful, achieved nothing with respect to the problem of the Polish frontiers, in spite of the fact that Sikorski afterwards told the British Foreign Secretary, Anthony Eden, that Stalin had said that Lwów should be included within the Polish frontiers and that Poland should obtain East Prussia.[281]

The outbreak of the Russo–German war was greeted with enthusiasm in Warsaw, although people saw different hopes and desires manifested in it. At that time, according to one report sent from Poland to London, the Soviets had a 'number of sympathisers either ideological or transitory' in the country. These people hoped for a quick Russian victory over the Germans.[282] The majority ('part of the thinking community') was reported as wanting the fight to be carried further into the east, ending in the exhaustion and defeat of both sides. However, there was also a fear of the Russians being defeated and above all of the implications of such a defeat.[283]

A new element in Poland's political life was also created by the German attack on the Soviet Union. The Polska Partia Robotnicza (PPR: Polish Workers' Party) which was in effect the Polish Communist Party came into existence in Warsaw in January 1942.[284] Its original leaders, Marceli Nowotko and Paweł Finder, had been parachuted into Poland in December 1941 to organise the party, which was established with the aid and approval of the Soviets, although there was already a rudimentary Communist organisation in existence.[285]

The PPR did not succeed in gaining many adherents, although it grew during the course of the war.[286] This growth in the number of Polish Communists was accompanied by a general radicalisation of the Polish community.[287] It is difficult to assess how much support the PPR commanded in Poland. In January 1957 Władysław Gomułka, who was on the Party Secretariat during the war, wrote that by July 1944 the PPR and the KRN (National Council of Poland) did not have the support of the majority of the nation.[288] The failure of the Communists to gain widespread support was probably due to the pro-Soviet attitude of the party, and general traditional anti-Russian feelings.[289] Nor did the Soviet Union's attitude towards Poland's eastern frontiers, as the PPR made clear, do much to endear that party to the people, but at the same time it was possible to find those who believed that these territories should be sacrificed in the cause of Polish–Russian understanding.[290] (Simultaneously Polish Underground publications did much to whip up anti-Soviet and anti-Communist feelings.[291]) For example, one article in *Biuletyn Informacyjny* told its readers that anyone who in the slightest degree supported co-operation with Communism was putting himself into the same category as the *Volksdeutsch*, and that since being a Pole and a Communist was incompatible, anyone who became a Communist ceased to be a Pole.[292]

In 1943 a contemporary observer summarising the situation in Poland wrote that in the towns and villages few people had been swayed by PPR propaganda, understanding the party to be 'a tool of the Soviets and that the PPR was isolated from the rest of society'. At the end of her analysis she wrote that it had been clear for a long time that the Soviets alone would liberate Poland and no one could prevent them. The form that liberation would take would depend on whether an understanding was reached between the Poles and the Russians. For that reason it was most important that the country should understand the necessity of coming to grips with reality, however, painful, e.g. the loss of Wilno.[293]

At the same time there seems to have been scepticism about the expediency of British strategy. The news of the first air attacks on London were reacted to by some people as being a good thing because it was necessary to show the English how the Germans made war, so they could prepare themselves for it.[294] As the war continued Warsaw impatiently awaited the opening of a Second Front by the Allies to bring a swifter end to the capital's sufferings. There were also complaints that the Allies made no demonstrations, such as sending Allied or Polish planes over Poland, which would be a great morale raiser.[295]

But Polish faith in the Allies was regarded as being the main source of optimism and the will to fight:

They believe and remember all the statements and declarations of the King, the British Prime Minister, members of the British Cabinet and eminent persons which have reached the country over the air. They are saying that Great Britain is fighting the war in defence of the principles of 'fair play' in international relations and against the principle that 'might is right'. The hopes of the Polish community are pinned on the belief of the victory of these principles and ideals.[296]

The Poles believed that Britain would stand by the ideals of the Atlantic Charter. What could now most affect Polish faith in the Allies was the latter's attitude to future Polish frontiers.

In January 1943 the Soviet Union announced that any persons present in Soviet territory in November 1939 were to be regarded as Soviet citizens. This move virtually put a stop to further evacuations of Poles, now considered to be Soviet citizens.[297] In March 1943 the Związek Patriotów Polskich (ZPP: Union of Polish Patriots) was formed in the Soviet Union, theoretically to organise and unite the remaining Poles in the USSR. In practice its role was to be far more political, and was later to form the basis of the future Polish government.

In April 1943 the Germans discovered the graves of about 4,800 missing Polish officers, who had been captured by the Red Army in 1939, on Soviet territory occupied by the German Army. The Germans were accusing the Russians of murder, and the Polish request for a Red Cross investigation into the matter led Stalin to suspend diplomatic relations with Poland.[298] Stalin's action made a strong impression on the Poles and in Warsaw it came as a great surprise.[299] One Varsovian described the suspension of diplomatic relations as a 'black horoscope'.[300] Anti-Russian feeling and fear of Communism was strengthened as a result of the Katyń revelation.[301]

In May 1943, General Berling started to organise a Polish Army from those Poles who still remained in the Soviet Union. This army was to fight alongside the Red Army. At the same time the Soviet Union started to demand the 'reconstruction' of the Polish government in London, which in effect meant they wanted the more anti-Soviet members of the Government in Exile to be replaced by politicians more amenable to the Soviet Union.[302]

In July 1943 General Sikorski was tragically killed in an air crash in

Gibraltar. He was replaced by the Peasant Party leader, Stanisław Mikołajczyk, as Prime Minister, with General Sosnkowski becoming Commander in Chief of the Polish Armed Forces. The death of Sikorski came as a great blow to the majority of Poles, who felt they had been deprived of their main hope.[303] His successor, Mikołajczyk, was still little known amongst his countrymen, although popular amongst the peasants. He and his government seemed, however, to have maintained the confidence of the majority of the Poles in their quest for an understanding with the Russians and the settlement of the frontier problems.[304] 'The majority of the Poles, although for the most part desirous of good Soviet–Polish relations, are deeply suspicious of Soviet intentions and are behind the Polish Government in resisting unilateral concessions.'[305]

In the months preceding the Tehran conference there was discussion between the Americans and Poles concerning the question of the eastern frontiers, and they tended increasingly to blend in with the already *de facto* situation created by the Soviet Union. At the Quebec Conference in August 1943 the Curzon Line, with Lwów lying to the west in Poland, was agreed by the US and Great Britain as the future Polish frontier to be discussed at the Moscow Conference in October. Mikołajczyk refused to agree to this saying that the Poles could not be expected to relinquish Wilno, and furthermore explained that it was not purely the question of Poland's frontiers which was at stake but the very independence of his country. Mikołajczyk did not give the British Foreign Secretary permission to discuss the Polish frontiers at Moscow.[306]

At the meeting of the Big Three in Tehran, however, the question of Poland's eastern borders was raised. The Soviet definition of the Curzon Line was accepted in principle as the future eastern frontier of Poland, if not agreed on formally, and Poland was to receive compensation in the west and part of Eastern Prussia.[307]

Little progress was made on any of these points between the beginning of 1944 and the outbreak of the Uprising. The Soviets did not lessen their demands on the Polish government and the attempts of the British government to mediate came to nothing. Mikołajczyk went to Washington in June 1944 and came back heartened. Roosevelt suggested that Mikołajczyk go to Moscow to discuss the problem with Stalin[308] and it was whilst he was on his way to this meeting that the Uprising broke out. On July 22 the Polish Committee of National Liberation (PKWN), recognised and supported by the Soviets, was set up to administer the liberated territories of Poland. According to one observer in Warsaw the population understood the necessity of agreement between Mikołajczyk and the PKWN in order to facilitate the setting up of a provisional government as soon as the country was liberated.[309]

The author has found that it is the opinion of many survivors of these times in Warsaw that the Polish Government in Exile enjoyed the confidence and authority of the majority of the population. This confidence was extended to the Underground, whose activity and influence was strongly felt in Warsaw.

As the war continued the Polish faith in the Allies weakened, especially after the news of the British acceptance in agreement with the Americans of the so-called 'Curzon Line' at Tehran became known, although it was felt that at least the Americans would help after the war.[310] And yet the basic faith and trust remained because the Poles believed that the Allies understood their attitude and would support it. They could not believe the Allies would not see the justice of their cause.[311] 'As a result of the support given by the English press to Soviet claims, there is bitterness and disillusionment in the country. In spite of this they [the Poles] believe with their whole heart that England will keep her word, they want to believe and hold on like grim death.'[312]

Churchill's speech in the House of Commons on 22 February 1944 about the Polish frontier led to much bitterness towards the Allies and many regarded it as a betrayal of the Allies' weaknesses.[313] The Poles felt they had been isolated in their dispute with Russia.[314]

Part of public opinion – mainly intelligentsia – feels that the attitude of England is only an expression of her politics to Russia necessitated by present events and is inclined to believe the further course of the war will reveal a basic pro-Polish attitude. Other groups, however, see in the attitude of England her basic attitude based on post-war co-operation with the Soviets.[315]

How great was the faith in the Allies by July 1944? The impression is that it was still strong and that the Poles felt that in the final analysis the British would support them. It was very difficult for the Poles to believe that they who had suffered so much and produced no quisling, whose forces had fought on all fronts alongside the Allies, should be let down. In April 1944 Colonel Perkins of the Special Operations Executive, dealing with sabotage and underground armies, after talking with a group of Poles recently arrived in England from Poland, wrote:[316]

People in Poland are generally suffering from a feeling of grave injustice, that they should be asked to give up any territories at all, but from a realistic point of view they know some sacrifice is inevitable ... people still entertain a considerable degree of faith in the honesty and fair play of the British Government, and in particular the Prime Minister himself.

As far as their eastern neighbours were concerned, the year preceding the outbreak of the Uprising was characterised by an attitude of fear and apprehension. Poles were apprehensive about the intentions of the Russians and what would come in the wake of Soviet liberation.[317] This disquiet was accompanied by a strong and universal desire for liberation, which would mean an end to the rule of Nazi terror.[318] Even the most anti-Communist elements were reported as wanting a 'Bolshevik victory' which would put an end to the German occupation.[319] But many of those who had lived in Soviet occupied territories believed that nothing could be worse and tended to fan an even greater feeling of antagonism towards the Soviet Union.[320]

A Polish student, who had been working in the Polish Underground in Warsaw, and went to London at the beginning of 1944, made the following remarks on the subject of public opinion and the approach of Soviet liberation for Warsaw. He said that there was a very strong anti-Communist mood in Warsaw and that only a very few, 'mainly workers and the scum of society [*męty*]', held Communist convictions. He added that the people of Warsaw expected the arrival of the Soviets 'but did not believe in the durability of their regime'. He described the attitude of his fellow citizens as being: 'we've coped with the Germans who are cleverer and we'll cope with the Bolsheviks'. The Germans were using Polish aversion to the Soviets in their propaganda, but it was not winning anyone over to the German side.[321]

A skilled worker, aged forty, who left Warsaw on 2 August and was interviewed in Stockholm summed up his attitude of his fellow Poles as follows:

very few Polish people left the city, although many of them moved across the river from Praga ... The population was favourably disposed towards the Russians despite some mistrust, because it was ready to even with the devil in order to be liberated from the Germans and their reprisals ... The population prepared for the Uprising with incredible enthusiasm, and gifts of money for the resistance movement were greatly increased during the weeks before August.

The attitude of Warsaw towards Soviet Russia was one of distrust and some people thought that once Germany was 'hors de combat' confrontation with Russia was inevitable. However, the population understood the necessity of agreement between Mikołajczyk's government and the Liberation Committee, in order that a provisional government could be formed as soon as the country was liberated.[322]

Alceo Valcini, an Italian journalist in Warsaw, described how some of his Polish friends in the city

felt their own kind of fears in the face of the Red Army crossing. You could not call it antipathy, but rather apprehension, maybe the same kind of disquiet that Christopher Columbus's sailors experienced before stepping on to virgin soil. However, here it was the other way round, because the new world entered into contact with the old Europe.

In Warsaw it was understood that the new Russia was different from and better than Tsarist Russia, but in spite of that people were afraid of her.[323]

It is difficult to assess how typical these opinions were due to the paucity of materials. It would appear, however, that there was apprehension and even fear, but that the Varsovians were awaiting the Soviet Army to free them from the Nazi yoke, although some still hoped the Allies might somehow carry out this task.

2

The outbreak of the Uprising and the implications of the first days

2.1 The Polish Underground State

[The Polish Underground State had its roots in the situation which developed during the siege of Warsaw in September 1939, when the Polish government abandoned the capital and the first steps towards the formation of the Polish Underground were taken before Warsaw fell.]Throughout September the Military Command of the Defence of Warsaw worked together with the various representatives of the political parties.[1] General Rómmel, Commander of the Defence of Warsaw, authorised General Tokarzewski to create an underground military organisation on 27 September.[2] As a result the Służba Zwycięstwu Polski (SZP: Victory for Poland Service) was created, which worked in co-operation with the main political parties: the Socialists (PPS), the Peasant Party (SL), the National Democrats (SN), and the Labour Party (SP).[3] Its general aims were as follows:[4]

1. To undertake a decisive and unrelenting struggle against the invader in every field of his activity in Poland and to continue this struggle with all the means at the movement's disposal until the liberation of Poland within her pre-war boundaries.
2. To reorganise the Polish Army.
3. To create the nucleus of a temporary national authority in Poland.

Between December 1939 and February 1940 a Główna Rada Polityczna (GRP: Chief Political Council) was established containing three representatives from each of the three main parties.[5] Its organs in the country, in the military districts, which were equivalent to *województwa* (voivodeships) and *powiaty* (districts), were Komisarz Cywilny (Civilian Commissars) who were subordinated to the military commanders.[6] The Socialist, Mieczysław Niedziałkowski, was the Komisarz Cywilny in Warsaw and functioned alongside General Tokarzewski.[7]

By the beginning of 1940 the SZP had been transformed into the Związek Walki Zbrojnej (ZWZ: Union of Armed Struggle) on the order of General Sikorski.[8] Later, in February 1942, the Armia Krajowa (AK: Home Army) was to develop from the ZWZ.[9]

The role of the ZWZ by February 1940 was not just to resist the occupier, but also to prepare in Poland an armed insurrection at the rear of the occupying army at the moment of entry into the country of the Polish Regular Forces'.[10] Its plans were long term and already envisaged some kind of Uprising.

The GRP was soon remodelled and transformed (26 February 1940) into the Polityczny Komitet Porozumiewawczy (PKP: Political Advisory Committee). General Rowecki, 'Grot', Commander of the ZWZ, was also a member of it. In June 1940 it was recognised by the Polish government in France as being the political representation of the nation, whose opinion had to be sought by the ZWZ Commander in all principal matters.[11]

The Army therefore dominated national and domestic affairs, and this military supremacy was disliked by the Polish politicians of the Underground as well as the Polish government. It smacked too much of the pre-war Sanacja system. The PKP was not independent of the ZWZ and tended to function alongside it.[12] In an attempt to gain greater independence from the ZWZ the PKP on 28 June 1940 formed itself into the Główny Komitet Polityczny (GKP: Chief Political Committee).[13] But this was not enough and therefore it was decided to set up a Delegatura Rządu[14] (Government Delegacy). First of all, however, a Delegatura Zbiorowa (Collective Delegacy) was established.[15]

The activity of the Delegatura Zbiorowa began in July 1940 with the publication of *Nakazy Chwili* (Orders of the Moment),[16] which proclaimed that the fight with the enemy still continued, and there could be neither compromise nor collaboration.[17] The Delegatura Zbiorowa, however, was not ratified by the Polish government because it still feared the supremacy of the Army and its competency.[18] Consequently it was dissolved in September 1940 and the PKP was reinstated.[19]

At the end of 1940 the first Delegat Rządu (Government Delegate), Cyryl Ratajski, was appointed.[20] The reason why it had taken so long to choose a Delegate was that the Polish politicians in London and Poland could not agree on the choice of a candidate.[21] Ratajski was chosen by London and his nomination provoked a great deal of opposition within Poland, although it was agreed to.[22]

The Government Delegate stood at the head of the Delegatura.[23] His task was to operate with the ZWZ but he was independent of it, and the Army was not to carry out any political activity, limiting itself to instructing its ranks in political and ideological matters. He had control over the ZWZ budget and had to ratify all death sentences passed by military courts. He likewise had to co-operate with the other parties and seek their advice on important decisions.[24]

It was not until 15 November 1942, however, that a Government Decree was issued establishing the precise activity of the Delegatura,[25] and it took some time for the various departments and local representatives to become organised.[26] Twenty departments were created:[27]

1. Department of Internal Affairs.
2. Department of Press and Information.
3. Department of Labour and Social Welfare.
4. Department of Culture and Education.
5. Department of Industry and Trade.
6. Department of Health.
7. Department of Agriculture.
8. Department of State Forestry.
9. Department of Justice.
10. The Treasury.
11. Department of Railways.
12. Department of Posts and Telecommunications.
13. Department of Post-war Construction.
14. Department of Public Works.
15. The Directorate of Civilian Struggle.
16. The Office for New Territories.
17. Budget and Financial Section.
18. Control Commission.
19. Advisor to the Government Delegate on Matters of Foreign Policy.
20. National Defence (established in November 1944).

The Delegatura represented the authority of the state. Its primary task was to organise the Underground administration.[28] Thus it can be seen that the government and administration of the Polish Underground State was based on a form of dualism of two equal agents: civilian-political and military. The civilian population was represented by the Government Delegacy and PKP, which was transformed in March 1943 into the Krajowa Reprezentacja Polityczna (KRP: National Political Representation). The KRP consisted of members of each of the four major parties, and the Delegatura and Commander of the AK were politically responsible to it. The Army was represented by the Commander of the AK.[29]

The authority of these agents was not always clearly designated and as a result there was overlapping in administration. The most obvious case of this, which led to conflicts between the Army and civilians, was over the question of the so-called *administracja zastępcza* (replacement administration). This was connected with the problem of arranging the administration of the operational zones, following the liberation of various areas of Poland. The creation of a body for administration was first discussed in 1940 and it was accepted that the competency for arranging its organisation should be in civilian hands.[30] At that time, however, since the Delegatura had not yet been formed, the civilian side of the Underground did not have any executive organisation for realising such a task. At the end of 1940 a Szefostwo Biur Wojskowych (Military Bureaux Administration) was established on the order of General Rowecki,[31] without the agreement or knowledge of the PKP.[32] General Rowecki was probably prompted to take such unilateral action as a result of his impatience with the inactivity of the civilians and no doubt his distrust of them.[33] Colonel Muzyczka, at the head of the Military Bureaux Administration, organised the administration of these operational zones.[34] However, his departments had their counterparts in the Delegatura and this led to overlapping and duplication of work as well as conflict with the Delegatura.[35] As a result the Szefostwo was abolished but only, and not without difficulty, on 2 February 1943,[36] and it was merged into the civilian structure of departments. The Army at each level was subordinate to the civilians and only the post and telegraphy services, railways and military industries remained under Army control.[37] Such mergers were not effected everywhere.[38] It will be seen that during the Uprising the Army was in fact organised to and did take over the administration.[39]

At the beginning of 1944 the civilian side of the Polish Underground was finally consolidated by the formation of the Rada Jedności Narodowej (RJN: Council of National Unity), which replaced the KRP.[40] It was larger than the KRP and contained three members from each of the PPS, SL, SN, and SP; one member from three other smaller parties, Zjednoczenie Demokratyczne (the Democratic Association), Chłopska Organizacja Wolności (Peasant Freedom Organisation) and Ojczyzna (Motherland; part of the SN); a representative of the clergy and a representative of Co-operatives. By the spring it had started to function. It was supposed to be an advisory body to the Delegatura but in effect it became the Underground Polish Parliament.[41]

On 26 April 1944 a Presidential Decree was issued establishing the legal basis in occupied Poland. It was only made public during the Uprising when it was published in the *Dziennik Ustaw RP* (Legal Code of the Republic).[42]

In May of the same year a complement to the Council of Ministers of the Polish government in London was formed in Poland as the Krajowa Rada Ministrów (KRM: National Council of Ministers).[43] It was composed of the Government Delegate and three other ministers chosen by him (Adam Bień, SL, Stanisław Jasiukowicz, SN, and Antoni Pajdak, PPS) and was entitled to issue temporary instructions concerning the occupation.[44] It can be seen as nearly equivalent to the British Cabinet.

The co-operation of the four parties was not a natural association and nor was it without antagonism. They decided, however, to act in unity during the war in the national interest until parliamentary elections would decide the future government of Poland.[45] In August 1943 these four parties published their programme, which was to be their guideline both for their political activity during the war and after it.[46]

On 15 March 1944 the RJN issued its most important declaration, a kind of manifesto explaining the aims and programme of the Council for the future of Poland. It was entitled *O co walczy naród* (What the nation is fighting for), and its main points were:[47]

1. A new international organisation should be set up for the political co-operation of all nations, based on democratic principles and having at its disposal an effective executive power. Lasting peace must be maintained by avoiding any kind of hegemony in Central and South Europe. To achieve this a kind of federation ought to be set up between the states of that area.
2. Future Poland should include East Prussia, Danzig, part of Pomerania and Opole Silesia. The Polish–Czech frontier should be established by mutual agreement of these two countries. The eastern frontier should be the same as established by the Treaty of Riga.
3. Policies towards other nationalities should be based on the principles of political equality.
4. Post-war Poland was to have a democratic parliament with a strong executive authority. The Army was to be an apolitical body.

5. In the future the system of a planned economy would be initiated. The degree of state control was to be expanded with the state having the right to nationalise public utilities, transport, key industries and banking, where it was in the public interest.
6. Future land reform was proposed including the requisitioning of all private estates over fifty hectares, which would be used to create small one family farms. Forests would be nationalised.
7. The state would release funds for public projects and re-training schemes.
8. Full employment, health, education, and social services were to be established.

This was the programme of the future which was to be further added to during the Uprising under pressure of the fear of growing radical-isation of the community and of loss of support to the Polish Com-munists and other left wing extremists.[48]

There were also four other very important spheres of activity going on in the Polish Underground State during the occupation. In April 1940 the Delegatura, in agreement with General Rowecki, set up a Kierownictwo Walki Cywilnej (KWC: Directorate of Civil Resis-tance), at the head of which stood Stefan Korboński.[49] The KWC was responsible for watching over the morale of the community and for maintaining an inflexible attitude towards the Nazi occupier. It organised boycotts of Nazi instructions, including those concerning contingents and forced labour, as well as boycotts of cinemas, lotteries etc. It established *mały sabotaż* (little sabotage) activities.[50] In July 1943 it was amalgamated with its military counterpart the Kierow-nictwo Walki Konspiracyjnej (KWK: Directorate of Underground Resistance), supposedly to avoid 'confusion and misunderstanding'.[51] From these two organisations the Kierownictwo Walki Podziemnej (KWP: Directorate of Underground Struggle) was established. The Commander of the AK was at the head of it and Stefan Korboński the only Delegatura representative in it.[52] Its creation in fact came as a surprise to Korboński and he and the Government Delegate, Jan Jankowski, tried to have it liquidated, but General Rowecki would not agree. Jan Jankowski decided not to force the issue as he wanted to have some bargaining power to make Rowecki yield over the *administracja zastępcza*. This was more important because it would mean that then the civilians would have control over the adminis-tration of the country and in effect, after the war, of the government.[53]

It has already been seen how the occupying authorities of Poland forbade the Polish secondary and higher schools to function.[54] To counter this secret schools were started. At the outset it was a purely spontaneous action on the part of teachers and professors.[55] In the autumn of 1939 the Tajna Organizacja Nauczycielstwa (TON: Secret Schooling Organisation) was established and started to function.[56] At the beginning of 1941, with the establishment of the Department of Education and Culture in the Delegatura, its activity received both official and financial support. Between 1940 and 1944 there were about 9,000 students studying in the underground institutions of higher education.[57] In the same period about 8,000 pupils matriculated from underground secondary schools and by 1944 there were about 30,000 pupils attending underground schools.[58]

Throughout the occupation an underground judiciary was in operation. It was started with the creation of the Wojskowy Sąd Specjalny (WSS: Special Military Court) in 1940. It was to continue its activity up until and during the Uprising, under the same Chief, Władysław Sieroszewski.[59] It could issue the death sentence.[60] In 1942 the Delegatura established Sądy Karne Specjalne (Special Criminal Courts) to deal specifically with civilian crimes and also to take some of the load off the WSS.[61] But their sphere of action does not seem to have been very large and in some areas of Poland no courts were set up at all.[62] The basis of the activity of such courts was the Polish Criminal Code of 1932 and special statutory laws concerning espionage,[63] and they too were empowered to pass the death sentence.[64] According to Stefan Korboński about two hundred sentences were passed and executed (about 90% of the cases were left to be settled after the war), mainly for collaboration, spying and anti-Polish activities. These sentences were published in the underground press, on placards in Warsaw and on the secret radio SWIT.[65] The KWC also set up Komisje Sądzące Walki Cywilnej (Judicial Commissions of the Civilian Struggle). These commissions dealt with smaller crimes, and also passed sentences of infamy, reprimand, censure.[66]

In 1942 another government organisation was established whose aim was to help mitigate the suffering of the Jews, called Rada Pomocy Żydom przy Pełnomocniku Rządu ('Żegota').[67] Thus it can be seen that the sphere and spread of the Polish Underground State was both wide and comprehensive. Everywhere, however, the predominance of the military both in and over civilian affairs is very evident. During the Uprising the Delegatura attempted to build a viable administration on the foundations established during the occupation, although it had not foreseen that it was going to have to function in an insurgent situation for over two months.

2.2 The staging of the Warsaw Uprising

It has been shown in the preceding chapter that from the outset the Polish Underground had been planning a general uprising, which would be launched when the German Army was forced to retreat from Poland. Throughout the occupation the plans for such an uprising and the forms it would take were gradually developed. Up until the death of General Sikorski and the arrest of General 'Grot' Rowecki in the summer of 1943, it was agreed that the rising would be started when the German Army collapsed.[1] According to this plan Warsaw was to be captured by the Polish Underground forces. After this date this plan was expanded and modified but never actually shelved. A new plan for an uprising evolved and received the code-name of *Burza* (Tempest). *Burza* was to be started when the German retreat from Poland had begun, if the staging of a national general uprising should prove to be impractical.[4]

The *Burza* plan had both political and military aims. Militarily it was to be a manifestation of the AK's will to fight against the Germans, to protect the civilian population from the retreating German forces, to aid the Soviet Army's advance and facilitate the open formation of the Polish Army, which would then fight alongside the Soviet forces.[5] However, at the same time the plan had a specifically political function in regard to the Soviet Union and the Communists, whom the Polish High Command wanted to exclude from political power after the German retreat. This was to be achieved by staging large scale operations against the Germans and thereby preventing the Communists from taking the lead in such activity, and by taking over the administration in the areas from which the German Army had retreated.[6] Furthermore if the Russians would not accept the Polish military and civilian authorities as the real authority and acted in a hostile manner towards them, the AK leaders hoped that the Allies might be forced to intervene in favour of the Polish government in London[7] (although the Polish Commander in Chief in London was still hoping that Poland would be liberated by an Anglo-American force from the west).

Fighting in large urban centres was not included in the *Burza* plan, and in March 1944 General 'Bór' also excluded Warsaw in order to avoid unnecessary losses and suffering amongst the civilian population and to safeguard historical buildings.[8] Polish armed units were supposed to leave their garrisons with only one unit remaining to protect the population and maintain order. In the case of Warsaw armed units were to leave the town when the Front crossed to the capital and go to the western regions around Warsaw, from where they were to undertake action along the most important communication lines. The task of the one strength left in Warsaw was to take the districts of Warsaw which did not contain German communication areas. The main route through Warsaw was to remain open so as to enable German movement to take place freely and unhampered and thus avoid any retaliation by the Germans.[9]

The idea of staging an uprising in large urban centres had previously been discussed and accepted within the framework of a general uprising. Both General Rowecki and General Kukiel, the Polish Minister of National Defence in London, had already suggested it. In February 1943, General Rowecki had sent an instruction to his eastern commanders concerning a rising against the Germans. He told them, amongst other things, that they must make a special attempt to take large and influential towns and establish AK garrisons in them.[10] General Kukiel in October was pressing his plan that the AK should concentrate its efforts on taking and controlling Warsaw. He wanted an uprising to be staged in the capital and not a general one in the whole of Poland, his motivation being that an attempt to forestall a Communist sponsored government from being set up there would be made by the establishment of an administration loyal to the Polish government in London.[11]

In July 1944, General 'Bór' reversed his decision of March 1944 not to stage an uprising in Warsaw.[12] He now believed that the control of the city was essential if the Poles were going to play the role of hosts to the arriving Russians.[13] His plan was very similar to that proposed by General Kukiel a year before.[14]

There are several reasons why General 'Bór' changed his original plan, which can be briefly summarised as follows. The *Burza* plan had already failed in the Volhynia, Wilno and Lwów areas, where it had already been seen that once the fighting was over the Soviet Army was not interested in collaboration with the Polish Home Army under the supreme command of the Polish Commander in Chief in London, nor was the existence of such an army tolerated behind the Russian lines.[15] Officers and soldiers in the AK were either arrested by the Russians or incorporated into General Berling's Polish Army fighting alongside the Soviet Army.[16] This made General 'Bór' appreciate the importance of taking towns in order to realise the political aims of *Burza*. The staging of an uprising in Warsaw was the ultimate realisation of this and the final attempt by the AK High Command to make the Russians understand that it was the Polish government in London who were the rightful authorities and to create a *fait accompli* in the case of Soviet hostility.[17] It was to be a last ditch stand. General Okulicki, the Chief of Operations, has written of the decision: 'An effort was needed that would stir the conscience of the world ... an effort which would display our extreme good will to Russia [and] which would even more strongly accentuate her behaviour towards us ...'[18]

The final decision to begin an uprising in the capital was taken some time between 21 and 25 July, but almost surely on 21 July.[19] Only one week previously, however, General 'Bór' had maintained that an uprising in the capital had no prospect of success.[20] The original plan to exclude Warsaw from *Burza* had resulted in arms being sent from the capital to other regions of the country, which helped to create an irremediable shortage of arms during the battle.[21] Communications had not been adequately prepared.[22] Diplomatic preparations had not been made.[23] General 'Bór' started the Uprising in the knowledge that Allied military and material help could not be relied upon.[24] And yet throughout the Uprising the people of Warsaw expected and waited in vain for this help. No prior co-ordination of strategy had been set up with the Soviets nor were they even informed of the timing of the outbreak of the Uprising.[25] Furthermore in June and early July the Polish authorities were considering the idea of declaring Warsaw an open city.[26]

The decision on the final timing of the Uprising was influenced not just by strategic considerations but by a combination of other factors. There was a fear amongst the High Command of the AK that the PPR in Warsaw might start the fight against the Germans, and thus take the initiative out of the hands of the government forces and authorities.[27] The German call for 100,000 men to carry out fortification work threatened to decimate the Polish Underground forces in Warsaw.[28] Furthermore both civilian and military leaders desired to give Mikołajczyk, who had gone to Moscow, some bargaining power with Stalin.[29]

It is not known if the Polish Communists were planning to stage some kind of armed action in the capital, but General 'Bór' believed that they were planning action of their own after the Soviet Army crossed the Curzon Line. He was afraid that in such an eventuality the Polish government in London would lose a substantial part of its popular support and preclude any hope of its authorities being able to establish themselves after the Uprising. The creation of the PKWN on 22 July 1944 only strengthened the conviction of the leadership of the AK that action was necessary to thwart any attempt by the Communists to strengthen their position.[30]

In 1949 General 'Bór' claimed that when taking the decision to start the battle in Warsaw he and his staff had believed 'that a struggle undertaken inside the city at the moment of the Russian attack from outside would shorten the battle and spare Warsaw the fate of Stalingrad'. He also believed that the Germans would defend Warsaw and that an Uprising would accelerate the arrival of the Russian and Polish Armies, which would avoid greater losses amongst the civilian population.[31] This consideration of staging the Uprising to help minimise as far as possible losses and suffering seems quite incompatible with the original attitude that for just that very reason armed action should not be staged in towns. This line of argument was also used during the Uprising, especially in the early stages, as an attempt to justify its protraction.[32]

The authors of the Uprising assumed that the battle would last not longer than a week to ten days and its failure was not reckoned with. Their thinking was geared only to a quick and successful Uprising; they were entirely certain of success.[33] The significance of this, added to the fact that two weeks previously no rising in the city centre had been anticipated, cannot be underestimated. There was little time to prepare for the Uprising, and no plans had been made for a long drawn out and unsuccessful Uprising.

But in fact a rising was staged in Warsaw which evolved into something far different from that originally conceived of. 'Bór's' original reasons for not staging an uprising in Warsaw, before his *volte face* of July 1944, were to save the civilian population and historical monuments. And yet in trying to 'spare Warsaw the fate of Stalingrad' approximately 200,000 Varsovians were killed or died and 83% of the capital was destroyed. The Uprising which was meant to forestall any possible Communist-led rising and their political ascension did much to hasten and aid it.

Due to the secrecy with which the Uprising was planned it was not possible to warn the inhabitants of Warsaw and advise them to prepare themselves by laying in stores. It would appear, however, that many had large reserves which they had learnt to collect during the occupation to hedge against any eventuality. Others knowing that there would be 'some kind of fight' collected stores in preparation.[34] It cannot be assessed how large these private stores were.

The RGO since the spring of 1944 had been functioning on very low stocks of food. By June it was going through one of the most difficult periods it had known since starting its activity. This was due to the fact that it had not received any of its usual official rations since March and growing financial difficulties made it hard for it to supplement depleted stores by buying on the free market. At the same time the size of communal donations had not been as high as usual. In a report of 14 July 1944, the Committee warned that it would have to close down some of it kitchens and limit or even cease issuing meals in others, if no stores were obtained within the next few days.[35] The AK quartermaster was also having difficulties in building up his stores, mainly because the retreating German Army was absorbing a lot of the usual available sources of supply and having to look for new ones, as it was unable to obtain them in Ukrainian and Russian territory.[36] It was estimated at the time that the Army had stores enough for seven to ten days fighting.[37]

Thus the Uprising broke out in a city which was totally unprepared psychologically and materially for the type of fighting which took place.

2.3 Warsaw in the last days of July 1944

The Soviet summer offensive of 1944 rolled forward at high speed carrying the Red Army into the Baltic States, up to the East Prussian frontier, into Southern Poland and on towards the Vistula.[1] The German defence was broken. On 22 July Chełm fell, followed by Lublin the following day. The German armies reeled backwards, not always managing to destroy bridges in their retreat. On 26 July the River Bug was crossed in the south in the regions of Dęblin and Puławy.[2] The defeated and routed German Army was retreating westwards in a disorganised and chaotic manner. Warsaw was bombed by Soviet aircraft on the nights of 21, 25, 27 and 28 July.[3]

Since the spring of 1944 Warsaw had been sensitive to the fact that the Germans were starting to evacuate the city. Fortification work had been in progress along the River Vistula, and within the town bunkers had been constructed in front of buildings used by the German Army and officials.[5] In June the news of the Allied landings in Normandy and their successes was received with great joy and approval by the Poles. They believed that soon something decisive would happen and that 1944 would be the last year of the war.[6] Warsaw during the second half of July was expectant and explosive.

[From the middle of July units of the German Army passed through Warsaw in retreat.)The German soldiers no longer presented themselves as the smart and disciplined units which had travelled through Warsaw in 1941 to go and fight on the Eastern Front. They were now in rags, some barefooted and carrying no arms. They appeared as ramshackle groups wearing various uniforms: next to the field grey of the Wehrmacht there were SS, Ukrainians, Hungarians and Cossacks. They were tired, stupified with exhaustion. They travelled on foot, on bicycles and on peasant carts, driving flocks of sheep, cows and dogs in front of them. 'They were no longer soldiers but moving human tatters: exhausted, horrified, inert, in a state of visible physical and moral decline. Perspiring, emaciated, covered in mud ... They wore long beards and had dispirited faces and sunken eyes.'[7] The Varsovians gathered to stand and watch the spectacle of the German troops as they slogged through Warsaw across the bridges: 'a heavenly sight was spread before our eyes, a sight which we had dreamed about during the long years of occupation'.[8] This feeling of joy was accompanied by a feeling of fear as to what would come in the wake of the defeated German columns.[9]

Warsaw was pulsating with movement. Not only was the German Army passing through but in greater panic their retreat was accompanied by civilians evacuating the eastern territories and Warsaw itself.)The town was full of rumours about the exit of the Gestapo, the German criminal police, the special German courts. Wages were paid to the *Volksdeutsch* for the month[10] and as a result the whole town was full of 500 złoty banknotes (so-called *górale*) and shops had no small change. All valuable equipment was being dispatched and documents were destroyed and burnt.[11] In the large factories the Germans were removing important machines and officials. By 4 July the dismantling of the Dzwonkowa, Philips and Lilpop factories had started,[12] whilst evacuation of other factories continued. [Polish workers were encouraged to hamper and sabotage these activities.[13])

Warsaw quickly learnt of the attempt on the life of Adolf Hitler on 20 July. In spite of its failure it was enough to make the Poles understand or hope that Nazi Germany was collapsing and that it would hasten the end of the war and the occupation.[14] At the same time disquiet was sown by the publishing of the July Manifesto by the Communist sponsored National Council of Poland (KRN) on July 21. This was followed two days later by the creation of the Polish Committee of National Liberation (PKWN).[15] On the night of 19 July an unsuccessful attempt to break out was made by a group of prisoners from the Gestapo prison, the Pawiak.[16] On 21 July the Nazis shot 154 male prisoners in retaliation and burned their bodies.[17]

The attempt on the life of Hitler created panic amongst the Germans in Warsaw.[18] The evacuation of the German civilians and civilian authorities was speeded up on 24 July, when they were ordered to evacuate to Łódź.[19] As a result of this the German civilian authorities virtually ceased to function in Warsaw. But the German Mayor Ludwig Leist did not hand over the administration of Warsaw to Julian Kulski as has been assumed.[20] Preparations for the evacuation of the Pawiak began.[21]

On 25 July Józef Dąbrowa-Sierzputowski wrote in his diary that in Warsaw the mood was 'tense' and that everyone expected something to happen at any moment.[22] However, the tempo of the evacuation quickly slackened.[23] The following day part of the German administration, police and SS units started to return.[24] Some of these units proceeded to carry out a series of arrests and to liquidate arms stores.[25] There was no real respite in the German terror. Dozens of Polish prisoners from the Pawiak were executed in the ruins of the Ghetto including Pawel Finder, one of the first leaders of the PPR.[26] Leist at a briefing of his personnel informed them that the evacuation had been called off and that everyone should return to work.[27]

The same day, 26 July, red posters signed by Fischer appeared on the walls of Warsaw. He appealed to the people of Warsaw not to listen to the slanderous rumours about the approach of the Red Army and not to leave their places of work. He reminded the Poles of the year 1920 and assured them that the German Army would repulse the 'Bolsheviks'. All acts of sabotage including absence from work and the closing of shops without permission of the Nazi authorities were to be punishable by death.[28] Police and SS units in the streets were strengthened and the main arteries of communication in the town were patrolled by tanks and armoured cars[29]. However, no longer were German police seen to be patrolling the streets individually but in groups of two or three.[30] At the same time German troop movements around Warsaw were continuing.[31]

In the evening of 26 July the Polish Premier left London for Moscow for talks with Stalin and the National Liberation Committee, in the hope of ending the existing political and diplomatic stalemate.[32] News of his journey was printed in the underground press on 27 July.[33] Warsaw awaited impatiently the outcome of the talks.[34]

In the afternoon of 27 July the Germans broadcast through megaphones an order calling 100,000 men between seventeen and sixty-five to come forward for fortification work.[35] This broadcast was decisive in bringing about the first mobilisation of AK troops by Colonel Chruściel, 'Monter', Commander of the AK Warsaw Area. He acted because he knew that the German call would break up his units needed for the Uprising, and make the staging of any Polish military action nearly impossible.[36] His units were ordered to collect at their assembly points and there await the announcement of the outbreak of the Uprising.

The following day the German call to fortification work was published in *Nowy Kurier Warszawski* and on posters.[37] The call evoked virtually no response. About seventy people turned up at the recruitment point in the Old Town. A few signed up but others only asked about the conditions of work. In some cases old and crippled people answered the call as a joke.[38] At the same time thousands of young people were moving in all directions by various means of transport to their mobilisation points. The mobilisation was effected quickly, quietly and efficiently.[39] When it became obvious that the Germans were not going to react to the boycott of their call Colonel 'Monter', on the order of General 'Bór', revoked his order and the units were dispersed and sent home.[40]

By 29 July the sound of artillery fire could be heard coming from the east and the Soviet Army Air Force was active over Warsaw.[41] The noise of battle was to be heard until the outbreak of the Uprising. The number of German patrols in the streets were stepped up and there were increasing numbers of German tanks.[42]

In the afternoon proclamations appeared on the walls of Warsaw signed by Colonel Julian Skokowski, Commander of the Polish People's Army (PAL), a left wing underground military organisation, notifying the city that due to the fact that the Commander of the AK and his staff had fled from Warsaw, he was assuming command of all underground units in Warsaw and called on them to mobilise for war with the Germans.[43] The inhabitants of Warsaw were not moved by this 'provocation'.[44]

By 30 July, Warsaw seemed relatively peaceful. One of the messages sent from Warsaw to London reported: 'After a few days of panic amongst the Germans all is quiet.'[45] The streets of Warsaw had the usual amount of Sunday movement on them, some were empty and generally all was quiet, although there seemed to be a greater number than usual of young people about. Although it was the height of summer they were wearing anoraks, coats, berets, and strong shoes. Girls were wearing grey trousers, sweaters, and windcheaters, carrying bags and knapsacks in their hands.[46] Food by then seems to have disappeared from the shops and public places.[47] Prices had soared.[48] There was no small change so it had to be given in kind. Clandestine papers were hawked and read openly. A feeling of complete freedom existed, in spite of German police and military patrols in the streets.[49] There was no postal service and no trains.[50] On the same day 1,400 men and 410 women were transported to concentration camps from the Pawiak.[51] In the evening a call from Moscow addressed to the people of Warsaw was picked up, telling the Poles that they could already hear the guns of the battle which would soon bring about liberation 'For Warsaw, which did not yield, but fought on, the hour of action has already arrived.' These calls were repeated and were also dropped as printed leaflets on the city from Soviet planes.[52]

This peaceful appearance of Warsaw was nothing more than a deceptive lull before the storm; Warsaw was in fact in a state of acute tension and excitement. This was due to the assembling of AK units on the 28 and 29 July and the generally hoped for outbreak of the Uprising on the night of 29 July, and because of the news of the appearance of Soviet regiments on the outskirts of Warsaw. The German radio communiqué about defensive fighting in Rembertów and the appearance of Soviet patrols in Wawer and Wilanów stirred up more feeling amongst the people.[53] According to one observer a general belief had begun to form that the Germans were going to abandon Warsaw without a fight, and had given up fortification work.[54]

Around 6 p.m. on 31 July the order went out from General 'Bór' that the Uprising was to commence at 'W' hour, 5 p.m. the following day, 1 August. But the order, although it was ready to be distributed by 8 p.m., was not delivered by messengers until the following morning because of the curfew.[55] Then the movement started. Suddenly the streets and trams seemed to be full of people, everyone going somewhere specific, everyone in a hurry. The streets were full of young boys and women wearing knee-high boots, anoraks, and coats under which they carried arms. They moved quickly through the streets in groups of two or three or more and they did not slow down when they met German patrols.[56]

Within the AK it seems that the realisation of the shortage of arms made apparent by the mobilisation of 28 and 29 July and the continual changing of orders, sometimes self-contradictory, had created astonishment and uncertainty. Some soldiers could not see the point of mobilisation and action when there were not sufficient arms and ammunition, a fact which was common knowledge.[57] It is not possible to assess how far these same sentiments could be found amongst the civilian population as a whole, although it is no secret that at the time there were certain sections of the population who did not want an Uprising.[58] According to one report which was written at 9 p.m. on 1 August, the original fervour and enthusiasm of the people was weakening.[59] But it is difficult to analyse this problem from the civilian point of view when it seems that few had any concept of what the Uprising would entail. They were only preparing themselves for some kind of armed action which would not last very long.

Throughout the whole day of 1 August men and women collected and prepared for the outbreak of the Uprising. There was no bread to be had in the morning as it was all given to the Germans. Only in the afternoon did the Poles receive their rations of bread.[60] One writer describes the atmosphere in Warsaw on that day thus: 'I walked around the town for a long time to find something to eat, but there was nothing to be had, everywhere was shut and empty. There was a feeling that something was happening in Warsaw, something threatening, something of promise that people had dreamed of.'[61]

2.4 'W' hour

The time of 5 p.m. in the afternoon of 1 August 1944 for the start of the Uprising was decided upon for a variety of reasons. It was felt that the element of surprise for the Germans would be greater because it would take place during the Warsaw rush hour, which would cause a distraction. It was believed that the earlier decision to start the Uprising under the cover of night was known to the Germans. Furthermore Colonel 'Monter' hoped this would give him the extra time to regroup his forces and consolidate his gains when it was dark.[1]

The preparations for the Uprising, which had been taking place throughout the occupation and were stepped up in Warsaw during the last two weeks of July 1944, were carried out secretly. Only those who were to fight, those in subsidiary and auxiliary organisations attached to the AK, and the members of the Delegatura Rządu and Council of National Unity were supposed to have been informed.[2] Needless to say knowledge of the outbreak could not be expected to remain such a tight secret and it was known to the majority of families with members involved in it.[3]

As the order to start the Uprising could not be distributed until the

Building a barricade in Powiśle.

morning of 1 August many soldiers did not succeed in reaching their
units and posts by 'W' hour.[4] The Government Delegate Jankowski
was only able to inform his deputies in the morning that the Uprising
would start that very day.[5] Many officials only learned by chance of
the impending outbreak of the Uprising.[6] Some hospitals were not
aware of the exact hour when the town was due to rise.[7]

In spite of the fact that some kind of armed action was anticipated
in the city the outbreak of the Uprising came as a surprise to the
majority of the inhabitants.[8] Not everyone understood the meaning of
the first shots. Some thought they signified a street round-up,[9] others
regarded the shots as the type of sporadic shooting they were used to
during the occupation,[10] and amongst others there was panic.[11] The
timing of the start of the Uprising could not have been more unfortunate for the civilian population. People were still travelling
home from work or finishing their afternoon shopping. Many people
could not get back to their homes and were cut off for the rest of the
Uprising as a result. Families were broken up, giving rise immediately
to the problem of coping with homeless people and children separated
from their parents. It also created a group of people who had cause to
be antagonistic towards the Uprising.

Antoni Chomicki, a bank employee, was one such victim. He was
cut off from his wife and had his niece with him. Throughout the

Building a barricade from paving stones on the corner of ul. Chmielna
and Nowy Świat – concern caused by German plane circling above.

Uprising, the majority of which he spent in cellars and shelters, he kept a diary in which he wrote on 1 August: 'Everyone was talking of an Uprising breaking out, but no one believed in it, because people had been talking like that for two weeks.'[12] Another diarist of the Uprising, this time anonymous, in Mokotów wrote: 'There was a lot of talk before about the possibility of an Uprising – yet it happened, quite unexpectedly.'[13] Kazimierz Szymczak, who was in Żoliborz when the first shots came, wrote: 'Everyone expected something undefinable, unknown, but not that which broke out, the Uprising.'[14]

In spite of the surprise, the outbreak of the Uprising was greeted with joy and enthusiasm by the inhabitants of all parts of the city. Movement stopped in the streets in the first moment of the fighting, shops closed and faces were to be seen looking through windows full of gravity and expectation.[15] Civilians were killed and injured in the firing and fighting.[16] But once the streets were taken and in the hands of the insurgents people rushed forward to volunteer and to build barricades.[17] Everyone helped with the construction of the barricades regardless of age and sex. Old and young men, women and children carried spades, shovels, pickaxes, broken bits of pavement and paving stones. They carried furniture, baths, buckets, barrels[18] and even typewriters and paintings.[19] The first barricades were not very professional.

On ul. Boduena an insurgent appeared on the pavement and unexpectedly unfurled a large red and white standard on a flag-pole. This action was greeted by a great applause from all the surrounding houses.[20] By 8 o'clock in the evening the Polish flag was flying from the highest building in Warsaw, the Prudential building.[21]

By the end of the day most of the Old Town was in the hands of the insurgents.[22] Once the German tanks were repulsed from pl. Krasińskich and the population saw the AK armbands and German prisoners of war, they came out of their houses and spontaneously volunteered to fight.[23] Barricades in the Old Town quickly grew. In the evening a bonfire was built and lit in the Market Square. It was piled high with furniture and wood, and Monika Żeromska, the daughter of the Polish writer, Stefan Żeromski, threw books on it.[24] The bonfire was, according to one witness, a sign to show the Russians on the other side of the river that the town was already rid of Germans.[25] Another says that it was a sign for the expected parachute drop – however, it later rained and the bonfire was extinguished.[26] The same scenes were repeated in other parts of Warsaw which were in the hands of the insurgents. At nightfall a glow hung over Warsaw from the fires started during the fighting.

It would not be presenting a true picture, however, to say that people were not frightened and uncertain in these early moments of what might result from the battle. A very few people even cursed the outbreak of the rising.[27] But the general enthusiasm and relief at being free at long last and the mass patriotic fervour and support did not permit doubts to be expressed, nor was there much time to do so.[28] But it has been recalled that when people were peacefully on their own in the evening it was possible to see in the eyes of some fear and even despair,[29] and one observer wrote: 'Whilst working we watched with great surprise the generally evident enthusiasm. In spite of that in moments of relaxation and peaceful meditation, voices expressing fear of defeat were to be heard.'[30]

This great enthusiasm and joy was a manifestation of the belief that the Uprising had heralded the end of the war. No one expected it to last long.[31] Even the authors and leaders of the Uprising had assumed that it would not last longer than seven days.[32] The wife of the eminent Polish professor, Prof. Manteuffel, has probably best summed up the situation when she wrote:

Today, when we know about the tragic course and ending of the Uprising, it is difficult to appreciate the understandable joy which we felt at the time. It arose as a result of the torment of the occupation, as a result of the pain and humiliation suffered for nearly five years. We were prepared for anything. We already had the experience of the 1939 siege of Warsaw behind us. The years of the occupation had taught us to be indifferent to the dangers that threatened us with every step. But above all the belief that the Polish armed movement would hasten the moment of the crossing of the Soviet Army to Warsaw and immediately force the Germans to leave the town invigorated us. The November days of 1918 came back to me, when Germans were disarmed in the streets. Whilst seeking the analogy I did not want to notice the differences. With joy I thought how the child I was carrying would be born in Free Poland.[33]

2.5 The first days of the Uprising

The rain continued to fall on Wednesday 2 August, but it did not manage to dampen the general enthusiasm and spirit of insurgent Warsaw.

General 'Bór' sent a message to London on 3 August in which he reported that the population was enthusiastically co-operating in the fight.[1] The following day he sent another message in which he was more specific:

The people of the capital join the Army in the fight and even the unarmed youth, carried away with enthusiasm, build anti-tank barricades. Women vie with the men to serve and fight, all of them in great obedience and with the spirit of sacrifice. Ammunition stocks diminish hourly and this accompanied by the shortage of arms is an agonising concern. As a result volunteers reporting *en masse* cannot be sent into action.[2]

The mood was such that any dividing line between those fighting and those helping was erased.[3] No one seemed to complain about the difficult conditions.[4]

The inhabitants of Warsaw came forward spontaneously, willingly, and voluntarily to help; they did not wait to be asked. They were busy putting out fires, repairing barricades, carrying out observation duties on roofs and at entrances, transporting wounded, and handing over stores of food.[5] Food, coffee, wine, fruit juices, clothes and blankets for the injured and homeless were donated.[6] Soldiers were fed.[7] Children also joined in the fight carrying food, arms and petrol bombs for the Army.[8] The latter were produced at home to make up for the deficiency of arms with which the insurgents had to fight.[9]

Examples of the type of atmosphere which prevailed in the city at this very stage are legion. But the following serves as well as any. The author was an AK officer during the Uprising.

On ul. Elektoralna German street names have been torn down as have German signs. On the walls of houses various braggish slogans of the enemy have been blacked out. It was all done with the same fervour with which the inhabitants built anti-tank barricades, organised soup kitchens at short notice to feed soldiers and those people not able to return to their homes, caught where the Uprising had surprised them.

The mood in the street reminded one of a continuous holiday. I will never forget those looks of delight which accompanied us wherever we went – full of words of hope and encouragement. One woman treated us with fresh rolls. She had mixed the dough and baked all night to be able to give them to the boys ... Everyone in their own way and within the limits of their ability took part in this decisive struggle. They gathered around us from all sides and invited us to their homes. One felt that we all made up one great family, and each hour brought us nearer to the moment of total victory.[10]

The inhabitants of Warsaw were thrilled to see Polish soldiers again and hugged and embraced them.[11] These first days of the Uprising were marked by a great affinity and co-operation between the civilians and the Army which was never to be repeated throughout its course. The soldiers had no need to worry about going hungry and anything they required was quickly produced. One soldier remembers how his pockets were stuffed with shortcake and how a kind old man holding a bottle of vodka took hold of him and insisted on them sharing a drink together.[12] Neither did the number of deaths weaken the enthusiasm. In the first day's fighting alone over 2,000 were killed.[13]

Barricaded streets under insurgent control were hung with Polish flags, which had been hidden at great risk during the occupation.[14] Colonel 'Monter' even issued an order that Polish flags should be put out to show which districts were fighting.[15] This order was soon recalled when it was realised that the flags marked out for the Germans where they should concentrate their fire.[16] Any Polish victory was greeted with great joy and celebration. When the 'Blank Palace' was captured from the Germans the people around cheered, sang the national anthem, laughed and cried. They went straight on afterwards to build more barricades.[17]

Liberated Warsaw throbbed with a kind of freedom that had not been known for five years. Even if this freedom was to be short lived it was very real at the time. A large proportion of the inhabitants were suddenly free, free from the fear of the Gestapo, free from the fear of street round-ups and arrests, free of the presence of the German police and gendarmes, and the Germans themselves. They were free of virtually any authority to begin with. But most of all they were amongst their own, although their own fate was far from being in their own hands.[18] 'Everyone is excited and exasperated with the joy, that at long last they can feel, think and talk aloud, freely. One's breath is taken away by the thought that we are finally free.'[19]

To the man in the street, to the average inhabitant of Warsaw, the Uprising had a very specific meaning, regardless of the motivation of its leaders. For the civilian population the Uprising was a fight against the Germans, a chance for the Poles to take part in the liberation of their own capital, and thus in the general victory over the Germans. It was an expression of patriotism, and they were prepared to die for the cause of freedom.[20] Fighting the Germans was good enough reason to support the Uprising.

If a graph were to be made of the morale and mood of Warsaw during the Uprising it would undoubtably show it to have been at its peak during the first few days. All information points towards this. There were some people who had doubts as to whether the outbreak of the Uprising had not been premature, but, in spite of this, according to one observer, there was a general conviction that the Germans were in a worse situation and on the defensive; that they did not have enough strength to attack.[21] Another relates that there was general agreement as to the necessity of the fight and this was manifested by the numbers who volunteered to join the AK.[22]

The proximity of the Soviet Army was taken by a great number of people to mean that a speedy liberation of the whole of Warsaw would be afforded. This added to the general enthusiasm. One internal report of 3 August regarded this enthusiasm as being dangerous because it resulted in a disregard of the German presence and threat. Furthermore, it led to a relaxation of discipline amongst the 'unorganised population', which included drunkenness. It was felt that propaganda was necessary to 'disseminate and dampen down this untimely enthusiasm, and to remind [the people] of the insecurity still existing'. Others felt unease as a result of the silence on the other side of the river.[23]

Insurgent newspapers published at this time unanimously stressed the great unity of Warsaw that the Uprising produced:

Warsaw is completely united, in hate, in revenge, in the common desire for freedom.
Workers and intelligentsia, women, men, and young people, all political groups – they are one people today, the people of Warsaw.[24]

The armed action, regardless of who started it and for what reason, has found support in the widest masses of the people of Warsaw and that is its strength.[25]

Nevertheless the reality of the situation tended to be lost in the wave of enthusiasm and fervour which gripped the city. 'Neither the population nor the insurgent units acknowledged nor did they want to acknowledge the unsuccessful attacks of "W" Hour and their possible tragic implications.'[26]

The original objectives of the Uprising had not been achieved. The fact that the greater part of the city was in the hands of the insurgents was an illusory achievement. The insurgents had failed to win the bridgeheads vital for the landing of the Soviet Army, nor were the main arteries of communication, the railway stations and airport controlled by them. None of the strongly defended German objectives had been taken. Units from Żoliborz and Mokotów had retreated to the forests, although they were later to return. Arms and ammunition were in short supply and being depleted daily. Friday 4 August, since

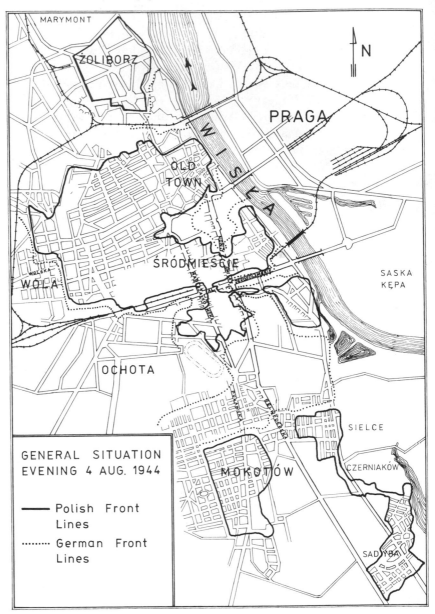

MARYMONT

ŻOLIBORZ

PRAGA

WISŁA

OLD TOWN

ŚRÓDMIEŚCIE

SASKA KĘPA

WOLA

OCHOTA

SIELCE

CZERNIAKÓW

GENERAL SITUATION
EVENING 4 AUG. 1944

—— Polish Front Lines

········ German Front Lines

MOKOTÓW

SADYBA

N

when there had been silence from the east, ended the period of the Uprising when the initiative was on the Polish side.[27]

In spite of the military failures good reports coming in on the morale of insurgent units and the enthusiastic support of the civilian population were vital to the continuation of the Uprising, if not decisive. The help of the population created a situation in which the fight was intensified. Their enthusiastic attitude strengthened in the units the will to fight, and influenced the whole character of the battle.[28] General 'Bór' in his memoirs writes how the co-operation of the civilians was often crucial for the success of armed action.[29] The initiative came from the community and not from above.[30]

General 'Bór', having appraised the situation with his staff, decided on the morning of 2 August to carry on fighting and await some decisive development, but instructed all unarmed soldiers to leave their units and return home, and only those still holding arms were to remain with their units. One of the main reasons for this decision was the failure of the initial objects of the Uprising.[31] Colonel 'Monter' mistakenly regarded the order as being tantamount to wanting to end the fight.[32] He therefore informed General 'Bór' that he would carry on fighting. His reasons for doing so are not clear but probably it was partly due to the attitude of the civilian population. In his report sent out to the district commanders on the same day, he wrote that the enthusiasm of the people and the splendid attitude of the Wojskowa Służba Kobiet (WSK: Women's Auxiliary Service) ought to spread to the units. This was the only favourable aspect in his estimation of the situation.[33] 'Monter' believed that time was on the side of Warsaw.[34] On the morning of 3 August, General 'Bór' again decided to continue fighting by going on the defensive, and waiting for help from the Soviets or the Allies, or for the collapse of Germany.[35]

This was the picture during the first four days of the Uprising in those parts of Warsaw in insurgent hands. The story was very different in those areas which had fallen or remained under German control. In the first days of the Uprising indescribable crimes were carried out by German soldiers. Rape, loot and murder had become the order of the day. On 3 August General 'Bór' in his message to London sent the first reports of the German practice of using Polish citizens as screens for their tanks when attacking Polish positions.[36] German snipers, usually *Volksdeutsch*, hidden in the roofs and attics of houses were menacing the population and claiming no small number of victims.[37] On 4 August the Germans dropped leaflets on Warsaw for the first time. They were written in the form of an appeal signed by General 'Bór', who supposedly called on his men to lay down their arms and stop fighting as Mikołajczyk's talks in Moscow had been abortive and the Russians were in consequence adopting a threatening stand. No one seems to have been at all influenced by these leaflets mainly because the Poles had become used to such methods during the occupation.[38] They tended to laugh at them as being full of lies and bad Polish grammar.[39]

In these early days life in Warsaw was somewhat chaotic and disorganised. Any organisation that existed was dependent on local and independent initiative.[40] It is not surprising that in view of this there were complaints about the lack of instructions and directives.[41] The first proclamation of the insurgent authorities was as follows. It was signed in the name of the Government Delegate for the District of the City of Warsaw by the AK Commander of the district:

The long awaited hour has come. AK units are fighting with the German invader in all parts of the City District.

I call upon the people of the City District to keep calm and cool in co-operation with the fighters and at the same time instruct:

1. After identification, fallen Poles and Germans must be provisionally buried and where necessary the authorities notified.
2. All kinds of lynch law is prohibited.
3. The enemies of the Polish nation, Germans and *Volksdeutsch* will be punished with great severity by appropriate courts. They ought to be temporarily put out of action and retained at the disposition of the security forces which have come out into the open.
4. The possessions of the German authorities and inhabitants should be officially secured in each house.

OPL and Straże Porządkowe [security unit] organs are responsible for seeing that the above is duly carried out, as well as for law and order in individual houses.[42]

The first instructions specifically for the inhabitants of the Old Town on 4 August were issued by the commander of the Łukasiński Battalion fighting there, and not by any civilian authorities. They were published in the Battalion's local newspaper. They started by saying that authority was in the hands of the AK and that during the fight everything and everybody was subordinate to them. The instructions continued: auxiliary service was to be performed by the Milicja Obywatelska (Citizen Militia), which had police powers; citizens not taking part in the fight must not endanger life by observing the action from windows and balconies, by walking in the street etc.; it was everyone's duty to help as much as possible in the armed action and preparing for it. Suggestions were given as to how preparations could be made, e.g. building barricades, collecting spades, pickaxes etc., making petrol bombs, organising medical posts and collecting dressings, organising soup kitchens. The people were instructed to put out national flags and not to spread rumours. Stores had to be reported to the military authorities and private requisitioning was forbidden. Shelter and help was to be given to the homeless. Finally people were reminded, when saying prayers in house chapels to pray for fallen Polish soldiers and the success of the Polish Army.[43]

All other instructions and orders of these first days originated from the Army and were signed by a military person, usually the AK Commander of the district. It was not until 10 August that the dividing line between military and civilian responsibility was clearly established.[44] Only on 9 August did the Government Delegate make his first announcement of the Uprising.[45] In spite of claims that the civilian authorities in Warsaw had been in operation since the beginning of the Uprising their activity seems to have been neither effective nor evident. Organisational initiative seems to have come either from the Army or from individual and independent community action.

Thus passed the first five days of the Uprising, which according to optimistic calculations should have already been over. Yet it was only beginning. However, out of the euphoria and chaos of the first days the civilian population developed an organised way of life and they would be forced by the battle to create totally new living patterns. But it was they who by their actions enabled the Uprising to continue.

All this time the inhabitants of Warsaw anxiously awaited news on the results of Mikołajczyk's talks in Moscow.[46]

2.6 The German reaction to the outbreak of the Uprising and their treatment of the civilian population

The Germans, although not surprised by the outbreak of the Uprising, were not adequately prepared for it and did not have the available manpower in Warsaw to crush it.[1] Ludwig Fischer, Governor of the District of Warsaw, had not believed that 'his Poles' would rise[2] and Himmler, the leader of the SS, had not reckoned with it.[3]

The counter offensive against the Uprising was not conducted and led by the Wehrmacht, but by Himmler. He described his reactions to the outbreak of the Uprising to a group of German officers and Area Commanders as follows:

When I heard the news about the Uprising I went straight to the Führer. You may take that as an example of how such news should be calmly received. I said, 'Mein Führer, the moment is unfavourable. From an historical point of view, however, it is a blessing what the Poles are doing. In five or six weeks it will all be behind us. Then Warsaw will have been extinguished, the capital, the head, the intelligence of 16–17 million Poles, the *Volk* which has blocked our way east for seven hundred years and had always lain in our way since the first battle of Grunwald. Then the Polish historical problem will no longer be a great one for our children and for all our descendants, yes, even for ourselves.'

Apart from that at the same time I ordered that Warsaw should be totally destroyed. You may well think that I am a frightful barbarian; I am, if you like, when I have to be. The order stated: every block of houses is to be burnt down and blown up, so no units can dig in any more . . .[4]

At 8.15 p.m. on the first day of the Uprising the Wehrmacht commander for Warsaw, General Stahel, had the following order broadcast over loudspeakers in the town: 'I order that as of this moment Warsaw is in a state of siege. Civilians who go out into the streets will be shot. Buildings and establishments from which Germans are shot at will be levelled to the ground.'[5] This order was thereafter used as a convenient pretext to shoot civilians regardless of whether shots had been fired at Germans or not.

Hitler on hearing the news of the Uprising is supposed to have flown into a terrible rage and demanded the withdrawal of the whole German Army from Warsaw to the edge of the town.[6] Warsaw was then to be razed to the ground and the Uprising thereby extinguished. He hoped by doing this to make an example to the whole of Europe.[7] But because there were Germans caught in the capital Hitler revoked this order and ordered that relief be organised for the Warsaw garrison. Once the Uprising had been crushed, regardless of the means, the town was to be *glattrasiert*. All the inhabitants of the capital were to be killed and no prisoners taken.[8] German aircraft were only to be used when it was clear which parts of the town were held by Germans and which parts by the insurgents.[9]

When the Uprising broke out the German forces available in Warsaw were insufficient to crush or even quell it. Himmler therefore had to send in units from outside to perform this task. It was his desire to keep the Wehrmacht out of such operations as far as possible.[10] He chose to send into Warsaw the police units from Poznań (2,740 officers and men) commanded by General Reinefarth, Dirlewangler's police and SS regiment from Lyck (881), Kamiński's SS Assault Brigade (RONA) from Częstochowa (1,700), Security Regiment 608 under Oberst Schmidt from the Wehrmacht (618), and finally an Azerbaijan Infantry Battalion (682). Thus by 5 August, the number of forces available to fight the Uprising had doubled.[11]

The significance of these units lay not in their numbers but in their character and quality. Barely half of the men of these units, although they wore German uniforms, spoke German. They were Ukrainians, Russians, Kalmuks, Cossacks, Turkomans, Azerbaijans and Muslims.[12] Dirlewangler's brigade was 'composed exclusively of condemned criminals and political prisoners, who were promised an amnesty if they proved themselves in the fight. They were people who had nothing to lose and everything to win. They therefore risked their lives without hesitation.'[13] Discipline does not seem to have existed. Dirlewangler himself had been imprisoned for molesting a minor.[14] Himmler personally wrote to Dirlewangler to tell him that Warsaw on the recommendation of Hitler was to be razed to the ground, and gave him full powers to kill anyone according to his liking.[15] Kamiński's RONA brigade was composed of Russians fighting alongside the Germans. Kamiński's men were not criminals but young, undisciplined and mainly untrained men.[16] Their primary interest was pillage and loot, 'the capturing of a "Schnappslager" was more important for them than capturing a dominant street position'.[17] They drank their way through the Uprising for as long as they were in Warsaw, committing indescribable crimes as they went. The soldiers were totally unaffected by death in any form and regarded rape as natural.[18] It is not easy to say whether it was with indifferent connivance or powerless disapproval that it was observed by the Wehrmacht in the diary of the German Ninth Army on 7 August that 'The Cossacks are obviously addicted to excessive plundering, which must be tolerated by us whether we want it or not.'[19] It was to these sorts of people that the orders of Hitler and Himmler were given. It is not surprising that as a result those areas and districts which fell into German hands during the first days of the Uprising, when about 40,000–50,000 people were killed,[20] should have been turned into Dantean scenes of orgy and destruction. The worst day for such crimes was 5 August, when the greatest excesses were committed by these groups, both in Ochota and Wola, around the main thoroughfares of ul. Wolska and ul. Chłodna.

It was probably on the evening of the same day that General von dem Bach-Zalewski, who was given the task of crushing the Uprising, arrived in Warsaw to take over command of the fighting.[21] He reconstructed his orders (after the war) from Hitler and Himmler as follows:

1. Captured insurgents ought to be killed regardless of whether they are fighting in accordance with the Hague Convention or not.
2. The part of the population not fighting, women and children, should be likewise killed.

3. The whole town must be levelled to the ground, i.e. houses, streets, offices – everything that is in the town.[22]

Nothing was to be left of Warsaw, all trace of the city was to be destroyed. But von dem Bach did not agree with the orders of Hitler and Himmler and therefore ordered the mass executions of the civilian population to be stopped immediately and all looting to cease. This was not, however, a humanitarian gesture, but one coolly calculated by von dem Bach to achieve Hitler's aims more effectively and undoubtedly agreed to by Hitler. Von dem Bach believed that the mass murdering of the Poles, apart from wasting ammunition and diverting his soldiers' attention from the real battle, would not win the Poles over to the German side but only strengthen their ranks. Civilians were to be forcefully evacuated from Warsaw to transit camps outside the town and thence to concentration camps for extermination or to penal labour camps. Warsaw was to be systematically emptied of insurgents and civilians in order to facilitate the seizure of public and private property and the destruction of the city. Thus the order of Hitler was only changed in that Warsaw was to be first emptied and then destroyed.[23] There was a discrepancy in attitude, however, as the order did not include non-combatants and the shooting of civilian men continued; on the morning of 6 August, people were driven from their houses and then the women and children were separated from the men who were shot. It was only after 12 August that the shooting of civilians was supposed to have ceased.[24] However, although after 5 August there was a decrease in the shooting and executions, they did not stop.

The bodies of the thousands of Poles executed were disposed of in a manner repugnant to the Catholic Pole who never practised cremation. The Germans used captured Poles to form a *Verbrennungskommando*, whose task it was under German supervision to collect the corpses into large piles and burn them like bonfires.[25]

The fate of those who managed to escape execution but remained in the hands of the Germans was also terrifying and inhumane. They were driven through burning streets littered everywhere with dead, burnt and charred bodies. From there they were usually sent to the transit camp in Pruszków (and later Ursus) just outside Warsaw or to St Wojciech's Church in Wola, which was also turned into a transit camp. On the way these unfortunate people had usually been stripped or robbed of any belongings they may have possessed. The conditions in these camps were abominable. They were without food, water, sanitation or medical care,[26] and the inmates were selected to work for the Germans or were further transported to labour camps or other camps such as Auschwitz and Ravensbrück.[27]

The events of the first days of August left an indelible mark on the Poles, so deep and strong that the order of von dem Bach came too late to produce any change of attitudes.

2.7 German crimes in Warsaw, 1–6 August 1944

There is no doubt that the worst crimes at the beginning of the Uprising were commited in Wola. This was the area which according to the Chief Signals Officer, Colonel Pluta-Czachowski, was supposed to have been the most peaceful part of the town.[1] The Uprising had hardly broken out when the killings of the civilians started. In the late hours of 1 August about twenty inhabitants were taken from their homes on ul. Powązkowska 41 and shot on the pretext that there had been firing from their house killing two German soldiers.[2] On 2 August about twenty-eight people were collected in the garden of ul. Magistracka and killed by a hand grenade. Next a seventy-seven year old man was led out and shot followed by four other men.[3]

Wola during the next four days was full of the sounds of gunfire and of smoke from burning houses and buildings – not just as a result of the fighting but because of the destructive exploits of the troops of the Reinefarth group. As they advanced into Wola along the main thoroughfare of ul. Wolska, they left behind them a trail of murdered Poles and burning buildings – actions systematically carried out. A priest lying in Wolski hospital was witness to the following execution on 4 August:

The Germans took the house opposite and executed all the inhabitants on the pavement in front of it, I suppose about sixty to a hundred people. I also saw how the Germans grabbed hold of one woman with a small child who in fear was visibly running away from the burning house, and threw them both back through the window into the flames.[4]

In the macaroni factory at ul. Wolska 60, crowds of people were sheltering from the fires and executions going on around them. At about 12 a.m. on 5 August the Germans started to burn down the factory and some of the people left. Those who stayed behind were soon driven out by German soldiers and dogs. In the courtyard, where a machine-gun was mounted, the women and children were separated from the men. The former were led off and later shot elsewhere, but the men were executed on the spot with new groups continually being led in to be shot. It is claimed that altogether between 2,000 and 4,000 Poles were shot there.[5]

No mercy was shown in the hospitals either. At noon on 5 August the German soldiers arrived at the Wolski Hospital and drove everyone out, having already killed some of the injured lying in the hospital. The injured and sick, even those who could not walk or were on stretchers, doctors, nurses, and people sheltering in the hospital were all hounded out.[6] They were driven along ul. Płocka and ul. Górczewska. All along the street 'in front of some of the houses lay partly burnt children, women, men and old people. The houses were already burnt.' They walked on up to the viaduct behind which lay 'murdered Polish men and women – even children and amongst them were cases, bags and other bundles. On the other side ... stood a machine-gun, which had obviously been used to shoot the people.' In a yard near the viaduct they were later all executed along with other inhabitants from the surrounding streets. As many as 2,000 were shot here, including women and children.[7] Wolski Hospital was burnt down, killing those hiding inside and the sick and injured who had been unable to move.[8] In the St Lazarus Hospital three hundred sick and injured were killed and burnt to death.[9] The same fate was also to befall the Charles and Mary Hospital the following day.[10] Only one hospital, the St Stanisław Hospital, was saved thanks to the intervention and pleading of a Polish doctor, although the director, one doctor and a priest were shot.[11] It was here that the German staff with General Dirlewangler established themselves, painting the Red Cross on the roof.[12] Needless to say red crosses on Polish hospitals were not respected by the Germans.

The same type of scenes were repeated throughout Wola. Inhabitants were dragged out of their homes and assembled for mass executions. One of the largest of these mass executions was carried out in the Ursus factory on ul. Wolska, where more than 5,000 people were shot.[13] A witness to the executions has described her experience:

Up until 5 August I stayed in the cellar ... On that day between 11 and 12 a.m. we were told to leave ... There was a terrible rush and panic. I was alone as my husband had not returned from the town; I was left with our three children, four, six and twelve years old, myself being in the last month of pregnancy. I lingered, hoping that I would be allowed to stay and was the last to leave the cellar. All the inhabitants of our house had already been taken to the Ursus factory ... and I was ordered to go there; I went on my own with the children; it was difficult to walk, everywhere were cables, wires, remains of barricades, corpses, cinders, and houses both sides of the street were in flames. With difficulty I arrived at the Ursus factory. Shots, shouting, begging and crying could be heard coming from the yard – there was no doubt that this was a place of mass executions. The people who were standing in front of the entrance were admitted or rather shoved in groups of twenty. A twelve year old boy on seeing his murdered parents and brother through the gate went mad and started to scream; the Germans and Ukrainians beat him and forcefully stopped him when he tried to get into the centre; he called for his mother and father. We could see therefore what awaited us. There was no chance of being saved or buying oneself out, Germans, Ukrainians and cars were all around us. I went in last and kept back, always lagging behind in the hope that they would not kill a pregnant woman. However, I was taken in the last group. In the factory yard I saw a heap of bodies about a metre high. There were several such heaps; the whole of the left and right sides of the large yards . . . were piled high with a mass of bodies. Amongst them I noticed killed friends and neighbours . . . In our group there were about twenty people, mainly children between ten and twelve years old; children without their parents; there was an incapacitated old lady who had been carried the whole way on the back of her son-in-law, next to her was her daughter with two children, four and seven years old; all were killed, the old lady literally on the back of her son-in-law. We were made to group in fours . . . and led up to the piles of bodies; when the four reached the pile, they were shot by revolver in the back of the neck falling on to the pile, and so on. After being placed in position people struggled, screamed, begged, and prayed. I was in the last four. I begged the Ukrainians around me to save me and my children. They asked me if I had anything to buy my life with. I had on me a considerable amount of gold and gave it to them. They took it and wanted to take me away, but the German who was directing the execution, saw us and would not allow them to. When I begged and kissed his hands – he pushed me away and shouted 'Quicker' . . . I went to the execution spot holding in my right hand the two small hands of my youngest children and in the left that of my eldest son. The children were crying and praying; the older seeing the dead bodies, cried out that we were going to be killed and called for his father. The first shot hit my elder son, the second me and the third my younger children. I fell on the left side, the shot that hit me did not kill . . .[14]

The witness did not die but lay alive under the mounting pile of dead until the next day, witnessing all the executions that took place.

It was scenes like these that repeated themselves in varying degrees throughout those days. It is claimed that 40,000 people were killed in Wola between 1 and 5 August although the source of these figures is not given.[15] In fact there does not seem to be any definite source, and calculations can only be made on the basis of witnesses' evidence, and due to the lack of such evidence it is not easy to assess the true figures.

Executions may well have taken place which left no witness. Hans von Krannhals puts the figure killed in mass executions at around 15,000,[16] which seems too low. Maria Turlejska estimates the numbers to be about 20,000,[17] and Borkiewicz quotes 38,000,[18] but Pobóg-Malinowski maintains that this figure is exaggerated.[19] However, on the basis of witnesses' evidence the number could easily be 30,000, and when the number of individuals shot in small groups or separately and those who died in the fires is added the total lies somewhere between 30,000 and 40,000.[20]

In Ochota, where the Kamiński brigade was on the rampage at the same time, the death toll was negligible in comparison. The units there were far more interested in rape and plunder. Iwan Waszenko, a soldier in the Kamiński brigade, wrote in his diary on 5 August, about Ochota: 'Mass looting is taking place in the town ... carried out by German as well as RONA troops. Speaking truthfully the RONA soldiers take things of value – watches and gold – the Germans, clothes, linen, coats, cases etc. Drunken soldiers are often to be found ...'[21] The worst crimes were committed in the Maria Curie Radium Institute, the residential area of Kolonia Staszica and the vegetable market, Zieleniak.

On 5 August soldiers in German uniforms entered the Maria Curie Institute shouting and shooting. They robbed and looted the hospital sparing neither staff nor patients. There were ninety patients in the hospital and a staff of eighty and their families. Everyone was ordered to leave the hospital under threat of arms and go into the garden. The staff and those patients who were able to walk left. This was followed by further looting and raping of nurses, sisters and the sick.[22] When one woman resisted she was shot. The following day the hospital was burnt down and the patients shot.[23] The staff were sent to Zieleniak.[24]

On 4 August, 160 men and boys were shot in the courtyard of ul. Grójecka 20.[25] Further down the street at number 104 about seventy people, including women and children, sheltering in the cellars were killed by hand grenades.[26] The following day about forty men were executed from Grójecka 24, having first been robbed of all their belongings and separated from the women and children, who were sent to Zieleniak.[27] Forty people were killed on ul. Korzeniowskiego 4 by being sent into the cellar, when shots were fired through windows and hand grenades thrown in.[28] On 6 August a group of RONA soldiers entered one of the houses on the corner of ul. Prezydencka and Langiewicza where there was a field hospital. All the patients escaped with the exception of eleven who were seriously ill. They were all killed by hand grenades and then the building was burnt down.[29] These are a few examples of the 'pacification of Ochota' which continued until about 12 August. It was the usual pattern there and the dispersal of the civilian population was always carried out with excessive brutality and terror.

The soldiers broke into the courtyard at noon either on 5 or 6 August and started to shoot in the direction of the house on ul. Mianowskiego 15. At the same time the order was given to leave the flats and cellars. The inhabitants were searched as they left. Pushing and shooting, watches and valuables were taken ... [two men] were killed by the Ukrainians in the cellar for refusing to obey the order to leave.[30]

It can be seen from statements made by witnesses that the shooting and terror differed from that in Wola. There were no large scale mass executions but instead fewer cases of shooting small groups of inhabitants, usually men. Many individuals were shot for such reasons as failure to obey orders, inability to move fast or keep up (this especially affected the old, sick, and disabled),[31] 'insubordination' and lack of co-operation (e.g. Count Czarnecki was shot for not letting his clothes be searched),[32] for resisting rape or after being raped in the case of women, or purely as a result of trigger happy drunk or sober soldiers.

Zieleniak, the place where those evacuated from Ochota were sent to, was a walled-in vegetable market with no medical or sanitary facilities. There was no organisation at all. During the day the hot August sun beat down and the nights were bitterly cold.

We were hungry. Not everyone had managed to take some bread with them. There was no water. Anyone having water sold it for 200 zł. a litre. At night there was ceaseless shooting. The Ukrainians shot women who resisted rape. They walked round with torches, which they shone in everyone's eyes and asked the same question, 'Where's your husband, your son?' If the answer was that they were in Warsaw the woman was straight away taken as being the wife or mother of a 'bandit', raped, and killed afterwards. One woman gave birth to her baby in the night. The screams of the woman in labour and the laughter of the drunken soldiers, who stood round watching, reverberated. The child died as the mother probably did. On the second day the people started to organise themselves somehow ... The Ukrainians drove a couple of cows in and a cow chase started. They shot at the cow from all sides. People were hit but who cares! When one of the cows fell people threw themselves at it with knives and cut pieces of meat from the still living animal and later sold it for a high price. The sight of it was ghastly. Hunger was as awful as the whole uncertainty about our fate. The Ukrainians shot above our heads and continued to rape women publicly. One woman was raped by fourteen Ukrainians.[33]

From Zieleniak the inhabitants were sent to a transit camp at Prusz-ków.[34] Altogether over 60,000 people passed through Zieleniak.[35]

In the rest of Warsaw equally foul crimes were taking place, although not on such a large scale. In Mokotów there were quite a few cases of the shooting of civilians, but among the worst was the massacre on 2 August of between thirty-five and forty Jesuit priests and several women in the Jesuit Monastery on ul. Rakowiecka.[36] Other figures put forward are that thirty civilians and eighteen priests were killed.[37] Between 400 and 600 prisoners in the Mokotów jail were killed on the same day although some did manage to save themselves by attacking their executors and then escaping.[38] On 5 August about 150 people were shot in the courtyard of ul. Puławska 11.[39]

At the same time and in the following weeks civilians in large numbers were shot in the Teatr Wielki, Ogród Jordanowski and in the Gestapo Headquarters on al. Szucha. Poles captured by the Germans were frequently used as human screens to German tanks attacking insurgent positions, or to dismantle barricades and remove Germans killed and injured under fire.[40] They were held as hostages, e.g. in the Muzeum Narodowe (National Museum),[41] by the Germans in attempts to force the Poles to stop fighting.

2.8 Results of the German action

As far as the Germans were concerned, it took them five days to organise themselves sufficiently before they could really start to sup-press the Uprising. It was then that German improvisation ended and systematic destruction of the Uprising began.[1] At the same time the initiative passed out of the hands of the insurgents into those of the Germans.[2] In retrospect it is also possible to see that those five days had a significant influence in crystallising the character which the Uprising was to take and in determining its length.

News and details of the terrible behaviour of the enemy units were transmitted by refugees escaping from Wola and Ochota to other parts of the town, i.e. Śródmieście and the Old Town. Insurgent soldiers who had been fighting in these areas and then retreated to other parts of Warsaw brought terrifying stories with them. News of the crimes circulated quickly.[3] Reports were published in the insur-gent newspapers although not on any great scale or in excessive detail.[4]

Civilians moving from destroyed areas of the city.

The German action against the civilian population had both immediate and long term effects. Firstly, the most direct result was the displacement of population. Thousands of people fled the districts of Wola and Ochota to escape falling into the hands of the Germans, which they believed meant certain death. From Wola refugees left their homes and flocked into the Old Town and Śródmieście, and from Ochota, in very small numbers, to Śródmieście. Whether they fled in the hope that a successful Uprising in other parts of Warsaw would afford them an escape from mass murder, as Krannhals claims, is difficult to say.[5] It was probably more a result of the fact that the basic human instinct of self-preservation drives the individual away from and not towards the enemy. Many of the inhabitants were warned by Polish soldiers to leave their homes and go on to other districts then in insurgent hands,[6] although there were also complaints about the failure of the Army to warn civilians of the impending danger and the chaos of evacuation.[7]

Secondly, the problem arose of organising the homeless refugees and fire victims who flocked into the other districts. It is not possible to assess what numbers were involved. General 'Bór' puts the figures

Refugees from other districts arriving in Powiśle.

by the second week of August in the Old Town at about 170,000
people, i.e. double the usual population.[8] In Śródmieście (Regions II
and III), out of a population of approximately 91,000 inhabitants,
21,000 were temporary.[9] But these figures also include people caught
by the outbreak of the Uprising. For all these people accommodation,
food, clothing and care had to be found. It was often spontaneously
supplied but not always.

Many homeless people lolled in doorways, filled up courtyards,
slept and rested on staircases and went into the shelters from which it
was often difficult to extract them. The problem of co-operation in
organising these people was aptly presented in *Biuletyn Informacyjny*:

The air of the overcrowded shelters stinks ... Rubbish and litter lie everywhere. Small children are crying. Someone is arguing, someone else com-

plaining. Next to healthy people others are now lying seriously ill from dysentery. Next to young people are indolent old people and pregnant women. The courtyard is dirty and here the homeless are sleeping. Pale and tired faces. Women's eyes are red from crying. Uncleaned entrances form perfect breeding grounds for epidemic diseases. There is no water and everyone is hungry.

On the first floor of the same house is a comfortable flat with several rooms. The large family runs its own personal kitchen. In the larder are substantial stores. It is the same on the second, third and fourth floor. The house commander accepts the homeless coldly. Grudgingly he provides them with accommodation in shelters and on the stairs. Daily food is whatever might come his way – one portion of watery soup at unspecified times, sometimes in the evening, sometimes in the afternoon.

... These people who have often lost their dear ones and all their possessions, have survived the bombing – they are totally depressed, often in despair. They hold on like grim death to the shelters. It is difficult to get them even to tidy up. An attempt to find volunteers in a certain house to carry thirty buckets of water for 150 portions of hot soup was unsuccessful. Attempts to separate dysentery sufferers came to nothing because of the opposition of the sick and their families. Pregnant women would not accept the proposition of transfer to a maternity clinic.[10]

Whilst not saying that this was typical of every house, shelter and cellar in Warsaw the article underlines the great problems created by the homeless. The object of the article was to call on those more fortunate to help the homeless and share their homes and stores with them. It was a call for a co-operative effort. This problem worsened as the Uprising progressed and the number of refugees increased, stores of food decreased and accommodation became increasingly scarcer.

The third result of the German action was the effect these waves of refugees and the stories and panic they carried had on the morale of the rest of the population. It seems to have been a short term effect, and although morale was undermined to begin with it soon returned to normal.[11] In fact the bitterness and panic often carried by the refugees did not have as decisive an effect on morale as other factors were soon to have. The danger was far more that these homeless refugees, unless adequately cared for, would form centres of discontent and therefore pose a threat to the positive mood and attitude then prevalent. It is for this reason that their effective organisation was so important.

The long term effects of German action, however, were far more significant in influencing the attitude of the civilian population to the Uprising. Firstly, it was quickly understood that no one would be treated with any compassion if they should fall into German hands and even if it did not mean death the prospect was still grim and miserable. The bitter memories of five years of German terror were still too fresh to make any trust between German and Pole possible, but at the same time a more positive and humane attitude from the German side might have resulted in a greater willingness on the part of the Poles to leave Warsaw, and thus cross to areas under German control, rather than risk their lives in the insurgent capital. Any calls by the Germans, no matter in what terms they were couched, were met with a general rejection and ignored by the Poles. There were only a few cases during the Uprising of the civilian population attempting to cross to the Germans, with the exception of the evacuation arranged by the Red Cross at the beginning of September, and those crossing after the fall of Mokotów and at the beginning of October. The determination to remain in the battle area in spite of the dangers involved was strengthened even more when information came through on the awful conditions in the transit camp in Pruszków.

Secondly, a strong solidarity between the insurgents and the rest of the population was formed. Civilian status carried no guarantees of safety, and therefore whether one was a member of the AK or not was immaterial, because to be Polish sufficed. Even a German informant in Warsaw recognised this point. He began his report by describing the unfavourable and unsympathetic attitude which the inhabitants of Warsaw showed towards the Uprising, but went on to say that when they saw that 'the Germans ruthlessly destroyed the lives and possessions of the inhabitants and razed the whole of Warsaw to the ground making no difference between those who were guilty and innocent, the whole attitude suddenly changed. From then on they placed themselves on the side of the insurgents, to fight against the unyielding deadly enemy of their nation.'[12] John Ward, AK officer and *Times* correspondent in Warsaw during the Uprising also stressed how 'The determination of the population to fight to the last man is only strengthened by this German barbarism.'[13]

Thirdly, German action probably prolonged the Uprising. Due to the fact that the soldiers engaged in these operations were not always well disciplined and were more concerned with loot and plunder, their own advance was hindered and delayed.[14] To say categorically that the German treatment of the civilian population resulted in a prolongation of the Uprising might just be conjecture, but the combination of the two preceding points add weight to the statement. Many potential opponents of the Uprising and groups of people who would have left Warsaw purely to avoid the fight did not withdraw their support from the insurgent cause, or at least did not desert it. If large groups of civilians had left Warsaw the whole Uprising would have taken on a very different character and probably not have lasted so long. Its leaders would have been deprived of the mass support which was also politically very necessary for them. The affinity between soldier and civilian was very strong and a mass voluntary civilian exodus would have had a very negative effect on the morale of the soldiers. Civilian support was not only vital to the wide base and significance of the Uprising for as long as it was to last, it in fact gave it such a significance.

Thus the behaviour of the Germans was of no small consequence in forming the character of the Uprising, having a solidifying rather than a divisive effect.

3

The course of the Uprising

3.1 Wola

It is not easy to draw any coherent picture of civilian life in Wola during the Uprising. The Uprising there lasted hardly six days, the shortest of all the left bank districts. There was no time, therefore, for any pattern of life or organisation to develop. The history of those days for the civilians was one of survival or escape from the Germans and the executions. Furthermore, there are hardly any materials available concerning the civilian population in the district.

Wola's boundaries were formed in the north by the Catholic cemetery in Powązki and by ul. Powązkowska, in the east by ul. Zamenhofa and in the south by the main arteries of ul. Wolska and Chłodna. It was from the west of Wola across ul. Płocka that the Germans advanced in an easterly direction.

The Uprising was greeted with the same enthusiasm and surprise as it was in other parts of Warsaw. People willingly and spontaneously joined in the building of barricades, even under fire:[1]

on their own initiative, civilians put up hundreds of barricades to hamper the movement of German tanks towards our positions, at least two or three on every street. They sprang up before our eyes in a couple of hours. It was quite simple. The inhabitants of neighbouring houses threw out from their windows tables, divans, cupboards, chests – in fact, everything movable they possessed. They tore up pavements and used the paving stones, and then, in front of this barrier of miscellaneous objects, they dug a deep trench.
... So great was the enthusiasm for this work that the Government Delegate had to appeal to the people not to use such objects as pictures, antiques, typewriters or other things of value. Houses on both sides of the street were covered with national flags.[2]

Soldiers were fed by the inhabitants:

Every day ... in one of the courtyards a fire was lit, on which was placed a large pot of water. It looked very ceremonial as women from the whole house emptied the contents of the bags in their hands into the pot. They poured in anything they had, different types of groats, oats, potatoes. When it was ready first of all the soldiers were called for and then the children.[3]

Underground passages were built to make communications easier in the cellars, and at the beginning everyone joined in happily, still believing that everything would soon be over and that the Germans would be gone for good. But at the same time there was disquiet about what was going on.[4]

On the first night of the Uprising refugees started to flow into the district, mainly from Koło. They filled up the doorways and some kind of help had to be found for them.[5] Civilians fleeing from the Germans and fires, often spreading panic with them as they went, sheltered in the hospitals and churches.[6] Refugees flocked into the hospitals in the hope that they would soon be able to return to their homes. They were all taken in, in spite of the chaos and deficiency in administration and feeding.[7] One of the medical staff in the Wolski Hospital recalls that they were a nuisance and were felt to be a potential panic threat to patients and workers. They filled up the lobby, which was an air-raid shelter. Later they were evacuated.[8]

Not all the hospitals had had any warning of the outbreak of the Uprising. In the Charles and Mary Hospital only one doctor was present when the Uprising broke out. The personnel of Wolski Hospital were only given one hour's warning. From the very first day the wounded started to arrive and had to be laid out on mattresses on the floor as there were not enough beds. As in the Charles and Mary Hospital, staff and organisation were also lacking in St Stanisław's Hospital.[9] In the hospitals of Wola there was no electricity, but there was at least water and gas. In the Wolski Hospital the operating theatre had electricity, because the director, Dr Piasecki, had installed a generator there as a result of his experience during the siege of Warsaw in September 1939.[10]

In the Wolski Hospital during the first days of the Uprising, in spite of the tension and unease, the mood was not one of despair. Everyone there continued to hope that something decisive would happen and that Warsaw would be liberated.[11] On 3 August two boys came in to visit an injured comrade, and greatly lifted morale by saying that the Russians would arrive either that night or the next day. Dr Janina Misiewicz comments on this event as follows: 'It can be said that nothing could have transformed the attitude of Warsaw to the Russians more favourably than their expected help in liquidating the Germans in the town, in the consolidation of the results of the

Uprising.'[12] By the following day the atmosphere in the hospital was peaceful. No one bothered to discuss the expediency of the Uprising any longer, but were far more concerned about their homes, their families and the people of Warsaw generally.[13] The next day, Saturday – a beautifully sunny day – was to see the massacre of the inhabitants of the hospital.

On the night of 4 August Warsaw received the first outside aid from the Allies. Two Halifax bombers dropped twelve containers with arms which fell into the insurgents' hands in Wola.[14] However, the Uprising did not last long enough there for any problems with the food situation to arise. There seems to have been no local organisation as far as the civilian population was concerned and there is no record of any. No civilian administration was formed.[15] Any organisation that there was must have been left to self-help and individual initiative.

There is only record of one newspaper having been published in Wola, *Warszawa Walczy* (Warsaw Fights). It was published by the AK battalion 'Zośka', but it is not known how many issues there were. It printed calls, appeals and instructions to the inhabitants of Wola, as well as radio news.[16] *Biuletyn Informacyjny* also got through,[17] but BIP did not function there[18] and so apart from the papers the civilian population cannot have received any official guidance. News was usually carried by word of mouth or picked up from outside stations on radios which had been hidden throughout the occupation.[19]

Those inhabitants of Wola who had managed to escape fled on to Śródmieście and the Old Town, taking with them only bags and bundles of the few belongings they had been able to gather together.[20] They left in fright, spreading panic and apprehension to other areas and districts,[21] undermining morale in the Army,[22] which at times they blamed for their plight and misfortune.[23]

3.2 Ochota

Civilian life during the eleven day Uprising in the district of Ochota seems to be even more poorly documented than that of insurgent Wola and therefore it is not possible to present a complete picture here, either.

The district of Ochota was contained in the boundaries of District IV of Warsaw,[1] which were widely flung and covered most of the area inside the railway lines to Skierniewice in the north and Radom in the west and south, and by ul. Żwirki i Wigury in the east. The majority of the fighting throughout the Uprising took place in the area between the streets of Wawelska, Kopińska, Szczęśliwicka, Grójecka, Niemcewicza and Filtrowa.

The Uprising in Ochota can be divided into two periods. The first period lasted from the outbreak of the Uprising to the morning of 4 August. The second period began there and ended with the general fall of the district on 11 August. The first phase, although not free from armed action or civilian executions, was relatively peaceful in comparison to what was to follow. On 4 August the soldiers of the RONA group started out on their drunken and bloody trail of plunder, loot, destruction, rape and murder.

The outbreak of the Uprising at 5 o'clock in the afternoon caught many people out on the streets, and the first hours of the fighting resulted in a high number of civilian casualties, especially on pl. Narutowicza.[2] The insurgent units failed to take any of the key positions held by the Germans.[3] Losses on the Polish side were high. As a result of these initial failures the Commander of the district, Colonel Mieczysław Sokołowski, 'Grzymała', ordered his units to leave and march to the Sękociński woods.[4] Other units in the area were not informed and were left behind.[5] Only the insurgents who had collected in the ZUS houses between the streets of Niemcewicza, Asnyka, Filtrowa and Grójecka left the district joined by some civilians.[6]

By 2 August there were three centres of resistance in Ochota, totally cut off from each other and from any other outside contact. The first was the so-called 'Kaliska Redoubt', where Lieutenant Andrzej Chyczewski, 'Gustaw', and his unit were fighting.[7] The insurgents were fighting in the streets between Kopińska, the west side of Grójecka, Niemcewicza and Szczęśliwicka. By 5 August the area had been reduced and was bordered by the streets of Jotejki, Białobrzeska, Kopińska and Kaliska.[8] The second centre was that of Lieutenant Jerzy Gołębiowski, 'Stach', and his unit in the 'Wawelska Redoubt', which encompassed the blocks of ul. Wawelska 60, ul. Adama Pługa 2, ul. Mianowskiego 15 and ul. Uniwersytecka 1.[9] The third centre was in 'Kolonia Staszica' where the unarmed unit of Lieutenant Juliusz Sobolewski, 'Roman', was caught.[10]

Both the 'Kaliska Redoubt' and the 'Wawelska Redoubt' housed large groups of civilians but Colonel 'Grzymała' had also left many behind in the ZUS houses. Civilians were trapped in other blocks and houses and it would seem from what evidence there is that they had to sit tight in their flats, shelters and cellars and do nothing. Movement on the streets was practically impossible due to shooting and snipers.[11] There was no barricading of the streets. Little has been written or recorded about these people before the arrival of the RONA groups. Consequently any description of 'civilian life' has to be restricted to that of the two redoubts and the ZUS blocks. But each case is an interesting example of independent civilian organisation and behaviour in an insurgent situation.

Whilst 'Grzymała' was still discussing the situation in his quarters on ul. Niemcewicza during the night of 1 and 2 August, a delegation of civilians entered the room. They asked him to evacuate the blocks because his unit's presence was exposing civilians there to repressions and reprisals. This request on the part of the civilian delegation seems to have been what finally made 'Grzymała' decide to order his men to march.[12]

There were about 2,000 civilians in these blocks,[13] including homeless refugees and fire victims from ul. Tarczyńska, Daleka, Raszyńska, Grójecka, the main railway station and pl. Zawiszy.[14] For the first ten days of the Uprising they remained virtually undisturbed.[15] A Samorząd Obywatelski (Citizens' Self-Government) or Block Committee was soon functioning.[16] It organised life there, finding accommodation for the homeless, gathering up food and clothes for them, establishing a collective kitchen and a medical point, and organising a small ward for the sick. Latrines were dug for the refugees, and basins, towels, and soap collected and general sanitation organised. Cigarettes were provided and child care arranged. A group of boy scouts, 'Zawiszy', were predominantly involved in all this work.[17] There were also two medical points in the blocks which had been prepared before the outbreak of the Uprising, at ul. Grójecka 45 and ul. Filtrowa 62. Civilians willingly took part in fire-fighting organisation.[18]

A daily newspaper was published by Professor Stefan Rygiel with news which he monitored from a neighbour's radio. Several copies were typed out by his wife and himself.[19] There was also a telephone which was still functioning.[20] Communication between ul. Niemcewicza and Filtrowa had to be through a tunnel because of shooting on ul. Asnyka. A central heating pipe under the street facilitated this. A very flat plank was placed inside which had a cable attached and was pulled by two people through the twenty-two metres of pipe.[21]

On 5 August the bombing started, which caused one witness to fear that they faced the same fate as the Ghetto. Mass was held in one of the shelters. After 7 August there was no water and in Grójecka . there was no well. For ten people there was one bath full of water. On 10 August the RONA units entered the blocks driving out the inhabitants, who were sent on to Zieleniak.[23]

In the 'Wawelska Redoubt', which was called at the time the alcazar of the capital,[24] there was no Block Committee but a general form of co-operation between the Army and civilians was established. There were about 600 inhabitants within the Redoubt.[25] Everyone took part in the fight by helping to put out fires, building and remaking barricades, carrying the injured and sharing their stores.[26] Only the sick and old were inactive.[27]

Irena Chosłowska and her daughter ran a kitchen for the Army and civilians in Mianowskiego 15, preparing between 500 and 600 meals daily. Stores came either from the Army or were requisitioned by the AK for the community from the flats of absent inhabitants.[28] The food situation was not easy and worsened daily.[29] An artesian well was sunk in the courtyard and a latrine built. In the moments when the Redoubt was not being attacked and the inhabitants were able to come up out of the cellars, barricades had to be strengthened and repaired, water had to be collected for washing and cooking, and the latrine used.[30] There was a medical point on Mianowskiego 15[31] which gradually grew into a little hospital.[32]

A newspaper was published in the Redoubt by Wilhelm Zwierowicz.[33] The telephone there was in operation but otherwise the Redoubt was totally cut off and news was continually awaited from the rest of the town.[34] After 6 August there was a radio and news started to come through.[35] It was possible to see what was going on in the surrounding houses – the 'evacuation' of their neighbours.[36]

Amongst the inhabitants of the Redoubt was a priest called Salamucha, who used to celebrate mass in the block.[37] When the Redoubt fell he refused to change out of his cassock into civilian clothes and tried to protect the inhabitants of the house. He left bearing a white flag but was killed.[38]

One witness has commented on the attitude of the inhabitants as follows: 'In spite of the very difficult situation there were not many people who were ill-disposed to the Uprising, and then really only when the situation proved to be hopeless ...'[39] On the other side of the street, however, in ul. Adama Pługa 2, the inhabitants had already started to become irritated by the situation by 4 August. Some were critical of the Uprising and others showed surprise that there had been no Soviet relief. They could see what was going on all around them and knew what fate awaited them. Some tried to escape to Filtrowa and a couple of *Reichsdeutsch* tried to arrange German protection for the inhabitants.[40] It was all in vain and the RONA soldiers arrived on 6 August.[41]

On 9 August the German attack began in earnest on the 'Wawelska Redoubt'.[42] It was directed from all sides and fires were started on the fourth and fifth floors, which civilians were responsible for putting out.[43] By 10 August 'the strain on the nerves of the inhabitants had reached breaking point. Those active and fighting managed to bear the repeated attacks considerably better than the old and the weak, who were forced to remain inactive . . .'[44] On the night of the same day the first attempt was made by the insurgents to cross to Śródmieście through the sewers.[45] In the afternoon of the following day the Redoubt was attacked with Goliath tanks.[46] White flags were put out but the attack continued.[47] In the evening the RONA soldiers arrived, driving the inhabitants out to Zieleniak.[48] They also shot and stoned about eighty people, men and the seriously injured.[49]

In comparison to these two communities little is known about the situation of the civilian population in the 'Kaliska Redoubt'. Wroniszewski has written: 'In comparison to the centre in Wawelska which a whole group of people organised peacefully and thoughtfully, it [i.e. Kaliska] was firmly organised above all by the activity and energy of both officers.'[50] There were about eight to nine thousand people collected in the 'Kaliska Redoubt'. The shortage of food was greatly alleviated there by the insurgents capturing the tobacco factory on ul. Kaliska on 2 August. Stores of flour, groats, animal fats, cigarettes, medical spirits and other articles were found. A bakery was established.[51] Witold Wolff and his wife published a newspaper called *Nowy Dzień* (New Day), which was printed on a duplicating machine. They had previously published a clandestine paper under the same name. A second paper called *Biuletyn Informacyjny* was produced by the AK unit there. Both papers contained news monitored from the radio.[52]

As in the other Redoubt the situation grew more difficult daily. German units attacked all the surrounding buildings and insurgent ammunition was running low. Problems with electricity and water grew worse and fires were left burning. At night the singing of drunken Ukrainians could be heard mingled with cries of the people they were capturing. Every day the inhabitants of the Redoubt saw groups of people, mainly women, children and the aged, moving from Zieleniak in the direction of the Western Railway Station.[53] The Redoubt fell on 9 August, its commander and unit having left.[54]

Lieutenant 'Roman' and his unit had left the Kolonia Staszica on the night of 3 August having made contact with the 'Golski' unit and together they crossed to Śródmieście.[55] They left behind them a group of civilians totally cut off and unable to move, not even into the courtyard due to shooting and snipers. No news got through to them – only gossip.[56] They heard stories of burning houses and the injured in other parts of the district, of the raping of nurses and the murdering of civilians.[57] The Germans arrived there on 12 August.[58]

Thus the Uprising in Ochota ended. It is difficult to see any true pattern emerging. Evidence is too scanty and narrowly based to draw any firm conclusions, although all cases show the extent of civilian sympathy for the military and civilian sacrifice. At the same time there are also inherent contradictions; co-operation on the hand and requests on the other that the Army should withdraw. Both support and criticism of the Uprising is to be found. There is evidence of civilians prepared to risk German assurances in spite of what was happening all around them. The Uprising, however, was too short and severe in Ochota to allow any firm conclusions to be drawn.

3.3 The Old Town

The change of mood and attitude of the people towards the Uprising was for me the most characteristic and deeply felt thing. I would think it was similar in all the districts, but in the Old Town where the fighting did not last so long the change appeared quickly and sharply.[1]

The Old Town is taken here to mean the area which remained in the hands of the insurgents for the majority of the Uprising. This area was contained within the streets of Konwiktorska (in the north), Wybrzeże Gdańskie, Bugaj, pl. Zamkowy, Bielańska, Nalewki, Świętojerska, and Bonifraterska. The narrow streets of the Old Town normally contained a large number of inhabitants, but during the Uprising these numbers were further swelled by refugees. There were between 75,000 and 100,000 people caught in this small area.[2]

The refugees arriving from Wola found a totally different situation and atmosphere from that which they had left behind them. There were no air attacks or bombing. Everyone moved around freely and the streets were full of happy faces. Shops, bakers, restaurants and chemists were open, and certain goods were being sold in the market square. Bread had been rationed. Flags were flying and portraits of national leaders were displayed. Walls were covered with posters and papers. Insurgent signs and billboards were hanging with such announcements as 'Władze cywilne' (Civilian authorities) or 'Fryzjer wyłącznie dla wojska' (Barbers – military only). Soldiers walked around in their uniforms. Jews who had been freed from the Gęsiowa camp were carrying sacks of dried potatoes found in the captured German stores on ul. Stawki. Children were playing on the round-about and swings in pl. Krasińskich. Underground passages had been built connecting the cellars and it was possible to travel quite far by them.[3] Various newspapers were in circulation – about eighteen papers were published and distributed in the district.[4] The morale of the inhabitants was good. They continued to be enthusiastic, to help and to share their stores with the Army and refugees,[5] although there was embitterment that the Russians had not appeared.[6]

On 9 August drops of arms and ammunition from the West were received.[7] This hoped for, indeed expected help filled the people with joy. 'One does not speak of hope, but of certainty in victory.'[8] On the same day the Germans started to bomb the Old Town and there was soon a marked change in the mood of the population. Life began to grow more difficult.[9] Houses were being destroyed. Water and food either ran short or ran out. There was no electric light, but candles and acetylene lamps were used instead. Stocks of dressings began to run low. As the printers were destroyed the flow of newspapers grew erratic. The number of dead and injured amongst civilians rose, and movement on the streets was restricted. People were forced to leave their homes and flats and go down to the cellars and shelters; the Old Town started to live underground. In the cellars and shelters there was an unpleasant atmosphere, for they were hot and stuffy and full of people who were often irritated, short tempered and pessimistic.[10]

Colonel Karol Ziemski, 'Wachnowski', commander of the AK Northern Group, seeking help with organising the civilians, sent an internal report on 12 August to Marceli Porowski, the Government Delegate for Warsaw, describing:

the situation … [of] the homeless civilian population in shelters in our district (hunger, terrible hygienic conditions, no organisation at all nor outside help). Such a state of affairs could have serious consequences, not only because of the danger of epidemics but also because of the spreading of defeatism and even in places antagonism towards the Army. These people display an unhealthy indifference. They survive the hunger quite passively (some have not eaten for 2–3 days) and show no initiative to try and find food. At the same time in spite of the terrible sanitary conditions and spreading disease, there is not the slightest initiative being shown in organi-sation, regular cleaning, ventilating and disinfecting etc. Against a background of hunger, bad air and disease the morale of the people continually worsens . . .[11]

On Sunday 13 August a booby-trapped German tank exploded on ul. Kiliński, killing over four hundred people who had crowded around it, believing it to represent an insurgent conquest.[12] Jan Dobraczyński, the Polish writer, who was the Deputy BIP Chief in the Old Town, regarded the tragedy as ominous: 'The explosion of the tank appeared to presage defeat in the Old Town. From that day on there was a considerable increase in the number of victims. More and more graves appeared in the courtyards and on the grass.'[13] Despair was beginning to show through. 'The fight had been going on for two weeks and yet our military situation is no clearer. We all feel like a lion in a trap; we are looking for salvation, salvation for our thoughts and the Uprising.'[14]

British aircraft dropped supplies on Warsaw on the night of 13 August.[15] These drops were enthusiastically received by the population, who in spite of the shrapnel came out into the streets crying, 'They are ours, they are British.'[16] The first Allied drops had been made on 4 August and this was followed by four more until 14 August, but they were not large. None of the containers from the subsequent sorties on 21, 27, and 28 August fell into insurgent hands.[17] The Varsovians were disappointed and disillusioned in their Western Allies in whom they once had so much faith, and from whom they had been led to believe help would come.[18]

By the middle of the month the food situation had become very severe. Shops were shut and some of the shop-keepers were selling off their stores to friends. Money had little value, barter being the only really viable form of trade. Goods used for barter were mainly bread, conserves, flour, cigarettes and vodka.[19] In the fighting units morale still remained good but amongst the civilians it was low and they were depressed.[20] The Signals Officer of the AK Headquarters, Major Wardejn-Zagórski ('Gromski'), then in the Old Town, summarised the feeling and mood of the population at the time: 'The Uprising is at an impasse. The AK is not capable of accomplishing victory alone, nor can it be sure of help from outside to such a degree as to bring it to an end. In this case the only way out is help from the Bolsheviks, which is generally awaited today with longing . . .' He added that although such a view was not held by the intelligentsia, the townspeople, small craftsmen, workers and stall holders were openly saying: 'The Bolsheviks will come with a real army, they will beat the

Germans and liberate us.' 'Gromski' considered that it was necessary to act against that kind of thinking with great energy.[21] He found that whilst these people had earlier reproached the Russians for not co-operating they now excused them on the grounds that 'operational considerations had not enabled them to cross earlier'.[22]

Saturday 19 August saw the real intensification of the German attack.[23] On the same day Marceli Porowski, the Government Delegate for Warsaw, wrote that the bombing which had been going on for two days was having a depressing effect on the population and that

Today at the very moment when I am writing, there are virtually no civilians on the streets. The Old Town, which is basically patriotic, is starting to fall under the influence of the AL [People's Army]. People are starting to lend an ear to talk about the rash starting of the Uprising, the lack of a previous agreement with the Soviets etc.

He went on to say that morale could be radically improved if there were some definite news about relief from external AK units, the appearance of Allied bombers, and the approach of Soviet forces.[24]

In the Old Town, Starost Władysław Świdowski, 'Wik Sławski', was responsible for organising and caring for the civilian population.[25] Marceli Porowski, in spite of the fact that he considered Sławski an 'usurper', confirmed him in his position as it had already been recognised by both the AK and AL, and because he gave the impression of being active and having the respect of the military as well as being popular and effective.[26] However, it seems that no real organisation was ever established and chaos rather than order prevailed. This may have been due quite simply to inefficient control or to the character of the people involved, but it was certainly also due to conditions prevalent in the district at the time. The bombing and continual movement of the population hampered any attempts at organisation.[27]

In his memoirs the Starost wrote that he organised the anti-aircraft and anti-fire defence, set up five soup kitchens and three distribution centres of powdered milk and sweets for children. The administration of the district was divided into four departments:[28]

1. Administration Department – responsible for the organisation of the district and personnel matters.
2. Department of Feeding – mainly responsible for organising and supplying the soup kitchens as well as feeding children.
3. Department of Social Care – collected clothes, shoes and linen for the needy.

4. Department of Health – controlled the distribution of medicines and disinfectants, and the burying of the dead.

Starost 'Sławski' was aided in his work by the PPS and Syndicalists. Members of the 6th Battalion PPS Militia were specifically appointed to help the civilian population. Their work was fourfold. Firstly, they organised two fire fighting companies, built wells and latrines and helped to distribute food and organise feeding,[29] the latter with the aid of the Pallottine Fathers.[30] Four soup kitchens were set up (on ul. Freta 39, Podwale 46 and 29, and Długa 17) issuing free meals to the refugees and the homeless.[31] Powdered milk from the captured stores of PWPW was distributed for babies and small children. The battalion was also instrumental in organising House Committees.[32] On 7 August the PPS newspaper published in the Old Town, *Warszawianka*, printed the following instruction concerning the establishment of House Committees:[33]

House Committees
1. Should be organised immediately in every house and the accommodating and feeding of the homeless arranged.
2. They are empowered to confiscate food from tenants who are not willing to help the refugees.
3. Confiscated food must be used in communal kitchens.
4. House Committees are responsible for fire defence, in which men and women exempt from military duty must work.
5. In cases of looting, the looters ... should be held by the House Committee and the Militia Commander informed.
6. An important task for the Committee is vigorously to counter all panicky rumours and gossip, and they should cheer and hearten other inhabitants and strengthen faith in the victory of our cause which is not far off.

These House Committees also played an important role in the building of underground passages.[34] The AL also tried to organise House Committees,[35] but on the whole the activity of these committees was minimal and deteriorated in conditions totally unsuitable to their efficient functioning.

The Company of Syndicalists in the Old Town, who were the best supplied with food during the Uprising, organised the feeding of civilians from their own stores. They also established committees to distribute food and medical care especially to the aged and sick.[36] Throughout the Uprising one of the main problems in all the districts was food. It was especially difficult when stores were continually being destroyed in the bombing and the Army also had to be fed.

Many stores were reserved specifically for the Army and hospitals.[37] Some inhabitants had private stores which they shared with others. The homeless were reliant on community action, others were fed from Church supplies and stores. At the beginning of the Uprising bread was rationed.[38] Later flour was taken to the bakery in exchange for baked bread or the bread was sold.[39] Bread became increasingly difficult to obtain and was often requisitioned by the Army.[40]

German stores of mainly tinned meat and sugar were captured on ul. Stawki, and formed the bulk of outside stores for the district. There were two other smaller stores in PWPW and in the Fuchs store on ul. Miodowa.[41] The inhabitants of the Old Town from the start learnt to eat just soup for lunch and drink ersatz coffee without milk.[42] Meals quickly became insufficient and monotonous and lacked nutrition. In the shelter of the Capuchin Church on ul. Miodowa the homeless taking refuge received the same meals every day: in the morning, coffee, sugar, biscuits; in the afternoon and evening a meal made from groats and flour.[43] Others had simply to close their eyes to the fact that they were eating noodles cooked in water which had flowed over dead bodies.[44] Others had nothing.

There seems to have been no centralised control for accommodating the homeless, who usually sheltered wherever they could. They moved from one place to another looking for somewhere safer – a church or a building already bombed.

The Old Town before the outbreak of the Uprising housed two permanent hospitals, Jan Boży Hospital on ul. Bonifraterska and the Maltański Hospital on ul. Senatorska.[45] Further hospitals and dressing posts were prepared before the Uprising or improvised during its course.[46] They had been organised primarily for the Army and no separate facilities had been prepared for the civilian population. Throughout the Uprising, however, the Municipal Centre for Health and Care was operating.[47] On 10 August Colonel 'Wachnowski' appointed Colonel Stefan Tarnawski, a doctor, to be medical chief of the Northern Group. He was told to start the immediate organisation of more hospitals and dressing posts, to cope with the growing numbers of injured amongst the fighting units and civilians. Further hospitals and posts were set up later on due to the destruction of others by bombing and fires and also the ever increasing numbers of injured. The problem was made no easier by the shortage of staff, many of whom were killed during the second half of August.[48] Indescribable conditions prevailed in these hospitals as a result of overcrowding, the bombing and fighting, shortage of medicines and dressings, and lack of sanitation. There were not enough beds and in many cases patients were left to lie on the floor.[49] Many stores were reputedly lost when the quartermaster at the store on ul. Stawki refused to issue materials without receipts or prescriptions during the evacuation there.[50] In addition the Starost organised a Department of Social Care in the fourth week of the Uprising. In August a list of doctors who were prepared to help civilians was printed in the *Warszawianka*.[51]

There were no field post in the Old Town, but in the offices of *Warszawianka* there was a receiving point for letters. Letters arrived there from Śródmieście and were distributed to the inhabitants of the district or were sent on to Żoliborz.

The lack of organisation at the time was strongly criticised – 'Wachnowski's' reaction has already been noted. It was followed by suggestions as to how to effect some kind of organisation.[52] 'Gromski' on 26 August complained about the civilian authorities.[53]

Conditions of life for the civilian population have got worse. Administrative authorities cannot cope. The Starost . . . is a very young and inexperienced individual and cannot take control of the situation. There is no water, light, gas, plumbing etc. People are starting to use corners to relieve themselves. There is a terrible stench, no lavatories are being built and in any case there is nowhere to build them – because in every square there are graves and more and more coming . . . No wells are being sunk, and the civilian authorities are quite silent about it . . .

Criticism was made of the increased bureaucracy of the authorities which resulted in their failure to distribute food.[54] Individual witnesses were also surprised by the lack of care and organisation.[55] This in turn led to criticism of and antagonism towards the Uprising, its leaders and the insurgent authorities.

On 22 August John Ward, a British airman and escaped POW in Warsaw working with the AK as a correspondent for the London and New York *Times*, radioed a long message to London. In it he described the situation prevalent at the time and said that the determination of the population to fight to the last man was only strengthened by German barbarism.[56] One day earlier, however, an internal report had described how the morale amongst the civilians was so bad that 'If the Germans were to give a little respite the population would be able to force the command to capitulate. Pro-Soviet feeling is growing and the people wait for the Soviet Army – as for their saviour.'[57] Morale seems to have totally broken down. Voices of defeat were increasingly heard and a few groups of people were seriously considering whether to give themselves up to the Germans.[58]

The reasons for this attitude were due not only to the living conditions in the district, but also to the fact that the inhabitants there felt totally cut off, and were receiving virtually no information about what was happening in the rest of Warsaw.[59] They were embittered by the failure of the Allies to bring help to Warsaw and had already given up hope of it coming.[60] Furthermore they could not understand why the Soviets had not brought any help.[61] The more favourable food situation of the Army and their ability to believe in victory increased the estrangement between military and civilians. Some of the inhabitants blamed the AK for their plight.[62] But what had even greater implications was that a crisis of confidence in the Polish government was growing.

After three weeks of fighting in Warsaw the situation resulting from the lack of effective help for the Uprising is taking on a character of political scandal. Public opinion accuses the government of having no great significance in the international arena. Aversion to the Allies is growing and an attitude of enmity is developing. The opinion is spreading that we have been sacrificed to English pro-Soviet policy . . .[63]

The Polish government in London was called upon to take stronger action to bring help to Warsaw.[64]

The original hunger for newspapers which had characterised the first days of the Uprising disappeared and people stopped reading the papers, and if they did it was only news monitored from the radio.[65] Broadcasts were listened to with increasing cynicism. The people had had enough of words – some kind of positive action was necessary.[66] The continual broadcasting of the song 'Z dymem pożarów' (With the smoke of fires) did not encourage anyone – quite the opposite.[67]

A good gauge of morale and support for the Uprising could be found in the attitude of the civilian population towards working for the various insurgent authorities and even in relief work. At the beginning they had responded willingly and often had to be turned away. During the course of the Uprising, disillusionment and fear of death led to continually fewer people coming forward, with the result that people died under the rubble as there was no one to dig them out. Men had to be dragged out of the cellars at gun-point to the accompaniment of pleading, begging, and cursing from the women.[68]

There was no respite in the bombing. On 23 August Professor Dzwonkowski walked out of his shelter during a lull in the six days of intensive bombing and recorded his impressions:

I walked out on the street; nothing but ruins, houses are burning. I went out from the corner of Freta, Nowomiejska and the Market Place, to the narrow streets of the Old Town behind Podwale – everything is one large pile of corridorless rubble, heaps of debris fill the street, burnt and bombed out houses, even the outline of the houses have been destroyed – only the odd chimney sticks out and one or two bricks.[69]

The cellars and shelters were overcrowded. Often there was no room to lie down and the inmates just stood crammed together. People became totally apathetic, never moving from the corner they occupied. They collected in houses where continual religious services were in progress. They prayed fervently and sang patriotic hymns, confessed and took communion. The sick were often deserted in terrible conditions and left lying in the dirt. An increasing number of voices cursing the Uprising and the authorities was heard. Discipline broke down, whilst larceny and petty crimes spread. People were killed in the artillery fire and bombing as they stood in queues for water. Individuals became indifferent to the suffering of others around them, even their own families. The dead were left unburied.[70]

On 25 August the morale of the Old Town improved when the sound of firing could be heard coming from the Right Bank.[71] In the early hours of the following morning General 'Bór', members of his staff, the Government Delegate and members of the KRM secretly left the district, crossing to Śródmieście through the sewers.[72] When the news leaked out it made a terrible impression: 'Everyone is aware that the rats have already left with the sinking of the battleship and that the Old Town is going to fall at any moment . . .'[73] But groups of insurgents had left the Old Town as early as 21 August and continued to do so after 26 August.[74]

People were by now vegetating whilst the bombing and attacks raged on. Water and food were practically impossible to obtain, and the former was usually contaminated. The price of a glass of fresh water was 600 zł.,[75] and the summer heat was intense. The cellars were full of the injured; by 26 August there were over 7,000 injured and 70% of those were civilians.[76] The Starost called on the people not to cook individual meals but to pool resources as the authorities only had very small stores of dried beetroot, potato flakes and coffee left.[77]

On 26 August Colonel Wachnowski in his order to the ranks of the Northern Group stressed that the Old Town had to be held at all costs until the enemy was repulsed.[78] At the same time a young courier in the Old Town described the life in the shelters as follows:

starving and thirsty children, whose mothers cannot forgive fellow shelter dwellers for not sharing their stores of food with them. They scowl at us, quite different from the beginning when they seized flowers from their pots and threw them at the soldiers. When Janusz was injured and we carried him into the cellar for a few minutes, I told the others to be careful not to stain the sheets, and someone said, 'It doesn't matter, the blood of a Polish soldier is like wine.'[79]

A delegation of civilians from the Church of Najświętsza Maria Panna and the Franciscan Fathers crossed to the Church of Siostry Sakramentki on 25 August where they asked the Canon and Mother Superior to leave the area with the inhabitants of the surrounding streets. They believed the insurgents would not shoot at such a large group. The Canon and Mother Superior explained that they could not act independently and suggested that a delegation should be sent to the insurgent authorities and the tragic plight of the civilians presented. The delegation went to the headquarters of Major Stanisław Błaszczak, 'Róg', Commander of that area. When they explained their position and advised that either the fight be stopped or the civilians allowed to leave, they met with a very strong reaction. They were told that if a whole group of civilians accompanied by representatives of the Church were to leave and cross to the Germans, the will to fight amongst the insurgents would be broken. Anyone leaving would be shot as a traitor.[80]

Under the influence of the knowledge of the evacuation of General 'Bór' and his staff the inhabitants of the Old Town were gripped by a kind of nihilism and some tried to revolt.[81] They tried to go down the sewers on their own, or wandered around the whole day looking for some kind of 'protection' or official 'function' which would get them out.[82] On 26 August Major Mieczysław Chyżyński, 'Pełka', seeing the hopelessness of the situation, called on his soldiers to join him in giving themselves up. Their attempt to cross to the Germans was unsuccessful, and became an open secret. As a result people maintained that if 'officers escape' the civilian population had the right to be taken out of the battlefield first and to be protected from massacre. Queues formed at the headquarters of the Northern Group Commander of people trying to obtain passes on any pretext. 'There were civilian officials cut off from Żoliborz, women and children, old and cowardly inhabitants not taking part in the fighting.'[83] Civilian men tried to obtain permission to go down the sewers in fear of German reprisals.[84] Colonel Wachnowski, fearing a general panic, banned the use of the sewers and treated it as an act of desertion. Under pressure, however, on 27 August he allowed certain groups to go, providing them with leaders.[85]

Some civilians were included in these groups but the Warsaw Delegate, Porowski, felt that their presence would aggravate the already difficult conditions in Śródmieście. On 29 August he sent the following message to Colonel Wachnowski:

> amongst the people arriving from the Old Town today in Śródmieście there were quite a number of women.
>
> As the feeding and housing situation in Śródmieście is getting very difficult, I consider the further directing of the civilian population to Śródmieście undesirable.
>
> In my opinion these people should be sent to Żoliborz . . .[86]

One woman with a two month old child is reported to have escaped through the sewers.[87]

Warszawianka on 28 August criticised the 'tendency' of a 'few' people to leave the town. It defended the insurgents by saying that their situation was not bad and that they had held their positions for four weeks without any great change. Furthermore there was no possibility of evacuating the civilian population from the area and any individual attempts to do so would be considered a naive and unfitting action.[88]

On 28 August in the Franciscan Church on the corner of ul. Franciszkańska and ul. Zakroczymska a white flag was put out, but was taken down after the visit of a PPS Militia representative, Captain Oleś Kaczyński. He told the people that they could cross if they wanted to but without a white flag. No one went.[89] There was also an attempted revolt by the civilians on the corner of Miodowa and Senatorska streets but again it was prevented by the visit of an Army officer, Captain Tadeusz Dąbrowski, 'Prus', and Father Alfons.[90]

On 29 August German aeroplanes dropped leaflets calling on the population to leave. The calls were repeated on loudspeakers. The most severe reprisals were threatened against those who stayed.[91] On the same day 'Wachnowski' wrote in his daily report:

> twenty-ninth day of the fighting, no food, little water, bad sanitary conditions, dysentery, and little sight of speedy help – all this creates very bad morale, which improves the moment the smallest piece of better news is received. According to observers, it is maintained that Soviet artillery fire was heard during the night and morning of 29 August from the east and south east (Wawer). This sound of artillery created much satisfaction amongst soldiers and civilians.[92]

On the night of the same day a group of civilians tried to force their way through the barricades on ul. Hipoteczna and cross to the Germans.[93] On ul. Świętojerska it is also recorded that some civilians tried to cross to the Germans or go down the sewers, some successfully.[94] On ul. Brzozowa a group left for the German side.[95] It is not known how large the numbers involved were.

Warszawianka on 30 August published instructions issued by the Starost stipulating that for security reasons lists of persons should be made and that inhabitants should be in possession of certificates issued by the Obrona Przeciwlotnicza (OPL; Anti Air Attack Defence); civilians could only move round the town during the day if they had been issued with a permit by OPL; every house should have a guard checking persons entering and leaving; latrines had to be built in every house; passages between houses had to be kept cleared; all oil and acetylene lamps with carbide had to be handed over to the authorities. It would appear that at this late stage these instructions were both impractical and impossible to carry out in the conditions existing at the time. It would be interesting to know why they were issued – perhaps as an attempt to try and bring some order to the situation, or to try to show the civilians that their authorities were still functioning.[96]

On the evening of 31 August 'Wachnowski' received the order from General 'Monter' to evacuate the Old Town with his units, leaving the injured and the civilians behind.[97] It is impossible to try to describe the scenes in the Old Town during the last days. People waiting to go down to the sewers, especially the Army, were made the subject of attack and criticism by those remaining.[98] The people were extremely antagonistic to the evacuation.[99] The district finally fell on 2 September.[100] One witness has written of the behaviour of the civilian population who were left behind in the Old Town: 'In spite of the knowledge of what was waiting for them, we did not see any kind of extreme cases of revolt, or any kind of demonstration which would have been justified in the situation.'[101]

There can be no doubt that the civilian population felt great anger towards the authorities for starting the Uprising which they came to see had no hope of success, but there was no great public manifestation of these feelings. Many reasons could be put forward in explanation: fear of the Germans, fear of the sewers, which although the only means of escape many people would not go down. It was impossible for them to organise themselves, and few went out into the streets because they were afraid of the bombing. But it can also be argued that a group of discontented people collected together in a cellar provides the ideal situation to create some kind of ferment. A strong feeling of patriotism seems to have formed an effective safety valve, although for many by the end of the battle this together with any kind of discipline had broken down. The explanation may lie in the type of people there, mainly shop-keepers and artisans whose ranks were swelled by people who had already fled equally ghastly experiences and would not be eager to cross to the Germans from whom they had already escaped once. Finally there was quite simply the lack of physical strength. These people had become apathetic and disillusioned as a result of defeat, failure of help from outside, hunger and illness. It was probably a combination of two main factors which determined the attitude of these people. They feared the Germans above all, but the majority of them did not have the strength to organise themselves to cross the barricades. Revolt would have achieved little. It was obvious to them that the fighting was going to carry on in the other districts and it would be better to show a patriotic, united front.

The losses amongst the civilian population in the Old Town cannot be established accurately. It has been stated that there were between 75,000 and 100,000 persons in this part of the city. The Germans claim that 50,000 Poles crossed their lines by 2 September.[102] Przygoński gives a figure of 60,000 Poles being evacuated to the transit camp in Pruszków from the Old Town, and the remaining 40,000 as having been killed.[103] However, Kirchmayer puts the number of fallen Poles in the district at around 30,000.[104]

The pattern which evolved from the fight in the Old Town – the initial enthusiasm, stepping up of the fight, moving down to the cellars and shelters, hunger and terrible living conditions, disillusionment with the Allies, pro-Soviet sympathies, conflict with the Army, disillusionment in the Polish government and insurgent authorities, and general lack of faith in any kind of help – was to be repeated in each of the insurgent districts throughout the rest of the Uprising. It was a pattern which had far reaching political and moral consequences.

3.4 Powiśle

In comparison to the Old Town, the area of Powiśle during the Uprising was not an isolated unit. It formed Region I of the AK district of Śródmieście.[1] Communication between Powiśle and the rest of Śródmieście was possible across Nowy Świat. The area remained relatively peaceful until 2 September, when the Germans were able to concentrate their attack there with forces released from the battle in the Old Town. Fighting, however, was going on the whole time on the periphery, and the district was bombed. In the first hours of the Uprising the power station was taken by the insurgents which meant that Powiśle and Śródmieście were supplied with electricity until the works fell to the Germans on 3 September.[2]

Powiśle here will be taken to include the area contained in the following streets: Oboźna, Browarna, Ks. Siemca, Lipowa, Wybrzeże Kościuszkowskie, to Czerwonego Krzyża, and along Smolna and Nowy Świat.

Although Powiśle was the first region of Śródmieście to fall, the experiences and reaction of the civilian population was similar to the rest of the district. Few separate reports and records remain concerning the morale and attitudes of the civilians there. At the same time it should be realised that good civilian morale was very often dependent on and relative to the degree and efficiency of the organisation in the area concerned. It has been seen how in the Old Town this worked in a negative sense. Powiśle on the other hand was reputed to have a high standard of organisation,[3] and therefore morale and attitudes were more controlled.

Life in Powiśle quickly returned to normal. Shops, bars, chemists and laundries were opened. Shoemakers put up notices that they would repair soldiers' boots free and tailors offered to make AK uniforms and do alterations. In the streets people were moving round freely, and mothers could take their children out. Various artistic performances were organised, and AK newsreels were shown in cinemas. There was a spate of weddings. The scout post functioned efficiently, and if a letter did not get through it was because either the scout or the receiver had been killed. Insurgent newspapers were being distributed.[4]

One woman who had escaped from the Ghetto and had been sheltered by Poles during the occupation wrote in her brief memoirs:

We had lots of papers the whole time. To begin with we read them full of faith and hope, but around 15 August that changed into doubt and even pessimism, which was not even dispelled by a radio broadcast from London. We listened to it on 20 August. In this programme apart from ciphers, which we wanted to believe designated places for drops, the tunes 'Z dymem pożarów' and 'Boże, coś Polskę' were played. These songs, which we listened

Insurgent newspapers being delivered. Note all the paving stones have
been removed for building barricades.

to looking at a city in ruin, filled us with acrimony and final doubt. That was
not what we had expected from them [the Allies].[5]

By the second half of August the morale of the civilian population
in Powiśle was summarised as follows in a BIP report:

the inhabitants of Powiśle can be divided into two distinct groups. The first
one includes the inhabitants of the upper regions of Powiśle, ul. Kopernika,
Okólnik, Szczygła and the whole of ul. Tamka, predominantly intelligentsia.
They distinguish themselves by their admirable attitude, and their great
political and civic efficiency. On the other hand, the morale of the inhab-
itants of the area of ul. Dobra and the streets crossing to and from Oboźna to
Karowa, representing mainly the lower middle classes and proletariat in
Warsaw, is worse. This is understandable as these streets suffer far more from

Boy scouts delivering newspapers.

fires and German terror, and they are constantly under fire from the university. These people hardly react to press propaganda. As a result mobile megaphone units have been sent into the area – the results are not bad.[6]

Powiśle had a reputation during the Uprising of being the area which was the quickest to effect organisation amongst the civilian population.[7] Immediately after the outbreak of the Uprising, the organisation of the administration of the area was controlled by the Komisariat Cywilny AK (AK Civilian Commissary).[8] After the creation of the Delegatury Rejonowe (Regional Delegates) on 9 August, civilian authorities, appointed by the Delegatura Rządu, took over.[9] The Delegate in Powiśle was Konrad Sieniewicz, 'Sokołowski'.[10] Powiśle was mainly administered by members of Unia (a Catholic

Posting and receiving letters through the Field Post.

Open air soup kitchen.

Megaphone units in Powiśle.

Food transport column on their way to collect supplies.

military-political organisation attached to SP) and SP, and as a result it came to be known as 'Republika Chadecka' (Christian Democratic Republic or 'Uniqua'.[11]

On 16 August there were 26,000 civilians living in Powiśle including approximately 4,000 refugees.[12] The administration of the district was divided up into ten departments:[13]

1. Administration and secretariat.
2. Security.
3. Propaganda.
4. Feeding.
5. Social care.
6. Health and hygiene.
7. Labour.

8. Technology.
9. Fire fighting and OPL.
10. Industry.

The region was divided up into sixteen blocks with a Block Commander at the head of each.[14] There were also House Commanders and House Committees, and later block officials attending to security. Each block was to a certain extent a self-governing and self-contained unit[15] and so the administration of the district was really at grass roots level, with its whole efficiency dependent on these committees. The Block Committees were established on the basis of the existing OPL organisation, and the Regional Delegate also appointed new people to them.[16] There was usually a briefing of Block Commanders every two days. All instructions were communicated to them and discussed with them.[17] By 24 August, the Regional Delegate claimed to have House Commanders in all the houses in the region.[18]

The Department of Security was mainly responsible for clearing the area of enemy persons (i.e. *Volksdeutsch*, *Reichsdeutsch*, Ukrainians, etc.) and criminals, and for the security of German property and that of Poles. The Department was responsible to the Państwowy Korpus Bezpieczeństwa (PKB: State Security Corps) and Straż Obywatelska (Citizens Guard). It organised camps for detainees.[19]

The Department of Propaganda had one of the most important functions to perform. It was responsible for fighting defeatism and depression, but above all for maintaining appropriate and responsible attitudes.[20] Its work was of great political significance. It was also responsible for providing information. In Powiśle its work was carried out in the following ways: it published a newspaper in the area called *Barykada Powiśla* and it also organised the circulation of other papers printed in the rest of Śródmieście; loudspeaker programmes were run daily to keep the community informed of current affairs; various types of entertainment for the Army, hospitals and civilians were also organised and public meetings were arranged.[21]

The Department of Feeding was concerned, above all, with the feeding of refugees and homeless persons.[22] By 20 August there were approximately 6,000 refugees and 2,000 inhabitants in need of help in the district.[23] The refugees came not only from the surrounding burnt out houses but also from Wola, ul. Krochmalna, ul. Śliska, ul. Żelazna, Zjazd and Mariensztat.[24] Food had to be found and requisitioned for them and the distribution of it arranged. The Department established a bakery which distributed bread to fire victims and refugees.[25] Flour and sugar amongst other items were handed out.[26]

There were special food distributions to children under ten years of age and mothers with babies. The Regional Delegate co-operated with the RGO which was functioning in Powiśle and by 3 September there were ten RGO soup kitchens in operation, feeding approximately 8,000 people daily, usually free of charge.[27] There had been at one time thirteen kitchens,[28] but three were destroyed.[29] There were also eight private kitchens functioning.[30] In spite of the difficulties with food supplies and the continual decrease in rations, there does not seem to have been severe hunger and everyone was somehow fed. Stores, although some ran out and others were destroyed, seem to have lasted.[31] The most basic needs of the population were satisfied.[32]

The Department of Social Care had three spheres of activity. Firstly, it was responsible for accommodation, providing information about free or partially occupied premises and allocating accommodation. About 10,000 adult refugees and 2,700 children were found accommodation by 24 August. Secondly, it helped to organise new kitchens and inspected them. Thirdly, it arranged clothing for the refugees and established shelters for the disabled and homeless.[33]

The Department of Health was concerned with the health of the civilians in the area. Two public baths were organised on ul. Drewnicza and Smulikowskiego. There were eighty-six doctors and seven dentists issuing free advice. Special care was arranged for inhabitants suffering from tuberculosis or venereal diseases and for infants. There were five hospitals functioning, on ul. Kopernika 43 (paediatric), ul. Smolna 8 and ul. Pierackiego 3/5 (both Red Cross hospitals) and ul. Pierackiego 10 and 11 – but they only had about four hundred beds altogether. In the more devastated parts of the district two mobile surgeries were set up. The Department also started to organise anti-typhus inoculations and set up another paediatric hospital.[34]

The Department of Labour was responsible for finding sufficient numbers of people to carry out military and administrative tasks. People were sent to work in the power station and for the Army, in transport columns and to help feed the homeless.[35] The Department of Technology arranged such matters as the inspection of buildings, rescue work, plumbing repairs and alterations, and the sinking and digging of new wells.[36] By 24 August twenty-five wells had been made operative and three more were being built in the region.[37]

As in the rest of the insurgent city, a great deal of organisation was left to individual initiative and charity. Many refugees never had to rely on the organised help of the Regional Delegate. The following excerpt, written by one of the Sisters of the Order of St Ursula, who lived in a building between the streets of Dobra, Gęsta and Ks. Siemca, is just one example of such activity in Powiśle:

> The shelter became more and more and more crowded every day, especially when the bombing began. Every attack . . . brought a new party of homeless. Some later left the shelter . . . others stayed longer, but they all had to be thought of and helped as far as possible. Hundreds of people – men, women and children – passed through our shelter during the Uprising. They had lost everything and most only possessed the clothes they wore. The most urgent matter was to feed and clothe them. In order to maintain cleanliness in such difficult conditions we allowed them to use our laundry, where they could wash and launder. But there were many who had nothing they could change into. Fortunately before the Uprising a whole load of materials was brought to us, which had been seized by the AK from a textile factory. The nuns started to sew underwear and dresses, and the women also helped, using sewing machines which were brought into the room next to the shelter. A collection of clothes, especially men's clothes, was made among other occupants. Thus when everyone had underwear and a change of clothes, they were protected against the lice, which were the torment of the shelters. The nuns took care of the children . . .[38]

By the end of the month morale had fallen and as in the Old Town people were being brought out to work at gun-point – but there were still others who came willingly.[39] People began to see the hopelessness of the situation and fear an intensification of the German attack which would come when the Old Town fell. They felt bitter towards the Polish government in London as well as their agents in Warsaw. The decorating of General 'Bór' with the Polish order, 'Virtuti Militari', was received coldly.[40] 'People from all classes are heard to be saying that the initiators of the Uprising must be in the pay of our enemies to destroy us.'[41]

On 2 September after the fall of the Old Town the German attack on Powiśle was intensified.[42] The incessant bombing and firing started. All movement virtually ceased outside the cellars and the shelters. Food and water was brought during the short respites between air attacks – but in large quantities to last the whole day.[43] Dirty, tired, sick and hungry soldiers and civilians, who had been through the sewers from the Old Town, started to arrive.[44] To add to the blow of the fall of the Old Town, many of the soldiers and evacuees arriving spread demoralising stories about the situation there, about the massive number of suicides being committed, about people being driven away from the sewers by the force of arms, about the injured left behind. Soldiers from AL units were reported to be

Civilians trying to rescue people buried in bombed buildings.

undermining the people's confidence in the leaders of the Uprising by 'whispering propaganda'.[45] At the same time news was published in the insurgent papers that Stalin had refused to allow the Allies bringing aid to Warsaw to use Soviet air bases. This further added to the general depression.[46]

Some people were quite happy to see the insurgents retreat because they thought it meant that the Germans would stop killing civilians.[47] Once again people could be found who were willing to cross to the Germans who were encouraging them through loudspeakers and in leaflets, promising them bread, work and good treatment.[48] Between seventy and a hundred persons, mainly women and children, set out to cross from somewhere on ul. Karowa.[49]

In panic many of the inhabitants clutching bundles left the district and tried to cross Nowy Świat.[50] In fact so many tried to leave that on 3 September pamphlets were distributed calling on people to stay put and not panic.[51] Others remained in the damaged and destroyed buildings awaiting the Germans. Some crept out with white flags and handkerchiefs and collected in the centre of the street, but that did not stop the Germans from firing on them.[52] Powiśle fell on 6 September.[53]

3.5 The Uprising in Śródmieście (1 August – 1 September)

... the barricades of Śródmieście appeared somewhat unreal to us, their perfect construction, their careful finish and the prevailing calm around them ... But strangest of all was the appearance of people in the streets. They did not creep around as if at any moment something would come crashing down, but walked along the pavements; they may have walked fast but their movements were controlled. They were normally dressed and clean. In spite of the simplicity of their dress the women managed to look elegant and the men wore ties.[1]

The sight which met the soldiers and evacuees emerging from the sewers was a strange one. Whole houses were still standing with their windows intact, there was a certain degree of organisation, soup kitchens, shops and wells were functioning. There were beds with clean sheets to sleep in. Plays, cinemas, concerts and lectures were advertised in the newspapers and on posters.[2] In spite of this, however, one witness maintained that the same level of participation did not exist as it had in the Old Town. In the cellars young and able men sat, not coming out to volunteer nor join in the fight,[3] nor was there the same faith and optimism that had characterised the fight in the Old Town in its earlier days.[4]

Although the inhabitants of Śródmieście had not had the experience of living in the centre of the battle under continual bombardment, by the time the Old Town fell they had lived in an insurgent situation for over four weeks. During this time a public opinion was recorded which forms the most complete picture of Warsaw during the Uprising.

Śródmieście together with Powiśle and the Old Town formed the military District I of Warsaw.[5] Here Śródmieście will be taken to be the area north and south of al. Jerozolimskie. The northern area was bordered by ul. Grzybowska in the north, ul. Nowy Świat in the east, ul. Chmielna in the south and around ul. Towarowa in the west. The southern area was bordered in the east by al. Ujazdowskie, from the corner of ul. Szopena to pl. Trzech Krzyży, where it bulged out to include parts of ul. Wiejska, ul. Frascati and ul. Książęca; the western boundary wound from al. Jerozolimskie along ul. Marszałkowska, ul. Wspólna to Emilii Plater, ul. Noakowskiego, ul. Polna to the corner of Mokotowska including pl. Zbawiciela. The majority of al. Jerozolimskie was held by the Germans, although a tunnel was built under the street from number seventeen to number twenty-two, and it was by this small passage that communication between the two sides of the district was possible.

The following analysis of morale in Śródmieście is based almost entirely on internal reports specially compiled at the time, mainly by the Information Bureau (BIP) or Community Service Information patrols. These patrols would hold talks and discussions in various houses and blocks, not only to inform people of the situation but also to check on problems and morale. The reports might concern one house, one block, one street, several streets or the whole area. It is not uncommon to find contradictory reports from the same area for the same time. There were very specific factors moulding morale and attitudes, and peculiar circumstances in each house and block could further change them. These factors concerned the nature of the people in each situation, for instance whether they were permanent residents, fire victims or refugees, what social class they came from, whether they were poor or rich, young or old. Attitudes were also influenced by individuals in the given situation, who may have been for political or other reasons undermining morale. When assessing a report it is necessary to appreciate whether the particular group of people were directly involved in the fighting, whether they were being shot at, whether there were snipers, the degree of organisation in the house etc. Furthermore, people may have acted during the compilation of these reports in a manner which they thought to be fitting and which may not have been genuine.

The contents of the reports were also dependent upon the objectivity of their authors, who may have been concerned with different problems. Some observers and patrols might have been more interested in the amount of food available, whereas others were solely concerned with political problems, so the stress laid on different problems varied accordingly. Likewise certain attitudes and problems might be over- or under-emphasised so as to obtain certain results and affect decisions, e.g. the problem of food supplies may have been reported as worse than it was so as to obtain quicker action, or other matters distorted for political ends. Finally it must be remembered that the compilers of these reports were primarily concerned with negative symptoms and attitudes, which may at times tend to give an unbalanced picture. Thus these reports must be used with great care and as far as possible on a comparative basis.

From the majority of reports written at the time, as well as from memoirs, it would seem that the generally wide enthusiasm that greeted the outbreak of the Uprising soon began to disappear, and depression set in.[6] This was mainly due to the fact that the Uprising had failed to produce the quick victory anticipated; it had run into an impasse and it did not seem that any external help was going to bring an immediate change in the situation. But the depression and the lessening enthusiasm were not marked by any parallel decline in co-operation on the part of the civilians at this stage,[7] although refugees and bomb victims were reported as being embittered and upsetting the other inhabitants.[8]

This decline in enthusiasm was accompanied by growing criticism of the Uprising and the timing of its outbreak. Such criticism seems to have come mainly from amongst the intelligentsia. Some regarded the Uprising as folly which had no chance of success.[9] This in turn led to criticism of the AK from certain sections:[10]

There is a danger of the Warsaw community breaking up into antagonistic factions indisposed towards the AK and this to a great extent depends on the further course of the Uprising. A quick victory avoiding further sacrifice and destruction of the town will win sympathy for the AK. Voices are being heard again that the Uprising was premature and too costly ... The activity and sacrifice of the AK soldiers prevents people for the time being voicing loud criticism against the Commanders of the Uprising. It would be considered unpatriotic and cowardly. We must strengthen our propaganda and widen its scope to all territories. Too much of our propaganda is concerned with heroism in comparison to our weaknesses. Concrete and non-stereotyped reasons should be used to explain the outbreak of the rising and reasons must be found to justify the prolongation of the fighting. The people must be convinced that the Uprising reduces the scale of destruction, which the Germans would have inflicted if they had been allowed to retreat freely from Warsaw ... The prolongation of the fighting must be accepted as a lesser evil than the drawing out of the occupation until the moment of German revenge ...[11]

The extension of the Uprising, the unfavourable fighting strengths of the AK, the lack of Allied or Soviet help, activity of the PKWN, fear of the Germans and the repression that would ensue if the

Uprising failed, bombing and fires, the forced inactivity of many men, insufficient information and propaganda, distrust and suspicion, the number of cases of plunder and theft, the abusive and incompetent behaviour of some of the AK commanders, too much or not enough suitable organisation and lack of OPL control (which was felt very strongly), fear of epidemics and hunger, lack of food and fuel, and disputes between the various Polish authorities were all influencing morale. Thus at such an early stage there were many diverse factors at work, which did not change greatly throughout the course of the Uprising but were only added to.[12]

By the end of the first week of the Uprising there seem to have been two dominant problems reflected in these reports. Firstly, there was the concern over Polish–Soviet relations, especially with regard to the outcome of Premier Mikołajczyk's talks in Moscow. This was coupled with speculation about the attitude of the Soviet Union towards the capital and about the timing of the arrival of the Soviet Army. The second problem was the lack of response of the Allies to the Uprising. By 5 August one report already mentioned the bitterness felt by the population against the Allies and Russians for their failure to bring help and drop supplies. It went on to say that the population impatiently awaited the arrival of the Soviet Army and news of the conference in Moscow.[13] By 8 August it was reported that even a compromise with the Soviets would be acceptable, if it would mean quick and effective help being afforded as a result. Both the Allies and the Polish government in London were criticised for their lack of help.[14]

On 9 August another report stressed again the anger felt at the failure of sufficient help to come from England and the impatience with which the Soviet liberation of Warsaw was awaited.[15] Although little pro-Russian feeling seems to have been displayed, one commander reported that although the population had grumbled about the 'Bolsheviks' 'they are so tired, that in spite of everything there is a danger of a joyful welcome for the Soviet Army, when they appear'.[16]

On 10 August the following summary of the situation was made: there was increasingly strong criticism of the failure of the Polish government in London to arrange help for the Uprising and of the inconclusiveness of the negotiations in Moscow. The tactless 'sugar coated words' of the Polish radio propaganda from London was upsetting and not regarded as fitting for the situation in Warsaw. The people wanted not only arms but tangible proof that the Polish government and the English were sincerely interested in the fate of

Warsaw. Many sections of the community, weary of the years of occupation and the perils of the Uprising, were indifferent to the type of government that would be established. They did not mind whether it was the Polish government or the PKWN as long as the fighting quickly ended.[17] The same report warned that the continual destruction of the city was swelling the numbers of people who had nothing to lose and so a further 'radicalisation' of attitudes could be anticipated. These attitudes if exploited by propaganda directed against the Polish government would push social and economic problems to the fore. That particular moment was regarded as being the last chance to introduce reforms as outlined in the declaration 'O co walczy naród'. Such a decree was regarded as giving the Uprising a social character and not just a military one, and of countering accusations about the reactionary character of government agencies.[18]

At the same time in some of the reports stress was laid on the great enthusiasm and encouraging attitude of the young. The Uprising had provided them with an outlet for their energy, suppressed during the occupation, and a chance for revenge.[19] Their fervour often encouraged and sustained their families and the older inhabitants.[20] They regarded the Uprising as a necessity, as a manifestation to the whole world of the Poles' desire to liberate their country with their own armed forces.[21]

It was against this background that the Government Delegate, Jankowski, sent the following message to London on 11 August:

We have received one tiny drop from you. Since 3 August all has been quiet on the Russo–German Front. Consequently we have neither material nor moral help, because apart from a short speech by the Vice-Premier on 8 August, you have not even shown any acknowledgement of our action. In vain the soldiers and inhabitants of the city gaze into the sky, expecting help from the Allies. Only German planes are to be seen in the smoke. The people are surprised, they are deeply disappointed, and begin to revile you.

We have virtually no communication with you, nor any estimation of the political situation, nor advice, nor directions. Has the matter of aid for Warsaw been discussed in Moscow? I repeat emphatically that if there is no immediate help, drops of arms and ammunition, the bombing of enemy positions, parachute landing – our fight will cease in a few days. But if help comes the fight will continue.[22]

Between 11 and 20 August there was a deepening of these attitudes amongst the inhabitants of Śródmieście. At the same time a kind of stabilisation set in as it was realised with increasing weariness that the Uprising was not going to end quickly. The situation was broken spasmodically by certain morale raising events, e.g. Allied drops on 12 and 13 August or the taking of the PASTA (Polish Telephone Corporation) building by the AK.[23] But a general desire to continue the fight was not lacking nor had the Uprising lost its civilian support.[24] Symptoms of defeatism were few in spite of the discontent of the people.

One journalist realised how difficult it was to dispel defeatist attitudes:

The fight against defeatism is most vital. I try desperately to fight it and possibly have some success. In our courtyard ... our national character which knows the value of sacrifice but does not know how to calculate soberly has started to be criticised. It is all aimed at the fact that the Uprising broke out prematurely. In my heart I agree with them, but will not say so. How would that help us today? 'Too early? Just in time. The Germans would have burnt the city and killed its inhabitants anyway. Meanwhile we have captured large parts of the town and there free Poland exists. Fewer of us will die in the attack than if we remain inactive.' Some of the people admit that I am right, others say nothing, they are ashamed of their attitudes and that is my small victory. But at the same time I know that no help will come, but I would not admit it to anyone. Perhaps there will be a miracle? One must believe in miracles.[25]

Disappointed by the failure of the Allies to bring any real help, the Varsovians attempted to find a suitable explanation for it. People were confused; some saw it as the Allies' unwillingness to expose themselves to the Russians whom, they feared, the Poles might begin to fight.[26] Talk of war between the Allies and the Russians was not uncommon. A pro-Soviet feeling was developing amongst certain sections of the community and others wanted some kind of understanding with the Russians, even if it were only temporary, because they believed that only with Soviet help could the Germans be defeated.[27] At this time the first mention of Communist activity in the city was made, which supposedly was directed against the AK.[28] But in most districts there were no reports of such activity.

On 15 August the first known public action was taken in response to the worsening situation in the capital. A Citizens' Committee from Region II (one of the regions of Śródmieście), which claimed a wide political basis, drew up a memorandum. It blamed the appalling living conditions in Śródmieście, the lack of water and food, the danger of epidemics and the spreading of fires on insufficient aid. It claimed that the people held the Polish government in London and the civilian and military authorities responsible for such a state of affairs.[29] Two days later on 17 August the Regional Delegate of Southern Warsaw received a deputation, which demanded help from London for fear that otherwise the population might take some drastic step.[30]

In Region III at this time morale amongst the civilians seems to have been especially low, due mainly to the problem of refugees fleeing in the wake of fires and 'Ukrainian' troops, as well as the lack of food, water, and organisation there. The refugees unable to cross to other parts of Śródmieście sheltered in the houses along ul. Śliska, Sosnowa, Złota and Chmielna. There does not seem to have been any organised help for them, and the old and sick were left without aid. Administrative agents were called on to alleviate the situation because it was undermining the morale of the other inhabitants.[31] One report from the region records how the administrator of the house at ul. Grzybowska 36 persuaded the inhabitants to cross to the Germans.[32]

On 20 August a BIP report summed up the situation in Regions II and III as follows:

The civilian population in our area continues to show a great deal of fortitude and sacrifice, but the initial enthusiasm is gradually disappearing, mainly due to weariness and a feeling of despair. Defeatism is still rare but nervous resistance is generally weakening ... Feelings towards the KRM have still not taken on a definite shape amongst the public. A certain contempt for the civilian authorities can be observed and there are complaints about too many overlapping 'authorities'. The community obeys the Army willingly and would like to see everything placed in their hands. The community is angry with the government in London ... One can often hear talk about the unresourcefulness of the government, of the inadequately prepared Uprising; the 'spineless' speeches and whining tone of our propaganda is criticised. The ending of broadcasts from London with the melody 'Z dymem pożarów' ... is especially irritating. Attitudes towards Russia change with news from the battlefields. Although the population is bitter and antagonistic towards the Soviet Union they desire the most speedy help from them. Voices calling for the opening of talks with Russia directly from Warsaw, by-passing London are not uncommon ... People are beginning to complain that too many publications are being circulated and that they contain mistaken and unreliable information. *Robotnik* and *Biuletyn* are the most popular. The anti-Soviet propaganda attempted by the newspaper *Szaniec* has had a hostile reception. The community at present keeps the possibility of war with Russia out of their minds. Complaints about the bureaucratic and often spiritless instructions of the OPL Commanders, PKB and other authorities are widespread ...[33]

By the middle of August, therefore, the Uprising had produced two results totally out of keeping with its original aims. Firstly, a crisis of confidence in the Polish government in London had developed and there was a danger of a possible power vacuum being formed.[34] Secondly, due to the hopeless situation and living conditions in Warsaw, and in spite of any fears and anti-Soviet feeling, a temporary pro-Russian attitude had developed amongst the population, as the Russians seemed at the time to hold out the last hope for the beleaguered city. Against this background the leaders of the Uprising and the Polish authorities in Warsaw were sending desperate pleas to London for aid, aid that was not just material or military, but political.[35]

The last ten days of August in Śródmieście brought a further decline in morale. At this time it is very obvious how diverse attitudes were and how dependent they were on local conditions. General living conditions were deteriorating all the time. Region III probably presented the most depressing picture at this stage. One local report of 21 August describes how morale 'changes from territory and circumstances. People who are continually under fire are depressed. However, there are others who cheer up those who have doubts. In safer areas complete faith and hope in the future can be found.'[36]

Generally there was embitterment and dissatisfaction,[37] but attitudes tended to vary between different social classes. The intelligentsia was reported as being dissatisfied and complained about the leaders of the Uprising, who had brought destruction on the town.[38] The working classes, however, were seen to have hope and certainty of a better future.[39] Another report qualified this by saying that those members of the intelligentsia who were dissatisfied were, on the whole, from the propertied classes, who had hardly been involved in clandestine life.[40] It is interesting to compare these reports with later ones. In these the morale of the working classes and the intelligentsia are regarded as uniform, i.e. poor due to the further destruction of the town and lack of outside help. But there was no desire to end the fight by surrendering to the Germans. As a result of their living conditions, refugees and fire victims were far more depressed and bitter towards the Uprising and its leaders. They were accused of spreading rumours that General 'Bór' and his staff had escaped from Warsaw.[41] Morale worsened as the bombing of the area was stepped up and the number of homeless increased.[42]

One of the reasons why morale was able to deteriorate faster in this area was reported to be the lack of efficient organisation. The OPL and House Commanders were not able to deal with the situation, and feeding and sanitary arrangements in many houses were deplorable. There was a shortage of water, soap, and basins. Typhus and dysentery spread,[43] with about 10% of the inhabitants of the region suffering from typhus. Lice were rampant. Many people wanted to go out to the country to lift potatoes. Some had not eaten soup or bread for several days, others had not had any bread for two weeks.[44] The RGO was unable to help on any large scale as it only possessed short rations of food.[45]

At the same time there was growing activity of groups antagonistic to the Polish government in London and to the AK. There were reports of an increase in the number of left wing newspapers, agitators, and soldiers with AL armbands appearing in the area.[46] One of the patrols summed up the situation in the area around the streets of Marszałkowska, Zielna, Złota, Chmielna, Pańska, Sienna and Żelazna on 26 August as follows:

The people in this region are at the end of their tether, and what is worse, they see the hopelessness of our efforts which is made apparent by their questions and ... they don't see any prospect of help ... We tried to convince them that we are not in such a hopeless position; we had some success and stressed that we must continue to rely on our own strengths which are considerable – twenty-six days of fighting being proof of that. For some reason we do not have to force people into a resolute desire to fight to the last, as we have observed how the people themselves display such an attitude. Little is expected from the English now, on whom they counted so much, and Russia is spoken of with great mistrust, although it is realised that the Soviet Army ... will be the first to enter Warsaw. The Communist press is read willingly and its statements are very moderate and cautious, which causes a great deal of confusion and people begin to believe in the sincerity of these pronouncements. It is strange that at this time a pamphlet of the 'Konwent' calling for a reasonable and favourable attitude towards Russia was received coldly. An opportunistic predisposition towards Russia and likewise her agent, the PKWN, is growing. It is perhaps at its strongest amongst the intelligentsia ... The problem of feeding everyone is very difficult. There is less and less food and more and more are going hungry. The situation with children is tragic ... and what is being done for them is insufficient.[47]

Meanwhile in the remainder of Śródmieście, as the population grew increasingly weary, morale was low although the news of entry of partisans from the woods to help the Uprising seems to have given it a lift.[48] The liberation of Paris provoked bitterness and jealousy, as did news about Allied help from Italian bases for Rumanian action in

Bucharest.[49] Bulgaria and Czechoslovakia received help and guarantees from the Allies but Poland, 'loyal and steadfast, received nothing'.[50] On 21 August Maria Gieysztor, commenting on Allied help for Warsaw, wrote in her diary: 'According to one report a hundred Allied aircraft, ours, English, and South African, took off with arms, but only half got through. Twenty-one did not return. When they were ten miles away from Warsaw smoke filled the pilot's cabin. Now they'll believe Warsaw is burning.'[51]

By that time some of the population had begun to consider the inactivity of the Russians as having political significance, which increased their resentment towards the Soviet Union.[52] Even Soviet supporters were reported as beginning to regard Moscow's behaviour as 'treacherous', aimed at destroying the most active Polish elements.[53] Part of the community was of the opinion that everything was all right for as long as the Uprising and fight against the Germans went on, but once the Soviet Army crossed over the river it would be necessary to leave Warsaw.[54]

On 28 August an increasing number of arguments were reported taking place between the civilian population and the government authorities. Life had been reduced to one of 'vegetation in the cellars' and the overcrowding and congestion helped a *sui generis* public opinion to form.[55]

By the end of August the situation in Śródmieście as presented in available reports was as follows. Morale was varied and dependent on local conditions.[56] People were growing increasingly tired and apathetic, but they had been conditioned by their predicament and had developed patterns of life to counterbalance their weariness. As supplies of food were exhausted a fear of hunger developed.[57] People were suffering from dysentery, typhus, nervous exhaustion and physical weakness due to inadequate feeding.[58] There was a clear dichotomy between the attitude of the permanent residents and that of the refugees and fire victims. The latter were far more critical and radical in their attitudes, and generally unco-operative.[59] They were regarded as being a vulnerable element which after the Uprising would side with the Communists and their followers. Many people were bored, especially those men not taking part in the fighting. Morale was, however, strengthened by religion and services were frequently held in the courtyards and cellars.[60]

The Polish government, the Allies and the Russians were all the object of attack. The general attitude to the Soviets had not changed, and although the community was split in its opinion, this was due

Evening prayers in a courtyard on ul. Drewniana.

mainly to fear of and not sympathy with the Soviet Union. People were afraid to express anti-Soviet opinions.[61] Public opinion was regarded in some quarters as being 'immature' and subject to the influence of 'demagogic agitators'. But everyone was anxiously awaiting the crossing of the Soviet Army to Warsaw. One observer maintained that the pro-Soviet members of the community kept their opinions to themselves due to the general bitterness felt towards Russia. The question was continually asked as to why the Allies did not force Russia to help Warsaw. Some blamed the Polish government. Suggestions were put forward for coercing the Allies into greater activity, e.g. Polish soldiers in England, France and Italy should ignore all Allied orders, or wear black armbands in mourning.[62]

The Polish press and propaganda were being treated with great scepticism.[63] There was criticism of bureaucracy and complaints about corruption.[64] Relations between the military and civilians deteriorated due to the high handed attitude of the Army, unauthorised requisitioning, stealing by soldiers, drunkenness and other abuses by the AK.[65] The methods used by the AK and PKB to recruit people for work created much ill feeling. Often it was only caused by the fact that too many men were made to report for work, but it was also due to the manner in which recruitment was carried out, sometimes reminiscent of German methods used during the occupation.[66] *Biuletyn Informacyjny* published an article complaining of the brutality with which people were taken to work, dragged from their beds in the early hours of the morning: 'How is it that in insurgent Warsaw this activity of stupid and brutal individuals, depraved by the occupation, can be tolerated.'[67] But these antagonisms were also due to jealousy of the Army, which was seen to be better fed and occupied than the civilians.[68]

Table 11 shows how in different houses on the same day morale and attitudes varied, in accordance with prevailing conditions. At the same time it also demonstrates the variety of information in reports. From this table a general conclusion can be drawn that at the end of August morale in Śródmieście was on the whole quite good, but the food supply was already beginning to present serious problems.[69]

The organisation of Śródmieście

As has been seen Powiśle formed Region I of Śródmieście. The civilian administration of the remaining three regions, Regions II, III and IV, was organised along the same lines as Region I, with Regional Delegates at the head of each. The main centre of administration of Region II was pl. Napoleona, where the Delegate was Major 'Wiktor'.[70] In Region III it was at ul. Śliska 6/8 with Józef Fabijański, 'Brzozowski', as Regional Delegate.[71] The Regional Delegate for Region IV was Edward Quirini, 'Stanisław Kulesza', who had his office on ul. Krucza 15.[72] Region II was further sub-divided into ten districts based on blocks where House Commanders were subordinated to Block Commanders.[73]

The combined population of Regions II and III during the first two weeks of the Uprising was about 91,000, of whom 50,000 were permanent residents. In Region IV on 28 August there were 150,000 people including 60,000 refugees.[74] By the end of the month, including the inhabitants of Powiśle, there were about 260,000 people, 125,000 of whom were refugees from other areas, and a further 55,000 had been impoverished due to the fighting and were in need of social care.[75] Region III had a population of about 87,000 at the end of August.[76]

Table 11. *Conditions and morale in various houses in Śródmieście, 31 August 1944*

Address	No. of inhabitants	Social background	Situation	Morale	Food supply	Sanitation	Complaints
Poznańska 3	permanent 103 temporary 106 (142 at talk)*	Moderately rich and rich intelligentsia.			70 using RGO. Stores of inhabitants nearly finished.		Brutalities of gendarmes. No. of newspapers disorientate public opinion.
Poznańska 5	permanent 75 temporary 28	Working class.		Good. Positive attitude to AK.	20 evacuees and 4 permanent using RGO. Stores of inhabitants nearly finished.		
Poznańska 7	permanent 41 temporary 8				2 using RGO. Stores being finished.		AK commander will not allow civilians to use well in house occupied by his unit. Complaining about forced evacuation of civilians by AK who did not give enough

Address	Population	Social composition	Military / special	Attitude	Food stores	Sanitation	Notes
							time to collect necessary food stores.
Marszałkowska 32	permanent 36 temporary 11	Intelligentsia and moderately wealthy.	Military position in house. Efficient commander.	Good.	Stores for 1 week. Kitchen being planned with RGO help.	Good. No disinfectant.	Army used threat of arms.
Marszałkowska 34	permanent 39 temporary 4	Temporary mainly artisans.	Very near front. Good commander.	People holding on and maintaining good spirit.	No stores.		
Marszałkowska 36	permanent 47 temporary 34	Intelligentsia. Temporary mainly artisans.	Snipers.	Good – willing to work, building well.	Temporary being fed by permanent. Stores for 5 days. No fats for several days.		Bureaucratic administration.
Marszałkowska 38	permanent 65 temporary 37	Majority intelligentsia.	Pluton post and medical unit in house.	Good.	Stores for a week.	Good. No disinfectant.	Electricity needed in cellar. No water or bread.
Piusa 40	permanent 42 temporary 19 (24 at talk)			Positive attitude to AK.	10 temporary using RGO. Stores are being finished.		
Piusa 42	permanent 143 temporary 36 (65 at talk)				All evacuees using RGO and 14 permanent. Minimal supplies.		

Table 11. (*cont.*)

Address	No. of inhabitants	Social background	Situation	Morale	Food supply	Sanitation	Complaints
Marszałkowska 69	permanent 22 temporary 32 (31 at talk)				Communal kitchen using stores of all inhabitants – enough left for 1 day.		
Marszałkowska 71	permanent 120 temporary 78 (70 at talk)			Attitude to AK positive and patriotic.	40 temporary using self-help kitchen – rest are being fed by others. Stores finished.		
Piusa 29, 35, and 37	253 at talk	All types.		Good spirits.	Running short.		
Wilcza 4, 6, 21 and Mokotowska 63		Many fire victims.		Irritated due to protracted insurgent action, exhaustion of food and destruction of houses.	Organised own feeding – stores of food exhausted. No one foresaw that it would be necessary to keep themselves in food for the next month.		Shortage of food and heavy drinking leads to arguments. Janitor in no. 6 did not want to fulfil duties – does not maintain order. Chaos and dirt. Threat of

Location	Strength	Social composition	Position	Morale / attitude	Supplies / other
Hoża 48	permanent 15 temporary 29	About 33% intelligentsia. At talks half intelligentsia.	Good.	Good.	arms by AK and PKB happens frequently for futile reasons, e.g. right of way and wells.
Hoża 50	permanent 90 temporary 61				
Marszałkowska 83	permanent 41 temporary 42				
Marszałkowska 85	permanent 20 temporary 17 (200 at talk)				
Wspólna 63b, 65, 65a, 67, 69	c. 120 at talk	All types.	On front line. Good House Commander.	Good. People support Army and decided to stay until the last possible moment, and leave with the Army.	Lack of water, newspapers, and rations.
Wspólna 27	permanent 53 temporary 56			Frightened but anxious to carry on. Good attitude to AK, willing to work.	c. 30 using RGO. Not enough food.

Table 11. (cont.)

Address	No. of inhabitants	Social background	Situation	Morale	Food supply	Sanitation	Complaints
Wspólna 29	permanent 84 temporary 53			Try to avoid work but good attitude to AK. Desire to carry on.	Permanent feeding temporary, but going to have to use RGO.		
Wspólna 31	permanent 30 temporary 75			Good. Willingness to carry on – no clash with AK.	Permanent feeding temporary. Many using RGO. Feeding situation bad.		In the house a certan woman in kitchen undermines morale and spreads depression.
Skorupki 4, 6, 8, 11, 12	432 refugees 5 fire victims			In one house good, in others 2 average and 2 less than average.	372 using RGO.		
Wspólna 33	permanent 58 temporary 69			Depression due to bad feeding situation. No clash with AK reported.	Permanent feeding temporary. Many using RGO.		Time people are kept, often 2–10 hours, when have to report for work. They are given nothing to eat.

Bracka 1 / Żurawia 2	permanent 47 temporary 18 (130 at talk)	Good.	26 using RGO but more want to.	
Bracka 3	permanent 44 temporary 11 (70% at talk)	Good.	30 using RGO.	Arguments caused by drunkenness.
Bracka 5	permanent 47 temporary 46	Good.	40 using RGO.	
Nowy Świat 5	permanent 6 temporary 2		No one using RGO.	No papers.
Nowy Świat 3	permanent 14 temporary 10		10 using RGO.	
Nowy Świat 1	permanent 16 temporary 16		9 using RGO.	
Nowy Świat 2/ Książęca	permanent 49 temporary 40		33 using RGO.	Robberies.
Nowy Świat 4	permanent 5 temporary 45		43 using RGO.	
Nowy Świat 6	permanent 12 temporary 5	Good.	17 using RGO.	No papers.

*The talks were those held by the BIP and Community Service Information patrols.

The steps taken to keep the population fed and supplied with food during August appear to have been adequate although the problem was never effectively solved. The situation in Regions II and IV was undoubtedly better than in Region III, where there was less organisation and a greater problem with the homeless and refugees. By the middle of August the problem of feeding so many people had started to become a serious one and was continually getting worse. *Biuletyn Informacyjny* reported on 13 August that due to the exhaustion of private stores of food the problem of feeding had become a burning question again.[77]

For the temporary inhabitants of ul. Śniadeckich 10, 12, 18 and 22 the following list has survived of their food supplies on 17 August:[78]

nine non-residents had enough food for seven days

nine	three days
five	fourteen days
two	six days
four	ten days
two	five days
one	four days

The temporary residents of ul. Śniadeckich 12 still had stores enough for an average of six days. The majority of them were feeding themselves or sharing with other inhabitants. Only two were using the RGO soup kitchen. The situation of the non-residents in no. 18 was similar. No one there was using the RGO and their stores were sufficient to last an average of five to six days, although some had only enough for two and a couple for twelve. In no. 22 five out of the eighteen non-residents were eating in the house kitchen and the rest ate with other tenants.[79] Thus it was obvious that within a week the shortage of food would become serious.

The type of food available, however, was not sufficient to provide a healthy diet. Śródmieście was cut off from both Mokotów and Żoliborz where vegetables and fruit could be obtained. The diet was very simple and monotonous. Normally no butter, milk, fats or meat were available, with the exception of slaughtered horses at the beginning of the Uprising. The most easily obtainable items were cereals, bread, groats, sugar and dehydrated vegetables.

A network of Block Kitchens was established, the majority organised by the House and Block Committees, others belonging to the RGO and supplied by them. By 4 September there were reported to be 134 registered kitchens in the whole of Śródmieście,[80] but the actual number must have been higher than this. A list compiled by the Department of Social Care on 30 September shows that at least ninety-seven kitchens were in operation by 31 August in Region II.[81] Stefan Sendlak, the Deputy Delegate of Region III, has written that in that region there were 175 Block Kitchens organised by the Block Committees.[82] The number of meals given out by these kitchens varied from about ten to a thousand.[83]

The development of the Health Service during the Uprising in Śrómieście has been divided by Dr Stanisław Bayer into five stages:[84]

1. Introductory period, when Health Service units worked and set up first-aid posts before 'W' Hour (1–2 August).
2. Period of improvisation, the starting of a number of first-aid posts developed by units, doctors and the community without any central or co-ordinated directives or commands (3–16 August).
3. Settling down period of the medical organisation (17–25 August).
4. Severe increase in the volume of work for the Health Service as a result of the growing numbers of injured, the influx of refugees, and the moving of hospitals down into the cellars (26 August – 24 September).
5. Pre-capitulation period of stagnation, caused by severe lack of food, water, dressing materials and medicaments.

The organisation of the regions, as in Powiśle, was effected by each one being divided into districts with a doctor to direct all the Health Service arrangements.[85]

Some of the medical posts and hospitals for the civilian population were to be found in the following places:[86]

ul. Koszykowa 28, 33, 37	ul. Nowogrodzka 6, 12, 19
ul. Wilcza 1, 7, 16, 26, 28a, 35	ul. Bracka 2, 5, 20
ul. Wspólna 2, 7, 20, 28, 30, 39	ul. Marszałkowska 56, 62, 68, 72, 79, 81, 86
ul. Żurawia 24a, 29, 31	ul. Chmielna 26
ul. Hoża 7, 13, 37, 76, 80	ul. Szopena 6
ul. Zlota 14, 27, 38, 62	ul. Pańska 53, 69
ul. Moniuszki 1a	ul. Górskiego 2, 3, 5, 6
ul. Warecka 9, 11	ul. Boduena 1, 2, 16
ul. Mokotowska 46a, 55	ul. Krucza 15
ul. Poznańska 15	ul. Sienna 84
ul. Piękna 24	ul. Śliska 51

Prescriptions were usually either issued to refugees, fire victims and the poor on the account of the Government Delegate, or the owner of the shop provided them gratis.[87] The newspapers carried lists of doctors' surgeries,[88] and instructions were printed concerning the use of water and the necessity of boiling it, on the building of latrines, on the maintenance of sanitation in cellars, cooking etc.[89]

Throughout August the health and sanitary conditions deteriorated.[90] The number of cases of dysentery and diarrhoea increased. They were especially frequent in Region III, but there were no epidemics,[91] and it would appear that the organisation of health care was as efficient and as effective as could be expected.

One of the most difficult problems to settle, not only from the organisational point of view, but also because it was disrupting cordial relations between the civilians and the Army, was the problem of water. The Army, hospitals, kitchens and civilians were all drawing water from the same wells without any set procedure. The queues for water were long and the Army tended to regard itself as privileged enough not to have to stand and wait their turn. This created arguments and friction between the civilians and soldiers. The hospitals were also unpopular because they had to draw large quantities of water which took a long time, often twenty-four hours.[92] In order to correct the situation a timetable was drawn up regulating the drawing of water:[93]

Army: 0600–0700 and 2130–2300 hours
Kitchens: 0500–0600 and 1500–1600 hours
Hospitals: 0400–0500 and 0800–0930 hours
Civilians: 0700–1500 and 1600–2000 hours

But this did not always alleviate the situation. Later on a new system was developed.[94]

By 24 August twenty-four wells had been built in Śródmieście North:[95]

ul. Koszykowa 43   ul. Mokotowska 5, 13, 15, 17, 21
ul. Noakowskiego 8   ul. Śniadeckich 8
ul. Lwowska 9, 8, 12   ul. Hoża 25, 28
ul. Wilcza 2, 6, 25, 61, 65   ul. Wspólna 44
ul. Żurawia 10, 81   ul. Poznańska 11
ul. 6-ego Sierpnia 9

Another thirty-two were being sunk:

ul. Żurawia 7, 8, 26   ul. Piusa 11, 13, 20, 21
ul. Nowogrodzka 26   ul. Krucza 3, 9, 13, 25
ul. Koszykowa 26, 28, 32, 34, 35, 37   ul. Mokotowska 55
ul. Marszałkowska 40, 78, 86   ul. Wilcza 21
ul. Hoża 6, 9, 10, 13, 22, 27   ul. Wspólna 10
pl. Trzech Krzyży 18

The alleviation of the water problem to a certain degree seems to have helped to improve morale.[96]

By the first week of September there was no electricity in Śródmieście.[97] Very strict regulations were imposed controlling the use of power for the civilian population.[98]

3.6 The September crisis and the civilian evacuation (1–10 September)

Between the fall of the Old Town and the fall of Powiśle there was a severe decline in the morale of the civilian population. At the beginning of September this decline was to precipitate a great crisis, nearly resulting in the failure of the Uprising.

The supply of food and health conditions in the town continued to deteriorate, against a background of a long drawn out Uprising, with no end nor help in sight. Generally there was loss of hope, but this does not seem to have been enough to spread defeatism amongst the majority who believed in perseverance and 'wszystko tylko nie kapitulacja' (anything but capitulation).[1] At the same time others were asking for arrangements to be made for women and children to leave with white flags to cross to the Germans, and slowly voices in favour of capitulation started to be heard.[2] They came mainly from fire victims, refugees and the hungry. The majority maintained, however, that they could carry on for another week or ten days, during which time, they believed, the Russians might force the Germans to retreat, or the Germans would be defeated in the west.[3]

During the first six days of September there were additional factors contributing to the depression of the Varsovians. Firstly, the full force of the German attack had been directed from the Old Town on to Śródmieście and many, who had previously been spared, were now feeling the full effects of it. Secondly, the fall of the Old Town had a strong impact. It was not just the toll in human life which its defence had cost but also the loss of some of the nation's most valuable architectural treasures.[4] Furthermore many realised that as a result of the fall of the Old Town the whole Uprising was doomed.[5] Thirdly, domestic factors played a significant role. The fall of the power station in Powiśle meant there was virtually no electricity after 4 September, and added to this was the problem of the great shortage of water.[6] With each day the food shortages also grew worse and people were starting to go hungry.[7] There was only enough bread for a few days, as the Germans had destroyed all the bakeries. Owing to the lack of milk, and the constant nervous shocks mothers could not feed their babies and the rate of infant mortality was extremely high. The lack

Checking of personal documents.

of water greatly hampered fire fighting. Accommodation could not always be found for all the refugees, many of whom were living in insanitary and unhygienic conditions. There was a danger of epidemics breaking out and many people were already suffering from dysentery.[8] Fourthly, the influx of refugees from the Old Town and Powiśle undermined morale.[9] Civilian refugees and soldiers spread alarming stories about the conditions in and the fate of the Old Town.[10] Many were demoralised and some soldiers went around drunk abusing their authority and thus fanning the flames of the military–civilian conflict.[11] There were others, however, who brought the fighting spirit of the Old Town with them and helped to raise morale.[12] But these groups of refugees created centres of ferment and were so critical towards the Uprising that they were regarded as

Movement during the Uprising through a labyrinth of passages leading
through buildings and cellars.

undermining national unity.[13] Finally, personal factors did not help.
Many people had seen at least one member of their family die, others
were cut off and could not make contact with their relatives and
friends.[14] The threat and prospect of death hung over everyone, not
just those who were fighting. Psychological as well as physical weariness made everyone more vulnerable. Discipline was breaking down
and the solidarity of the community breaking up. Some of the inhabitants of Warsaw were growing antagonistic towards the authorities
and their work, and there was a great desire for an end to the fighting
regardless of the results.[15]

Attitudes depended very much on what individual people had
already gone through during the Uprising. One internal report summarised the two varying attitudes thus:

The population which has already survived bombing and heavy shooting
desires that the fight should not last long and that some kind of formal
capitulation should be concluded . . . The population that has still not been
affected by the fight desires to continue but considers its physical and
psychological endurance to be at the longest a week to ten days. This group

still believes that during that time the Russians may force the Germans to retreat or the Reich to capitulate in the west. Some believe that some surprising 'miracle' will save the situation.[16]

On 3 September a certain Colonel 'Sulima', who was on the south-west side of al. Jerozolimskie, sent a message to General 'Monter', in which he reported that a crisis of confidence in the Army and the Uprising had developed and that people had left their homes carrying white flags to give themselves up.[17]

Even amongst the majority of the members of the Delegatura Rządu it would seem that the general feeling was that there was no hope for the Uprising. The Government Delegate himself had, although strongly opposed to such an attitude, lost hope that the Russians would liberate Warsaw and believed it was necessary to save the rest of the population.[18] Józef Stopnicki, the Deputy Regional Delegate of Southern Warsaw, has written that after the fall of the Old Town individuals and even deputations came to the office calling for an end to the fight.[19]

On 29 August, General 'Bór' wrote to the Commander in Chief of the Polish Armed Forces, General Sosnkowski, and Premier Mikołajczyk, in response to the latter's suggestion for an agreement with Russia:

The plan is tantamount to total capitulation and anticipates a whole series of most important political moves based on the good will of the Soviets, without any prior guarantees from the USSR and the Allies. The plan forms a departure from the political line which we have followed up to now ...

At such a momentous time for the future of Poland when decisions of historic importance will be made, I consider it my duty to state, in the name of the AK, which I command – and undoubtedly in total agreement with the opinion of the patriotic thinking community – that Poland did not fight the Germans for five years, in the most difficult conditions, bearing the greatest losses, just to capitulate to Russia.

Warsaw has not been fighting for a month with the most minimal external help and has not fallen into ruins so that the government could bow to the pressure of circumstances and throw at the nation a submissive attitude in the face of outside pressure, an attitude which history condemns.

Our fight against the Germans has shown us that we can manifest our hard and unswerving desire for freedom, which we love more than life.

If it is necessary we shall repeat that manisfestation for anyone who wants to destroy our independence ...[20]

This document shows very clearly General 'Bór's' attitude to the Uprising and the value of the fight. A stubborn defiance is manifest in it and it was this defiance which was decisive in spite of temporary waverings. Whilst never being prepared to capitulate to Russia, the prospect of Russian liberation of the capital was enough for the fight to continue.

On 3 September, General 'Bór' sent the following message to London:

I have decided to defend Warsaw to the limits of possibility. We have enough food to last until 7.IX and bread until 5.IX. Ammunition is being exhausted – its sufficiency depends on the intensity of the fight.

The spirit of the soldiers is good, the civilians are suffering due to shortage of food, water, accommodation, clothing and bad state of health. Morale is falling and is dependent on the degree of help for a quick ending to the fight, or the intensity of the help.

The possibility of carrying on is not dependent exclusively on our endurance, but also on your material help or the speed of successful Soviet operations in our area.[21]

On 4 September, General 'Bór' maintained at a meeting of the RJN that the exit from the city of its inhabitants would have its advantages, because 'the fewer civilians there are, the easier it is for the Army to fight'. Most members of the Council shared his view, although one of the leaders of the Peasant Party said that such a step would have a sad end because it would lower further the morale of the Army.[22]

The following day a leading article appeared in *Biuletyn Informacyjny* saying that there was still time to save the rest of Warsaw. All that was needed was for the Allies to release their front line airforce to help Warsaw. It continued by explaining that it would be enough if planes were sent at once in great strength to attack German positions, and if Russia offered the same kind of good will that Marshal Tito received from England.[23] It cannot have provided much solace. In *Rzeczpospolita* an article appeared calling on the population not to let their spirit weaken and thereby make the fight more difficult for the Army. It appealed to them not to succumb to the German call to capitulate five minutes before the Germans themselves would capitulate.[24]

The Germans had meanwhile been dropping leaflets, signed by General von dem Bach, calling on the civilians to leave the city and promising them safe protection.[25] These pamphlets were taken seriously by some people and considerable numbers were reported to be preparing to go.[26] In one report concerning the morale of the population in Śródmieście it was written: 'The leaflets dropped by the

Germans have had quite a different effect on the population than any previous ones. It ought to be reckoned with, that a large number will cross to the German side.' [27] In response to the German appeals and because of the prevailing situation negotiations were started between the German commander, General Rohr, and the Polish Red Cross, to arrange for the evacuation of the civilian population. This move was agreed upon at the meeting of the RJN on 6 September.[28]

On the same day posters appeared in the city signed by the District Government Delegate concerning the German pamphlets. They said that the German action was a desperate one aimed at driving a wedge between the civilians and the Army, and at breaking the morale of the latter. He told the population that there was only one answer to von dem Bach's appeal – 'We fight until the final victory not only of the capital but of the whole nation.' [29]

On 6 September when Powiśle fell the crisis came to a head, and General 'Bór' assessed the plight of Warsaw as follows:

The situation is reaching a climax. The civilian population is undergoing a crisis, which could have a fundamental influence on the fighting units. Reasons for the crisis: the attacking and bombing of the town, which continues with no retaliation, worsens, awareness that the enemy is trying to destroy the whole town ... the ceaseless battle, the increasingly smaller hunger rations for fire victims, and the speedy exhaustion of food for the permanent inhabitants, the high death rate amongst infants, hostile agitation by unfriendly agents, lack of water and electricity in all districts. If we add that ammunition is being exhausted, then you have a full picture of the situation of our struggle which grows more difficult hourly and daily. It is difficult to imagine what could be the result of a mass exit of the population from the districts under the terror of fire, and their congestion in districts from where there is no exit. In agreement with the announcement of the Premier could you let us have an exact time as to when promised help will come, or let us know if we are not going to receive it. This will be the most important factor in our ensuing decisions.

Do you think that action in the west will bring about the end of the war within the next few days?

We are not counting on a quick conquest of the city by Soviets.[30]

This was followed on the same day by a joint message from General 'Bór' and Jankowski:

Our situation as explained to you in previous telegrams makes it necessary that we should warn you about the possibility of a crisis and inform you of our views on such an eventuality.

The duration of resistance in the inner part of the city north of al. Jerozolimskie, a district which was heavily attacked during the last days, cannot be foreseen. In the most favourable conditions it might last as long as seven days but a collapse in the morale of the civilian population, who suffer enormously, may force the Polish forces to withdraw to the district south of al. Jerozolimskie, and this may even happen within the next two to four days.

After the fall of the northern part of the inner city the defence of the southern part, after the total strength of the German forces had been thrown against it, would only last a matter of hours. We cannot sacrifice the large numbers of inhabitants, who are sheltering here from all the other districts of Warsaw, for such a short gain in time. Therefore, in the case of the loss of the northern part of the inner city we would be faced with the following alternatives:

1. After the removal by agreement with the Germans of the civilian population – to fight to the end.
2. To surrender unconditionally.
3. To capitulate by district (Śródmieście, North, South, Mokotów, Żoliborz) in turn, depending on where the Germans are concentrating their attack. This solution would gain a little time, but at the same time destroy the whole city.

The choice of the above alternatives will depend on the degree of resistance and *on the bearing of the population* and on the amount of food and ammunition available.

We are presenting you with these possibilities in good time so you can prepare the English statesmen for it. We maintain that the collapse of the rising in Warsaw would have both military and political implications. An early awareness of this on your and the Allies' part may help in any political bargaining. It is obvious that after the fall of the Uprising power will pass into the hands of the Communists not only in Warsaw, but in the whole country. Immediate help from you in the form of bombing and supplies may lift morale and delay the crisis somewhat.[31]

The word 'capitulation' had started to be used amongst the leaders of the Uprising for the first time.[32]

By now many civilians were prepared to leave Warsaw at the first possible moment and, therefore, when a ceasefire was arranged to allow the evacuation of the civilian population as a result of the negotiations between the Polish Red Cross and the Germans, there were people ready to go.

From the two messages quoted above it can be seen that the end of the Uprising and the capitulation had been considered and anticipated. A kind of indifference is also visible. No longer was help asked for in desperate and demanding terms to save the Uprising, but rather in the hope that it might lift morale and put off the final hour of reckoning. At the same time this may also show a total disillusionment and disbelief in any help coming from the Allies. Unlike at the beginning of the Uprising when the enthusiastic support of the civilian population had made the continuation of the battle possible, their depressed and low spirits and in many cases antagonistic attitude now aggravated the already serious military situation, without being directly responsible for bringing about the possibility of capitulation.

On 7 September it was announced by the Regional Delegate that negotiations were going on concerning the evacuation of the civilian population.[33] He did not say, however, who was negotiating. This led to both confusion and criticism of the manner in which the authorities were acting.[34] Only the previous day the District Government Delegate had told the Varsovians that the Germans were not to be trusted and that Warsaw would fight until victorious.[35]

The evacuation of the civilians took place on 8, 9, and 10 September. On 8 September *Biuletyn Informacyjny* carried the following article concerning the evacuation, and voiced the opinion that all German assurances must be treated with great care – but the Polish authorities, civilian and military, do not want in this matter to interfere with those who wish at their own risk to test the value of these assurances. It went on to say that the authorities had applied to the Polish Red Cross to come to an agreement with the Germans on an evacuation, and as a result all units had received instructions not to interfere with women, children, the aged and sick leaving the area in AK hands and going out in the direction of German posts. Young men and men in good health were not allowed to leave. Evacuees were permitted to take one day's food supply so as not to upset stocks in Warsaw. The paper was very careful to point out that the Polish authorities took no responsibility for such action, that each individual was leaving at his own risk and that he would only be under the care of the Polish Red Cross until crossing the German lines.[36] *Robotnik* also stressed this point.[37] *Armia Ludowa* told its readers that it did not trust the Germans and their promises.[38]

There were no calls to dissuade people and nothing was said about the treatment these individuals might receive. Only the newspaper *Rzeczpospolita* carried an article reminding its readers how the Germans had treated Poles who had previously crossed to them – some had been shot at, others robbed of their belongings, those who were fit had been sent away to work.[39]

On 9 September, the second day of the evacuation, leaflets were distributed signed by the District Government Delegate concerning the further possibility of civilians leaving. It also explained what had happened to those who left the day before:

According to news received the Germans confiscate all larger pieces of baggage from those leaving, therefore there is no point in burdening yourselves with large amounts of food, clothing, linen etc.

It has been ascertained that men are separated from their families by the Germans.

Everyone must spend a few days in the camp at Pruszków and from there the men are sent to do fortification work and women and children will be sent west.

All those who want to take advantage of this opportunity to leave Warsaw can do so without any obstacle from the Polish authorities with the exception of men of working age.[40]

Thus it can be seen that whilst no one was openly encouraged to leave there was no official manifestation of discouragement. Everyone was left to decide for themselves. The sick, old, mothers and their children, however, were advised to leave, according to Stefan Korboński. No one was forced to go.[41]

Fewer than 10,000 left, according to published Polish figures. German figures put the number at nearly three times that amount.[42] However, it would seem from contemporary sources that the German figures may have been closer to the true number. In a report Korboński sent to London he stated that *kilkanaście* thousand old people, women and children left with the silent approval of the authorities.[43] The word *kilkanaście* is ambiguous and can mean any number between ten and twenty. Jankowski, in a report sent to London on 22 September, quotes over 20,000 people as leaving the city, although he gives no dates for when they left.[44]

The reason put forward for such a sharp fall in evacuations on 9 and 10 September is that the sound of the fighting on the eastern side of the city filled the people with a new hope of being liberated.[45] This is probably true but it must also be borne in mind that those who decided to leave would have left on the first day and not spent any longer making up their minds. Other people who were considering crossing may have been put off by the reaction of those who had no intention of leaving the city. One or two groups were stopped from leaving by an AK Commander.[46] Others who had prepared to leave and went to the crossing points changed their minds and turned back at the last minute.[47]

Thus it seems that between 20,000 and 25,000 people left out of a population of about 250,000, i.e. $8-10\%$. This is probably the most telling figure concerning the attitude of the civilian population towards the Uprising. The majority of the inhabitants decided to stay in Warsaw; not as many left as had been feared by the authors of internal reports.

The problem as to whether to leave the city or not caused great heart searching, due to a combination of fear and distrust of the Germans and patriotic reasons. No one was sure what awaited them on the other side. They had already heard or been warned about the way civilians had been treated and of the appalling conditions prevailing in the transit camp at Pruszków. Apart from that the inhabitants of Warsaw had the whole experience of nearly five years of Nazi occupation behind them, and they knew about the Pawiak, Auschwitz, Majdanek, Dachau and other camps. For some, however, the choice was easy for they felt that nothing could be worse than what they had already gone through in the insurgent city. In fact it was sometimes found that those who left had not suffered as much in the Uprising as others had, but they simply could not put up with the deprivations of insurgent life.[48] Others went in the hope of saving their children or of finding members of their families who were missing.[49] Many were breaking down and thought it was the best thing they could do for themselves, or believed that Warsaw would capitulate any day.[50] One woman left because she felt alone and uncared for.[51] Criminals and *Volksdeutsch* left under the cover of the evacuation.[52]

The majority of evacuees were reported to be women, children, the aged and the poor – mainly, shop-keepers, artisans and servants,[53] but according to witnesses and reports a surprisingly high number were members of the intelligentsia and the wealthy classes.[54] Young and strong people left including young men,[55] which led to scuffles between them and AK soldiers.[56] In some cases officers and soldiers escorted their families to the assembly points.[57] At least one House Commander is alleged to have crossed.[58] Many left in shame and tears,[59] others were quite indifferent and showed no emotion.[60] Some were proud of the fact that they had managed to avoid death in Warsaw.[61]

On 10 September at 7.00 a.m. General 'Bór' sent a note to the German Commander of the South of Warsaw, General Rohr, as a result of the latter's initiative, in an attempt to reach a possible capitulation agreement subject to three main conditions:

1. Recognition of combatant rights for AK soldiers, without any reprisals for their anti-German activity before or after 1 August 1944.
2. Clarification of the fate of the civilian population which remained in the city.

3. Clarification of the German attitude to the Polish civilian authorities and their activity during the Uprising.

General Rohr's reply at 10.30 a.m. assured General 'Bór' that:

1. All AK soldiers would be granted combatant rights and held in prisoner of war camps.
2. There would be no reprisals for the activity of insurgents before 1 August 1944.
3. The civilian population would be sent westward out of the area of fighting with the Soviet Union.
4. Persons working for the civilian authorities would be evacuated together with the civilian population and there would be no reprisals.

General Rohr demanded capitulation by 4.00 p.m. on the same day, but General 'Bór', playing for time, sent another note demanding additional conditions:

1. The civilian population which still had property and lived in undestroyed houses could stay in Warsaw.
2. The declaration should be endorsed by General Reinhardt as Commander of the whole Centre Front and not just General Rohr, who was Commander of the southern part of the town.
3. The declaration should be announced on the German radio.

General Reinhardt stated that he had nothing to add with regard to the previous conditions agreed by General Rohr. He warned the Polish Commander that if he had not capitulated by 1.00 a.m. on 11 September, the fight would be continued in an even more severe form – 'those are my last words'.[62]

The ultimatum was totally ignored by the General Staff of the AK,[63] and the note was answered the following day. It said that the additional Polish demands of guarantees had not been answered and that it was the Germans who had broken off the negotiations by their unrealistic time limit and threats of intensifying the fight.[64] All negotiations came to an end.

Although General 'Bór' had wanted capitulation, not all his staff agreed with him and this is why he had been playing for time. By 10 September he had reason to believe that capitulation could be avoided. There were again sounds of fighting coming from the eastern bank of the Vistula, messages had been received from London saying that help was on its way, and the reports coming in from his unit commanders were more encouraging than before. Furthermore he did not have any real faith in the German assurances.[65]

In spite of the fact that General 'Bór' had believed that the fight would be easier if the civilian population were evacuated, this does not seem to have been one of the factors leading up to his decision to fight on. The civilians had helped to create the crisis at the beginning of September but had never really been taken into account in determining whether the Uprising should continue or not. It is not known whether by 10 September the opinion of the leaders of the Uprising was influenced by the relatively small numbers of evacuees. Only in the combined report of General 'Bór' and the Government Delegate is any mention made of the influence of civilian behaviour.[66] However, if there had been a mass exodus of civilians at this stage would not the command have had to adopt a different attitude? Was it not rather the fact that the civilian population did not abandon Warsaw that made further fighting possible? It is impossible to know what would have happened if large numbers had deserted the Uprising, but there is no doubt that it would have had a very profound effect on the morale of the fighting soldier and the international reputation of the Uprising, as well as depriving the authors of the Uprising of important 'political' support.

It can also be maintained, however, that in view of the political situation at the time it was most important to the leaders of the Uprising that the fight should continue, regardless of its prospects. General 'Monter' had written to General 'Bór' saying that anyone who helped the fight was worthy of Poland's gratitude, that everything else would somehow fall into place and that even co-operation with General Żymierski, Commander in Chief of the Polish Army fighting alongside the Red Army, was preferable to capitulation: 'in the history of the Polish Army they are but fragments'.[67]

One survivor of the Uprising has written that those who stayed behind prepared themselves for a new occupation and the start of Russian–German fighting in Warsaw.[68] The people of Warsaw were filled with a feeling which he called *likwidacyjny* (winding-up). They began above all to think of survival and organising themselves after the Uprising.[69] Others were reported to believe still in the ultimate victory of the Uprising.[70]

The evacuation did succeed in ridding the town of certain elements of the population who had been undermining morale.[71] The people who left were regarded as being weak, as traitors and deserters by those who stayed behind.[72] One report wrote of the attitude of the Army to the civilians who left:

The soldiers were enraged by the exit of civilians. They made caustic remarks at those leaving and would not allow them to be given cigarettes.

One soldier at his post on ul. Lwowska told me that if he saw his mother in the crowd he would shoot her. He complained about the fact that the authorities had allowed such a shameful thing to happen and above all that so many young people were leaving.[73]

But afterwards a considerable easing of tension was noticed.[74]

Why did the majority decide to stay behind, to share the town's fate, to await events or some miracle? Most of the remaining inhabitants still had members of their family fighting or actively involved in the fighting and therefore felt a strong personal tie. Many still had their homes and were living in them, and, for as long as they were still left standing, would not leave. There was the indescribable fear and distrust of the Germans; no one knew what would happen on the other side of the barricade. There was a general feeling that it was preferable to die in the rubble then by a Nazi bullet. Added to this was the fact that in spite of the difficult living conditions and dangers of insurgent Warsaw, they were at least amongst themselves, under Polish authorities, and they had the protection of the Polish Army, whose fate they wanted to share. Some still hoped that help would come: they remembered Mikołajczyk's broadcast of 1 September,[75] and the sound of battle could be heard again on the other side of the river. Finally, an incredible faith and even belief in the impossible, a very strong characteristic of the Polish nation, gave these people the strength and courage to carry on. Some saw their fight not just as a military battle but also as a moral demonstration of the Polish desire for freedom, which ought to be supported even if it brought no immediate military victory. Many of these Varsovians were imbued with Polish insurgent traditions. Five years of Nazi occupation and their acute sense of their national history made the choice easy for them.

3.7 The Uprising in Śródmieście (10–30 September)

After 10 September, as a result of losses of territory during the fighting, the district of Śródmieście mainly consisted of the area south of al. Jerozolimskie, although insurgents still held positions in the northern part.[1]

On the whole in the second ten days of September morale was improved. The inhabitants of the district seem to have had a responsive and positive attitude towards insurgent life and were determined to carry on. This was partly due to the departure of certain malcontents during the evacuation, but also to the revival of Soviet activity on the other side of the river and the appearance of Russian planes fighting over Warsaw on 9 September.[2] There was new hope as well as the overnight improvement in morale. The mood was such as to even remind one observer of the first days of the Uprising.[3] Ominous signs, however, were seen to reveal themselves in this upsurge in morale: 'The situation has changed to the advantage of Russia. The people in no way hide their sympathy for Russia. This is quite a dangerous symptom and ought to be fought . . .'[4] In the early hours of 13 September the first Soviet drops of arms, weapons and food were received, and these continued until 18 September.[5]

At the same time in the district various rumours circulated, which alternately sustained or undermined morale. Stories were spread that the Sadyba pump stations in Czerniaków, Mokotów, and Góra Kalwaria were in the hands of the Soviets. These stories were received 'with joy but without enthusiasm'.[6] Others were circulating that AK units were leaving Warsaw through Czerniaków, to go to the woods, or that AK officers and soldiers had crossed to PAL formations with the aim of avoiding the 'gniew Stalina' (the wrath of Stalin), after the arrival of the Soviet Army. Some connected this with Monter's announcement and others with the forty-fourth day of the Uprising, as a symbolic number in the Polish poet Adam Mickiewicz's classic poem 'Dziady'.[7]

A lengthy and detailed report in the middle of September made the following observations: amongst the civilian population both General 'Bór' and the civilian leadership had lost their authority. The Polish government in London was also losing support, because it did not appear able to relieve the situation or give a lead. The German threat of greater destruction only strengthened the determination of Warsaw to continue the fight whilst the Allied failure to bring help raised expectations of Soviet aid. The PKWN propaganda did not provoke any opposition and the prospect of Polish–Soviet co-operation was met with 'approval and great joy'. All anti-Soviet articles in the insurgent papers were read with dissatisfaction and a fear of a worsening of relations with the USSR, although public opinion regarded the criticism as being 'objectively valid'. The KRM and RJN were regarded as having no influence whatsoever on the situation. The author of the report concluded: 'I am virtually certain that when the Red Army enters the people of Warsaw will violently turn against the present leaders of the Uprising if no compromise is reached with PKWN. The political stand of the community is breaking up.'[8] Relations between the Army and civilians were still some-what strained.[9]

On 12 September it was possible to report that the food supply in Śródmieście was not too bad, and that although there was general undernourishment, fainting as a result of it was rare. Stores of flour were exhausted and the majority of the inhabitants were living on a monotonous diet of groats.[10] Two days later the situation began to grow worse and, as always, those who were most badly hit were the poor, refugees and fire victims. But still many felt that it was better to go hungry than fall into the hands of the Germans.[11] As more and more private food stores were depleted and no quick end to the Uprising was foreseen, new feeding posts were organised in practi-cally every house for the civilians by House and Block Committees.[12]

On 14 September the Department of Social Care of the Regional Delegacy for Warsaw North reported that by 13 September all the Department's stores had been exhausted, with the exception of sugar and coffee. Minimal amounts of these products had been issued to the kitchens, but neither barley, coffee nor sugar were suitable ingre-dients for soup. The previous night the special food transport columns carrying food from stores had not been able to cross over from ul. Czerniakowska, due to the fighting there. On that day, therefore, there had been no barley for the Block kitchens. The transport from ul. Ludna 9 had come through but due to lack of containers there was only 250 kg of wheat, 200 kg of sugar and 12 kg of marmalade, not enough to supply all the RGO kitchens. Thus only some were provided with coffee and sugar on 13 September. It was the same with the Block kitchens. This represented at least a 25% fall in the number of meals being issued, whilst the number wanting meals rose considerably. It was impossible to feed them all in the public kitchens and, therefore, they were sent to the Block Commanders. The report was concluded by the remark that it was necessary to mobilise further permanent inhabitants to help the kitchens feeding refugees.[13]

After this date the numbers of people going hungry began to increase and hospitals felt the shortage of food acutely.[14] It was maintained at the time that morale could be raised if even a minimal food ration were distributed.[15] On 15 September, the same day as the Red Army entered Praga, the Warsaw AK radio station, 'Błyska-wica', put out the following broadcast:

The most tragic moment has come. Warsaw faces hunger. The inhabitants, left for several days without adequate nourishment, are exposed to this most

Movement in Śródmieście under the protection of barricades.

cruel torture. After forty-six days of ferocious fighting the city has no food left. The small stores saved after five years of occupation have been seized by the Germans or destroyed by fire. The remnants dug out from under the rubble are being distributed to the famished people. Warsaw must be immediately supplied with food . . .[16]

Government representatives were also sending appeals to London for supplies of food and clothing.[17] By 18 September, all the public kitchens had ceased to function, as all their stores were depleted. The full onus of supplying meals thereafter fell on the House and Block kitchens.[18]

By the same time water was only obtainable from wells and the drawing of it involved standing in long and slow moving queues. The desperate lack of water and the dangers in drawing it were having a very adverse influence on morale.[19] One survivor of those days has written that the problem with water was worse than the lack of food. Obtaining it was the worst part, especially as she had no bucket, but just two one-litre bottles. She stood in the queue all night,

and waited several hours to fill up my bottles. The water trickled out in a faint stream. There was always less and less water; new wells were built – the water was filmy and virtually unfit to drink, but it was drunk, there being no choice. People waiting for water were usually shot at ... Every morning several bodies were lying alongside the well, but the following day more people were always standing with their buckets. The water trickled out in drops, the buckets filled up slowly, every moment threatened death, and yet no one hastened, no one complained . . .[20]

Another witness remembers how, because of the shortage of water and difficulties in obtaining it people went unwashed and unshaven. Washing up after tea or coffee was done in the remaining water in the bottom of the basin. Afterwards everyone took it in turns to wash their hands in it – 'in that way our hands got dampened at least once a day'.[21] Others cleaned their dishes with paper.[22]

On 17 September, General 'Bór' sent a message to London pointing out the implications of the situation:

The long and exhausting fight in Warsaw, the political bargaining in the international arena as well as echoes of the internal strife in the Polish Government in Exile has a great influence on and continually affects civilian and military morale and political opinion. Our fight is taking place in the most difficult conditions, and the fact that negotiations with the Germans were broken off by us has formed in everyone a determination to persevere. This is all the more reason why both soldiers and civilians are not only waiting for some concrete decision regarding help for Warsaw but also

The drawing of water from wells specially sunk during the Uprising;
civilians carrying buckets to the well.

demanding indications as to how an independent and sovereign existence is
to be regained in the face of Russia's aggressive attitude to Poland. There are
increasingly frequent accusations about the impotence and inactivity of the
political and military bodies here, as well as the Polish authorities in London.
This is due to the lack of information from the government about our international situation when the Soviets are about to enter Warsaw, as well as the
lack of visible help and care from our Western Allies, and increasingly
popular Soviet propaganda.

The lack of sufficient help from the West and the numerous disillusion-
ments and disappointments which this has caused us induces the community
here, including some Commanders, to look for salvation in the east. The few
Soviet drops which we have received and the Soviet air and artillery support
at the present stage of our fight has further strengthened the desire for some
kind of agreement with the PKWN. A deepening of such attitudes and ten-

dencies may push us into the Soviet orbit of influence and consequently totally cut Poland off from the English ...

Soldiers and civilians have ceased to believe in the long and patiently awaited help from the West, and as a result they have grown angry with and distrustful of the emigré authorities.

It is foreseeable that when Soviet units enter Warsaw, public opinion affected by Soviet propaganda will turn against our highest authorities in London and the Western Allies ...[23]

At the same time an internal report of the Department of Information and Press reported a fall in morale again after the lift it had been given by Soviet activity. This was attributed to the bombing, hunger, long drawn out Russo–Polish negotiations and lack of Polish decisiveness. The report concluded that these factors were creating a suitable atmosphere for the growth of Communist propaganda, especially amongst the homeless, which was even more effective because the only hope for the Uprising would be the arrival of the Soviet Army.[24] But there was a general willingness to last out until that day.[25]

On 18 September, 107 American Flying Fortresses in a daylight sortie appeared above the city to drop supplies.[26] They provided the necessary propaganda which the Polish authorities wanted to balance Soviet activity.[27] The sortie was greeted with great enthusiasm:

With the exception of the sick and wounded, everyone had emerged from the cellars. Basements and cellars were deserted; courtyards and streets were jammed with people. Everyone able to stand on his feet had rushed into the open. At first the people were quite certain that they were watching parachutists coming down. We had a splendid exhibition of Allied air-power, but the majority of the containers fell beyond our lines ... The vast crowds of people who had been shouting and cheering, bowed their heads and returned to their cellars and shelters after the planes had disappeared.[28]

Only 15% of the containers fell into insurgent areas,[29] but still morale improved instantly.[30] One witness has written that it created a new hope in some kind of miracle.[31] However, this action on the part of the Americans had a very short term effect on morale.[32] The sortie was not repeated and the appeal of the Government Delegate, the RJN and KRM, that the American planes should come not just once for political reasons, but regularly to supply Warsaw with food and ammunition, went unheeded.[33]

On the same day the Second Polish Division, fighting alongside the Soviet Army, attempted to cross the Vistula.[34] The attempt failed.

By the beginning of the second ten days of September nearly all the inhabitants of Śródmieście had moved down to the cellars. No one went out into the streets unless it was necessary, all communication being by the underground passages.[35] An assessment made of the situation at the time compared it to 'the lull before the storm'. The civilian population was seen to be expecting some great event, which would at last radically change the situation in the capital.[36] Some still believed that the Russians would come.[37] The following is an extract from the diary of a Warsaw bank employee, an invalid, who had been caught away from home by the outbreak of the Uprising and had been in a cellar for practically the whole of the Uprising:

19 September ... strong criticism made against those who started the Uprising.

21 September ... Everyone is saying that the Bolshevik units and the Soviet Army have crossed the Vistula in the district of Siekierki, and that our units have made contact with those units that have crossed from Praga. If it is true a quick capture of Warsaw by the Red Army can be depended upon.

22 September ... If the insurgents link up with the Soviet units landing on the left bank, the whole population would leave for Praga. Some of the refugees in the cellars are ready at any moment for their journey. There is great joy in the cellars because it appears we will be liberated at any moment. I myself would also go to Praga if there were such a possibility, I would not wait an hour.[38]

Between 18 and 21 September no drops were made by the Russians. They started again on the night of 21 September and continued until the night of 28 September.[39]

Meanwhile the newspapers had, to a certain extent, been trying to sustain the hope that the liberation of Warsaw was at hand and that the Russians would soon be in the capital. On 16 September *Barykada Wolności* (Freedom Barricade) explained that the Soviet Army had not been able to help Warsaw earlier, as it had only just arrived at the outskirts of the town.[40] *Biuletyn Informacyjny* the following day announced that the Uprising was entering its final and victorious phase. The Russian attack was to be expected in the next few days. It went on the say that those days would mark the last of the Uprising and the first of preparing to work together with the Red Army.[41] On 22 September *Nowy Świat* (New World) likewise wrote that the end was approaching and that in the coming days the Russians would enter Warsaw.[42] Three days later *Barykada Wolności* wrote: 'The last act of the tragedy of Warsaw is being unrolled and probably before long the happy ending, brought about by the Red Army's liberation of Warsaw, will give rise to certain questions.' One of those questions was why there was no co-operation with Russia from the Polish side.[43] The PPR newspaper *Głos Warszawy* (Voice of Warsaw), wrote that Poland was standing on the threshold of liberation.[44] *Armia Ludowa* after 15 September was continually stating that the moment of liberation was at hand.[45]

By the third week of September, however, a doctor observed that Warsaw was taking its dying breath; people knew there was no hope of any help or victory and therefore just awaited their fate.[46] Another Varsovian described the state of the civilians as expectant[47] and an elderly lady wrote at the same time in her diary that the support the civilians were giving to the Uprising was incredible and without it the Uprising 'wouldn't last a week'.[48] She added that everyone dreaded capitulation.[49]

On 22 September Czerniaków fell and the last possibility of access to the Vistula was lost. Hope of any landing from the eastern bank had to be abandoned.[50] Exhaustion and hunger spread. Many kitchens had neither food to cook nor issue.[51] Dogs, cats and pigeons were being eaten.[52] Confusion reigned. Many people were sick and sanitary conditions deteriorated. Once again there was a fear of an outbreak of epidemics, there already being an epidemic of dysentery.[53] There was a shortage of clothing. As a result of the lack of soap and water increasing numbers of people were becoming lousy.[54] There were still clashes with the Army over the allocation and drawing of water,[55] which led to accusations from civilians, e.g. one woman shouted at a soldier, 'You only joined them to eat, drink and do nothing.'[56] There was great depression, and people felt themselves to be caught up in a vicious circle, not knowing where to go for help.[57] Others managed to keep their spirits up. No one knew how much longer the Uprising was going to last and, therefore, it was difficult to plan the use of stores.[58]

In an attempt to alleviate the desperate shortage of food, instructions were sent out on 21 September empowering the Regional Government Delegacy to requisition all foodstuffs (flour, flour products, legumes, groats, fat, meat, and meat products, tinned food, sugar, salt, and marmalade) still in shops in the city. These stores were supposed to be reported by their owners.[59] It is difficult to believe this move had any effect nor is there any evidence that it did.

A report of the Department of Information and Press on 22 September clearly shows the problems involved in organising the feeding of the population. Due to the shortage of food an attempt was made to open new house kitchens. It was unsuccessful, due to several factors. In the eighth week of the Uprising it was impossible to base the supply of kitchens on offers from tenants, who themselves had hardly any stores. The only means by which it was theoretically possible to supply these kitchens was by transporting dried food from the other side of al. Jerozolimskie, but this involved other difficulties. The majority of the people who used the kitchens were fire victims, usually with little resilience and afraid to leave the shelters, and attempts to persuade them to leave for their own needs were usually fruitless. Furthermore hunger and the unhealthly living conditions had weakened them and they were not strong enough to carry supplies. The stronger tended to sell and exchange the provisions they received and in that way maintained themselves and their families. Queuing for water, often to no avail, took up so much time that the possibility of a whole day's expedition for provisions was excluded. Thus the only feasible solution was to force those who wanted to use the kitchens to carry food and water. Two permanent transport groups had to be formed by the House Committees, whose co-operation was necessary but hard to get due to their own physical and psychological exhaustion and the personal difficulties of their members. Meanwhile water was being traded (for about 100 zł. a litre) or bartered, which tended to result in an unjust social distribution of water, favouring the rich. It also created a run on the number of utensils available.[60] Thus the problems got worse and not better.

On 23 September John Ward sent the following message to London:

The inhabitants of Warsaw are now virtually living only in ruins ... Civilians are in a worse plight [than the Army]. Private stocks are largely buried under the ruins. Hospitals are in what were coal cellars a few weeks ago. Many thousands of wounded lie there, perhaps more civilians than military. The conditions in which they are lying are really terrible.[61]

Two factors became very clear at that time. Firstly, the criticism of the leaders of the Uprising was steadily increasing. Secondly, support for the Polish Communists, the AL and the PAL also increased markedly and, with the prolongation of the fight, greater distrust and lack of support for the AK authorities was revealed. One of the manifestations of this was the growth in the circulation of the Communist press, which was more and more widely read and accepted.[62] The newspaper *Armia Ludowa* had come to be regarded by some as the only reliable paper, whilst *Biuletyn Informacyjny*, whose readership was falling to a minimum,[63] and *Rzeczpospolita* were regarded as being 'trash, lies and fraud'. Furthermore, some individuals now considered that only the AL could create a Poland friendly to Russia. They read in the papers that the population in Praga was being fed, clothed and treated justly.[64] The forces of the left were reported to be growing larger every day,[65] and these opinions were allegedly not limited to any one section of the community.[66]

The increasing popularity of the Communist press was not seen as a turn towards Communism by the people, who continued to be afraid of it, but was rather a manifestation of criticism and disillusionment with their own authorities. The people believed that Warsaw should be taken out of the direct field of battle at any price, which was only possible if an agreement were concluded with the Russians. Criticism of the insurgent authorities grew because they were seen to be hampering all attempts at Russo–Polish understanding.[67] It must be stressed that it is not known how general these feelings were and there were those who remained uncritically loyal to the Polish authorities.[68] It was reported that the people were saying that everyone would leave for the country when the Soviet Army entered.[69]

By the last days of September discipline was breaking down. Every day the number of cases of looting and stealing increased.[70] Organisation was disintegrating and it was extremely difficult to find people to work. If they did turn up they often soon went away, because conditions of work were unsuitable.[71]

Such then was the situation in the last week of the Uprising. The will to hold out still existed and if the spirit of some people had broken they were not all without it.[72] One report contained the following observation:

An increasing number of people await the end of the Uprising with growing impatience. Often one hears doubts as to its quick ending and as a result faith in the ability to hold on declines. At the same time the number of people who do nothing else but pray and meditate, being totally indifferent to current events, increases.[73]

General 'Bór' has described conditions in Śródmieście at the end of September as follows:

The state of the hospitals was indescribable. Wounded poured in all day and every day. The doctors could hardly cope with the work. Surgical operations were performed without anaesthetics, in cellars, by the light of a few candles or even in exceptional cases carbide lights. When dressing materials were short, paper was used to stop haemorrhage. Exhaustion reached such a pitch that even the first aid service, which hitherto had worked very well indeed, slackened. People became indifferent to everything – even to the cries of those buried in the basements of destroyed houses. All strength had been used up and there were no more men to clear the rubble. In the cellars, where altruism reached the extreme point of sharing the last pound of wheat, a few men utterly devoid of scruples would part with a scrap of food for gold or jewels to people ready to pay any price for something to eat.[74]

The food situation had become catastrophic.[75] The basic diet of Śródmieście was *plujzupa*, a soup made from either cooked oats or barley.[76] The death rate amongst small children rose and as a result of hunger two adults died.[77] People were fainting and collapsing from weakness,[78] and there were cases of pediculosis and swelling caused by malnutrition.[79] Even front line soldiers were going without food.[80]

General 'Bór' telegraphed to London on 26 September: 'The spectre of capitulation or the crossing of the civilian population to the Germans, this time due to hunger, haunts us again. Food supplies will last a week without daily drops and at the longest ten days. There are a dozen odd cases of scarlet fever.'[81] Three days later he telegraphed that there were only sufficient food rations for three days.[82] This figure corresponds with the calculations of the RGO at the same time, who maintained that they had enough stores for three days of minimal rations. At that time the RGO was feeding through its own and House and Block kitchens about 20,000 people.[83] (Compare 17,000 reported by the Department of Social Care including RGO on 27 September.[84] According to another register 22,544 lunches were issued on 30 September by communal kitchens registered in the Department of Social Care[85] – this represented about 75% of the maximum amount issued at any one time during the Uprising. These figures do not include non-registered kitchens. But even so a large number of people were still feeding themselves.) There was the continual problem with water. New wells could not be sunk or made operative due to lack of equipment. Every day more people were killed queuing for water.[86]

On 29 September the Department of Information and Press reported that the preceding days had been marked by a strong fall in morale amongst the civilians.[87] Complaints were being made not just by the so-called *schronowcy* (shelter dwellers) but even by people who had managed to keep going and had not succumbed to the strain. The reasons put forward for this were the usual ones; length of the Uprising, hunger, shortage of food, failure of the Allies to help the city and no sign of liberation by the Soviet Army. The Polish authorities were strongly attacked and the articles in the pro-government news-papers were described as being 'cheap supplication'. There were growing demands that people in leading positions should be relieved of their posts, as they were not considered capable of discharging their duties. The Army was attacked by the general public as they had been seen bartering products from Soviet drops for vodka, dollars and złoties. In turn the authorities were blamed for allowing such abuses to be practised alongside hunger and misery.[88] One report (concerning some of the inhabitants of ul. Mokotowska, Koszykowa, Piusa and Emilii Plater) divided the community up into three types of people:[89]

1. The more strong minded who, in spite of everything, believed in a happy ending to the Uprising, assessed the current political and military events calmly, and appreciated the necessity for all the present sacrifices and efforts as the nation's contribution to the war.
2. People tired of the Uprising, often homeless and having little or nothing, blaming everything around them for their plight. They saw salvation only in an immediate submission to the will of the USSR and in consequence had a hostile attitude to the Polish government in London and its policies.
3. People totally absorbed in their own affairs and difficulties, not at all interested in current problems.

The author of the report did not say which group was the largest.

The Uprising was seen to be collapsing.[90] There was apathy, exhaustion and lack of co-operation.[91] Some people were trying to arrange ways of crossing to the German held areas.[92]

The stories of the German attacks on Mokotów and Żoliborz brought about great depression.[93] It led to panic and people started to cross to the northern area of Śródmieście.[94] They feared that the German attack would be concentrated on the district after the fall of Mokotów, and that the inhabitants of Mokotów would be left to their own fate as had happened in the Old Town.[95] The Varsovians ceased believing that the Russians would come or that any kind of speedy military help would reach them.[96] The majority considered that the Russians were too weak to bring about a successful offensive and expressed the opinion that the Germans were in a position slowly to liquidate the Uprising. They believed that the entry of the Soviet Army would result in the AK being incorporated into the Red Army, but if there were a capitulation a bearable fate would await Polish soldiers in POW camps.[97] Voices were heard in favour of unconditional surrender and the question of whether to cross to the

Germans or not was openly discussed.[98] The recent successes of the Soviet Army in the Baltic states led, under the influence of the press, to the conviction that the Russians were holding back for political reasons. The news that General Sosnkowski had resigned as Commander in Chief of the Polish armed forces spread new hope that Polish–Soviet difficulties would be resolved, although lack of news about any further developments in Russo–Polish negotiations was regarded as new procrastination. Depression was further deepened by the strong German artillery bombardments, which hampered movement and the barter trade, which for many was the only way of obtaining food.[99]

It was obvious by then that Warsaw was breaking up, but she was still not broken. Although there was no hope for a quick end to the nightmare of the Uprising, there was still a willingness to hold out and there was still a sustaining spirit. This is why the end came as such a shock to many.

3.8 Mokotów

The materials available for study of the civilian population in Mokotów during the Uprising are as limited as they were for Powiśle, Ochota and Wola. There are very few original documents surviving. Consequently any attempt at such a study must be narrowly based and incomplete. However, there does not seem to be any great divergence in the information provided by such materials as do exist.

Mokotów formed District V of Warsaw and was contained in the following area: Fort Mokotów, Wierzbno and Wyględów and through the districts of Służewiec, Siekierki and Miasto Ogród Czerniaków.[1] By 4 August the front lines were formed by the following streets: in the north ul. Szustra across ul. Puławska, in the east a double bulge through the area lying between the streets of ul. Belwederska-Sobieskiego and Puławska, in the south along ul. Woronicza and in the west al. Niepodległości.[2] In comparison to other parts of the city Mokotów housed a large number of Germans, not just the Army but SS and civilians.[3] Furthermore it was not an area of blocks of flats like Śródmieście but a larger, more spacious area, containing villas belonging to the wealthier inhabitants of Warsaw, each one usually surrounded by a garden.[4] Thus the whole physical layout of the district was conducive to different organisation, morale and attitude of its inhabitants than in other parts of Warsaw.

Because of the failure of the insurgent units to take the area lying between Śródmieście and Mokotów, Mokotów was cut off from the town centre for the whole of the Uprising. On 6 August communication with the town centre was established through the sewers.[5]

The outbreak of the Uprising was greeted with the same enthusiasm as in the rest of Warsaw, but this enthusiasm was soon to disappear.[6] Maria Manteufflowa has written:

The optimism which accompanied the first minutes of the Uprising was soon extinguished. The news of the fighting in the town, the bloody battle, heavy losses, lack of arms and ammunition, all pointed to the fact that the Uprising was going to be a longer one than we foresaw at the beginning, especially after the silencing of the cannonade on the other side of the Vistula. (The unfulfilled hope of external help.)[7]

As in the rest of Warsaw the longer the Upriing lasted and the nearer the German units advanced, the more the population lost hope and the more critical it became of the Uprising.

According to existing memoirs and reports it does not seem that the same degree of co-operation or the same attitudes were to be found in Mokotów as in the rest of Warsaw. Mokotów was not a happy island 'breathing peacefully', as one author has described it.[8] Jan Dobraczyński, who was the Deputy BIP Chief in the Old Town, crossed to Mokotów by sewer on 6 September, to be BIP Chief of the area. He immediately noticed the different atmosphere there in comparison to that of the Old Town and the lack of enthusiasm.[9] On 16 September he published an article in *Komunikat Informacyjny* stressing this anomaly:

Those arriving in Mokotów are struck by the complaining, whining and moaning, which are to be heard here much more often than in other parts of Warsaw ... in the Old Town there was nothing like that. There the hard fight with the enemy – the fight, which claimed hundreds of victims and which left houses in piles of rubble – did not give rise to half the number of complaints that are heard here. In the Old Town there was nothing to eat, nowhere to sleep, and the harassing strength of the artillery fire was incomparably greater than the fire directed on Mokotów. Also in Śródmieście the large number of mines, grenades and bombings did not upset the district, and there is no moaning or complaining. It is a pity that one or two of the inhabitants of Mokotów do not have a chance to see how people stand all night to fill a bucket of water, or how they vainly try to find something to eat, but even so the morale of the average inhabitant was much better and the will to resist the effects of the fight much greater.[10]

Dobraczyński has likewise written of the lack of enthusiasm and ingenuity in Mokotów, how in the large open spaces of Mokotów, in the well-to-do houses and in their gardens, people were living who up till then had lost nothing and hoped to survive the Uprising without endangering themselves. They thought their best defence would be to stay quietly at home. There was no enthusiasm about the fighting and when the final German attack on Mokotów began the AK Commander was met with violent demands for capitulation, and the populace put out white flags.[11]

Amongst reports held in the archives of the Polish Underground Study Trust there is an anonymous one which is in very much the same style as the above quotations. It is the opinion of the present author, based also on other references in the report, that the author was Jan Dobraczyński. In this report dating from 1945 it is written:

The social problems in Mokotów were not straightforward ... There was an underlying conflict between the population of Górny Mokotów [Upper Mokotów], the more prosperous intelligentsia, and the working class of Dolny Mokotów [Lower Mokotów], who were forced by the fight in Powiśle to move to Górny Mokotów. Antagonism grew daily, and was added to by forced work – the digging of potatoes, which the Army forced anyone capable of working to do. As some people managed to 'get off work' and other were released from it, there were conflicts, arguments, and even complaints to the authorities. The people of Górny Mokotów were on the whole critical of the AK – they continually talked about the unnecessary staging of the Uprising. One felt that these people, who were the owners of small detached villas, feared the destruction of their property. On the other hand the population of Dolny Mokotów, whose homes had already been destroyed, stole and used property still intact, whilst threatening Bolshevik aggression and creating a feeling that the Bolsheviks were coming to settle up with the bourgeoisie. They were either showing their true Communist faces or – and more often – displaying one of two attitudes: a form of self-defence or a cover up for their appetite to steal and loot.[12]

Another witness involved in the publishing of underground newspapers during the occupation has written:

Unfortunately the civilian population of Mokotów was left entirely on its own without any kind of adequate ideological propaganda direction on the part of the responsible military authorities, who reserved for themselves the exclusive right in this sphere. This caused a disorientation in the minds of the people, who painfully felt the lack of idealistic-social impulse and succumbed to rumour and panic, and were partly indisposed towards the young insurgents ...[13]

But it must be remembered that in the open spaces of Mokotów propaganda work was not easy.[14]

The appearance of Allied aircraft over Warsaw on 18 September was greeted with the same tremendous enthusiasm as in the rest of Warsaw.[15] People ran out of their homes to watch the planes and gained from this display of Allied power all kinds of optimistic ideas.[16] But outside help was treated sceptically and without any faith once the first week of the fighting had passed.[17] The newspapers were read less and less.[18] Groups of people could be found who were ill disposed towards both the Uprising and AK.[19] However, one of the few reports coming out of the district claimed that the morale of the civilian population was good and the attitude to the Army 'good natured, but there was depression and complaining'.[20]

It is not easy to say why such a reaction was to be found in Mokotów. As we have seen, Mokotów was a garden suburb of Warsaw containing a large number of villas owned by the more prosperous inhabitants of the city. The owners of these houses did not make up the majority of the population, although their proportion was high relative to the rest of the district. Nor is there any real proof of a great divergence in attitude and behaviour between the various classes during the Uprising. The wealthier members of the community tended to suffer as it was more difficult for them to adapt their life style to insurgent conditions. An important factor may have been the layout of the district with its scattered and detached houses. This hampered propaganda and organisational work, and created a greater feeling of isolation among the inhabitants. There was no real 'block psychology' nor group psychology to sustain them as in other parts of Warsaw, and the bombing of the small houses gave rise to panic. The feeling of isolation was aggravated by the severance of Mokotów from the rest of the town. The proximity of the Germans and the knowledge of their terrible crimes must also have created greater fear and depression than in the rest of Warsaw. It is probably true to say that nowhere else in the city was the closeness and threat of the Germans felt so strongly for such a long period of time.[21]

The degree of organisation in the district would have had its effect on morale. It will be seen that the administration of Mokotów was not efficient and it was for some time under the control of the Army. Likewise, because of geographical problems there was very little propaganda work or morale boosting activity conducted by the authorities there.

One of the best diaries written during the Uprising was that of an anonymous woman who probably lived on the corner of ul. Olkuska and Puławska. She wrote in detail about various problems. It is not known what type of person she was but from her writing it can be supposed that she was not very old, perhaps twenty to thirty years of age. She does not appear to have been very enthusiastic about the Uprising. The following extracts illustrate not only the situation in Mokotów but life for the civilian population in Warsaw in general.

5 August ... Still no news of the Bolsheviks. No bread ...

8 August ... Water only on the first floors and in the cellar. No electricity since yesterday ... In the shelter people are burning paraffin lamps so as not to sit in darkness. But supplies are running low fast ... and that awful lamp pollutes the air. Furthermore there is nothing to cook on. Twenty-three people cannot cook on the small stove in the cellar ... not everyone has coal and hardly anyone has any wood.

9 August ... Yesterday we had our first air attack ... Everyone was praying in the cellar and clutching their beads. Some make reproaches at the Uprising ...

18 August. Today we went out to find some bread. A bakery on ul. Olkuska is issuing it on ration cards ... A few of us left together when it was still dark. At four in the morning having crossed through streets and gardens wet with the morning dew we arrive there. Dawn breaks. There is an enormous queue and it is quite clear that only half those waiting will get bread. Precedence is given to those people like us who were there for the second day and who the previous morning received a number in the queue. But even so we have to stand until seven o'clock before we are let inside. Whilst waiting various planes circle above creating fear that they might drop a bomb on our group; only one person leaves the queue, however, as the need for bread is so great, and [whilst waiting] people talk about their experiences. Someone got burnt, someone else ran out of a collapsing house ... When the door to the bakery was opened everyone squabbled and struggled so much that literally ribs were broken. The lack of discipline and feeling of injustice is terrible here.

20 August. Life is beginning to get organised. Houses have been grouped into blocks and bread is distributed through the block system, the OPL Commanders collecting bread for each house, 200 grammes per person. It is a great improvement ... and we have bread regularly. Men capable of working are listed. Every authorised house receives a communiqué every day.

24 August ... One of the most terrible things is to experience ... the frightful nervous strain amongst people of such different mental and cultural backgrounds as there are in this shelter. There are those who never believe in what Poles write or do, there are those who have the mentality of a kicked-about dog and believe that they would be able to survive and have their daily potato soup if the Germans had not disturbed them, and there are others, being good Poles, who foresee the most terrible events which might happen in this awful situation. But what about all the continuous political discussions and conversations! The more unqualified someone appears to be to talk on the subject, the more precisely he knows that the Uprising broke out too

early, that the Soviets have such and such intentions and the Allies such and such strengths ...

25 August. Everyone in the house thinks that the Bolsheviks will not bring freedom, but at least salvation. If the Germans are to win it means extermination ...

26 August. Everyone doubts that the insurgents on their own can expel the Germans ... Without the Bolsheviks we cannot get rid of the Germans, unless they themselves lay down their arms. As far as I know the second alternative cannot be counted upon in the short run and therefore the first remains sad but unavoidable. People are saying more and more openly that the Uprising was made without the agreement of the English or the Bolsheviks, and that only the latter can help us ... This state of affairs has been going on for three weeks now and people are inhumanly tired. When one looks at the figures in the shelter as the sun rises in the morning – yellow faces, red eyes, pale lips, uncared for hair, creased up clothes – one feels sympathy and fear. And yet everyone holds on, despite the shortage of food, the continual danger, the sleepless night, the smells, the bugs in the shelter ... There is a general lack of discipline and knowledge about communal living, e.g. our shelter, everyone leaves stools, chairs and even folding beds in the corridor and entrance. Curtains, they should not be hanging in the windows as they fan fire, and yet not all the inhabitants have taken theirs down, and no one induces them to do so. Four weeks ago every soldier was greeted as a hero, who due to the fact that he was shedding his blood was beyond criticism. Now they call him nothing else but a *gwardia*, because they have come across one or two who were not up to standard.

2 September. We take it in turns to wash in the kitchen, first the women and then the men ... Even worse is living in such cramped conditions, people are irritated and argue. They are very base people, really in these conditions it is social torment. Our janitor does not know how to answer a simple question other than brutally ... Semi-intellectual conversations are held and it is not safe to start a conversation, because it can lead to an angry frenzy.

6 September ... people are not allowed to go out as such movements attract aircraft fire – amongst us there are several people who walk out into the courtyard saying it is not their duty to conform with the will of the majority, even if the majority are exposed to danger.

10 September ... Morale raised due to the proximity of the Bolsheviks.

12 September. What is the day like for us? We get up at 5.00 a.m. before sunrise to cook breakfast (black ersatz coffee and potatoes without any fats), and lunch (soup, potatoes and tomatoes). The soup is wrapped up in paper, blankets, pillows to keep it a little warm until the afternoon. If there is water we wash a little. After that the bedclothes are shaken and the shelter swept. Afterwards nothing. If someone has a light they read, others talk, doze, walk out to see what is going on outside. There is no end of quarrels about pouring water, closing the closet door, about saucepans and about space in the kitchen ... About 12.00 people start feeling hungry for the soup. Before 6.00 p.m. the communiqué arrives, which is read out, and ten out of ten times

leads to discussion. 'Supper' consist of groats (with fats) or potatoes, but it is eaten late because only at dusk can we light the fires ...

20 September ... Everyone cooks for themselves and their families, which leads to problems in the kitchen.[22]

The organisation of the civilian population seems to have taken longer in Mokotów than in other parts of Warsaw. Up until 27 August it was in the hands of the Army. Major Zenon Beyer, 'Zenon', issued various instructions concerning curfew hours, anti-air and fire defence, and the sanitary situation.[23] A system of House and Block Committees was established.[24] Instructions were issued to the Block Commanders in Mokotów which form an interesting comparison to those in other parts of insurgent Warsaw. They were as follows:[25]

1. To organise observation posts, an observation and intelligence service, and to forward the results.
2. To prepare the block for defence and build necessary fortifications; barricade entrances and doorways; use all available wire netting and barbed wire.
3. To organise and carry out OPL services.
4. To collect all kinds of arms.
5. To observe and strengthen morale and fight defeatism.
6. To keep control over all inhabitants permanent and temporary.
7. To secure the possessions and homes of foreign and absent inhabitants.
8. To allot quarters to the Army.
9. To maintain hygienic and sanitary conditions.
10. To arrange the rational use of products from surrounding allotments and fields. To combat profiteering. To report hidden food stores.

The PKB in Mokotów not only fulfilled its police role, but it was also responsible for the feeding and accommodation of the civilian population.[26]

A great deal was left to individual initiative. Antoni Boliński and two other PPS colleagues organised a Komitet Opieki nad Uchodźcami (Committee for the Care of Refugees).[27] Its main centre was at ul. Pilicka 24 with other smaller ones at ul. Puławska 140, Lenartowicza 4 and Racławicka 10. The committee provided food and medical help and distributed clothes. Food was supplied to it by the community and collected from stores, shops and deserted private flats.[28] Also a *Społem* (co-operative) directed by Józef Jasiński was created, whose soup kitchen provided meals.[29] The OPL system functioned, carrying out its stipulated tasks as in the rest of Warsaw.[30]

Otherwise individuals organised themselves and their houses without external instructions.[31]

On 27 August a Komisarz dla Spraw Ludości Cywilnej (Commissary for Civilian Affairs) was set up with Antoni Hanebach, 'Antoni Gruby', at its head. The Commissary was divided ito five departments:[32]

1. General Department – concerned with internal and legal affairs and matters concerning the supervision of state and deserted properties.
2. Department of Security – all general affairs of administration and security, PKB, population mobility, matters of law, administration and military association.
3. Department of Feeding – compiling of lists and making collections of food, requisition of articles of greatest need, distribution of food, supervision over the food industry and price control.
4. Department of Social Care – concerned with refugees, help for the very poor, child care, orphans, supervision of care institutions.
5. Department of Health.

The food supply in Mokotów was one of the best in insurgent Warsaw. The diet was less monotonous than elsewhere, with the exception of Żoliborz, and fresh fruit and vegetables were available. The gardens and fields in Mokotów provided potatoes, cabbage, tomatoes and even grapes.[33] Often, however, these vegetables had to be dug up under fire sometimes resulting in loss of life.[34] In the previously quoted anonymous diary the authoress complains of lack of food, but in comparison to what was being suffered in the Old Town and Śródmieście it was not at all bad. Bread was received, although not always regularly, until the second half of September.[35] By then the food situation had seriously deteriorated,[36] because of the exhaustion of supplies and the fall of Sielce.[37] Hunger began to be felt.[38]

The Commissary on 27 August set a norm as to how much food was necessary for one person:

Starch items (flour, macaroni, kasza)	5 kg
Legumes	1 kg
Sugar	2 kg
Fats	1 kg
Salt	1 kg
Tinned meat or fish	2 kg
Condensed milk	1 kg
Fruit and honey preserves	2 kg

Potatoes	10 kg
Vegetables	8 kg
Coal	20 kg
Wood	10 kg
Candles	5 kg
Cigarettes (for adults)	300 or 200 grammes of tobacco
Matches	5 boxes
Spirits and vodka	1 litre

It was not stipulated how long these supplies were supposed to last, but anyone holding stores in excess of these amounts had to report them to the Commissary by 3 September.[39] It is not recorded whether this policy was effective. As in the rest of Warsaw food was distributed from central stores.[40]

The Chief Medical Officer of Mokotów, Dr Klemens Gerner, was cut off by the outbreak of the Uprising in ul. Chocimska and was unable to assume his duties. In his place Dr Edward Loth, 'Gozdawa', was appointed.[41] It was his task to organise improvised field hospitals, as the facilities in the Hospital of the Sisters of the Order of St Elisabeth on ul. Goszczyńskiego were far from sufficient and no large hospital had been prepared for the Uprising.[42] Dr Loth appointed Dr Stanisław Radwan to help him. A hospital was organised on ul. Lenartowicza with fifty beds.[43] Further hospitals were set up on ul. Racławicka in the convent of the St Elisabeth Sisters and another on ul. Puławska 91.[44] A hospital was also opened for civilians on ul. Tyniecka.[45] A dispensary was run by the Komitet Opieki nad Uchodźcami.[46] The hospitals were mainly supplied with gifts from the community and by chemist shops in the area, and the 'Alba' factory provided bandages and cotton wool.[47]

The following is only a fragment of what conditions were like in one of the hospitals, a wing of the Hospital of the Sisters of the Order of St Elisabeth:

civilians suffering from burns started to be carried in more and more. We looked with horror at the stretchers on which lay half burnt human forms, small children with black faces, festering and swollen. We discovered that the Germans had taken a street somewhere, driven the inhabitants into a mined shelter or shut them into the cellars, where they threw grenades. Some of these poor unfortunate people lay for several days, alone, wounded in the rubble, before they were found by a medical patrol and carried under fire to the hospital.

Soon we started to run out of beds. We laid the injured down, side by side, on straw mattresses, in one room and then a second and before long in the hall and corridor. Needless to say there was a shortage of blankets and bed linen. We tried to cover the straw mattresses at least with a sheet, but the scalds festered so badly, that the sheets were saturated within hours and there was no possibility of changing them. Some of the patients were unconscious and in no time insects were everywhere in these overcrowded conditions. We could only gaze at it hopelessly, as trying to bring any order was an unattainable dream.

August was hot and sweltering. On the one hand this was a relief as we had nothing to cover the patients with, they usually lay under their own coats, but on the other hand as a result the air in the ward was foul and we were afraid of an epidemic.[48]

The problems with water and electricity were the same as in the rest of Warsaw. In the anonymous diary the authoress notes on 8 August that there is electricity and water only on the first floor and in the cellars.[49] Thereafter the supply of water became more erratic and unreliable. Wells were to be found in Mokotów in the following places: ul. Olkuska 11, Racławicka 14, Misyjna 6, Wiktorska 2, 63, and 73, in the 'Makarewicza' Factory, ul. Rózana 9, al. Niepodległości 36, Wielicka 27, Ksawerów 20, Krasickiego 6 a., and 29, in the St Elisabeth Hospital, ul. Puławska 107 and 113, Lenartowicza 4, on the corner of ul. Goszczyńskiego and Pilicka, ul. Wejnerta 32, 26, and 19, and on the corner of Naruszewicza.[50] It was the responsibility of the Block Commander to see that the wells were maintained in good and clean condition as well as seeing that the hours for drawing water were observed. Military units, hospitals and kitchens drew their supplies of water between 7.00 p.m. and 5.00 a.m., and between 2.00 and 3.00 p.m.; civilians between 5.00 and 8.00 a.m., 12.00 a.m. and 2.00 p.m., and 4.00 and 7.00 p.m.[51]

A field post operated in Mokotów until about 18 September.[52] Letters were sent through the sewers to Śródmieście and as elsewhere boy scouts were used for delivering them. However, in Mokotów, according to Tadeusz Gryżewski's finding, the field post sending letters to the town centre was organised by the AK and not by the scouts.[53] One of the scoutmasters in the area has also written that the postal service was started by two men unconnected with the scout movement.[54]

A Special Military Court was in operation throughout the Uprising in the district, but no similar civilian court seems to have been established.[55]

During the Uprising in Mokotów there were several insurgent newspapers in circulation at various stages. The main one was

Komunikat Informacyjny published by BIP. The Leftist PPS group started to publish a paper from the middle of September called *Robotnik Mokotowski* and at the same time PAL started putting out a paper, *Kurier Mokotowski*. There were two small papers published by AK units, *Baszta* and *Granat*, as well as a paper for children, *Dzieci Mokotowa*.[56] Some papers were also brought through from Śródmieście.[57] Liaison girls returning to the town centre from Mokotów in the middle of August describe the area as being without either civilian authorities or any political life. They described the four papers in circulation as not having a very high standard and said that the copies of the papers they took with them created a 'great sensation'.[58]

By the middle of September Mokotów was suffering from all the maladies of the Uprising – destruction, lack of food and water, disease, worsening hygienic conditions, and an ever increasing and uncontrollable flow of sick and injured going to the hospitals and dressing points. Some inhabitants had started to escape by night and were led across the German lines by 'professional guides' who charged 500 zł. per person.[59] The population was fearful of its fate, expecting the same outcome in their district as in the others.[60]

The German attack on Upper Mokotów began on 24 September.[61] On 25 September two Polish prisoners of war were sent by the Germans to the AK Commander of the area, Colonel Józef Rokicki, 'Karol'. They came to put forward General von dem Bach's proposition for an evacuation of the entire civilian population from Mokotów, as the Germans had started their attack on the district, intending to destroy it. The two Poles also had tried to arrange a meeting between General von dem Bach and General 'Bór' on neutral ground. The former was convinced that 'in the future Poland and the German Army would fight together against Bolsheviks'.[62] Colonel 'Karol', when passing this information on to General 'Monter', wrote in his report that he intended to fight to the last man.[63]

On 26 September at 6.00 a.m. General 'Karol' sent the following report to the AK Command in Śródmieście through London: 'Morale in the Army creating panic, a tendency to put out white flags, one of the commanders has not carried out his orders. I intend to evacuate gradually through the sewers.'[64] The remaining area of Mokotów was under incessant fire, being bombed and attacked by tanks and Goliaths. Later on in the day civilians started to put out white flags in many of the houses. Colonel 'Karol' ordered all the flags to be taken down by AK gendarmes.[65] This did not prevent further ones being put out later and in places mob law broke out.[66]

At 12.30 a.m. Colonel 'Karol' reported that he intended to evacuate his units.[67] He had previously received permission from General 'Monter' to evacuate the lightly wounded and any civilians wanting to leave, but 'Monter' adamantly forbade the evacuation of the units. 'Karol' received this information when he was already moving through the sewers.[68]

At 4.00 p.m. a two hour cease fire was arranged by General von dem Bach, and according to German figures 9,000 civilians left[69] but a 'considerable number' still stayed behind.[70] In the evening the evacuation through the sewers began. Among the evacuees were members of the civilian administration of the area.[71] Around the manholes crowds gathered and in the chaos civilians managed to slip down, although they had no knowledge of the layout of the sewers. Others had managed to forge passes.[72]

On the following day Major Kazimierz Szternal, 'Zryw', who had been left in command by Colonel 'Karol', seeing no sense in fighting on sent representatives over to the German side to discuss conditions for a capitulation. At 11.00 a.m. the battle came to an end and the insurgents' status as combatants was recognised.[73]

According to German figures 5,000 civilians left the district after the capitulation. They were collected together with the lightly injured in the stands of the race course and thence sent to Pruszków.[74]

3.9 Żoliborz

There is even less material available on Żoliborz than on Mokotów, but what exists is very much of the same kind. Few original documents remain and any analysis of the Uprising can only be based on memoirs, reports, published and press sources.

The district of Żoliborz formed the military District II, which included not only the district of Żoliborz, but also the smaller ones of Marymont and Bielany.[1] The Uprising in Żoliborz broke out earlier than in the rest of Warsaw on 1 August due to a clash between German and Polish troops near pl. Wilsona. At the end of the day the AK Area Commander, Lieutenant Colonel Mieczysław Niedzielski, 'Żywiciel', ordered his units either to disperse or march to the Kampinos Forest, as they had failed to capture their objectives, stores of arms and ammunition were insufficient and the fighting had cut Żoliborz off from the rest of Warsaw.[2] Not many of the civilians knew about the exit of these units, but amongst those who did there was consternation at the thought of being left to the wrath of the Germans. It was taken by some to mean the breakdown or end of the Uprising.[3]

The Germans also retreated on the night of 1 August fearing an insurgent attack, and therefore Żoliborz was deserted both by the Polish units (except for one small unit of Captain Adam Rzeszotarski, 'Żmija') and the Germans. 'Żywiciel' was ordered by 'Monter' to return immediately to Żoliborz, which he did but not without fighting and further losses. On the night of 3 August these returning units linked up with that of 'Żmija' in pl. Wilsona. By the following day they had brought under their control pl. Inwalidów and the area on either side of ul. Mickiewicza.[4]

Żoliborz will be taken here to mean the area which remained in insurgent hands throughout virtually the whole Uprising. The area was bordered in the north by ul. Potocka and in the east by ul. Gwiaździsta, across ul. Krasińskiego to ul. Kaniowska. From there the southern limit ran below pl. Inwalidów along ul. Wojska Polskiego to ul. Stołeczna, which formed the western boundary.

Life for the inhabitants of these streets returned to 'normal' quite quickly after the outbreak of the Uprising and remained so. There was no great fighting until the middle of September and snipers alone posed a constant threat. Although the area was cut off from the rest of Warsaw it was not closed in, as the Kampinos Forest and the surrounding countryside could be reached without too much difficulty.[5] In comparison to the rest of the capital there were no German points of resistance within these streets and the insurgents controlled the whole area.[6] Cut off from the rest of Warsaw the inhabitants of Żoliborz developed a specific life style of their own for nearly two months.[7]

The initial reaction of the civilian population to the battle was very much the same in Żoliborz as in the rest of Warsaw. The Uprising was greeted with enthusiasm and there was faith in victory. Relations between the Army and civilians were good.[8] But these feelings soon disappeared and misunderstandings arose.[9] Refugees coming in from Wola with their horrific reports were accused of being *agents provocateurs*.[10] However, by the beginning of September one of the soldiers from Żoliborz wrote that people there had had enough of the Uprising and were badly disposed towards the Army, and had to be threatened at gun-point to be made to work.[11]

Although people coming out of the sewers from the Old Town found life in Żoliborz 'normal',[12] one witness found it very different to that which had prevailed in the Old Town. The people there did not show as much enthusiasm and the patriotic spirit was mixed with selfishness and reluctance to assist the insurgents.[13] But generally the morale of the inhabitants of the area seems to have remained fairly good. This may have been due to the efficient and good organisation of the district.

Żoliborz was known as the Republika Żoliborska (Republic of Żoliborz) due to its isolation and independent organisation.[14] There are no figures of the number of people living or caught in the area, except in the middle of September 1944 the Starost quoted a figure of about 6,000 families.[15] The Starost of the area, known as Ekspozytura Starostwa Warszawa Północ (Branch Starost of Northern Warsaw), was Robert Froelich, 'Góral', who represented the government authorities.[16] He was later joined by one of the Government Delegates from the Old Town, Stefan Zbrożyna.[17] As a result of KRN initiative a council called the Samorząd Ludności Dzielnicy Żoliborza (*Samorząd* for the people of the District of Żoliborz) was established. It worked in co-operation with the Government Delegacy. In order to facilitate organisation and administration the district was divided up into six settlements.[18]

Each settlement, all of them together containing between 6,000 and 12,000 people, further subdivided into colonies representing 500–2,000 inhabitants. The inhabitants of the colony had to choose an *opiekun klatkowy* or *opiekun sąsiedzki* (staircase guardian), whose task it was to be aware of his neighbour's needs and the material situation of those in need of help, to prepare temporary shelter for anyone who might lose their home, etc. These guardians in turn elected a *Samorząd* for the colony containing three members, a Director, his Deputy, and the Secretary, one of whom was responsible for order in the colony, one for providing food, and one for health and child care.[19] The Directors of the *Samorząd* for the colony formed the *Samorząd* for the inhabitants of the settlement, which elected its presidium of three members, Chairman, Deputy and Secretary. There were also two other delegates, one responsible for food and the other for health and child care, who were elected by their counterparts in the colony *Samorząd*.[20] The Chairman of the settlement *Samorząd* formed the Presidium of the District. Stanisław Tołwiński was Chairman and Feliks Zelcer Secretary.[21] They worked in co-operation with the AK Area Commander, with a conference being held every day at which all matters were discussed.[22]

It is difficult to judge how widespread this action was and whether the district organisation was actually carried out along these lines. According to a local paper, by 16 August *Samorząd* had been set up in all the WSM settlements.[23] It is important to note, however, that the *Samorząd* was established on the initiative of the Polish Communists. The Government Delegate and the *Samorząd* were two totally independent institutions,[24] although the Secretary of the Presidium has written that: 'the Starost only existed nominally, because it did not undertake any lively activity. We did not have any contact with them ...'[25] Stanisław Tołwiński has written that due to the fact that the Ekspozytura members knew that the PPR and RPPS (Leftist PPS) would protect them when the Russians arrived the Government Delegacy was both cautious and increasingly amenable to both groups. However, Tołwiński has also written that 'we organised our own authorities in opposition to those of London in agreement and after consultation with our colleagues in the KRN with a view to later taking over the whole direction of the Warsaw *Samorząd*.'[26]

In order to maintain law and order in Żoliborz a security organisation was formed by the government authorities with three organs:[27]
1. Obywatelska Straż Bezpieczeństwa (Citizens Security Service).
2. Milicja PPS (PPS Police) functioning in the WSM.
3. PKB functioning in Lower Żoliborz.
Two special courts were established: Wojskowy Sąd Specjalny (Special Military Court) and Cywilny Sąd Specjalny (Special Civilian Court).[28] They were concerned with the controlling of mob law, lawlessness of insurgent gendarmes, security organisation, the security of the population, espionage, the examination of Gestapo agents, *Volksdeutsch*, collaborators, snipers and criminals.[29] There was also a Komisja Sądząca (Judicial Commission) dealing with small matters and petty crimes, e.g. looting or shirking from work, and handing out appropriate punishments. These courts and commissions were all established according to the Government Decree of 1942.[30]

The food supply in Żoliborz was not as plentiful as would be expected. This was mainly because the numerous allotments in the district were usually under fire. Żoliborz possessed no stores of food although food was smuggled in from German held territory.[31] There was a shortage of vegetables and potatoes,[32] as garden vegetables were soon used up.[33] There seem to have been some quantities of beef, horsemeat, oil and bread.[34] During the first weeks of the Uprising a kilo of bread per person was distributed daily, but this had later to suffice for two people and by the end there was only black-bread, a kilo of which was shared by four people.[35] Food was later distributed from Soviet drops[36] when they started, consisting mainly of dry biscuits, pork fat, tinned food, fats, and tobacco.[37] By the second half of September the food and water supply was causing serious concern, and there was a shortage of bread.[38]

Canteens were opened in cellars for the civilian population by the *Samorząd* and soup kitchens were organised.[39] Refugees and the homeless were fed in these kitchens, for it was amongst them that the greatest lack of food and water was felt.[40] Collections of food and clothing were arranged for them as for the Army and the amounts collected were large.[41]

Żoliborz had no permanent hospital and the four field hospitals which the Germans had were evacuated before the Uprising.[42] From the beginning, therefore, there was a problem of organising a health and hospital service; help had to be arranged and facilities improvised. The nuns of the Order of the Resurrection in their convent on ul. Krasińskiego had started to organise a hospital but it was not complete when the Uprising broke out. Flats were opened to the injured and beds, linen, fruit, cigarettes and sweets were donated to them.[43] Patients with minor wounds and illnesses were nursed privately.[44] But there was a shortage of doctors, nurses and operating facilities.[45] Sanitary and medical conditions were inadequate. Dr Ludwik Zaturski organised a hospital, primarily for civilians, in a house on the corner of ul. Śmiała and ul. Mierosławskiego.[46] There was a small hospital on the corner of ul. Dziennikarska and Dygasińskiego.[47] A military hospital was organised in the building on ul. Czarnieckiego by Dr Szulc.[48] There was a dressing point at ul. Gdańska 2 with four beds mainly for civilians. At the end of August Dr Szulc set up a hospital in the Sokolnicki Forts where many civilians were sheltering. At the end of September a crowd of people from the forts tried to plunder the small food stores there, but they did not succeed.[49] By early September there was a cholera epidemic and both soldiers and civilians were suffering from scurvy.[50] The number of cases has not been recorded. General medical consultation was organised by a team of doctors.[51]

Communication with the rest of Warsaw was by radio and telephone, and later through the sewers.[52] Newspapers from Śródmieście were brought through – *Biuletyn Informacyjny, Wiadomości Radiowe, Rzeczpospolita, Syndykalista, Żywią i Bronią.*[53] Local papers were also published with news and information collected and monitored from the radio.[54] Four main papers were published: *AK Dziennik Radiowy*

XXII, Biuletyn Podokręgu No. 2 AL, Biuletyn Okręgu IV PPS i OW PPS Warszawa Północ and *Nowiny Żoliborskie*. Also a paper for children was published, *Jawnutka*.[55] A library was opened by the youth branch of the PPS in Żoliborz for the Army and civilians.[56] Radios were used again and public ones were set up in front of which people collected to hear the news.[57]

The proximity of the Soviet Army on the other side of the river was strongly felt in Żoliborz. It was possible to observe the fighting and the retreat of the Germans from the rooftops. As a result the feeling of expectation of a quick liberation by the Soviets was strong.[58] This hope grew stronger when the first drops of food and ammunition were received.[59] On 18 September a German appeared in the area with a letter from General von dem Bach addressed to the Commander of the Żoliborz units proposing a truce and the evacuation of the civilian population 'in the name of humanity'. Colonel Żywiciel did not receive the German representatives but sent a reply quoting examples of the type of inhumane behaviour that the Germans had already displayed and suggesting a German capitulation.[60]

On 24 September in the *Biuletyn Okręgu IV PPS i OW PPS Warszawa Północ* an article was published describing conditions in Żoliborz:

In pl. Wilsona we are greeted by the sight of stumps of burnt apartment blocks of the First Colony of the WSM. We turn into ul. Dziennikarska and in front of us lie rubble and ruins . . . in the area nearest to the Vistula. The inhabitants are living mainly in the cellars.

The people whom we spoke to told us that the lack of water is the most painful problem and food availability was not the best. There is no danger at present with the sanitary situation. Apart from the water problem there is also that of the plague of stealing and thieving. The number of inhabitants of the area is only a fraction of the usual and grows smaller every day as people move up to the higher areas.

The greatest destruction is in the area starting at ul. Tucholska and ul. Dygasińskiego up to ul. Bohomolca. There is not one house here that could be slept in. However, we only caught sight of the existence of hell in Żeromski Park and the forts. Collections of the most diverse social groups are living there in desperate conditions. Hunger is written all over their miserable grey faces. Many people have had nothing in their mouths apart from water for several days. The lamentable state of children cries out for help.

In these smelly damp holes about 25,000 people are living in the open air. The lack of water and medical care spreads illness and death . . .[61]

Another witness has also described Żeromski Park during the Uprising:

It looked like a large gypsy camp. Due to the fact that the barracks for the unemployed next to Dworzec Gdański [Gdański Station – a main railway station] were burnt to the ground in the first days of the Uprising, all of its inmates descended in panic on Żeromski Park and Fort Sokolnicki, in whose old tsarist walls and dungeons they found safe and ample shelter. However, in the early morning they all emptied out into the park and camped. The weather in August was good and warm, and at the beginning there was no artillery fire or air attacks. The *Barakowcy* set themselves up in the open air ... with their plentiful supplies of food. On stoves built of bricks they cooked tasty smelling soups and potato pancakes, and muffins sizzled away. When the time of hunger started, these people always had something to cook. At the risk of their lives they went into the allotments around Żoliborz gathering potatoes, vegetables, and tomatoes ...[62]

The same witness also relates how these people were especially representative of the criminal elements of society and did not want to cooperate or work.

By this time, as in the rest of Warsaw, the people of Żoliborz had lost hope and many were seized by anger for and enmity of the Uprising.[63] On 28 September the Germans sent a delegation of Poles from Mokotów, a professor from the Polytechnic and two nuns, with a note proposing capitulation, but Colonel Żywiciel turned it down with the unanimous support of his commanders.[64]

On 29 September the final all-out German attack on Żoliborz began.[65] The following day the district capitulated.[66] Colonel Wachnowski was appointed by General Bór on 29 September in connection with the negotiations concerning the evacuation of the civilian population from Warsaw, to arrange for the exit of the civilians from Żoliborz, and to take the decision as to whether to continue the fight there or not. When Colonel Wachnowski met General von dem Bach on the morning of 30 September, the General informed him that there was no longer a problem of the evacuation of the civilians from that part of the town as most of the district was already in German hands and the civilians were being evacuated immediately. The capitulation of the district was arranged, and Wachnowski later crossed into the area to consult Colonel Żywiciel, who agreed to the capitulation, seeing no other way out.[67]

The capitulation received a varied reaction. One woman remembers it as a terrible experience. Even though for the preceding two months they had lived under the most awful conditions they had lived amongst their own and had seen no Germans. They had believed that somehow they would survive the worst without abandoning their posts.[68] One of the priests in the district remembers how the young were always full of enthusiasm but the older people varied in their behaviour. Some sat in their cellars throughout the whole Uprising full of fear and blunt resignation. Only when they knew the fight was over did they come out fearfully and timidly, waving white flags, creating committees, organising boards and negotiating with the Germans.[69]

3.10 The capitulation of Warsaw

By 1 October both Mokotów and Żoliborz had fallen. Śródmieście with its two isolated centres of fighting was left as the last redoubt of the Uprising. The remains of insurgent Warsaw were surrounded on all sides by the enemy. Cellars and passages of the remaining houses were full of civilians who had escaped from other districts. They were threatened with starvation, and were without light and water.[1] The previous day rumours had been circulating that Warsaw was finally going to surrender, but they were often met with accusations of defeatism and panic-spreading.[2] However, on 1 October, General 'Bór' decided to discuss capitulation with the German commander, General von dem Bach.[3] On the same day, he sent the following message to London: 'Warsaw no longer has any hope of defence. I have decided to start negotiations . . .'[4] Before this, however, talks sounding out the German attitude to the battle had been going on between the Poles and the Germans, along with the arrangements between the two sides for the evacuation of the civilian population.

On 27 September, the Germans had made contact with the Poles, proposing talks with them, but not on the question of capitulation. General 'Bór' delegated Lieutenant Colonel Zygmunt Dobrowolski, 'Zyndram', with an interpreter to go and hear General von dem Bach's proposals.[5] The meeting took place during the morning of 28 September. General von dem Bach explained that further resistance on the part of the insurgents was pointless, and therefore he was giving General 'Bór' two choices. The crux of the matter was whether the Polish Commander wanted to continue to fight or not. If he wanted to pursue the battle, General von dem Bach wanted it to be as humane as possible. If General 'Bór' decided to halt the fighting he proposed:[6]

1. The recognition of combatant status for all Polish soldiers in accordance with the Geneva Convention.
2. Granting officers the right to keep personal arms.

3. To enforce these regulations under the control of the International Red Cross.

4. The evacuation of the civilian population from Warsaw, which, being the forward defence line, could not contain civilian persons. These people would be treated in the same way as previous evacuated persons. They could take with them what they wanted. After the evacuation the authorities would wherever possible remove by carts cultural and church possessions beyond the area of battle, and where possible private possessions.

If General 'Bór' decided to continue the fighting, General von dem Bach declared that:[7]

1. Regardless of this he wanted to evacuate the entire civilian population.

2. The fighting would be carried out with every available means until the town and the Army were totally destroyed.

After the return of Colonel Dobrowolski, General 'Bór' held a conference in the evening. The Vice-Premier and Government Delegate, Jankowski; the Second in Command to General 'Bór', General Pełczyński; the AK Chief of Staff, General Okulicki; the area Commander of Warsaw, General 'Monter'; Chief of the Operational Bureau, Colonel Szostak; Chief of Operations, Colonel Iranek-Osmecki, and the Head of BIP, Colonel Rzepecki, were all present. Colonel Dobrowolski reported on his talks with General von dem Bach.[8]

'Monter' spoke on the military situation, the morale of his troops and the food situation. He stressed that his troops' morale was still high, and that there was still a strong desire to fight to the last. He admitted that after the fall of Mokotów, Śródmieście would be weakened, but the defence there was good and better than in Żoliborz. He maintained that his units had enough arms and ammunition to fight for several days. The food supply on the other hand was critical and the district food stores had no more supplies to issue. He estimated that general hunger would start within three days. He was very adamant in his opinion of the projected evacuation of the civilian population, which would

have a negative influence on the psychology of the soldiers. The insurgent soldier is part of that very community, into which he has become integrated; he feels the throbbing of the life of the capital by observing its inhabitants and his contacts with them. The cold and dampness of the cellars and trenches full of people today would not have the same effect on the soldier if they were empty. Today the soldier knows that at the same time as fighting, he is defending the capital's people. We may anticipate that if Warsaw is to be emptied of its inhabitants these soldiers will feel alone and incapable of defending this heap of rubble which forms Warsaw today.[9]

Thus in 'Monter's' opinion any evacuation would have a negative effect on the fighting.[10] Jankowski, who had been a staunch opponent of any capitulation at the beginning of September, was of a totally different opinion.[11] To him any continuation of the fighting was quite senseless and 'pure madness'. He believed firmly that the fighting should be ended, and thereby the 'biological substance of the nation' saved. This was of additional importance because Warsaw was the home of the Polish cultural and scientific elite. If the Germans were going to crush the Uprising ruthlessly as von dem Bach had warned, he felt that at least the people should be saved. He believed the fighting should be quickly ended and that both London and the Soviets should be informed, and if the Polish Command in Warsaw procrastinated the Germans might impute bad will towards them and lay the blame on the people, as they had done already.[12]

Pełczyński agreed with 'Monter' that the spirit in the Army was good, but pointed out that the critical food situation should not be overexaggerated as the soldiers had various means of obtaining provisions. Whilst it was undoubtedly worse amongst the civilian population, especially the fire victims, there was no great alarm. He still believed that the Russians might attack. In spite of this he agreed with 'Monter' and Jankowski that there was a 'capitulation mood' in Warsaw. Whilst acting with caution so the Russians would not take advantage of the situation in their propaganda, he agreed that talks on the evacuation of the civilian population should be opened, and the occasion could also be used to test the Germans' attitude to concluding the fighting.[13]

Following Pełczyński, 'Monter' made two very valid observations. Firstly, the situation then differed markedly from that between 6 and 10 September, when advantageous results of Russian activity were expected, including the liberation of Warsaw. By the end of September it was known, however, that a quick liberation of Warsaw by the Soviets could not be counted on, and about this there could be no doubt. He agreed with Jankowski that 'biological extermination' must be avoided, and that after the fall of Mokotów and Żoliborz the full weight of the German attack would be centred on Śródmieście, entailing heavy losses amongst the civilians.[14] But 'the difficulty in doing so will be that the inhabitants of the city, for as long as the Army remains in the town, will not want to leave of their own free will'. This remark complemented his previous argument and he was to be proved right.

In conclusion 'Bór' agreed that negotiations should be started concerning the evacuation of the civilian population and at the same time the door to negotiations on the ending of the fight should be kept open. In order to gain a few days' time before making the final decision they would take advantage of the German proposals that the Poles could inspect the camp at Pruszków and the hospitals and meet prisoners from Mokotów. It would be made clear that any final decision was dependent on the Polish government in London, which would give them two to three days, and the question of the evacuation of the civilian population would be treated similarly.[15]

General von dem Bach agreed to these demands of the Poles on 29 September, which meant that a Polish delegation could be sent to inspect the camps and hospitals straight away and also that the evacuation could be organised.[16] On the same day General 'Bór' sent the following message to London:

1. We have established that the rations of food will suffice for only three days. We do not see any chance of the Russians taking Warsaw within that time, nor of their ensuring the city sufficient cover from bombing attacks or providing supplies of food, which would enable the town to last out until its liberation.
2. I have informed Marshal Rokossowski about the situation and asked him for help. However, if I do not immediately receive it in great quantity, I will be forced to surrender on the German guarantee of granting combatant status.
3. Due to the fact that after the fall of Mokotów the Germans took the initiative in talks on removing the civilian population from the town and the possibility of ending the fighting, which they consider to be senseless, I agreed to the talks. The evacuation of the civilian population is expected to take place from the morning of 1 October and will last, I should think, three days.
4. . . .
5. If the Red Army attacks within the next few days the evacuation will be stopped and I shall still engage in the fighting.[17]

Although the Polish Commission investigating conditions in Pruszków and the hospitals returned dissatisfied with what they had seen, they recommended that the evacuation be carried out in order to save the population from extinction.[18] General 'Bór' appointed a delegation to arrange and organise the evacuation. It was primarily made up of representatives of civilian organisations – Stanisław Podwiński, Vice-President of Warsaw, Countess Maria Tarnowska,

Vice-President of the Polish Red Cross, Dr Stanisław Wachowiak, Vice-President of the General Council of RGO, Col. 'Seweryn Janicki', Edward Lubowicki, the delegate of AK Command and Dr Hieronim Bartoszewski.[19]

The delegation arranged with the Germans that the evacuation would take place on 1 and 2 October, between 5.30 a.m. and 6.30 p.m. To facilitate it a ceasefire was arranged in the whole of Śródmieście between 5.00 a.m. and 7.00 p.m. The population was to leave in a westerly direction by the following streets: Grzybowska, Pańska, Sikorskiego, Piusa and Śniadeckich. Evacuees were permitted to take personal possessions and food with them, bearing in mind the difficulties on their journey which would be on foot. A later announcement was to be made concerning the evacuation of sick and injured. The regulations concerning the evacuation were preceded by the explanation that due to the difficult feeding, medical and tactical situation in Warsaw, the Polish authorities, in order to reduce losses amongst the civilian population, had accepted the German proposals to evacuate the civilian population. It was concluded by a rather mild report, veiling the true conditions in Pruszków and the hospitals.[20]

The announcement of the evacuation produced for the first time throughout the whole Uprising strong controversy in the press over the problems of the civilian population; the unison which the newspapers had always shown was broken.[21] The Communist press criticised the evacuation for breaking the bond that had always existed between the Army and the civilians and for the fact that the civilians were to be handed over to the enemy, in spite of the fact that the Uprising had been started to defend the lives of the capital's inhabitants.[22] However, the AK paper *Biuletyn Informacyjny* no longer saw civilian sacrifice as a 'necessary contribution to the fighting' after sixty-three days of incredible dedication.[23]

The evacuation came as a surprise to many people; they did not believe it was happening.[24] Furthermore they did not trust the Germans and were reluctant to leave. Debates started again as to whether to leave the city or not.[25]

On 1 October, a Sunday, Warsaw was silent; there were no shots to be heard. A sad and depressing atmosphere hung over the city.[26] People slowly moved around over the rubble, looking for friends or families. Many cried,[27] but the lull in the fighting brought relief to many, who were 'happy that the moment has come when they can look at the sun. Documents are being thrown away and burnt. People are packing. Everyone knows it is the end and if anyone talks of

Cease fire.

further defence it is only to maintain morale, but no one believes it.'[28] People were destroying documents and suddenly there seemed to be plenty of food.[29] Reserves were opened and all that could not be carried was eaten.[30] One woman walked out of the shelter to take a last look at Warsaw. Around her she saw women digging graves, somewhere she heard a lively waltz being played,[31] whilst on ul. Krucza perfume, soap, shoes and butter were being sold and bartered. People were walking around carrying onions.[32] Barter tended to disappear in the first days of October and shops were open, clothes and food were being sold, tomatoes, potatoes and cabbage brought in from Pole Mokotowskie were traded. Crowds of people were wandering around previously deserted streets.[33]

But news of the evacuation was received negatively. Few wanted to leave, preferring to share the fate of their Army,[34] and only about 8,000 people went, mainly women and children.[35] There was an outcry against the civilians leaving without the AK.[36] General von dem Bach himself complained that hardly anyone left on 1 October. He was told that such a reaction had been anticipated, because after two months of siege arm in arm with the soldiers, the population was not going to want to leave on their own and would wait to see what would happen to their defenders. Furthermore there were still quite a

The civilian population leaving Warsaw after the capitulation.

few people who had their homes and possessions intact and could not decide whether to leave them or not.[37] The fact that the population knew that they had two days in which to leave and therefore could put off their departure until 2 October does not diminish the solidarity that was displayed between the Army and the civilians.

On 1 October, General 'Bór', seeing no sense in continuing the fight, decided to negotiate with the Germans.[38] The capitulation agreement was signed on 2 October, and the evacuation of the Army and the remaining civilians began the following day. The AK was assured combatant rights, no collective responsibility was to be imposed on the civilian population, no reprisals were to be brought against anyone who had been part of the government or its administration, or social or charitable organisations during the Uprising, or who had been politically active before.[39] General 'Bór' sent telegrams informing both London and the Soviets of the ending of the fighting in Warsaw due to the complete lack of food and the overwhelming technical superiority of the enemy.[40]

On the second day of the ceasefire, by which time news about the capitulation negotiations had become known, the evacuation started properly, and by the afternoon of 2 October it had taken on a mass character and thousands had to be held back.[41] About 24,000 persons left.[42] 'The peace after the capitulation and the order to leave the city did not cheer anyone up. People collected their bags together, but no one wanted to leave ...'[43] Their energies and thoughts were directed to deciding what to take and how to save as much as possible.[44]

One survivor has written that people could not believe that it was really the end, and were prepared to stay even longer in Warsaw – anything not to fall into the hands of the Germans. They waited a bit longer hoping for some change which would save them from the sight of the Swastika.[45] An AK officer saw in the capitulation a reuniting action between the civilian population and the Army. Another witness, however, said the attitude of the civilians still varied: some gave the soldiers all they could and bade them a moving farewell, whilst others continued to blame the Army for the destruction.[46]

Maria Gieysztor has described her last moments in the city thus:

2 October: At 2.00 today I left home with Janusz. I was barely conscious of what I was doing: ...

... the expected capitulation of the Army, the wasted two months of effort of the Uprising, the sea of tears and blood, such great material loss and, in my own case, the abandonment of everything I possess has made me so apathetic as to be incapable of concentrating on what to pack and how; consequently I did many silly things, which I now reproach myself for. I left winter things behind: a woollen dress, warm underwear, nightgown, shawl, galoshes etc. I tell myself I had too little time to decide, and also I was afraid of having too heavy a load. A lot of things which I had already in my knapsack I threw out agains because I felt I wouldn't be able to lift it.

We walked along streets covered in rubble, around barricades, alongside which there were only narrow paths, slippery from rain. People pushed from behind, and everyone was in a hurry; the going was very difficult for me due to my bad legs and aching back. I fell several times and had to pick myself up again. We walked through ul. Żurawia, and then Krucza to Koszykowa, and further along Śniadeckich. A long trail of many thousands of people, dragging bundles, knapsacks and cases with them. Small children were pushed in prams, the weak were taken by hand. Our Polish exodus could probably be compared to the exit of the Jews from Egypt. At dusk we arrived at the Marshal Piłsudski hospital . . .[47]

It is difficult to judge how these wretched people felt as they left the capital, or what the atmosphere was really like. According to Stefan Korboński, they were filled with a mingled feeling: relief and joy at the fact that they had managed to survive, but also uncertainty as to what fate held in store for them.[48] In Warsaw there was a relaxed atmosphere of a sort, with the tension of the fighting and the ever present fear of death gone. Korboński maintains that the civilians of Warsaw still had hope that their government and the Allies would do something to save the situation. They believed in England, and especially America, who they thought would not allow the Soviets to occupy Poland and prevent the independent existence of Poland. But this was partly due to the fact that they were not well informed of the real state of international affairs.[49]

Colonel Bokszczanin, the Deputy Chief of Staff to the AK from January to July 1944, has described the feeling of the inhabitants of Warsaw and the Army as worse than after the September defeat of 1939.[50] There was depression and bitterness especially about the blood spilt and lives lost. People were broken down and held a grudge against everyone and everything, and blamed the AK Commanders for their misfortunes.[51] Stanislaw Ziemba has also written about the bitterness felt towards the Uprising amongst the refugees in Kraków.[52] Both the Army and society as a whole began to be filled with defeatist feelings.[53]

The number of civilians left in Śródmieście by the beginning of October is not easy to estimate. Mikołajczyk in London had a figure of 260,000 civilians which was supplied by Korboński.[54] Colonel Dobrowolski quoted a figure of 500,000 in his talks with General von

dem Bach. The German Major Fischer, who was also present, estimated it to be about 200,000. Von dem Bach maintained that both
these figures were too high and he was probably right.[55] The RGO
gives a figure of 280,000.[56] In the German Ninth Army Diary, however, the following figures are given concerning the evacuation:[57]

3.x.44.	48,000 civilians left Śródmieście
5.x.44.	To the figure of 65,000 civilians, 15,000 more added today
6.x.44.	37,000 inhabitants transported from Warsaw
7.x.44.	51,000 inhabitants transported from Warsaw
8.x.44.	Since 1.x.44. 153,519 persons evacuated from Śródmieście

On 4 September the number of civilians in Śródmieście was estimated
to have been about 260,000.[58] This number would not have increased
due to the fact that after this date there was no large inflow of refugees
into Śródmieście. However, it would have been decreased by the
evacuation of Powiśle, the numbers leaving at the beginning of
September, and the deaths caused by bombing, fires, injury, and
disease. Any evacuation figure would not be truly representative of
the population of Śródmieście at the end of the Uprising due to the
fact that some people managed to escape, especially members of the
governmental and civilian authorities, and a few stayed and hid in the
rubble of Warsaw, especially Jews. About 4,000 injured were left
behind to be evacuated.[59] Therefore it must be supposed that the
population in Śródmieście at the beginning of October was between
150,000 and 160,000.

It is impossible to calculate how many civilians died during the
Uprising. Many perished without any trace, or with only a heap of
ashes remaining. According to the RGO about 150,000 civilians died
due to air attacks, artillery fire, fire, diseases, mass executions etc.[60]
According to Hitler and Goebbels over 200,000 inhabitants were
killed[61] and it is not likely that they should want to exaggerate their
crime, though it cannot be known on what source and information
they could possibly base their assessment. Official sources at the time
put the numbers killed at between 200,000 and 250,000.[62] Over
15,000 Polish insurgents died.[63] The accepted total figure today is
about 200,000 and is often quoted to be as high as 250,000, including
the Army. In Wola and the Old Town alone over 90,000 died or were
killed. Many hundreds more died afterwards from wounds or diseases
contracted, or remained sick and maimed, physically or mentally, for
the rest of their lives. It cannot be calculated how many children and
babies died or were stillborn. Here was a tragedy in which a whole

generation, on whom the hopes of a new Poland had been based, was decimated. It was amongst the young, men and women, that the losses were so high. The flower of the Polish youth and intelligentsia had been destroyed, families had been broken up and often obliterated.

4

Life in insurgent Warsaw

The administration of insurgent Warsaw

The administration of Warsaw during the Uprising had been planned to cover the whole area of the liberated city. This plan could only have been part of the original concept of a quick and victorious rising. The failure of the insurgents to gain control of the whole of the town hindered the establishment of the administration as well as dividing it up into unconnected and unco-ordinated fragments. Consequently it took some time for any kind of official control or organisation to appear from the civilian authorities.

During the Uprising Warsaw was divided up into administrative units based on the pre-war *Starostwa grodzkie* (City boroughs). These units formed *Rejony* (regions) of the *Obwód* (district) of Warsaw.[1] At the head of them stood the Delegat Stołeczny (Delegate for the Capital), Marceli Porowski, 'Sowa'. He carried out functions similar to that of the Mayor of Warsaw.[2] However, as has already been seen, in certain parts of Warsaw no administration existed at all, i.e. Wola, Praga and Ochota (although in the latter some type of organisation was effected as a result of local and individual initiative). In Śródmieście, the Old Town, Żoliborz, Mokotów and Czerniaków a centrally controlled administration was established in some form or another.

The Government Delegate, Jankowski, being also the Deputy Premier, was responsible for seeing that his ministers arranged the administration and care of the civilian population. Although the Uprising was expected the actual timing of the outbreak came as a surprise to the members of the Delegatura, which at the last moment was split in two, and this greatly affected its functioning in the first days.

On the morning of 31 July 1944, at a meeting between General 'Bór', Jankowski and the Presidium of the RJN, 'Bór' told the polideclans that the outbreak of a rising within the next few days was not foreseen.[3] Later in the day, at 4.00 p.m., the meeting Jankowski had arranged with his three KRM ministers was surprisingly interrupted by General 'Bór's' aide-de-camp, asking the Government Delegate to leave immediately to go to the General.[4] The meeting of the KRM was therefore postponed until the following day at 1.00 p.m.[5]

When Jankowski arrived at the headquarters of General 'Bór', he was informed that the Uprising was to commence at 5.00 p.m. the following day and his approval was sought.[6] According to Adam Bień, a member of the KRM, Jankowski, when he informed his ministers of the decision at their meeting the following day, said that the information had been 'communicated' to him the day before.[7] Colonel Pluta-Czachowski, however, has written that Jankowski told his ministers that General 'Bór' had ordered the starting of the Uprising with his approval and said:

The C. in C. took the decision suddenly yesterday in the early evening (6.00 p.m.). This was as a result of military factors, reported by Colonel 'Monter', including the fact that the Soviet Army was already attacking Praga and our intervention might be too late ... The die has been cast and nothing can be changed. Yesterday due to the curfew the information could not be distributed. All Department chiefs have been alerted this morning.[8]

Pluta-Czachowski obtained this information from Stefan Pawłowski, director of the Cabinet of the Delegatura Rządu.[9] All available evidence, however, suggests that the decision about the timing of the outbreak of the Uprising was a joint one between General 'Bór' and Jankowski.[10]

The news of the imminent outbreak of the Uprising came like a bolt out of the blue, not only because the ministers had been informed the day before that it was neither feasible nor likely, but also because the final decision had been made with only one government representative present.[11]

Since Jankowski died without leaving any writings on the subject, the truth will never be known about how much influence he had on the final decision. He is recorded as saying that he himself took the decision to start the Uprising and authorised 'Bór' to do so, and afterwards stated that he was entirely responsible.[12] Jan Hoppe, the deputy leader of the SL, has written of that decision: 'It is difficult to believe that Jankowski agreed willingly to surprise his colleagues with the timing of the outbreak of the Uprising.'[13] It would seem, however, that there was no calculated plan to surprise the Delegatura, but rather it was a result of the panic and haste with which the final decision was made.

The three members at the meeting on Tuesday 1 August were given less than four hours in which to prepare themselves. They were not alone in their surprise. Stefan Korboński, the Head of the Civilian Resistance, received the news from his wife at about the same time. Several years after the event he wrote: 'I could not make out why I had not been notified, except for a piece of unpardonable negligence on someone's part.'[14] He had no contact with the High Command nor the Government Delegate for the first days of the Uprising, nor did he know where they were.[15] Bagiński, the Director of the Department of Internal Affairs, arriving too late at the meeting at the AK Headquarters because of police and Gestapo action, only heard about the timing of the Uprising in the early morning of 1 August. It was then his task to inform the President of the City, Marceli Porowski, who before the outbreak of armed action was meant to take over authority in the Town Hall from Kulski. Stanisław Tabisz, Commander of the State Police of the Delegatura, also only heard the news by chance.[16]

Jankowski, at the meeting with the three KRM ministers on 1 August, informed them that he was going to stop working in the Delegatura and go together with the Chairman of the RJN, Pużak, to the AK Headquarters for the entire duration of the Uprising. He transferred the control of the civilian authorities to Adam Bień, who was to stay in Śródmieście and make contact with Colonel 'Monter', Commander of the District of Warsaw. In consequence, Bień maintained that in spite of a prior understanding that the Delegatura during the Uprising would function as a whole in close co-operation, it was broken up into two parts at the last moment.[17] Pluta-Czachowski says, however, that this decision was in agreement with previous plans, as does Stefan Korboński. Thus two centres of the main Delegatura were formed, one at the AK Headquarters and the second in Śródmieście alongside the Commander of the Uprising. The first was of a symbolic nature displaying unity amongst the highest directors of the Uprising. The second, in the hands of Bień, was the real functioning part of the Delegatura and it was there that true responsibility lay in organising the civilian population.[18]

By 3 August Jankowski, Stefan Pawłowski, Bagiński, and Leopold Rutkowski from the Department of Internal Affairs, and Pużak were all at the Headquarters of the AK in Wola.[19] The unexpected outbreak of the Uprising and the splitting of the Delegatura resulted in considerable disorganisation. Bień claims that he was left totally on his own with no contact addresses. Only by coincidence did he meet Pawłowski's liaison girl, who gave him the required information. He managed to make contact with all the other departments except Internal Affairs.[20] On 3 August, Stanisław Jasiukowicz, the Deputy Government Delegate, arrived and a few days later the arrival of Antoni Pajdak completed the KRM.[21] As of that moment the organisation and 'rebuilding' of the Delegatura started, but it still had no contact with Jankowski.[22]

It was Bień's primary task to make contact with Colonel 'Monter' and immediately afterwards, when the insurgents had taken over the building which housed the Presidium of the Council of Ministers, to set up the KRM and the departments of the Delegatura in it. It was also his task to go with Colonel 'Monter' to greet the Soviet Army when they entered Warsaw on the Poniatowski Bridge.[23] This was also the most important task for Porowski.[24] But at the same time as it became obvious that the Soviet forces were not going to arrive the main preoccupation became to set up and organise the administration and to make contact with the local inhabitants after the surprise of the Uprising.

It took the Delegatura several days to start functioning and during that time if there was any visible attempt to organise the civilian population it was done by the Army. The AK before the outbreak of the Uprising had organised an *administracja zastępcza* (replacement administration) which was supposed to fulfil the provisional function of organising the administration of the conquered territories during the battle for the liberation of Poland. This led to duplication and conflict of authority. Porowski has written that he learnt of the AK's organisation of a civilian administration by accident and added: 'I do not think the Government Delegate was informed about it.'[25] Also before the outbreak of the Uprising the AK, according to Bień, without any agreement with the Delegatura, had organised their own security corps. The Delegatura was supposed to call the PKB (State Security Corps) into existence.[26]

At the beginning of the Uprising appeals and orders were signed in the name of the civilian authories by a Komisarz Cywilny (Civilian Commissary) and countersigned by the Commander of the district of Warsaw.[27] The Komisarz Cywilny was, according to Korboński, illegal.[28] On 5 August an article was published in *Biuletyn Informacyjny* saying that the Polish authorities were coming out from underground and that the Polish officials and the Komisarz Cywilny under the supervision of the AK District Commander were functioning.[29] The article was not referring to the Delegatura but to the Army's own agencies. Nothing was said about the Delegatura.

Stanisław Ziemba, who was head of the Polish press agency, PAT (Polska Agencja Telegraficzna), during the Uprising, has written in no uncertain terms that the Army did not want to let the civilian authorities run the administration in Warsaw during the Uprising and that it was 'their kind of Sanacja coup' against the pre-war opposition.[30]

During this time little had been heard from the Government Delegate, Jankowski. On the evening of 8 August, Stanisław Kauzik, the Director of the Department of Information and Press of the Delegatura, told his workers that a text had to be prepared to be read on the radio by the Government Delegate the next day. It was especially urgent as a week of the Uprising had passed and apart from individual calls to fight there had been no separate speech by the Government Delegate, which the community must have been expecting.[31]

In the course of the next few days two significant steps were taken which brought the administration under Delegatura control and established it on some kind of organised basis. On 9 August Regional Delegates were created to control the administration of the regions which were formed. This new office was founded as a result of the capital being split up into unconnected areas by the fighting. The Regional Delegates had the same authority and carried out the same activity as the old Starost of Warsaw.[32] This step, however, in reality only affected Śródmieście, which was split up into four regions. The Regional Delegates acted through House and Block Committees, with the house being the basic unit of administration. Their tasks were to organise anti-fire and anti-air attack defence, security, social welfare and propaganda matters.[33]

On the same day Colonel 'Monter' ordered that the Army restrict itself to purely tactical matters and some anti-air attack defence.[34] All matters not directly concerned with military operations were to be the sole domain of the civilian authorities, whose only executive organ was the PKB. It was their task to organise the care and security of the civilian population, to arrange their evacuation in connection with military matters and provide them with food and accommodation.[35] Thus was the delegation of authority established. The accompanying chart shows how the administration of the town functioned according to the system that evolved.

Government Delegate
|
District Delegate
|
Regional Delegates
|
Block and House Commanders
|
OPL-Block and House Committees

It has already been seen in the preceding chapters that this system of administration was quickly established in the regions of Śródmieście. In the Old Town, however, conditions made it very difficult for a lasting and effective administration to be organised.[36] In Mokotów and Żoliborz independent but similar systems evolved. In Mokotów on 29 August a Commissary for Civilian Affairs was organised, and in Żoliborz, although there was a Government Delegate, totally separate *Samorządy* were established.[37] Thus really only in the centre of the town was government controlled administration effected.

The only example available of the functioning of these delegates is from Region III. The offices of the local Delegatura were on ul. Śliska 6/8 and later moved to ul. Złota 59. Fifteen officials were employed on the spot, and the rest, about eighty-five, functioned in different parts of the town. All important decisions on policy were made jointly, whilst smaller matters were settled separately. The office was open from 8.00 a.m. to 4.00 p.m., regardless of the military situation, and at 6.00 p.m. its officials met to discuss the current problems and the following day's programme.[38]

On 14 August the first briefing of the Regional Delegates was held in the Ministry of Internal Affairs.[39] Similar meetings were held every two to three days so that current problems and questions could be settled.[40] The overall efficiency of the administration was dependent on the activity of the individual Block and House Committees and their commanders, and in turn on individual initiative. Since the very outbreak of the Uprising some committees had been organised and continual calls were made asking the inhabitants to make sure such committees were elected.[41] After 17 August special instructions were issued in an attempt to make the system of committees function everywhere. In each house with more than seven inhabitants committees had to be formed; houses with fewer inhabitants had to form joint committees. Three to five people in each house had to be elected. The committee then chose its chairman. The OPL chairman of the house had to be a member of the committee.[42]

The duties of these committees included organising air-raid precautions and a fire fighting service, and ensuring adequate supplies of sand and water at all times. In the event of houses collapsing or fires the Commanders were empowered to call people out to work. In the sphere of security, they had to act in accordance with the appropriate PKB and Straż Obywatelska (Citizens Guard). The Regional Delegate was empowered to hold and arrest people and requisition suspect premises or those belonging to suspect persons, premises for communal and welfare purposes as well as goods and materials to supply the civilian population. In the same sphere House Commanders were supposed to oversee the security of property of persons living in or having business in the given area, to secure German possessions which were put at the disposal of the Polish authorities and secure empty premises and their contents. They were empowered to check the identity of people wandering in or around the area or house and hold people who did not have sufficient proof of identification. These people had to be taken immediately to the PKB Station. In the sphere of social care the Commanders were responsible for finding and allocating accommodation and compiling lists of inhabitants. In cases of necessity the Block Commanders in agreement with the House Commanders could carry out partial and provisional requisition of premises with access to a kitchen and necessary equipment. The Regional Delegate was responsible for organising through the committees the feeding of temporary and permanent inhabitants. The Commander had to draw up lists of people and their supplies of food. People with no means of support had to be sent by the House Commanders to the nearest functioning RGO kitchen or to other families. Commanders were empowered, with the assistance of two other people, to check the stores in their area and to supply the Regional Delegate immediately with a list of all articles of food (in warehouses and at wholesalers). Stores had to be secured by the House Commanders without delay and if the Regional Delegate decided to requisition them, they were to be distributed amongst the needy. Special care had to be taken of mothers, babies and lost children and medical stores organised. It was the Commanders' responsibility to maintain the cleanliness of shelters, courtyards, and staircases, and to see to the building of shelters and thoroughfares. They had to see that sufficient newspapers and propaganda materials were distributed, and organise readings of the papers and communiqués as well as chats for the aged and children. Morale had to be maintained and defeatism fought. They had to make sure that no blackmarketeering took place and control the consumption of water. Finally, it was their task to arrange for the burial of the dead. Later on in the Uprising it also became their responsibility to organise 'drop' observations and searches, and to hand over any containers and their contents from drops to the authorities.[43]

In the centre of Warsaw it would seem that the system of House and Block Committees was generally established. The efficient running of the civilian administration was dependent on both the Committees and the character of the Commander. His ability was vital not only to the smooth running of his house or block but also in maintaining morale. The majority of Commanders fulfilled their duties well. Some fell victim to the pressures of the Uprising – drank too much, argued with other inhabitants, were indifferent to illegal activities, or failed to maintain suitable conditions within the house.[44]

The office of each Regional Delegate was divided up into the following departments:[45]

General Department
Department of Security
Department of Fire Defence and OPL
Department for the Organisation of Communal Activities
Department of Feeding
Department of Health
Department of Accommodation
Department of Social Care
Department of Technology
Department of Information and Propaganda
Department of Industry
Department of Liquidation

The functions of these departments have already been largely explained. The Department for the Organisation of Communal Activities was responsible for matters arising from the co-operation between the network of House and Block Committees, the registration of persons and the organisation of labour, i.e. compulsory work. The Department of Industry was concerned with securing and establishing industry, craft and trade institutions, and with matters of raw materials, circulation of goods, registration of industrial stores necessary for the Army, control over prices, control over speculation, and co-operation with the existing private and government domestic organisations in the sphere of industry, craft and trade. The Department of Liquidation was responsible for securing and controlling the personal and public German estates and documents.[46]

Instructions, orders and information were passed on to the civilian population by four means. Firstly, there was distribution through the organisation of House and Block Committees. Secondly, posters and communiqués were put up on walls and in courtyards. Thirdly, various insurgent newspapers were published. In Śródmieście the Delegatura Rządu published a paper, *Dziennik Obwieszczeń*, which contained instructions for the civilian population. Fourthly, information was broadcast on the civilian radio station, Polskie Radio Warszawa.[47]

The Delegates worked alongside and with the help of other civic and political organisations. The RGO, continuing its work from the occupation, helped with feeding and clothing. The Polish Red Cross was mainly concerned with the sick and injured, although it did also establish Missing Persons Bureaux during the Uprising.[48] The PPS Milicja was especially active in the Old Town along with religious and charitable organisations.[49] The scouts also played an invaluable part in helping the civilian population. They formed the Wojskowa Służba Społeczna (WSS: Military Community Service), whose aim was to organise help for the civilian population.[50]

Thus the organisation of Warsaw, although ostensibly controlled by the Delegatura, was very much a co-operation of various groups and only such a co-operation made any organisation possible. Even so a great deal was left to individual initiative and in fact such initiative was imperative for successful organisation. Large numbers of people went through the whole Uprising without having to turn to any outside authorities, purely as a result of their own activity and ability. Much of this work was done by women.

It is not easy to judge how effective the organisation and administration of the Regional Delegates proved to be. The task which had to be carried out was not an easy one. There were complaints about lack of organisation, bureaucracy, carelessness, lack of realism, inefficiency and general disregard by the authorities. In Region III this was especially true. It has been seen that the lack of resourcefulness and activity on the part of the insurgent administrators often resulted in the lessening of their authority and hence that of the Polish government. But the picture which appears in Śródmieście is one more of organisation than chaos, and it would seem that, bearing in mind the very difficult and extraordinary conditions, the civilian authorities in fact functioned as best they could.

4.2 The infrastructure and internal trade of insurgent Warsaw

The efficient organisation of the infrastructure of Warsaw during the Uprising was as much in the military as the public interest and the two were interconnected. Due to the military importance of electricity, plumbing and fire fighting, preparations had been made in these areas before the outbreak of the Uprising.[1]

Electricity, plumbing, sewerage and gas

Preparations for an Uprising had been going on in the power station in Powiśle since 1942. Not only had the necessary materials and equipment been collected, but also stores of food, shoes, clothes, drills etc.[2] Until its fall on 5 September the power station supplied those parts of the city controlled by the AK with electricity and also served as a bastion of defence for Powiśle. The workers in the station were not only occupied keeping up the electrical supply but also had to repair damages, very often in difficult conditions under fire; they set up telephone lines between fighting districts and established electrical current for hospitals and the Army. After the destruction of the power station at the beginning of September, which left Warsaw virtually without electricity, accumulators were built and recharged in the insurgent factories by motor engines. These were used to supply hospital X-ray units, mechanical workshops for the Army, mills, laundries, and water pumps with electricity, and provided light for underground passages, e.g. the one underneath al. Jerozolimskie.[3]

At the end of August specific instructions were issued concerning the use of electricity. Electricity was only allowed to be used in factories working for the Army, in hospitals, at important radio posts, for the lighting of entrances to cellars and to a limited extent by the civilian population. The use of heating appliances and electrical motors was prohibited except for medical use, for preparing food for babies under eighteen months, or for motors driving water pumps or workshops charging batteries. It was the responsibility of the House Commander to see that these instructions were carried out, and to take charge of these appliances and motors, ensuring that each apparatus carried a card showing ownership and that the owners were given a receipt. He also had to record the number of kilowatts used in each flat, as the permitted consumption of electricity was one or two kilowatts depending on the size of the property. In barber shops the use of electrical appliances was forbidden, although at the discretion of the House Commander one hairdryer was allowed in ladies' hairdressers. The use of lifts was forbidden except in the case of accidents or for the quick transportation of rescue teams. Hospitals had to obtain permission from the Electricity Office to use lifts, which were allowed only to transport the heavily injured, not to carry any other personnel or equipment.[4]

The problem of supplying water during the Uprising was one of the most difficult to solve. The Municipal Waterworks on ul. Filtrowa was captured by the Germans who cut off the water supply on 14 August.[5] The Sewer Pump Station on ul. Dobra only remained in insurgent hands until 10 August, the Inspectorate for the plumbing and sewerage network fell with the power station on 5 September, and the Experimental Station was held by the insurgents from 31 August until 14 September. The water meter on ul. Niemcewicza was held by the Germans. The filters worked until 20 September. Furthermore as the fighting divided Warsaw up into separate districts the central organisation was broken up and, therefore, it was up to the individual stations to solve their own problems.[6]

A repair group was formed from the workers of the Inspectorate for the plumbing and sewerage network, and throughout the whole of August and part of September it operated in Powiśle and Śródmieście and sometimes made contact with Mokotów. Its work was mainly concerned with the shutting off of pipes damaged in the fighting and with closing parts of the network which were supplying water to areas in German hands.[7] It made necessary repairs to supply hospitals, feeding posts and homes with water. The most important task in the sphere of plumbing and sewerage, apart from maintaining the network in active operation and repairing damage, was to prepare other means of supplying the population with water, when the normal supply was damaged or broke down. This was done by using wells already in existence, bringing disused ones into operation, and sinking new ones.[8]

The Department of Technology was responsible for matters concerning buildings and communications (i.e. keeping streets and thoroughfares clean), and for maintaining and repairing the electrical, plumbing and sewerage systems. It was responsible for organising work squads to carry out these tasks.[9] The members of the squads were either employees of the municipal institutions, OPL members, volunteers or men who had to report for compulsory work and were

Table 12. *Allocation of water*

Street	Well	Hours
Hoża 45, 47, 49	Poznańska 11	5.00–6.45 p.m.
Poznańska 11, 13, 15, 17	Poznańska 11	5.00–6.45 p.m.
Hoża 53, 55, 57	Hoża 53	6.00–7.45 a.m.
Hoża 59, 61	Hoża 59	6.00–7.45 a.m.
Emil. Plater 8	Poznańska 11	5.00–6.45 p.m.
Emil. Plater 10, 12, 14	Hoża 59	5.00–6.45 p.m.
Wspólna 49, 51, 53	Marszałkowska 91	1.00–2.00 p.m.
Marszałkowska 83, 85	Marszałkowska 91	2.00–3.00 p.m.
Poznańska 22	Marszałkowska 91	4.00–5.00 p.m.
Hoża 54, 56	Hoża 56	5.00–6.45 p.m.
Hoża 46, 48, 50, 52	Marszałkowska 91	8.30–10.00 a.m.
Poznańska 21, 23	Poznańska 11	6.00–7.45 a.m.
Wspólna 57, 59	Poznańska 11	6.00–7.45 a.m.
Hoża 58, 60, 62	Poznańska 11	6.00–7.45 a.m.
Wspólna 63b	Hoża 66	5.00–6.45 p.m.
Hoża 70, 72, 74	Hoża 66	5.00–6.45 p.m.
Wspólna 65, 65a, 67	Hoża 66	5.00–6.45 p.m.
Hoża 76, 78	Hoża 66	5.00–6.45 p.m.
Wilcza 38, 40, 42, 44, 46	Wilcza 44	5.00–6.45 p.m.
Marszałkowska 77	Marszałkowska 79	6.00–7.45 a.m.

recruited by the OPL.[10] The Department of Industry also helped with matters concerning gas, plumbing, electricity etc.[11]

The building of wells was continually fraught with problems. There was a lack of building materials, no plans of the city's water pipes, insufficient numbers of workers, usually due to the fact that they were not well enough fed for such hard work, and lack of electrical current.[12] German soldiers captured by the AK were sometimes used for building wells.[13] By 11 September the Hydraulic Section of the Department of Technology claimed that the water system in Śródmieście was in general under control and a 'catastrophic shortage of water' had been averted. By that date forty-two wells had been completed and another forty-eight were near completion.[14] But by 25 September it was estimated that another thirty to forty wells were still necessary.[15] As a result of the shortage of water Warsaw tended to be further subdivided into smaller districts, the nucleus of each one being the well.[16] To begin with water was allocated at certain hours to the Army, hospitals, kitchens and civilians separately. Later on it was allocated on the basis of individual houses and blocks. Table 12 shows how this system worked.[17]

It must also be mentioned here that the valuable knowledge of the sewer workers was extensively used in the employment of the sewers during the Uprising as a means of communication and evacuation. These workers helped in plotting out new routes or leading groups through the sewers. Their knowledge of the layout was indispensable, they held plans and maps of the sewers, and above all could advise on the dangers of the underground tunnels and what precautions were needed in their use.[18]

There were two gas works in Warsaw, the larger on ul. Dworska in Wola and the second on ul. Ludna in Śródmieście.[19] The former remained in the German held part of Warsaw throughout the whole Uprising and the latter fell to the Germans on 13 September 1944.[20] Little reference is made to the supply of gas in materials available for the study of the Uprising. At the beginning of the battle there was gas in some houses,[21] but a report sent to London by Jankowski on 22 September stated that there had been no supply of gas for a long time.[22]

Postal service and telephones

A postal service, a field post, was run during the Uprising by boy scouts. Its creation was not based on any governmental instruction but purely on their own initiative.[23] Later it was given official recognition by the Regional Delegate in Śródmieście.[24] It was started on 6 August.[25] At the beginning the centre of the field post was in the Scout Headquarters on ul. Wilcza until the Head Post Office on pl. Napoleona was taken by the insurgents. When it was later destroyed by a bomb the scouts moved back to their original 'post office'.[26]

Letters were posted in special boxes, alongside which books were placed to be given to the injured lying in hospital. This was the only form of payment.[27] There were two collections daily at 9.00 a.m. and 4.00 p.m.[28] Letters which were posted in Śródmieście were delivered to addresses in that same district on the same day, whereas mail to Żoliborz and Mokotów took two to three days. Letters were also delivered to the Old Town and Czerniaków.[29]

Instructions were issued regulating the writing and posting of letters. It was not permitted to send heavy letters, they had to be written clearly and not on scraps of paper, they were not supposed to exceed twenty-five words, all post was subject to military censor (the censoring of letters was usually done by the scouts' parents),[30] and it was forbidden to write about the fighting.[31]

The following are two examples of letters posted:

our flat has been bombed. Mother was killed under the rubble and we cannot reach her at present. The rest of the house is burnt.

how are you all? Are you well? I am asking because I know you live near the bridges. All is well with us. Father is an OPL Commander and does nothing but shout! Generally there is a lot going on. Stephan, Uncle Stasiek, Aunt Zosia, Janek, Główka are all in the AK. Our area is held by the Poles. Now the whole house is like one family. If you have a spare moment write a letter. They are distributed by the scouts. I send you all much love and look forward to seeing you in the 'Free Fatherland'.[32]

By 1 September a total of 116,317 letters had been posted, an average of 3,000–6,000 daily. The heaviest collection was on 13 August when about 10,000 letters were posted.[33] The figures for the preceding days were:[34]

August 8	3,659
August 9	2,153
August 10	3,058
August 11	6,654
August 12	9,721

Stamps were specially printed for these letters at the insurgent printers on ul. Szpitalna.[35] The first stamps appeared on 2 September.[36] One of the scouts carrying mail even tried to trade some of the stamps for food.[37]

The field post played an invaluable role in bringing together families and friends who had been cut off from each other by the fighting. It took its toll, however, of the lives of young scouts[38] who carried out their work enthusiastically regardless of the risks involved. One of them managed to cross several times during the day from the Head Post Office to Żoliborz. He used to slip through the allotments in the region of the Gdańsk Railway Station, where he stuffed his pockets full of fruit to bring back to the town centre.[39]

After the beginning of September the activity of the field post declined and it functioned only in Śródmieście. By that time the Headquarters of the AK had left the Old Town and established themselves in Śródmieście and as a result the scouts were more often used to carry military reports than private correspondence. Furthermore the people who had previously been using the post had by then moved down into the cellars, where they were able to move around by a labyrinth of underground passages. The volume of mail fell as the city's inhabitants became increasingly accustomed to insurgent life and their lack of contact with kith and kin.[40]

At the beginning of the Uprising a few telephones were still opera-tive,[41] but very quickly all telephone communication became impossible.[42]

Fire fighting

The organisation of an efficient fire fighting force during the Uprising was imperative although not easy to effect. Preparations had been made prior to the outbreak of the Uprising, but on 29 July 1944 the Germans had requisitioned most of the fire engines from the Warsaw Fire Brigade.[43] At the outbreak of the fighting few motor pumps, hoses or sprays were available.[44]

The Department of Air and Fire Defence or OPL and OPL Pożarnictwo, the equivalent of the ARP in London, quickly under-took the responsibility of arranging a fire service. The fire fighting service during the Uprising was drawn from four organisations:[45]

1. The six fire units of the Warsaw fire brigade.
2. Military fire fighting detachments.
3. OPL and OPL Pożarnictwo.
4. Volunteer rescue squads.

This organisation was responsible not only for the extinguishing of fires, but also for rescuing people buried under buildings destroyed by bombing and fires.

On 9 August the following instructions were issued by the District Government Delegate:[46]

1. Each Block and House Commander has to appoint two guards to be on continual alert against fires and air attack.
2. All inflammable materials and wooden partitions must be re-moved from attics.
3. Sufficient quantities of sand and water must be placed in the attics.
4. During dry weather water must be sprinkled to prevent fires from spreading quickly.
5. Water and sand must be placed in containers in courtyards.
6. The nearest well must be allocated to be used if the water supply fails.

Most of the information available on the fire service concerns Region III. In that part of the town squads comprising eight persons and a commander were formed in every house or block as the fire fighting service. They were supplied with very basic equipment: spades, axes, and buckets (there was a great shortage of the latter). These squads were inspected regularly and their members were exempt from any other work, military or civil.[47]

It was a losing battle, however, to fight the fires as their numbers grew, water became difficult or impossible to obtain, and the physical strength of the squads weakened. By the beginning of September the task had already become very exacting due to the shortage of water and by the end of the month fires were being left unfought. The fire squads devoted their energies mainly to rescuing and evacuating people.[48] One case had been recorded of a fire being extinguished with vinegar as nothing else was available.[49]

The internal trade of insurgent Warsaw

The outbreak of the Uprising upset the internal trade and rationing system which had come into existence during the occupation. On 4 August instructions were issued ordering all shops and stores to open as soon as the Germans left town. All basic food articles could only be sold in a limited amount, e.g. one day's supply of bread was to be rationed according to the system already in existence. Hoarding was explicitly forbidden as were speculation and blackmarketeering. Failure to comply with these instructions would be punished by closure of the shop concerned and confiscation of all goods.[50]

On 14 August further instructions were issued by the Regional Government Delegate. All ration cards issued by the Germans were rendered invalid. All such goods and products as stores of flour, groats and legumes had to be registered and could not be sold until further instructions were issued. Likewise all horses, cattle and pigs had to be registered and it was forbidden either to slaughter or sell them. The same was applicable to all stores of textile and leather articles. All proprietors were called upon to open their shops, restaurants, work-shops and fuel stores. All goods were to be put on sale with the exception of those which had to be registered. People were encouraged to barter goods on the widest possible scale. Shop-keepers were asked to maintain prices wherever feasible at the level they were in July 1944 on the free market, and not to speculate.[51]

Many shop-keepers, however, did not co-operate. There were various reasons for this. Some of them were not in Warsaw at the time, others feigned absence in order to avoid requisition, as they wanted to hold back their goods as currency for a later date. They preferred to trade 'under the counter' amongst people known to them, and thereby avoid controls and fix their own prices or method of transaction. There were also shop owners who had nothing in their shops to sell, and some of them complained that it was too dangerous to open their shops and that they had no staff to work in them.[52]

Money quickly ceased to have any value whilst barter and speculation flourished.[53] The most highly sought after goods, mainly fats,
cigarettes, vodka and water, were the most important forms of currency. In Śródmieście in the second half of August, one litre of vodka
bought two kilogrammes of bread.[54] In Mokotów at the end of
September, five cigarettes bought one kilogramme of potatoes.[55]
Food from the Soviet drops in September was also sold or bartered –
biscuits were sold in exchange for vodka and cigarettes.[56] Dogs and
cats were bartered for cigarettes and sausages.[57] By the very end of the
Uprising a kilogramme of sugar was being exchanged for five kilogrammes of bread.

As the Uprising progressed bartering increased and flourished.[58] In
the courtyards notices were put up offering goods for exchange. In the
Palladium Cinema on ul. Złota 7 and at ul. Wilcza 41, ul. Krucza 9,
21 and 24 special 'markets' were established for exchanging articles.[59]
The only real money which held any value was the gold dollar and
roubles.[60] The following list shows some examples of prices after
20 September and demonstrates how worthless the Polish złoty had
become:[61]

12.5 kg wheat	2,000 złoty
$\frac{1}{2}$ loaf of bread	100
1 kg of pork fat	6,000

    (On 14 August the same amount had cost about zł. 1,000.)

1 packet of matches	30
1 cigarette	30

    (On 21 August 950 cigarettes had cost zł. 900.)

Other comparable prices at the beginning of September are butter
which cost zł. 2,500 a kilogramme and potatoes which fetched zł. 200
for the same amount.[62] But these prices were usually only theoretical
as barter was the main form of trading used. Only at the very end of
the Uprising did money come back into circulation, but then only
gold and gold roubles had any real value.

This kind of profiteering was an unavoidable evil of the situation
and a continuation from the occupation, and although many were
only in it for gain and it was an unsocial activity it seems to have
helped to alleviate the problem of food supply for some.

Transport and communication

During the occupation all taxis, private cars and cabs disappeared
and heavy vehicles were requisitioned by the Germans.[63] Likewise in

June 1944 the rickshaw which had become a popular means of transport was also banned.[64] However, the battle in insurgent Warsaw would have made the use of any form of mechanised or horse drawn transport extremely difficult. As a result the inhabitants of the city moved round on foot during the Uprising, and more often than not via a network of underground passages.

A whole complex of passages and thoroughfares was developed during the Uprising which ran overground through interconnected houses and courtyards and underground through tunnels and cellars specially constructed. These passages were formed right from the outset of the Uprising, even before official instructions were issued.[65]

On 21 August 1944, House Commanders were given the following instructions by the Regional Government Delegate:[66]

1. Street movement
   a. Holes formed in the pavement where paving stones have been removed must be levelled to facilitate street movement and make movement at night safe.
   b. Streets must be swept daily and, water supplies permitting, sprinkled. Each house is responsible for the area in front of it up to the middle of the street.
2. Passages between houses
   a. All houses should have cellar passages linked to their neighbouring houses and, where technically possible, connected to the network of underground passages along the street.
   b. All doorways linking passages ought to be at least 75 cm wide and 120 cm high to facilitate the transport of the sick and injured as well as speedy pedestrian movement.
   c. All houses and properties between two parallel streets ought to have sufficient external thoroughfares and where possible also underground.
   d. Cellar thoroughfares ought to be sufficiently lit at each entrance and corner. Electric lighting is compulsory. House Commanders must have sufficient stores of other means of lighting in case of an electricity failure.
   e. All cellars and courtyard passages and each turn must be clearly signposted. The signs must be distinctly written either on a board or on the wall.

These passages greatly aided and facilitated communication during the Uprising. The eminent Polish Socialist, Zygmunt Zaremba, has described this underground communication maze in his memoirs:

The people ... have knocked through openings from one cellar to the next, and they have dug small tunnels under the streets. They have even put up signposts with explanations as to the situation of the given passage and the direction in which it is going. It was possible to get from ul. Bielańska to pl. Zbawiciela, from Nowy Świat to the Polytechnique with only having to emerge rarely into various courtyards and then descend again below street level following the chalk-written signs. In these passages there was as much movement as on a normal street. Around the edges of these low cellars people were camped on pallets, mattresses and sometimes on real beds ...[67]

Inter-district mobility was virtually impossible, except through the sewers, which were only opened for couriers and groups having official permission to use them.

Employment

The outbreak of the Uprising brought all normal work to an abrupt halt. Many people had already left their normal places of employment to join their units, others were cut off from their places of work, whilst for others it was impossible for them to continue with their normal jobs in insurgent conditions. But there were some who continued at their work for as long as it was possible if in a slightly changed capacity, e.g. electrical, gas and sewerage workers, printers, bakers etc. At the same time totally new employment necessities arose. People were called upon to build barricades, dig wells, form rescue squads, transport columns etc.

In Śródmieście during the Uprising the organisation of work was controlled by the Department for the Organisation of Social Administration in the Regional Delegatura Rządu. This department was responsible for matters arising from co-operation with the network of House and Block Committees and the Department of Census and the Department of Work.[68] In turn OPL and the House Committees were responsible for organising and recruiting work squads to carry out duties. In other districts the same obligation fell on the committees and volunteers.[69] It would appear that the first instructions concerning the duty of each individual to work were issued in the Old Town:

All citizens regardless of sex and age, not taking part in the battle with the enemy, are called on immediately to start work to hasten a victorious end to the fight. There is a lot which needs to be done, e.g.:
1. Start work in such places which should be functioning – food shops, bakers, chemists etc.
2. Build and repair barricades.
3. Run kitchens for soldiers and the homeless.
4. Care for the injured and bomb victims.

5. Clear footpaths through the rubble.
6. Fire defence.
7. Burying the dead.
8. Distributing of Polish publications.
...[70]

Just over a week later the Regional Government Delegate in Śródmieście issued a far more detailed instruction, which made it obligatory for all men to report for work:

1. All men between the age of 17 and 50 on 18 August 1944 are compelled to work in AK work squads.
   Everyone must report for work at points listed below at 12.00 a.m. The following persons are excluded:
   a. AK members or people serving in the AK.
   b. Persons holding exemptions issued by the Government Delegate for Warsaw-Śródmieście.
   c. OPL.
   d. Persons qualified as medically unfit for work.
2. Persons failing to report will be punished.
3. Persons working in the AK work squads must work six hours daily, the hours will be allocated by the Director of the AK work squads. While working full daily meals will be supplied (3 meals).
4. In connection with the above OPL House Commanders must draw up lists of permanent and temporary inhabitants who are bound to work ...
5. Men and women who are not bound to report for work may volunteer.
6. ...[71]

Later these instructions were modified and made even more detailed as a result of complaints.[72]

The system of recruitment for work was continually and often bitterly criticised. To prevent people from evading these squads the work was publicly propagated as being the duty of each individual, and avoiding it was synonymous to a soldier deserting his post.[73] The authorities who were responsible for organising work complained that too many medical exemptions were issued by doctors, which in turn was causing a low turn out for work.[74] At the same time there were cases of people refusing to work because they were not told how much they would be paid.[75]

Throughout the Uprising calls were made for specific workers to come forward. On 24 August Polskie Radio Warszawa broadcast a request for tailors to go and work in the sewing shops set up by the military authorities. Tailors, seamstresses and women were asked to go and sew uniforms and underwear for soldiers. People having sewing machines were also invited to help.[76] Mechanics were asked to join teams building wells, and appeals were made to radio and other electricians, plumbers and gas workers to come forward to work.[77] Calls went out for people to volunteer to work in the transport columns bringing in the much needed food supplies.[78] In the Old Town engineers, technicians, plumbers etc. were reminded that they should register for work.[79] Doctors were likewise appealed to.[80]

Payment for these services was usually made in kind.[81] Furthermore the form of payment was very important. In September people carrying stores of food (barley and wheat) were allowed by the Regional Government Delegate to keep 20% of the amount carried as payment.[82] But there were other institutions which paid up to 50% of goods carried over fifteen or twenty kilogrammes. This resulted in an unfavourable situation being created for the regional authorities and a loss of labour.[83]

The organisation of these work squads came under heavy criticism during the Uprising. Although there are no detailed statistical materials available on the subject it would appear from other sources that the attempts at arranging these teams did not prove easy nor always successful, and resulted in conflict and acrimony.

Social care

Social care during the Uprising was organised by the Department of Social Care, which was mainly responsible for caring for the homeless, feeding, clothing, housing, missing persons, and mother and child care. The problem of looking after the homeless and refugees was in effect carried out while the other activities of the Department were taking place.

Before discussing these different aspects of the administration of insurgent Warsaw, a few words should be said about the Military Community Service teams (Wojskowa Służba Społeczna), whose activity facilitated and aided the work of the other departments.

Wojskowa Służba Społeczna (WSS)

Leon Marszałek, one of the main organisers or the WSS, has best defined it:

The name [WSS] belonged to the activity of boy and girl scouts during the Warsaw Uprising ... aimed at organising help and care for the civilian population. The area where the WSS functioned was Śródmieście, although in other districts cut off from Śródmieście scouts undertook similar activity.

The initiative for this work was only started during the Uprising. Nobody before its outbreak had thought about preparing community action for the civilians as no one imagined that it would take such a course.

The WSS was arranged in the second week of the Uprising in the Boy Scouts' Headquarters. It functioned in close co-operation with the military and civilian authorities and could in many cases be regarded as their executive.[84]

The tasks of the WSS were manifold. They would take special care of civilians in front line areas, bringing them clothes, food, disinfectants, medicines and newspapers; they evacuated front line stores. One of their main duties was to look after babies and small children, collecting food and clothing for them and organising milk kitchens. These groups also cared for the aged. In addition to these tasks the scouts would also help put out fires and rescue people buried under the rubble. As they went about their work they were supposed to help maintain morale and raise the spirits of the civilians and also distribute newspapers.[85]

It was the activity of these scout groups which enabled the administration of the town to be carried out more efficiently than might have been expected in insurgent conditions.

Feeding

The outbreak of the Uprising brought an abrupt halt to the system of provisioning and feeding the city. Rationing stopped immediately and it became impossible to bring any fresh supplies of food into the capital. The inhabitants and the Army had to be supplied from existing stocks and their own private stores, which in many cases were to be totally destroyed during the battle.

It had been calculated before the outbreak of the Uprising that there were sufficient stores of food assembled (tinned meat, fats, flour, sugar, dried potatoes, vegetables and groats) for the Army (*c*. 45,000 soldiers) for three days, and what would be captured from German stores would feed the units for a further seven days.[86]

It is impossible to assess how large the private stores were which were held by the inhabitants of Warsaw during the Uprising, although it has been seen that they were quite extensive. Many Varsovians had accumulated basic stores at home as a result of a kind of 'occupation mentality' and generally most people who had the means to kept reserve stocks of food.[87]

The food available for insurgent Warsaw came from five sources: stores collected by the Army before the outbreak of the battle; stores (mainly German) captured during the fighting; private stores; food requisitioned from shops and stores, and from private accommodation, e.g. *Volksdeutsch* flats; food left behind by people who left Warsaw at the beginning of September, and minimal amounts of food which were brought in from gardens and allotments. Later on food was also received from drops.[88]

The main stores which were taken and used during the Uprising were: Haberbusch and Schiele, ul. Browarna (wheat and barley); the Związek Mleczarski (Milk Union), ul. Hoża (sugar and fats); Społem (Co-operative), ul. Czerniakowska (sugar); RGO stores on ul. Ludna and the stores on ul. Stawki (tinned meat and sugar) and in the mint (PWPW) on ul. Miodowa.[89]

As soon as the civilian authorities started to function the problem of feeding the civilian population was one of the first to be dealt with. In Śródmieście it was announced that the Delegatura would be opening soup kitchens in the district. At that time there were already two functioning, feeding about one thousand people daily, mainly fire victims.[90] In order to help people having difficulties feeding themselves each house was called on to supply a list within the next twenty-four hours showing what stores each resident had. The inhabitants were to be broken down into the following categories: those having enough for four weeks, for two to four weeks, for one to two weeks, for less. At the same time it was announced that bread was going to be rationed.[91]

There was also another instruction asking House Commanders to register all stores in their properties and to check with tenants how large their stocks were. Lists were to be made of people who had no stores and who were not being helped, and of those who were being helped but for whom that help might cease at any moment.[92]

Instructions, however, were far from enough to solve the problem of the shortage of food. Many people had their own stores and means of feeding themselves but thousands more, especially the homeless, did not have such facilities. These people had to rely on the help given to them and the system of soup kitchens which was developed during the Uprising. The system which evolved was based on a network of kitchens providing meals, including private, community, and RGO kitchens as well as ones specially set up by the Delegatura. There were also separate childrens' kitchens.

At the outbreak of the Uprising private soup kitchens were spontaneously started in various blocks and houses to feed the homeless and soldiers. Mrs Polak, an inhabitant of ul. Senatorska, organised one for soldiers and for refugees coming in from Wola. At the beginning most of the food came from her own supplies and later on from her neighbours.[93] On ul. Hoża 28 the wife of the manager of the Department of Social Care in Region IV ran a kitchen from RGO stores and those brought in by other inhabitants.[94] In the Old Town the Capuchin Fathers ran kitchens from their own stores.[95] Maria Müllerowa opened one in Żoliborz, where she fed refugees, single mothers and people who did not have their own stores, until it was destroyed by a bomb at the end of August.[96] These are just a few examples of this type of private activity.

As the organisation of Warsaw got under way and the need for soup kitchens increased, the number of Delegatura and RGO kitchens also increased. The figures available on the number of these kitchens and the amount of meals they were issuing are given below. In the Old Town by 11 August the Wydział Pomocy i Opieki nad Ludnością organised by the PPS had started four kitchens for the homeless.[97] The number of meals issued by the RGO soup kitchen on ul. Złota increased as follows:[98]

10.VIII	300 portions of soup
11.VIII	1,500
12.VIII	3,000
13.VIII	3,500
14.VIII	6,000

By the middle of August the main RGO kitchens were reported as supplying nearly 2,000 meals daily of which 700 were for the Army.[99] At the same time private communal kitchens were recorded as having issued the following:

ul. Hoża 9	1,000 dinners daily
ul. Hoża 19	1,000
ul. Krucza 5	100
ul. Krucza 6	50
ul. Wspólna 31	50
ul. Koszykowa 37	200

By 20 August the RGO kitchens on ul. Solec, ul. Polna and ul. Lwowska were each issuing 1,500 dinners daily.[100] At the end of August there were ten RGO kitchens in Powiśle with about 8,000 people using them and 13,000 meals being issued daily.[101]

In the second month of the Uprising as the problems of food became greater more and more kitchens were opened.[102] However, it is interesting to note that by the end of September the number of meals being served at any one time was still 75% of the peak figure. Most kitchens still managed to issue a uniform number of meals. Even after 21 September another thirty-four kitchens had been established. The approximate figures of people using these kitchens in the southern area of Śródmieście were:[103]

4.IX   17,000 people (134 kitchens)
15.IX   13,958   (115)
24.IX   15,000   (102)
27.IX   17,000   (121)
30.IX   20,000

There were at this time about 150,000 people in this part of Śródmieście and therefore it would appear that a very large number were still managing to feed themselves, and that the food problem was under control although the diet was monotonous and lacked nourishment.

By this stage of the Uprising, government food stores contained only sugar and coffee and the food transports, when they came through, were bringing mainly barley, but also wheat, sugar and a little marmalade. By 18 September all stores of food had been exhausted in the public kitchens.[104]

There are no similar figures for Region III, although soup kitchens were in operation there.[105] The RGO kitchens on ul. Poznańska and Śliska had ceased to function on 5 September due to lack of supplies.[106] In Żoliborz in the WSM, in each of the colonies a canteen was organised, where soup was issued in the middle of the day.[107] Kitchens were also organised in Mokotów.[108] The authorities helped the civilian population with their food supplies by distributing provisions from their own stores. The stores were allocated to them by the AK quartermaster.[109] The following is a description of most of these distributions made in Śródmieście during the Uprising. Special attention was paid to children.

On 28 August it was announced that permanent inhabitants of each block or house would receive 200 grammes of sugar and the temporary inhabitants 400 grammes and 50 grammes of butter. Children under eighteen months were to be given powdered milk and 2,000 kilogrammes of honey, which was also for the sick and nursing mothers.[110] By 22 August all children in Region III had received a quarter litre of fruit juice, four eggs and 250 grammes of sugar. Mothers with infants under two years were also given sago and wheat flour, and half a kilogramme of flour for each adult.[111] In the Old

Town eighteen tons of dried potatoes and sugar from the Fuchs store on ul. Miodowa were distributed.[112]

But the greater part of the rations would be sent directly to the kitchens, which received dried beans, groats and flour, as well as fats, dried vegetables, meat when it was available, coffee and sugar.[113] Bread was rationed in most districts of Warsaw at the beginning of the Uprising, but as the battle continued its supply dwindled and the rationing system broke down. Sometimes bread was issued on an exchange basis for flour.[114]

Thus it can be seen the rations of food which were distributed were extremely small and would only feed one person for a few days. As a result it is clear how dependent the inhabitants of Warsaw were on their own stores or the soup kitchens. What then did the people of Warsaw eat for sixty-three days? Obviously it varied from district to district where different products were available, e.g. Mokotów had fruit and vegetables, but in Śródmieście a diet of soups with groats and macaroni had to suffice. In the Old Town the soup kitchens supplied coffee, sugar, and biscuits for breakfast, and for lunch and supper some kind of meal prepared from groats and flour.[115] In the soup kitchen in Region III coffee, bread and marmalade were served for breakfast and hot soup with groats or macaroni as a main meal.[116] In the southern part of Śródmieście the kitchens were issuing coffee and sandwiches or groats for breakfast, for lunch vegetable soup with meat or animal fats, and for supper coffee, sandwiches and dumplings.[117] But all these examples come from documents from the first half of August and the menu was to become much less varied and appetising thereafter.

Another example of insurgent victuals has been given by the owner of two chemists' shops on ul. Marszałkowska, where there were no food stores, and medicine was issued to the staff instead. Amongst his medical supplies the owner had some sugar which was mixed with dried blueberry and raspberry powder to make a kind of jelly, and wheat flour pancakes were fried in medical oils.[118]

By the second half of September all reports described the desperate situation with regard to the supply of food and stated that hunger was posing a real threat to both the city and the battle.[119] The only food which was available in large quantities was barley and many of Warsaw's inhabitants were living on a diet of *plujzupa*, whilst others had already been reduced to eating dogs, cats and pigeons.[120] However, it is questionable how grave the threat of starvation was when so many people were still able to feed themselves from their own supplies and when the stores of food revealed at the capitulation in October are remembered. This is not to say that the population was not undernourished and weakened by inadequate meals. The problem may have been more a question of the failure of people to share their stores, especially with the homeless. Repeatedly it was stressed in official reports that as the government stores were empty the only hope of alleviating the situation was to appeal to the population to open up more kitchens with their own stores.[121]

Clothing

The duties of the Department of Social Care with respect to clothing during the Uprising were mainly connected with finding clothes for the homeless. Clothing which had been requisitioned was available from military stores to be distributed. Appeals were also printed in the press and on posters calling on the town's inhabitants to donate spare clothes and material to the homeless and refugees.[122]

In Śródmieście clothes – sweaters, anoraks, trousers, handkerchiefs, dresses, gloves – and summer material for women and children were distributed.[123] By 4 September one thousand pairs of shoes had been handed out, but these consisted mainly of wooden clogs.[124] A report from the Department of Social Care records the following amounts of clothing as having been distributed by 13 September to 13,500 poor people:[125]

socks, stockings etc.	557 pieces
children's underwear	4,704
ladies' underwear	3,840
men's underwear	65
material	3,836
other pieces of clothing	1,052
wellington boots and galoshes	178
wooden clogs	1,746

There seems, however, in Śródmieście to have been a shortage of men's clothing, warm clothing and shoes.[126] The shortage of warm clothing was already worrying the authorities in view of the approaching winter. On 23 September Jankowski sent the following message to London: 'in view of the incredible destruction we shall not be able to guarantee on our own a minimal essential existence to the tens of thousands of victims ... especially a roof above their heads, warm clothes and underwear.'[127] In the southern part of Śródmieście it was reported a few days later that the WSS patrols had managed to satisfy the region's needs of warm clothing for small children and babies.[128]

The shortage of clothing was, like other shortages during the Uprising, never rectified and as a result many people were unable to change their clothing which aggravated hygiene problems.[129]

Housing

Housing during the Uprising was one of the most difficult problems due to the continual destruction of property and movement of people. It has already been seen how the population of each district was swelled with refugees and people who had lost their homes in the bombing.

At the beginning of the Uprising there was no special organisation to help the homeless. They would move in with relatives, friends, or anyone willing to give them accommodation, or quite simply settle into any free space available.[130] But there were continual complaints about the lack of facilities and the terrible conditions in which people were forced to live.

In Śródmieście there was a Quartering Section in the Department for War Relief. It was their responsibility to provide information on free or partially occupied accommodation which could be allocated.[131] They were helped in their work by other civic agents, e.g. the RGO. By 26 August, the RGO in southern Śródmieście had found accommodation for 2,740 people.[132] But this activity was insufficient and by the middle of August the situation was worsening daily and it was recognised that it needed to be reviewed.[133] The responsibility was then transferred to the Department of Social Care and on 29 August ten mobile Społeczne Komisje Zakwaterowania (Community Quartering Commissions) were established with the task of finding and allocating accommodation.[134] Each Commission consisted of three people whose job it was not only to investigate the general conditions already in existence, but also to arrange harmonious relations between permanent and temporary inhabitants, to find accommodation in cellars and to develop a system of reallocation of people from overcrowded places.[135]

The findings of these commissions were registered at the Department of Social Care.[136] Within the first three days of its work 3,671 free places were registered and 763 people accommodated, and a shelter was also arranged for the homeless.[137] By 12 September another 316 persons had been housed.[138]

In the other districts of Warsaw the problem of finding accommodation was mainly left to each individual or arranged by the House Committees. In the Old Town OPL Commanders were instructed to allocate available living space.[139] In Żoliborz the *Samorząd* arranged for the refugees from Marymont and the area to be accommodated in empty flats.[140] In Mokotów likewise this duty lay with the House and Block Commanders, although the Komenda Mokotów arranged a rendezvous point on ul. Lenartowicza 4 for those who were unable to find accommodation.[141]

Missing persons

The outbreak of the Uprising cut many people off from their homes and families, and in the course of the battle more families were to be split up. As a result Missing Persons Bureaux were organised. To begin with they were arranged by the Polish Red Cross in compliance with the Geneva Convention and the Red Cross statutes. Later the Department of Social Care and the Department of Information set up their own offices.

In the Old Town the Department of Information opened an office to register information about lost persons on ul. Hipoteczna 3. There were other similar offices on ul. Długa 9 and 25, Freta 16, Koźla 7, Piwna 45 and Podwale 27.[142] In Śródmieście the Polish Red Cross organised two information centres supplying news about dead, killed and injured persons on ul. Śniadeckich 11 and ul. Pierackiego 15.[143] The main Red Cross office for the whole of Warsaw was later moved to ul. Kopernika 13, after the bombing of the other localities.[144] On ul. Ks. Skorupki an assembly point for missing persons, mainly children, was set up.[145]

Further offices were opened by the Department of Information on ul. Tamka 36, Chmielna 7 and Złota 59a. Information registered at these points would be posted up in different parts of the town or printed in the press.[146] The following is an example:

Władek, Jurek, Zygmunt, Jasio, Tosiek, Benito, Czarny and Bolek are waiting for news from Ząb, Stefan, Kazik, Kulawy, Lis – Warecka 18, OPL Committee.

Antoś, Jasio, Staś, Władek, and Zdzisław working in Printers DI please report to Warecka 15, OPL Committee.

Wacław Wasilewski informs his wife that he is at Mietek's on ul. Złota.

Janina Malessa seeks information about her sister, Irena, Chmielna 56/44.

Lost Irena Kędzierska – news to ul. Chmielna 31, Hotel 'Royal'.

Alexander Kaniewski, Siewierska 17, news at Widok 9.

Janina and Józef Machalski, Adam Piekarski – news wanted: Widok 9.
Zenon Falkowski seeks information about his wife, Eugene, his mother,
Marianna, and Emil and Helena Hauser, Chmielna 27/11.
Maria and Basia Romantowska, Karolkowa 84. I am well – Gienek.[147]

Offices were also opened by the Department on ul. Krucza 15, Hoża
30 and Poznańska 13.[148] In Żoliborz the *Samorząd* kept a card index of
missing persons.[149] In Mokotów the Komitet Niesienia Pomocy
Uchodźcom on ul. Pilicka 24 also had offices. The Red Cross opened a
bureau as well on ul. Pogonowskiego 12.[150]

At the beginning of the Uprising lists of missing persons would also
be printed in the press, notices were posted up by individuals on
doorways and noticeboards, and announcements were broadcast
over the radio.[151] By 4 September information concerning 1,300
people had been published in the press.[152]

Mother and child care

Child care in insurgent Warsaw was not only extremely difficult but
often hopeless. Children were born in insanitary conditions and their
mothers were very often unable to breastfeed them.[153] There was a
shortage of suitable food and milk in the city for babies and children.
In the press it was continually being stressed how much extra help
was being given to pregnant women, nursing mothers and children
by the authorities. The main form of help came from special food
distributions of powdered milk, milk, sugar, fruit juice, eggs, honey,
sago, wheat flour, marmalade, 'owomaltine', porridge and medicaments.[154] Later on condensed milk was distributed from Soviet
drops.[155]

Appeals were frequently published in the newspapers asking
people to hand over stores of condensed milk and milk generally for
newborn babies, who were dying.[156] On 29 August an appeal was sent
to the Polish government in London to send food for the children in
drops.[157]

The WSS organised a special children's centre on ul. Ks. Skorupki
12, where homeless and lost children were cared for, and where
parents could come to find missing infants. Food for them was also
distributed from this centre. On ul. Zielna 11 there was a baby care
centre, where food was specially prepared and taken to homes where
there were babies. A day centre was started on ul. Piusa 58/60
organised by girl scouts. After 3 September, however, it ceased to
function as parents were too reluctant to let the children out of their
homes, due to the fighting and bombing. On ul. Pogonowskiego there

was another centre for children and the aged.[158] The inhabitants of Warsaw were also called upon to arrange special baths for babies in each block.[159]

In Mokotów the Komitet Niesienia Pomocy Uchodźcom organised a milk supply service for children. The milk was obtained from a cow kept in a cellar.[160] The *Samorządy* in Żoliborz also tried to arrange special medical care for children and extra food for them. The allotments in the district enabled the children to be supplied with high vitamin food.[161]

All this help and effort in the long run had little effect as it could not stop the high mortality rate amongst small children who died from dysentery and lack of milk.[162]

The Health Service and sanitation

No detailed description will be made here of the Health Service arrangements in insurgent Warsaw, as this subject and its organisation in each district has been discussed in the preceding chapters. The task of the authorities during the Uprising to maintain a good level of hygiene was extremely important in order to avert the outbreak of any epidemics and also to create as healthy living conditions as possible in the specific conditions existing in the town.

The organisation of public hygiene in Warsaw was based on a series of instructions. These instructions laid down the following regulations: houses had to be cleaned daily with special attention being paid to the cleanliness of staircases and passages; pavements and streets (up to the middle of the road in front of each house) had to be swept and sprinkled with water daily; rubbish and the remains of food had to be burnt and buried; the passages had to be washed with a lime liquid and rubbish bins emptied and sprayed with lime chloride daily. As there were usually large numbers of people crowded together in the cellars and shelters it was imperative that strict hygiene was maintained. No form of ablution was permitted in the cellars unless the nearest facilities were too far away. People were instructed to take special care of their own personal hygiene, wash their hands often and be on the alert for lice.[163] In Żoliborz they were told also to drop the habit of shaking hands as it spread diseases.[164]

Strict instructions were issued concerning the use of water. All drinking water had to be boiled and people were warned not to drink water from wells not under the control of the insurgent authorities. All food had to be cooked and fruit and vegetables carefully washed. In every house boiled water had to be held in clean containers for persons passing through who needed a drink. It was the duty of each individual to report persons suffering from infectious and venereal diseases, injured or in need of medical care, and children suffering from diarrhoea. Regular inoculations especially against typhoid and dysentery were to be continued.[165] Further instructions were issued concerning the burial of the dead. All corpses had to be buried quickly and deeply and where possible in a coffin. The place of burial and details of the dead person had to be registered with the House or Block Commander.[166] Extra lavatories had to be built and disinfected daily.[167]

It was the overall responsibility of the House Commanders to see that these instructions were carried out.[168] At the end of August Sanitary Commissions were also created in Śródmieście. Their task was to supervise the cleanliness of courtyards, stairs, pavements, streets, public lavatories, rubbish disposal, to inspect the cleanliness of empty properties, to form a watchdog service for infectious diseases and epidemics and to oversee the burying of the dead. Each commission consisted of three persons, usually led by a doctor.[169]

These various instructions, however, were often totally impractical and could never be fully carried out due to the shortage or complete lack of water, detergents, disinfectants, and soap.[170]

It is not easy to judge how effective the authorities were in coping with the problem of sanitation in insurgent Warsaw. It would appear, however, that, bearing in mind the difficult and specific situation, public hygiene was kept to a great extent under control. Although by the end of the Uprising, and the end of August in the Old Town, most people had not washed for days and many were lousy, no epidemics had broken out. The fact that large numbers of people were suffering from dysentery was as much a result of inadequate feeding as bad hygiene. No epidemics on any scale were recorded during the Uprising.

Entertainment and schooling

There was little organised public entertainment during the Uprising as conditions were unsuitable. It would appear also that there was no specific attempt made to arrange concerts, films, plays etc. for the civilian population, although more was done for the Army. Productions for the latter were usually also open to civilians.

A BIP report of 22 August on entertainment for the troops made the following observations:

Thirty-five concerts have been staged for soldiers, half of which were arranged by us [i.e. BIP Artistic Department], the rest, especially in the first two weeks, were spontaneously and incidentally arranged.

The concerts took place in AK quarters or soldiers' canteens. The celebration for Soldiers' Day took place in larger facilities with a larger audience.

... in the hospitals about twelve concerts have been performed.

... Music has been arranged at field services four times by us ... No concerts have been arranged for the civilian population yet, but they are being organised.[171]

The Government Delegate from Region I recorded in his August report that the Department of Propaganda for the area had organised concerts by the Warsaw Philharmonic Orchestra for the Army, hospitals and civilians and a very successful travelling puppet theatre for children.[172] Similar activities were also taking place in the rest of Śródmieście.[173]

Polish artists formed special travelling groups to entertain both soldier and civilian. They included such well known names as Jan Ciecierski (actor), Jan Ekier (musician), Mira Zimińska (singer) and Mieczysław Fogg (singer).[174] All these artists had to obtain official permission to perform, and anyone who had performed during the occupation for the Germans was denied such permission.[175]

In the insurgent press a few articles can be found commenting on entertainment arranged. The following are two examples:

On Friday a concert was performed by well known artists. The programme contained music banned by the Germans.

It was a strange experience. Like a dream, as if it had not happened. A garden, beans climbing up the fence, vegetables around the base. The blocks around are scarred by shrapnel. The history of 1939 and 1944 is written on the walls. There is a piano on the balcony of the ground floor flat. The entertainers stand around it. The excellent group is made up from inhabitants of Mokotów, from fire victims, from people who were caught in the area by the outbreak of the Uprising. Here is part of an orchestra, a very good singer, a specialist club entertainer, a violinist ... and a superb compère. That was the stage but the audience – soldiers in grey dungarees predominate, there are groups of civilians practically indistinguishable from the soldiers ... and of course there are children ...[176]

In Mokotów on 20 August a call went out to all musicians, dancers and actors to come forward and help by using their talents.[177]

On 15 August special arrangements were made by artists in the city to celebrate Soldiers' Day.[178] On 3 September a concert was held to commemorate the fifth anniversary of the outbreak of the war. It was opened by a short talk from a chaplain followed by another from a unit commander. Afterwards the concert started and Chopin's 'Polonaise in F Minor' and 'Revolutionary Studies' were played, poems recited and then the soldiers sang their own songs.[179] Often entertainment would be arranged by the Block and House Commanders as part of their effort to keep up morale. This usually involved some form of community singing.[180] A special newsreel film was made during the Uprising of the battle and this was screened several times in August at the Palladium Cinema on ul. Złota.[181]

Thus entertainment for the civilian population, although it was recognised that it was important as a morale raiser, was not organised on a large scale by the authorities.

There was no schooling during the Uprising as the school holidays were still in progress. However, it seems improbable that schooling could have functioned effectively at this time due both to the difficult insurgent conditions and to the fact that many pupils and their school teachers were directly involved in the fight.

The administration of justice

Before the outbreak of the Uprising plans had been made for Sądy Wojenne (War Courts) to function during an uprising. However, due to the fact that the AK was not granted combatant rights until 30 August, by which time it was no longer feasible to organise the courts, the Wojskowe Sądy Specjalne (WSS) continued to function.[182] The WSS were a continuation of the clandestine judicial system which had already been active during the occupation.

At the beginning of the Uprising General 'Monter' asked the head of the WSS for the district of Warsaw, Witold Majewski, to organise a court, which became the WSS Śródmieście North. At the same time spontaneously and on the initiative of local commanders similar courts were established in other districts on the basis of a Decree of General Sikorski of 1 January 1942.[183]

In Śródmieście a Komisja Sądowa (sometimes called Komisja Sądząca – Judicial Commission) was also established. It was a kind of 'people's tribunal' governed by no written law.[184] It was organised by the judge, Tadeusz Semadeni.[185] The commission dealt almost exclusively with the Gestapo, confidants, spies and *Volksdeutsch*.[186] This commission, however, was only active until the middle of August as in practice it proved difficult to operate. Thereafter it was absorbed into the WSS system.[187] A commission under the same name was also functioning in Żoliborz, but it dealt with smaller matters, e.g. looting and shirking work.[188]

On 16 August a Judicial Service was established with Władysław Sieroszewski at its head.[189] The first task of the service during the Uprising was to standardise the legal basis of the jurisdiction, and set up courts as far as possible in areas controlled by the AK. This was necessary to frustrate any attempts by the police or gendarmes to establish illegal courts.[190] WSS courts were either created, therefore, or their existence attested in seven districts of Warsaw: Śródmieście North and South, the Old Town, Powiśle, Żoliborz, Mokotów and Czerniaków.[191]

In the middle of August a Sąd Specjalny Okręgu Warszawskiego (Special Court of the District of Warsaw) was established in Śródmieście South by the Government Delegate. Its jurisdiction covered all crimes not covered by military courts and committed after 31 August 1939. The court was empowered to pass the death sentence and impose terms of imprisonment.[192]

During the Uprising the WSS courts were able to function more openly than under the occupation. Judgement no longer had to be passed behind closed doors nor by default, as wherever possible the accused was present. But the practice of there being only two possible sentences, death penalty or not guilty, was confirmed. Sentence could be withheld until normal legal services were introduced, i.e. after the war. The courts could hold people in preventive arrest, although when Warsaw capitulated everyone was released.[193]

The courts during the Uprising dealt mainly with the following types of crime and criminals: treason, Poles working for the Nazis, Gestapo agents, *Volksdeutsch*, Polish policemen during the occupation, 'Granatowy' who had gone beyond the demands of their service in the interest of the occupier, spies, snipers, armed and unarmed theft and robbery etc.[194] Only serious crimes were dealt with, as conditions did not permit smaller and petty crimes to be brought to law.[195]

Records and materials from the Sąd Specjalny Okręgu Warszawskiego are not available for research, but the following are examples of some of the types of civilian cases dealt with by the different courts:[196]

1. 'Execution of sentence. On 7 August 1944, the following persons were sentenced to death by a Field Court ... Szymon Jóźwiak, aged 23, and Wacław Molend, aged 38, for armed robbery of civilians. The sentence will be carried out at 6.00 a.m. today.'

2. 'The Wojskowy Sąd Specjalny Okręgu Warszawskiego has sentenced to death: Zofia Halina Kutyna, Alicja Kamińska, Henryk Kamiński, and Jadwiga Krzyżanowska for collaborating with the enemy during the Uprising, and for stealing property of Polish citizens.

   '. . . Stefan Prościński, Jerzy Grzegorz Kuziw and Henryk Petz, Polish citizens, who entered German service and took part in action against the Polish Uprising.'

3. Sentence of WSS Court of 7 September 1944: death sentence passed on Lubow Jachwicz, who from the end of 1939 until 1 August 1944 was a confidant of the Gestapo and denounced two Polish citizens who were killed.

   Zofia Jabłońska for collaboration with the Gestapo and for causing the arrest of a Polish officer in hiding (sentence passed 11 September 1944).

4. Case of Kordian R. He was arrested by the Gestapo during the occupation and in order to save his own life agreed to collaborate with them and work as a code breaker against the Polish Underground. The Polish counter espionage discovered this. At the beginning of the Uprising he was caught on pl. Zbawiciela crossing to the Polish side from the German side. His explanation was that he had only made a pretence at working for the Gestapo and had betrayed no one. However, he was not able to put forward a convincing enough case and was sentenced to death.

5. Case of the prostitutes from Hotel Japoński. Four young girls working as secret prostitutes were caught at the outbreak of the Uprising in the Hotel Japoński in the company of German soldiers. The soldiers started to shoot from the hotel windows. The girls, instead of escaping, 'stayed with them, cooked for them and handed them ammunition' (according to witnesses). After a couple of days the soldiers surrendered and the girls were tried. Goods were also found on them which were probably stolen. The prosecutor in an attempt to be fair recommended that the case be transferred to the Komisja Sądząca and that the girls be sentenced for infamy and have their heads shaven. The court, however, found them guilty of having collaborated with the enemy during the Uprising and of stealing property of Polish citizens. They were sentenced to death.

6. Death sentences passed on 25, 26, and 28 April 1944: Franciszek Słomiński, Adolf Kitzman, Henryk Marks, Leotij Korec,

Zbigniew Kordyłowski, Aleksander Krakowski, and Roman Srokczyński. Polish citizens who entered the SA or SD or became German police or gendarmes.

Józef Gradecki, a Polish citizen, who worked for the enemy taking part in extermination actions against the Poles, as a 'Granatowa'.

Zdzisław Wasiak and Marianna Chachólska who worked for the German police, handing people over to the Gestapo.

During the Uprising police activity was carried out by the Państwowy Korpus Bezpieczeństwa (PKB: State Security Corps). They were the only legal police force.[197]

4.3 The press during the Warsaw Uprising

The insurgent newspapers printed during the Uprising are an invaluable source of information on the period, an important reflection of the character and life of insurgent Warsaw, and they played a significant role in the daily lives of the city's inhabitants. During the Uprising about 130 insurgent publications, including dailies, weeklies, magazines, radio communiqués and agency news, were printed.[1] The majority of these papers were published by organs representing the AK, Delegatura Rządu and other political organisations sympathetic to them.[2] Examples of the numbers printed are as follows:[3]

Biuletyn Informacyjny	25–28,000 copies daily
Robotnik (PPS–WRN)	5–10,000
Rzeczpospolita	5–10,000
Walka (Śródmieście)	6,000
Armia Ludowa	3,000
Kurier Stołeczny	2,000
Nowy Świat	1–1,500

It would appear that the more popular papers were *Rzeczpospolita* and *Robotnik* (*Warszawianka* in the Old Town), but as the Uprising continued the newspapers representing the Polish Communists became more sought after.[4]

The greatest number of publications were to be found in Śródmieście, including the Old Town and Powiśle, where about 75% of the known published papers originated.[5] Even in the smallest communities papers were published, as we have seen. In Ochota, in the redoubt on ul. Wawelska, Wilhelm Zwierowicz wrote a paper, and the Gustaw Unit in the same area produced one called *Nowy Dzień*.[6] Likewise in the ZUS house on ul. Niemcewicza Professor Rygiel and his wife typed out a daily paper with radio news.[7]

The editors of the various newspapers and the Department of Propaganda were prepared for the Uprising and in most cases their work was a continuation of the underground clandestine newspapers, which had been printed during the occupation.[8] Papers were printed in increasing numbers right from the outset of the Uprising, although many of them were only of a short duration. There were many new papers, however, which were started either for political reasons or to provide a source of information for areas cut off from the main centre of fighting or where no regular supply of papers came through, e.g. *Nowy Świat, Biuletyn CKL, Barykada Wolności, Komunikat Informacyjny* in Mokotów, *Nowiny Żoliborskie* in Żoliborz, *Czerniaków w Walce*.

All the papers were published and printed in difficult conditions. In Śródmieście the best and most numerous printers were to be found.[9] The largest printers at the time were situated on Marszałkowska 3/5, but were held by the Germans throughout the Uprising.[10] There was a continual shortage of paper, ink, materials and machines.[11] The papers usually had at the most four pages, but by the middle of the Uprising most had restricted their size to two pages.[12] In September the number of copies printed was reduced and by the end of the month most papers had been reduced to one side only, more like posters.[13]

The information for the insurgent papers was obtained from local reporters, official press conferences at the Department of Propaganda of the AK, monitored radio news, Reuters and verbal information obtained on the spot. In Śródmieście there was also a PAT (Polska Agencja Telegraficzna: Polish Telegraph Agency) information centre. In addition to this the Department of Information and Propaganda also produced daily a *Serwis dla Prasy* (Press Service) for the newspapers with information.[14]

The newspapers, however, although the most widespread, were not the only form of information during the Uprising, although other forms were really only available to the inhabitants of Śródmieście. There were two radio stations, Błyskawica (Lightning), the military one, and the civilian Polskie Radio (Polish Radio). They broadcast programmes with local and overseas news as well as BBC programmes and music.[15] It was these stations which sent out appeals to the world for help.[16] Programmes were listened to on radios which had been hidden away during the occupation. The Polish authorities appealed to radio owners to place them where they could be heard by a larger audience as there was such a shortage of wirelesses.[17]

In the Old Town there was another station operative from the middle of August called Warszawa Walczy (Warsaw fights). The following is an example of the type of programme content it presented:[18]

12.00–12.20 Polish communiqué from the Department of Information.

13.40–14.45 Programme in the German language.

14.30–14.35 Communiqué in English.

18.30   Polskie Radio.

19.30–22.00 Programmes for soldiers.

22.30   Programme in English.

At the beginning of August a megaphone service was organised by BIP in Śródmieście and operated by military patrols.[19] The following is an example of the type of programme compiled:

Record – 'Marsz Lotników' (The Airmen's March).

Reading of a Broniewski poem.

'After the retreat from Paris' – a discussion on the general situation.

News from the Warsaw Fronts.

The Barricades of Warsaw.

These programmes lasted about fifteen minutes each.[20]

Another source of information was provided by the BIP patrols, whose task it was to give talks to the population and chat with them, and to find out what their problems and opinions were. Usually at the beginning of such a talk one of the members of the team would give a short lecture on such questions as the current political situation both in domestic and foreign affairs, the course of the war, the situation in Warsaw, general information to help the inhabitants in their daily lives etc. The reaction to these talks varied; often they were received enthusiastically and warmly, sometimes they resulted in very heated discussion and arguments, and sometimes the reception was anything but friendly.[21]

The newspapers were delivered for no charge by a network of couriers and messengers, mainly women and scouts, who often worked under fire and would carry their papers through the sewers to get them into other districts. The papers were usually read in groups, or read out aloud in doorways and cellars, or posted up on notice-boards and passed on from hand to hand.[22] The newspapers seem to have been well distributed especially bearing in mind the difficulties involved. It is possible to find complaints about the excessive number of papers (especially in Śródmieście) being distributed,[23] as well as appeals from other areas where they would be totally non-existent.[24] Antoni Chomicki wrote in his diary on 11 August that people found it strange that there were so many papers all giving the same news.[25] Where there were shortages, however, it was usually because the areas were front line districts or heavy firing was going on, or they were cut off, all of which made it difficult or impossible for the papers to be brought through.[26]

The newspapers published in insurgent Warsaw in August and September of 1944 can be seen as having four distinct roles: they supplied news, they provided the town's inhabitants with a source of information for the organisation of their daily lives, they were used as a form of propaganda, and finally they had the task of maintaining morale in Warsaw.

Throughout the war up to August 1944, the underground newspapers had published news monitored from secret radios and from a network of correspondents and information agencies. In Warsaw at the same time the German newspapers had been generally available, but during the Uprising the only form of printed information was these insurgent publications. There was always a great demand in Warsaw for news, not only because of the five years of occupation but also because the battle had finally cut the city off from the rest of the world as well as dividing it up internally. Thus papers were published separately and independently in the areas of Warsaw where the main papers, e.g. *Biuletyn Informacyjny* and *Rzeczpospolita*, did not get through. Even in parts of Śródmieście these papers did not always arrive and they were supplemented by others e.g. *Wiadomości z Miasta i Wiadomości Radiowe*.[27] In Czerniaków and Sadyba there was discontent caused by the lack of news,[28] but in Czerniaków on 22 August the first issue of a local AK paper, *Czerniaków w Walce*, appeared.[29] In Żoliborz, cut off from the centre of fighting, four papers were quickly started, *Dziennik Radiowy AK*, *Nowiny Żoliborskie*, *Biuletyn PPS*, and *Biuletyn AL*.[30] In Ochota three papers were published.[31]

Insurgent Warsaw was to a great extent organised through these papers, as they were used by the authorities to pass on their instructions to the people. Here could be found announcements about the Health Service, about hygiene, the consumption of electricity, food distribution points, how to strengthen buildings, appeals, warnings, instructions for the election of 'Self-Help Committees', instructions on the use of wells, announcements about church services, concerts, and lost and found columns. These papers fulfilled a role which would today be carried out by radio, television and motorised megaphone announcements. If there had not been such a newspaper service during the Uprising the organisation of the city would have been considerably more complicated.

The propaganda provided by these papers was obviously of great importance when not only the fate of Warsaw was at stake but the future of Poland hung in the balance. Each political group or interest group had some kind of publication during the Uprising, even if its life may have been short lived. The papers representing the Polish government in London and the AK were in the majority, although the groups and parties represented in the PKWN controlled a substantial share.

At the outbreak of the Uprising the newspapers showed a united front towards the battle, and all the papers stressed and applauded the unity of the city, for example:

Although this is not the first time Warsaw has risen the will to fight has never been so widespread before. Warsaw is totally united in hate, in revenge, and in an undivided desire for freedom. The working class and intelligentsia, women, men, young people of all political beliefs and classes are all one people, the people of Warsaw ...[32]

The armed action regardless of who started it and why, has found the support of the widest masses of the Warsaw people and that support is its very strength ...[33]

Throughout the fight there was no real change in this attitude although its emphasis varied and new elements entered the scene. As the days of the Uprising ran into weeks the press became more politically orientated; articles started to appear in the second half of August which betrayed the deep and underlying political divisions and differences.

On 7 August *Robotnik* told its readers how the 'working masses' ought to act at the moment of the crossing of the Soviet Army. They were told to 'assemble around the legal state authorities, namely the government in London,... which represents the most important groups in Poland'. Young workers were to report to Army units of the PPS which were part of the framework of the AK.[34]

After 10 August *Biuletyn Informacyjny* began to attack the Soviets. It accused them of wanting to overthrow all that Poland had striven for during the war and to replace the government by its own organisations. The article added that the Polish people were fighting not only

for peace but also for freedom and quoted Kwapiński, the
Deputy Prime Minister: 'The nation demands that its sovereignty
respected and that no decision as to its fate is made without the
nation's agreement.'[35] Two days later *Biuletyn Informacyjny* printed a
very critical article on the Polish Army fighting alongside the Red
Army. It attacked the method of recruitment and political aims of the
Army. The difference between it and the Polish Army in England,
legally formed by the Polish government under the Allied High
Command, was strongly emphasised. The article concluded by
saying that when the Polish units from Russia arrived the Polish
people would have to behave with great caution towards their political and military attitudes, but 'We will not refuse a brotherly hand
and friendly congenial advice to the kind of soldier who has found
himself in the Berling units either out of necessity or by being tricked
by propaganda . . .[36]

Biuletyn Informacyjny attempted to justify the timing of the outbreak
of the Uprising, its motivation, and value, especially in aiding the
Soviet advance,[37] although *Barykada Wolności* (a left wing Socialist
pro-PKWN paper) was quick to attack the claim, saying that the
Uprising had neither an important influence on the course of the
action on the Eastern Front nor lessened the military strength of the
German Army.[38]

The papers affiliated to the PKWN devoted most of their leading
articles to the aid the Soviet Army was providing and the imminent
crossing of that Army, and to the future of Poland, a future which it
claimed could only be successful if it was in alliance and friendship
with the Soviet Union. *Barykada Wolności* on 22 September published
an article praising Soviet aid, saying that in the previous two weeks
the Soviet Union alone had helped Warsaw not only by drops but by
its fighting action on all fronts. Furthermore it wrote that a wide mass
of people had turned away from the Polish government in Exile
because they 'see quite clearly that reactionary agents are responsible
for the tragedy of Warsaw'.[39] Earlier the *Biuletyn CKL* (of the Central
People's Committee which had by then recognised the PKWN)
argued that the Polish nation knew it could not fight on two fronts
and ought not to. Its geopolitical position was one that such a battle
would be catastrophic and therefore it was an historic necessity to put
an end to the Polish–Russian dispute and to create the best conditions
for a co-operative defence against their common enemy.[40]

Towards the very end of the Uprising the PPR *Głos Warszawy*
reiterated its support for co-operation with all other 'socialist coun-

Soviet Union, and stated that 'Only with con-
co-operation with the Soviet Union might Poland
estern territories and regulate the question of the
ern borders, and secure herself against a new cata-
rman aggression.' [41]

paganda published was conflicting, with each side
y its own action with no real facts or events to back
net result was increasing disbelief in the papers.

papers had to help maintain the morale of the population
in Warsaw as most papers do during war-time. This was as true of the
government controlled papers as for the others. It was achieved not
only by publishing popular patriotic articles but also by a deliberate
falsification of the facts, as well as, towards the end of the Uprising, by
writing less about events in Warsaw.

Two people who were concerned with publishing papers during
the Uprising have commented in their memoirs on this topic. Janina
Dunin-Wąsowiczowa, who worked on an insurgent paper in Żoliborz, recalls that all the papers in the district printed comforting
news, although they 'understood that there was no question of a quick
end to the Uprising'. The fall of the Old Town was portrayed as some
kind of honourable desertion of lost positions and 'we were glad to see
that so many insurgents had got through to Śródmieście'.[42] At the end
of September Janina Dunin-Wąsowiczowa's husband held an interview for *Nowiny Żoliborskie* with Professor Kipa, who had come
through the sewers from Śródmieście. From what the professor said he
obtained the impression that all was well, that Warsaw was holding
out perfectly with enough food, and that the civilian population was
well organised and disciplined. Furthermore the spirit of the Army
was splendid and there was certainty of victory.[43]

Jan Rosner, the editor of the Old Town *Warszawianka*, wrote that
'We obviously wrote a lot to raise spirits especially in the first period of
the Uprising, when it appeared that there were hopeful grounds for
an optimistic estimation of events.' After the fall of the Old Town he
worked on the PPS paper *Robotnik* where he says the task of the
journalist became an increasingly thankless one. It became continually more obvious that they were fighting a losing battle and that the
Varsovians were losing faith in their articles, which talked about the
effect of help for the city and the latest successes of the Uprising. He
believed that by the middle of September the morale of the Uprising
was already broken and because of this the task of the press to sustain
it was almost impossible.[44]

Papers which had been snatched up and were in short supply at the outset of the Uprising were later to be read sceptically or not at all.[45] As early as 4 August General 'Bór' had complained about the *Biuletyn Informacyjny* printing front page articles giving a totally false picture of the situation with the comment: 'You may only write what is factually true, as each reader is quite capable at any time of checking the accuracy of the *Biuletyn Informacyjny* and losing faith in it. I forbid the printing of such rubbish!' He did not complain about only that paper.[46] Janina Misiewicz, a doctor working in the Wolski Hospital, also complained about the *Biuletyn Informacyjny*. On 2 August a copy was brought to the hospital in which it was written that all of Wola was in insurgent hands. They knew, however, that this was not true, and therefore 'the whole of the rest of the paper was treated sceptically'.[47]

BIP reports also highlighted the dissatisfaction amongst the population with the official press:

Sensational headlines of some papers like 'Politechnique is ours', when it is known we have lost it, or 'Poniatowski Bridge in our hands', when tanks drive along al. Sikorskiego and fire on our districts etc., instead of raising morale sooner depress it and undermine at the same time confidence and faith in the accuracy of our propaganda. Public opinion demands that the truth be spoken, even the worst. It is generally felt, 'there is no retreat, therefore, we want to know what our plight is, we are not children who listen to fairy tales'.[48]

Other reports claimed that the people were embittered by information in the press about Allied help, which they could not see,[49] and that they were generally tired of the papers and critical of them and their cheap appeals.[50] Furthermore they were critical of the aggressive attitude of the government papers to the Soviet Union, maintaining that such articles should be consistent with the foreign policy of the Polish government.[51] By the end of August there were complaints that faith in the official press and information was lacking, and by the end of September the problem was summarised as follows: 'The efforts of the official propaganda having as its aim the maintaining of morale by serving certain news with a bias is not finding a suitable response amongst the population, which is tired by the drawn out Uprising and believes only in facts.'[52]

The reaction was the same in each district of insurgent Warsaw, and happened more or less simultaneously, although more quickly in the Old Town. A young girl who hawked newspapers there has written that by the second half of August, although the papers were still grabbed at, only the radio news was read. Grażyna Dąbrowska, a student liaison girl for the Peasant Battalions (B.Ch., Bataliony Chłopskie), recalls how the people had increasingly less desire to read the papers, which they considered 'skimpy' and unreliable.[53] A reader from Śródmieście was also complaining by the middle of August that the papers were short of external information, and that they contained 'a lot of propaganda, many phrases and words but little concrete information'.[54] In Mokotów Jadwiga Krawczyńska, a journalist, complained likewise that the local BIP paper, *Komunikat Informacyjny*, 'had too many mistakes . . . In comparison to the painful reality, which everyone could see, any kind of attempt at an optimistic falsification caused illusive hope and had quite the opposite result to that intended.' She also claims that the people read less and less, not wanting to read about hope and help when they themselves knew what was happening.[55] Another reader in Mokotów recalls how the papers provided them with no consolation for their plight.[56]

One of the results of this was that the left wing papers supporting the PKWN became increasingly popular and more people started to read them instead of the papers supporting the Polish government in London. The situation at the beginning of the Uprising had been very different.[57]

4.4 Religion

The feeling of despair and desolation has always led man to seek consolation and find reason for hope. This may be manifested in various ways. Poland, whose main religion was Roman Catholicism, turned to her religion and Church for consolation. During the terror and difficulties of the occupation Catholicism was very strong, prayer often being the only form of relief and support.[1] During the Uprising this process continued. The Church was very active and the people's faith was a crucial factor in maintaining morale.

On 11 August 1944, General 'Monter' in his 14th Order gave instructions as to how he considered morning and evening prayers should be taken and told his soldiers to go to mass, communion, and confession as often as possible. Furthermore on 22 August he issued another order as to how the Holy Day (26 August) of the 'Black Virgin of Częstochowa' should be celebrated.[2] In the Old Town on 4 August, one of the first instructions issued was for the civilian population to remember fallen soldiers in their prayers and to pray for the Polish victory.[3]

Normal services were held in churches whenever possible. When this was no longer feasible services were held in houses or cellars.[4] Sometimes they were held in cinemas.[5] At the end of August a special mass was arranged in the cinema 'Uciecha' for the 'Black Virgin of Częstochowa's Holy Day', and the order of service included mass, a sermon, confession, a talk by a representative from the Delegatura Rządu and the singing of the Polish patriotic hymn, 'Boże coś Polskę'.[6]

The following list shows how many masses were organised daily in the middle of August in Śródmieście North:[7]

Nowy Świat 37	daily at 08.00	Sunday 10.00
Czackiego 19	08.00	08.00
Chmielna 14	08.00	10.00
Królewska 35	08.00	08.00
Mazowiecka 7	07.00	10.00
Warecka 11	07.30	07.30 and 09.00
Górskiego 3	07.00	08.00

In all the memoirs and reports written about the Uprising it is rare not to find some recollection of the religious fervour in insurgent Warsaw. In the cellars and shelters people would pray all day long, in courtyards and shelters if there were not already small altars new ones would be built.[8] One memoir recalls: 'There were field altars all the way down Marszałkowska, where, regardless of bombing and air attacks, a chaplain would take a service every day.'[9]

Special chapels were built.[10] Collective prayers would be arranged in the morning and in the evening, and public services held in the courtyards.[11] The numbers attending these services increased daily.[12] One report at the end of August comments on the religious strength of the community and also notes 'appearances of religious and mystic exaltation'.[13] Adam Bień, the Government Delegate's Deputy, has recalled how he

saw endless human suffering, suffering devoid of any hope. I watched the Dantean defence of it, which took place in the cellars packed out with the people of Warsaw. I saw a crowd of people gathered in a large gloomy room in the cellars, kneeling on the ground and praying aloud to a black cross hanging on the wall.[14]

Religion and faith, as well as providing relief, were also part of an organised action in insurgent Warsaw to help the population and maintain morale. Most of the services are recalled as having kept up people's spirits and raised morale,[15] but some witnesses to such scenes also claimed that the singing and praying increased the feeling of depression and despair.[16] But for many undoubtedly it was their religion that kept them going during the Uprising.[17]

Only two recollections have been found of what priests told their congregations in sermons to help lift morale and what they considered fitting advice during the Uprising. An elderly lady, Zofia z Grabskich Kirkor-Kiedroniowa, notes in her diary how the priest told them only to think of Poland, their Motherland, and not of themselves.[18] A young scout, however, remembers with foreboding how the priest warned them to 'trust and believe in the care of the Virgin Mary, because if she were to desert us, if the Uprising were to collapse, we would have no Holy Mother but a wicked stepmother'.[19]

It is also known that during the Uprising special prayers were said and written, but few have been recorded. The following is one that has:

Our Father which art in heaven, have mercy on us. O Lord, have mercy on our sons fighting for Poland and on our brothers dying from bombs and shrapnel. O Lord, who has given the smallest bird its nest and the peace of the sky above its head, save our homes from being destroyed and our walls from crumbling. Turn thine anger away from us as we have already suffered so much. We beg Thee, O Lord, to help Warsaw. We beg Thee, O Lord, to deliver a speedy end to the war and grant a free and independent Poland. O Lord, Thou who hast commanded us to love our enemies, grant that peace and justice and Thy Divine law may rule in the world, and those whom Thou dost early call to Thy Kingdom, grant them an early death and eternal peace, and ensure that through their blood shed and innocent sacrifice, the White and Red Polish banner may shine with fresh glory.[20]

Part of another prayer written during the Uprising has also been remembered and recorded:

> From bombs and fighter planes – save us, O Lord,
> From tanks and 'Goliaths' – save us, O Lord.
> From bullets and grenades – save us, O Lord,
> From mine throwers – save us, O Lord,
> From fires and being burnt alive – save us, O Lord,
> From being shot – save us, O Lord,
> From being buried alive – save us, O Lord ...[21]

Throughout the Uprising the Church played an important role in all spheres of communal activity as well as taking services and hearing confession. Priests, monks and nuns opened the doors of their cloisters to refugees and the homeless, who were fed and cared for by them. They organised hospitals, carried out nursing duties and generally helped to provide a medical service. The nuns helped look after children, and collected food and clothing for the homeless. A few examples may be cited. The Capuchins in the Old Town sheltered and fed the homeless, and provided them with medical care.[22] The nuns of the Ursuline Order in Powiśle likewise housed the homeless, feeding and clothing them. They also started a laundry and ran a hospital and RGO kitchen and cared for children.[23] In Mokotów the Sisters of the Order of St Elisabeth helped in the hospitals[24] as did the Sisters of the Order of the Resurrection in Żoliborz,[25] and in Śródmieście the Franciscans.[26]

Thus the religious life of Warsaw continued with great fervour during the Uprising. The strength and importance of religion and the Church was manifested openly and helped to create and maintain a propitious morale during the battle.

Conclusion

It is clear that during the Uprising a distinct pattern of social behaviour emerged. There were variations from district to district, but its overall development was the same. The outbreak of the Uprising was greeted with enthusiasm by everyone. This enthusiasm resulted in the spontaneous, voluntary and united co-operation of the whole community in the insurgent cause. It was this warm reaction which was probably decisive in enabling the fight to continue after the initial failure of the insurgents to expel the Germans and take the whole of the city. However, it must be added that such a reaction did not automatically imply an unqualified demonstration of support for the Uprising but rather overwhelming relief at the end of the terror of the occupation, which it was thought to herald.

As the Uprising, which was expected to last only a few days, began to drag on with no visible sign of a conclusion, the initial enthusiasm and euphoria began to cool. By the middle of August it had generally disappeared. The inhabitants of Warsaw had begun to grow accustomed to the conditions of insurgent life. They were busy coping with their day-to-day problems. Morale steadily declined throughout August, reaching a crisis point in the first week of September with the fall of the Old Town and Powiśle.

The crisis was defused by the evacuation arranged by the Polish Red Cross on 8, 9 and 10 September, which gave those civilians who wished to the chance to leave the beleaguered city. This evacuation succeeded in freeing the town of certain elements who had been undermining morale and others who could not cope with the strains and stresses of insurgent life. The fact that only 10% of the civilian population of Śródmieście decided to leave demonstrates that the majority preferred to stay in the capital rather than risk the mercy of the Germans, although this cannot necessarily be taken as approbation of the Uprising.

Immediately after the evacuation there was a strong upsurge in morale mainly caused by the renewal of Soviet activity on the other side of the river. The hope of an imminent liberation of the city thereafter helped to sustain morale although it slowly declined until the third week of September, when it became clear that all attempts to cross the Vistula had been fruitless. As all faith in liberation and help disappeared and the Germans stepped up their attack, morale worsened and continued to do so until the final capitulation on 2 October 1944. But it never seems to have fallen as low as it did during the so-called September Crisis at the beginning of the month. This maintenance of morale seems to have been due, firstly, to the fact that those people still in the city had stayed voluntarily and were therefore psychologically prepared and conditioned for the worst, and, secondly, to the fact that the longer the Uprising lasted the more people learnt to live with it and adapt their lives to it.

However, the inhabitants of Warsaw not abandoning the fight is not synonomous with their support of it. The choice for the citizens of Warsaw was between staying in the city, which although a risk to life at least kept them among their own people in a small piece of 'Free Poland', and leaving the city and crossing to an unknown fate. Neither during the occupation nor during the Uprising had the Germans behaved in a manner which might reduce Polish hostility towards them. The German treatment of the Poles during the Uprising resulted in a rejection of all their calls on civilians to leave the city, and united rather than drove a wedge between the population and the insurgents. This in turn prolonged the rising. Many political opponents of the Polish government, and it has been seen that they were not in short supply, and groups of people who might have left Warsaw to avoid the fight did not. If a large group of civilians had left the whole Uprising would have taken on a very different character and probably would not have lasted so long. Its leaders would have been deprived of their mass support, which was politically necessary for them. The bond between soldier and civilian was very strong, with at least one member of many families being directly involved in the fight. Soldiers and liaison workers lived at home or often only a few streets away. Therefore most people were voluntarily or involuntarily involved in the battle and its course. A mass exodus of the civilians would have had a destructive effect on the morale of the insurgents.

If it is accepted that the Uprising had not only a military function but also a political one – to take the city and to demonstrate, before the Soviet Army arrived, that the Poles were masters in their own house, by setting up an administration in Warsaw loyal to the Polish government in London; to gain for that administration and Mikołajczyk's government the widest possible popular support; to forestall the establishment of any government by the Polish Communists with the help of the USSR; and to force the hand of Stalin in recognising the Poles loyal to the London government as the rightful leaders of the country – it can only be seen that the results of the fight were totally contrary to such intentions.[1]

It has been explained that most Poles in occupied Poland had a strong faith in their Western Allies. They had been disappointed by the attitude of the British over their eastern frontiers, but believed that Britain would see that right and justice prevailed. Furthermore, the majority were so convinced of the right of their own cause that they could not conceive of being let down. By the end of the Uprising the Varsovians were totally shaken by the failure of their Allies to aid Warsaw and their faith in them was in ruins. There were still a few individuals, however, who clung to the last hope that the tragedy of the Uprising would finally force the Allies to realise what was happening in areas of Poland liberated by the Soviet Army and what the Soviet Union's real intentions were. Others believed that the Americans could still be relied on to help. But the majority were bitterly disappointed and disillusioned by the passivity of the English. The Uprising did not bring support for the Polish government in London. The government's inability to secure any real help for Warsaw and its failure to come to an understanding with the USSR discredited it. This led some people to turn to the Polish Communists for a solution. If this was a transitory step for some, the overall change in attitude by the majority was permanent. With the fall of the Uprising the citizens of Warsaw understood that only with co-operation between Poles and the Soviet Union was any peace for Poland possible and, regardless of the form it would take, it was already a *fait accompli* that Poland's future lay in Stalin's hands.

At the same time the attitude of Stalin towards the Uprising did not do anything to endear the Soviet Union or himself to the Varsovians. Before the outbreak of the Uprising, Warsaw had expected to be liberated by the Russians, although there was apprehension as to the form the liberation might take and what would come in the wake of it. Once the battle for Warsaw had begun, the arrival of the Soviet Army was awaited daily. This expectation grew with desperate impatience as the fight continued. The Varsovians were praying for the crossing of the Soviets 'as if for their saviours'. Fear and apprehension did not diminish the longing with which their arrival was awaited, if only it would put a stop to the terrible toll in human life and the destruction of the city. It is difficult to say whether it was a mistake on the part of Stalin not to help Warsaw on a greater scale. Specific and political reasons can be put forward to explain his action. But it can also be argued that he lost an ideal chance to win the support of a very important section of the Polish nation. Stalin did not show the 'generous gesture' which Mikołajczyk had claimed would 'win the hearts of the Poles for ever'. The bitterness felt by the Poles towards the Soviet Union as a result of the Uprising was very deep and it has left an indelible mark on the city and nation. This virulence was demonstrated publicly again in 1956 and 1968.

Thus an ambivalent attitude arose amongst the Poles of Warsaw. They realised that the future of Poland and its development was dependent upon the co-operation of and good relations with the Soviet Union, whilst at the same time they felt no gratitude to nor respect for that state. It was this ambivalence which convinced sixteen key figures of the Polish Underground to accept an invitation from the Soviets for friendly discussions on 'important matters', which resulted in their arrest and trial in Moscow.[2]

It is difficult to assess these developments as there is no yardstick by which to measure them. No opinion polls were taken. It will never be known if the Polish government in London really lost substantial support, because the ensuing history of Warsaw and Poland was to exclude it as an element in Polish politics. A totally new situation arose. The elections in 1947, which did not represent the same party structure as existed in 1944, cannot be regarded as being a true reflection of the situation, and were not conducted according to the principles of free elections.[3] Only speculation as to the effect of the Uprising on the Polish political scene can be attempted.

The role of the civilian population during the Uprising cannot be underestimated nor can the Uprising be considered a purely military problem. Throughout the course of the Uprising it is possible to see certain circumstances influencing the overall morale of the city and moulding public opinion. There were also other short lived moods which were determined by the immediate situation and only reflected morale for a few hours or at the most a couple of days.

The overall morale of civilian Warsaw seems to have been formed by the following factors:

1. General economic problems, i.e. shortages and availability of food clothing, water and medicine.

2. The activity of the Allies in response to the Uprising, not only with regard to the supply of airborne aid but also at a diplomatic level.
3. Soviet military activity. The failure of the Soviet Army to liberate Warsaw and supply the city with greater material aid was probably the most decisive factor influencing morale.
4. The development of Soviet–Polish negotiations in Moscow led by Mikołajczyk, which proved to be fruitless, and the lack of any viable initiative towards a Russo–Polish understanding.
5. The activity of the Polish government in London in trying to alleviate the situation.
6. The overall organisation of the capital not only as established by the offices of the Delegatura Rządu but also in every individual house and block.
7. The availability of news on the immediate battle in Warsaw and also on the general progress of the war and on the diplomatic scene. Not only the news itself but also its presentation and credibility were important.
8. The behaviour of the Army towards the civilian population.
9. Religion and the activity of the Polish clergy.
   More immediate and particular moods, however, were formed by such circumstances as:
10. The fighting not only in the immediate vicinity, but also in other parts of the city. Insurgent military successes boosted morale. Likewise, when General 'Bór' announced that the Polish partisans were to come to the aid of the beleaguered capital morale was raised.
11. Individuals in the house or block undermining morale.
12. Rumours and gossip.
13. The weather, e.g. when it rained in the Old Town spirits were raised as it was hoped that rain would dampen the fires.

It has been seen throughout the course of this study how it was possible to divide the civilian population of Warsaw up into three groups, although the dangers inherent in such a clear cut division must be appreciated. The first group was made up of people who remained active throughout the battle and did not allow themselves to succumb to the strains and stresses of insurgent life. They even joined in the fight, helped keep up the spirits of their fellow inhabitants and participated in the general organisation of the community, whilst maintaining or demonstrating a favourable attitude towards the Uprising and the Polish authorities. The second group was composed of people, mainly refugees, fire and bomb victims who spent the majority of their time sitting in the cellars or shelters, the so-called 'shelter dwellers' who barely saw the light of day. Nothing could induce them to go out, not even for their own good. Many of them were suffering from shock or were ill, most had lost all they possessed, and others simply did not have the stamina to withstand the demands of insurgent life. These people were nearly always considered to be dangerous centres of ferment and dissent, as well as being most vulnerable to the propaganda of the Left. This was all the more reason why right from the outset when individuals were cut off from their homes by the outbreak of the Uprising, it was acknowledged by the Polish authorities in Warsaw how imperative it was to feed, clothe and house them, so as not to allow centres of opposition to form amongst them. The third group, the smallest of the three, consisted of people who were hostile to the Uprising or people who felt no affiliation either way and were only interested in surviving and even gaining as much as possible from the misfortune of others.

Whilst not underestimating the suffering borne and the stupendous endurance displayed by the inhabitants of the insurgent city, Warsaw was a city of contrasts. Alongside superhuman sacrifice and selfless-ness, there was selfishness and shirking; where many gave of every-thing they possessed, others hoarded and capitalised; unprecedented communal solidarity was marred by intrigue and betrayal; whilst some people treated the insurgents as faultless heroes others regarded them as the instigators of their suffering and the murderers of their families and children.

The virtual annihilation of Warsaw as a result of the battle and ensuing systematic destruction by the Germans, as well as the heavy loss in human life – all to no avail – had two significant effects on post-war Warsaw and Poland. Firstly, the Varsovians returned to the city to live in the rubble and cellars and started to rebuild their capital, often with their own bare hands. This demonstrated their determi-nation to show that Hitler had not succeeded in his aim to destroy Warsaw and Polish culture. This action also established Warsaw once again as the real and traditional capital of Poland. Secondly, the Poles seem thereafter to have abandoned 'their attitude of insisting on everything or nothing and shared a surprising spirit of compromise'.[4] In other words they had ceased to be advocates of 'romantic revolu-tion' and, as happened after the nineteenth-century insurrections, reverted to a so-called 'neo-positive' attitude again. The 1944 Warsaw Uprising had painfully demonstrated the tragedy of such a hopeless battle and injected a weariness into the nation of risking or provoking a repetition. Even as recently as 1976 an eminent Pole, working for the Workers' Defence Committee established after the troubles in Poland on 25 June 1976, remarked: 'We are always afraid of one thing. We do not want a Czechoslovakia on our soil. It would be real war ... I've seen Warsaw levelled once in my lifetime and that's enough.'[5] The events of 1980 in Poland, characterised by a spirit of realism and compromise, are further evidence of this.

Notes

The following abbreviations are used in the notes. For those not listed here, see also the bibliography.
Where no source is given in the notes, documents are in private possession.

ADR – Akta Delegatury Rządu
Arch. Hist. Med. – Archiwum Historii Medycyny
AWIH – Archiwum Wojskowego Instytutu Historii
DOT – Documenta Occupationis Teutonicae
Dzieje Najnow. – Dzieje Najnowsze
Gaz. Krak. – Gazeta Krakowska
Gaz. Lud. – Gazeta Ludowa
GKBZH – Zbrodnie okupanta hitlerowskiego ..., Główna Komisja Badania Zbrodni Hitlerowskich w Polsce
Król. Apost. – Królowa Apostołów
LCPW – Ludność Cywilna w Powstaniu Warszawskim, vols. I–III
NDP 1914–1939 – Najnowsze Dzieje Polski. Materiały i Studia z okresu 1914–1939
NDP II Wojny – Najnowsze Dzieje Polski. Materiały i Studia z okresu II Wojny Światowej
Pol. Zbroj. – Polska Zbrojna
Prze. Hum. – Przegląd Humanistyczny
Prze. Kul. – Przegląd Kulturalny
Prze. Lek. – Przegląd Lekarski
PSZ – Komisja Historyczna Polskiego Sztabu Głównego w Londynie, *Polskie Siły Zbrojne w Drugiej Wojnie Światowej*
Rocz. Warsz. – Rocznik Warszawski
TP – Tygodnik Powszechny
Tyg. Dem. – Tygodnik Demokratyczny
Tyg. Warsz. – Tygodnik Warszawski
WTK – Wrocławski Tygodnik Katolików
Wojsk. Służ. Info. Społ. – Wojskowa Służba Informacyjno – Społeczna
ZH – Zeszyty Historyczne
Ziem. Pom. – Ziemia Pomorska

Introduction

1. APUST, 3.9.2.8, Radio messages received from John Ward, 24.VIII.44.
2. Borkiewicz, A., *Powstanie Warszawskie 1944*, 3rd edn, Warsaw, 1969;

Kirchmayer, J., *Powstanie Warszawskie*, 4th edn, Warsaw, 1970; Komisja Historyczna Polskiego Sztabu Głównego w Londynie, *Polskie Siły Zbrojne w Drugiej Wojnie Światowej; Armia Krajowa*, vol. III (hereafter cited as *PSZ*), London, 1950.

3. Krannhals, H. von, *Der Warschauer Aufstand 1944*, Frankfurt am Main, 1964; Skarżyński, A., *Polityczne przyczyny powstania warszawskiego*, 3rd edn, Warsaw, 1969; Ciechanowski, J.M., *The Warsaw Rising of 1944*, Cambridge, 1974.
4. Serwański, E., *Życie w powstańczej Warszawie*, Warsaw, 1965; *Ludność Cywilna w Powstaniu Warszawskim*, vols. I, II, and III (hereafter cited as *LCPW*), edited by Prof. C. Madajczyk, Warsaw, 1974.
5. For a full bibliography of works published in Poland up until 1969 see Kiedrzyńska, W., *Powstanie Warszawskie w książce i prasie*, Warsaw, 1972.
6. 'Meldunek BIP, Rejon III (?), Patrol V', 5.IX.44.

1 Warsaw during the Nazi occupation, October 1939–July 1944

1. Once you were beautiful, rich and splendid, now just a pile of rubble remains. Bombed hospitals, burnt out houses, where will the injured shelter?

   Bombs fly down from the sky, there is no bread for the people. We must die not just from bombs but from hunger. When poor Warsaw was left in ruins it was then that poor Warsaw had to give herself up.

   But she defended herself for three weeks, and God will yet avenge your crime. Listen people, God is with us and we shall rebuild Poland from shore to shore.
2. Drozdowski, M.M. and Zahorski, A., *Historia Warszawy*, Warsaw, 1972, p. 366. For a detailed description of the siege of Warsaw see *Cywilna obrona Warszawy we wrześniu 1939*, Warsaw, 1964, and Drozdowski, M.M., *Alarm dla Warszawy*, Warsaw, 1964.
3. Bartoszewski, W., *The Warsaw Death Ring 1939–1945*, Warsaw, 1968, p. 18.
4. Krajewska, B., 'Ludność Warszawy w latach 1939–1945' in *Warszawa lat wojny i okupacji*, vol. III, p. 195.
5. GSHI, A.9.III.2a/31, Report on Warsaw after one year of German occupation.
6. Drozdowski and Zahorski, *Historia Warszawy*, p. 366.
7. Bartoszewski, *Warsaw Death Ring*, p. 18.
8. GSHI, A.9.III.2a/31, Report on Warsaw after one year of German occupation.
9. AMW, Amt des Distrikts Warschau, File no. 5.
10. *Ibid.*; IH PAN, A/152/61, Pawłowicz, H., 'Samorząd Społeczny w okresie okupacji hitlerowskiej', Warsaw, 1974, p. 101.
11. Quoted in *Cywilna obrona Warszawy we wrześniu 1939*, p. 123.
12. Iranek-Osmecki, K., '"Ptaszki", "Zrzutki"', *Kultura* (Paris), no. 1/27,

1950, pp. 133–9; Komisja Historyczna Polskiego Sztabu Głównego w Londynie, *Polskie Siły Zbrojne w Drugiej Wojnie Światowej*, vol. III, London, 1950, pp. 820–1

13. Szarota, T., *Okupowanej Warszawy dzień powszedni*, 2nd edn, Warsaw, 1978, p. 315.
14. Pomian, A., *Jozef Retinger: memoirs of an eminence grise*, Sussex, 1972, p. 162.
15. Szarota, *Okupowanej Warszawy dzień*, pp. 58–67.
16. *Ibid.*
17. *Ibid.*; cf. p. 61.
18. *Ibid.*, p. 480.
19. *Ibid.*, p. 67.
20. *Ibid.*, p. 70.
21. *Ibid.*, p. 75.
22. *Ibid.*, p. 76.
23. Madajczyk, C., *Polityka III Rzeszy w okupowanej Polsce*, vol. I, Warsaw, 1970, p. 238.
24. Drozdowski and Zahorski, *Historia Warszawy* p. 383. On 30 October 1939 Himmler ordered all Jews and certain undesirable sections of the Polish population, to leave Polish territories annexed to Germany and go to the Generalgouvernement.
25. Szarota, *Okupowanej Warszawy dzień*, p. 76.
26. *Ibid.*
27. *Ibid.*, p. 78.
28. Madajczyk, *Polityka III Rzeszy*, vol. II, p. 337.
29. Szarota, *Okupowanej Warszawy dzień*, p. 81.
30. *Ibid.*
31. Bartoszewski, *Warsaw Death Ring*, pp. 358–60.
32. Krajewska, 'Ludność Warszawy' in *Warszawa lat wojny i okupacji*, vol. III, p. 199.
33. Drozdowski, *Alarm dla Warszawy*, p. 11.
34. Szarota, *Okupowanej Warszawy dzień*, p. 82.
35. Madajczyk, *Polityka III Rzeszy*, vol. II, p. 239.
36. Bartoszewski, *Warsaw Death Ring*, pp. 454–60.
37. See pp. 30–2.
38. Drozdowski and Zahorski, *Historia Warszawy*, p. 334.
39. Drozdowski, *Alarm dla Warszawy*, p. 11. These socio-economic groups are used in the original information compiled before 1939.
40. Drozdowski, M.M., 'Skład i struktura społeczna ludności Warszawy międzywojennej' in *Warszawa II Rzeczypospolitej: Studia Warszawskie*, vol. I, Warsaw, 1968, p. 57.
41. *Ibid.*, p. 9.
42. Unless otherwise stated all these percentages are calculated on the basis of table 8 in Drozdowski, 'Skład i struktura ludności Warszawy', p. 42.
43. Hoppe, J., *Wspomnienia, przyczynki, refleksje*, London, 1972, p. 236.
44. Drozdowski, M.M., 'Struktura społeczno-zawodowa ludności

Warszawy w latach 1918–1939', *NDP 1914–1939*, no. 5, 1962, pp. 16 and 46.

45. Kobielski, D., *Warszawa międzywojenna*, Warsaw, 1969, p. 52.
46. Drozdowski, 'Skład i struktura ludności Warszawy', pp. 39–40.
47. *Ibid.*, p. 40.
48. Calculations of the author.
49. Drozdowski, M.M., 'Struktura społeczno-polityczna ludności Mokotowa w latach 1918–1939' in *Dzieje Mokotowa*, ed. J. Kazimierski, Warsaw, 1972, p. 130.
50. *Ibid.*, p. 133.
51. Jacobmeyer, W., *Heimat und Exil*, Hamburg, 1973, p. 30.
52. For a detailed account of German policy towards Poland during the war see Madajczyk, *Polityka III Rzeszy*, vol. I, pp. 64–206.
53. *Ibid.*, pp. 27–71.
54. *Ibid.*, p. 129.
55. AMW, Amt des Distrikts Warschau, File no. 5, p. 2.
56. *Ibid.*, p. 5.
57. Bartoszewski, *Warsaw Death Ring*, p. 16, quoting Nuremberg Document no. 2325.
58. *Dziennik Hansa Franka*, vol. I, Warsaw, 1970, p. 309.
59. Bartoszewski, *Warsaw Death Ring*, p. 15.
60. Madajczyk, *Polityka III Rzeszy*, vol. I, p. 121.
61. AMW, Amt des Distrikts Warschau, File no. 5, p. 10.
62. *Dziennik Hansa Franka*, vol. I, p. 248.
63. IH PAN, 'Raporty Fischera; Zweijahresbericht 26.X.39–1.X.41', p. 106.
64. AMW, Amt des Distrikts Warschau, File no. 5, pp. 3–5.
65. *Ibid.* For a full discussion of the German plans for the future of Warsaw see Sobczak, K., 'Warszawa w planach niemieckich po stłumieniu Powstania' in *NDP II Wojny*, no. 6, 1962, pp. 183–98.
66. AMW, Amt des Distrikts Warschau, File no. 5, p. 21.
67. Drozdowski and Zahorski, *Historia Warszawy*, p. 372.
68. Pomian, *Jozef Retinger*, p. 159. Comparable figures in other Nazi occupied countries are given in table 13.
69. GSHI, A.XII.3/89, Report on Polish community, Ldz.3211/43; Madajczyk, *Polityka III Rzeszy*, vol. I, p. 121; Duraczyński, E., *Wojna i okupacja, wrzesień 1939 – kwiecień 1943*, Warsaw, 1974, p. 49.
70. Bartoszewski, *Warsaw Death Ring*, pp. 348–9.
71. Szarota, *Okupowanej Warszawy dzień*, p. 99.
72. PAN, Srokowski, S., 'Zapiski, wrzesień 1939–sierpień 1944', p. 208.
73. *Głos Warszawy*, no. 93, 1.1.44.
74. Unless otherwise stated all the information in this sector comes from Bartoszewski, *Warsaw Death Ring*, pp. 349–51 and 354–60, and Krajewska, 'Ludność Warszawy' in *Warszawa lat wojny i okupacji*, vol. III, pp. 198–202.
75. Bartoszewski, *Warsaw Death Ring*, p. 29.
76. AZHP, 383/11–4, Krahelska, H., 'Praca Publicystyczna 1943', p. 10.

Table 13. *Comparison of losses in human lives in countries under Nazi occupation*

Country	Losses per 1,000 Inhabitants	Total number of losses
Poland	220	6,028,000
Jugoslavia	108	1,706,000
Greece	70	558,000
Czechoslovakia	25	360,000
Albania	24	28,000
Holland	22	200,000
Luxemburg	17	5,000
France	15	653,000
Belgium	10	88,000
Norway	3	8,600

Source: *Encyklopedia II Wojny Światowej*, Warsaw, 1975, p. xxix.

77. Szarota, *Okupowanej Warszawy dzień*, p. 108.
78. IH PAN, 'Raporty Fischera; Zweijahresbericht', pp. 66–7; Drozdowski, M.M., 'Klasa robotnicza Warszawy' in *Warszawa lat wojny i okupacji 1939–1944*, ed. K. Dunin-Wąsowicz, vol. III, Warsaw, 1973, pp. 245–8.
79. 'Położenie gospodarcze Warszawy. Marzec 1940', Report of the Delegatura Rządu, p. 1.
80. Misztal, S., 'Przemysł Warszawy' in *Warszawa lat wojny i okupacji*, vol. III, p. 306.
81. *Ibid.*, p. 312.
82. *Biuletyn Informacyjny*, 11.X.40.
83. Madajczyk, *Polityka III Rzeszy*, vol. I, p. 576.
84. 'Położenie gospodarcze Warszawy. Marzec 1940', p. 1.
85. It is difficult to establish how large these numbers were. See Krajewska, 'Ludność Warszawy' p. 188.
86. AZHP, Krahelska, 'Praca Publicystyczna', p. 5.
87. Madajczyk, *Polityka III Rzeszy*, vol. II, p. 16. Madajczyk also states that the number employed by industry in Warsaw up until the spring of 1944 was lower than at the height of the depression in 1932. For further discussion see pp. 7–23.
88. Szarota, *Okupowanej Warszawy dzień*, pp. 105–6.
89. *Ibid.*, p. 95; IH PAN, A/152/61, Pawłowicz, 'Samorząd stołeczny', pp. 56 and 59.
90. IH PAN, 'Raporty Fischera', May 1942, p. 107.
91. GSHI, A.9.III.2a/37, Letters from Poland, Ldz.1898/42, 5.v.42; 'Położenie gospodarcze Warszawy. Marzec 1940', pp. 3–4; *Biuletyn Informacyjny*, 30.V.41; *A Worker's Day under German Occupation*, London, 1941, p. 12; Szarota, *Okupowanej Warszawy dzień*, p. 119.

92. *A Worker's Day under German Occupation*, p. 12.
93. *Robotnik*, no. 108, 22.III.43; *Dzień Warszawy*, no. 545, 21.IV.43.
94. Szarota, *Okupowanej Warszawy dzień*, p. 174.
95. *Biuletyn Informacyjny*, no. 156, 7.I.43.
96. 'Sytuacja materialna ludności Warszawy, a działalność Rady Opiekuńczej Miejskiej', Report of Delegatura Rządu, 30.IX.41, p. 4.
97. 'Sytuacja aprowizacyjna Warszawy; wrzesień 1941', Report of the Delegatura Rządu, p. 4.
98. *Ibid.*; cf. Madajczyk, *Polityka III Rzeszy*, vol. II, pp. 65–6.
99. Written memoir entered for competition in *Polityka*, 'Byli wówczas dziećmi', by Ryszard Hładko.
100. Pomian, *Jozef Retinger*, pp. 160–1.
101. 'Sytuacja aprowizacyjna miast', Report of Delegatura Rządu, 30.VIII.41, pp. 2–3; Kroll, B., 'Organizacja polskiej samopomocy społecznej w Warszawie, październik 1939–lipiec 1944', in *Warszawa lat wojny i okupacji*, vol. II, p. 93.
102. Szarota, *Okupowanej Warszawy dzień*, p. 251.
103. GSHI, A.9.III.2a/31, Report on Warsaw after one year of German occupation.
104. AMW, Amt des Distrikts Warschau, File no. 5, p. 5.
105. GSHI, A.9.III.2a/31, Report on Warsaw after one year of German occupation.
106. Szarota, *Okupowanej Warszawy dzień*, pp. 491ff and p. 316.
107. *Biuletyn Informacyjny*, no. 21, 27.V.43.
108. Szarota, *Okupowanej Warszawy dzień*, p. 315.
109. *Ibid.*, p. 317.
110. *Ibid.*, p. 318.
111. IH PAN, 'Raporty Fischera', August and September 1942, p. 158.
112. 'Położenie gospodarcze Warszawy. Marzec 1940', p. 1.
113. IH PAN, A/152/61, Pawłowicz, 'Samorząd stołeczny', p. 101.
114. Szarota, *Okupowanej Warszawy dzień*, p. 321.
115. 'Położenie gospodarcze Warszawy. Marzec 1940', p. 2.
116. Szymczak, K., 'Dni zgrozy i walki o wolność' in *Pamiętniki robotników z czasów okupacji*, Warsaw, 1948, p. 26.
117. *Ibid.*, p. 34.
118. Szarota, *Okupowanej Warszawy dzień*, p. 322.
119. *Biuletyn Informacyjny*, 16.X.41.
120. 'Sytuacja aprowizacyjna Warszawy; wrzesień 1941', p. 3; Szarota, *Okupowanej Warszawy dzień*, pp. 323–33.
121. GSHI, A.9.III.2a/37, Letters from Poland, Ldz.1898/42, 5.V.42.
122. AMW, Dąbrowa-Sierzputowski, J. 'Wspomnienia wojenne Warszawa 1939–1944', p. 47.
123. Madajczyk, *Polityka III Rzeszy*, vol. II, p. 84.
124. Szarota, *Okupowanej Warszawy dzień*, p. 326.
125. Karski, J., *Story of a Secret State*, London, 1945, pp. 205–6.
126. *Polityka* competition, 'Byli wówczas dziećmi', entry by J. Ciecha-

nowicz, p. 2.

127. 'Sytuacja materialna ludności Warszawy, a działalność Rady Opiekuńczej Miejskiej', p. 2.
128. AMW, Dąbrowa-Sierzputowski, 'Wspomnienia wojenne', p. 35.
129. IH PAN, 'Raporty Fischera, Zweijahresbericht', pp. 7–8.
130. 'Sytuacja materialna ludności Warszawy, a działalność Rady Opiekuńczej Miejskiej', p. 2.
131. Szarota, *Okupowanej Warszawy dzień*, pp. 233–4.
132. 'Sytuacja aprowizacyjna Warszawy; wrzesień 1941', p. 1.
133. AMW, Dąbrowa-Sierzputowski, 'Wspomnienia wojenne', pp. 33–4.
134. Sytuacja aprowizacyjna Warszawy; wrzesień 1941', p. 1; Szarota, *Okupowanej Warszawy dzień*, p. 236.
135. 'Sytuacja aprowizacyjna Warszawy; wrzesień 1941', p. 1; cf. IH PAN, A/152/61, Pawłowicz, 'Samorząd stołeczny', p. 151.
136. Madajczyk, *Polityka III Rzeszy*, vol. II, p. 70.
137. PAN, Srokowski, 'Zapiski', p. 148; cf. Madajczyk, *Polityka III Rzeszy*, vol. II, p. 71.
138. Kroll, 'Organizacja polskiej samopomocy społecznej w Warszawie', in *Warszawa lat wojny i okupacji*, vol. II, p. 91.
139. Szarota, *Okupowanej Warszawy dzień*, pp. 245–46.
140. *Biuletyn Informacyjny*, no. 156, 7.I.43.
141. Madajczyk, *Polityka III Rzeszy*, vol. I, p. 598; IH PAN, A/152/61, Pawłowicz, 'Samorząd stołeczny', p. 152.
142. *Biuletyn Informacyjny*, no. 137, 20.VIII.42; Madajczyk, *Polityka III Rzeszy*, vol. I, pp. 598–9.
143. GSHI, A.9.III.2a/37, Letters from Poland, Ldz.1898/42, 5.V.42; Madajczyk, *Polityka III Rzeszy*, vol. II, p. 82.
144. Jastrzębowski, W., *Gospodarka niemiecka w Polsce*, Warsaw, 1946, p. 240.
145. Szarota, *Okupowanej Warszawy dzień*, pp. 278–9.
146. 'Sytuacja materialna ludności Warszawy, a działalność Rady Opiekuńczej Miejskiej', p. 1.
147. *A Worker's Day under German Occupation*, p. 4.
148. 'Sytuacja aprowizacyjna Warszawy; wrzesień 1941', p. 3.
149. Szarota, *Okupowanej Warszawy dzień*, p. 307.
150. Madajczyk, *Polityka III Rzeszy*, vol. II, p. 84.
151. Pomian, *Jozef Retinger*, p. 162.
152. *A Worker's Day under German Occupation*, p. 4.
153. GSHI, A.9.III.2a/37, Letters from Poland, Ldz.1898/42, 5.V.42.
154. *Biuletyn Informacyjny*, no. 197, 21.X.43.
155. *Polityka* competition, 'Byli wówczas dziećmi', entry by J. Ciechanowicz, p. 2.
156. GSHI, A.XII.10/30, Report on medical and sanitary conditions inside occupied Poland, April 1944.
157. IH PAN, A/152/61, Pawłowicz, 'Samorząd stołeczny', pp. 141–2.
158. 'Sytuacja aprowizacyjna miast', pp. 2–3; Kulski, J., *Zarząd Miejski Warszawy 1939–1944*, Warsaw, 1964, p. 124; Madajczyk, *Polityka III*

Rzeszy, vol. II, p. 87; IH PAN, A/152/61, Pawłowicz, 'Samorząd stołeczny', pp. 136, 143, 146.

159. GSHI, A.XII.10/30, Report on medical and sanitary conditions inside occupied Poland.
160. 'Położenie gospodarcze Warszawy. Marzec 1940', p. 1.
161. *Biuletyn Informacyjny*, 9.X.41.
162. GSHI, A.XII.10/30, Report on medical and sanitary conditions inside occupied Poland.
163. 'Zdrowotność ludności Warszawy (1939–IX.41)', Report of Delegatura Rządu, p. 2; *Rzeczpospolita*, 16.XI.41.
164. *Ibid.*; 'Zdrowotność ludności Warszawy', p. 3; IH PAN, 'Raporty Fischera', October and November 1943, p. 376.
165. 'Zdrowotność ludności Warszawy', p. 3.
166. GSHI, A.XII.3/90–2, Information given by Mr K., 20.I.44.
167. *A Worker's Day under German Occupation*, p. 8.
168. Madajczyk, *Polityka III Rzeszy*, vol. II, p. 87.
169. Kroll, 'Organizacja polskiej samopomocy', pp. 96–8, and p. 103.
170. GSHI, A.9.III.2a/31, Report on Warsaw after one year of German occupation; Madajczyk, *Polityka III Rzeszy*, vol. II, p. 104.
171. Galast, S., 'Działalność społeczno charytatywna ks. Władysława Łysika w latach 1939–1945', M.A. Thesis, Lublin, 1972, p. 35.
172. Manteuffel, E., 'Zapiski na temat pracy społecznej w Warszawie podczas okupacji i w latach poprzedzających II wojnę światową', *NDP II Wojny* no. 8, 1964 p. 112.
173. Madajczyk, *Polityka III Rzeszy*, vol. II, pp. 113–15.
174. Kroll, 'Organizacja polskiej samopomocy', p. 124.
175. Szarota, *Okupowanej Warszawy dzień*, pp. 281–2.
176. Kroll, 'Organizacja polskiej samopomocy', p. 124; Ossol., 3319/II, Gawiecki, B., 'Wspomnienia', p. 485.
177. Gawiecki, 'Wspomnienia', p. 487.
178. *Ibid.*
179. AAN, RGO.518, Reports on PKO activity in Warsaw 1944; Szarota, *Okupowanej Warszawy dzień*, pp. 280–1.
180. *Ibid.*, pp. 280–3.
181. 'Sytuacja aprowizacyjna Warszawy; wrzesień 1941', p. 5.
182. *Ibid.*, p. 6.
183. Kroll, 'Organizacja polskiej somopomocy', p. 128.
184. *Biuletyn Informacyjny*, no. 197, 21.X.43.
185. Kroll, 'Organizacja polskiej samopomocy', p. 128.
186. 'Sytuacja materialna ludnosci Warszawy, a działalność ROM', p. 4.
187. Kroll, 'Organizacja polskiej samopomocy', p. 129.
188. Ossol., 3317/II, Gawiecki, 'Wspomnienia', pp. 487–90.
189. 'Sytuacja materialna ludności Warszawy, a działalność ROM', p. 3, and 'Sytuacja aprowizacyjna; wrzesień 1941', pp. 5–7.
190. IH PAN, 'Raporty Fischera. Zweijahresbericht', p. 109.
191. AMW, Amt des Distrikts Warschau, File no. 5, pp. 4–5; Szarota,

Okupowanej Warszawy dzień, pp. 358–9.

192. IH PAN, 'Raporty Fischera. Zweijahresbericht', pp. 110–13; Madajczyk, *Polityka III Rzeszy*, vol. II, pp. 129, 135, 148–9.
193. IH PAN, A/152/61, Pawłowicz, 'Samorząd stołeczny', p. 132.
194. IH PAN, 'Raporty Fischera', January 1942, p. 31 and October and November 1943, p. 376.
195. *Biuletyn Informacyjny*, 1.XI.40 and 13.IX.40.
196. *Ibid.*, no. 197, 21.X.43; Manteuffel, 'Zapiski na temat ...' p. 107.
197. *Ibid.*
198. For further details see Szarota, *Okupowanej Warszawy dzień*, pp. 360–6.
199. *Biuletyn Informacyjny*, 10.V.40.
200. See p. 61.
201. Szarota, *Okupowanej Warszawy dzień*, pp. 365–6.
202. *Ibid.*, pp. 347–52; Kann, M., *Niebo nieznane*, Warsaw, 1968, p. 83.
203. Szarota, *Okupowanej Warszawy dzień*, pp. 425ff and p. 435.
204. Dobroszycki, L., 'Studies of the underground press 1939–1945', *Acta Poloniae Historica*, no. 8, 1962, p. 101.
205. GSHI, PRM.46a/1941/5, Report of emissary Antoni, Ldz.1820/41, April 1941.
206. Madajczyk, *Polityka III Rzeszy*, vol. II, pp. 156 and 160.
207. Sroczyński, K., 'Szpitale warszawskie w okresie okupacji hitlerowskiej', *Prze. Lek.*, no. 1, 1976, p. 115.
208. Madajczyk, *Polityka III Rzeszy*, vol. II, p. 156.
209. See pp. 10–12.
210. Ossol. 3319/II, Gawiecki, 'Wspomnienia', p. 487; Szarota, *Okupowanej Warszawy dzień*, pp. 98–9.
211. Szarota, *Okupowanej Warszawy dzień*, p. 103.
212. *Ibid.*, p. 105.
213. 'Sytuacja aprowizacyjna Warszawy, wrzesień 1941', p. 4.
214. Giełżyński, W., 'Dziennikarski ruch oporu' in *Wspomnienia dziennikarzy z okresu okupacji hitlerowskiej*, ed. E. Rudziński, Warsaw, 1970, pp. 81–2.
215. Bień, A., *Wspomnienia* (1953), pp. 56–7.
216. Dobraczyński, J., *Tylko w jednym życiu*, Warsaw, 1970, p. 201.
217 Blätter, F., *Warschau 1942: Tatsachenbericht eines Motorfahres der zweiten schweizerischen Ärtzenmission 1942 in Polen*, Zurich, 1945, p. 45.
218. Kulski, *Zarząd Miejski Warszawy*, pp. 163–4.
219. GSHI, PRM.46a/1941/23, Delegate's Report, no. 3126/11/43.
220. Szarota, *Okupowanej Warszawy dzień*, p. 111.
221. *Ibid.*, p. 105.
222. Szarota, T., 'Inteligencja warszawska', in *Warszawa lat wojny i okupacji*, vol. III, pp. 268–9.
223. *Ibid.*, pp. 271–2.
224. BN, Rps. syn. IV.6400, Kirkor-Kiedroniowa, Zofia z Grabskich, 'Wspomnienia i notatki pisane w czasie powstania warszawskiego', p. 7; Madajczyk, *Polityka III Rzeszy*, vol. II, p. 27.
225. Cf. Szarota, *Okupowanej Warszawy dzień*, pp. 103–4, 111.

226. GSHI, PRM.46a/1941/23, Delegate's Report, no. 3126/11/43.
227. Szymczak, 'Dni zgrozy i walki o wolność', p. 37.
228. *Biuletyn Informacyjny*, no. 147, 5.XI.42.
229. Szymczak, 'Dni zgrozy i walki o wolność', p. 56.
230. *Biuletyn Informacyjny*, no. 147, 5.XI.42; *A Worker's Day under German Occupation*, p. 11.
231. *Biuletyn Informacyjny*, no. 147, 5.XI.42.
232. Szarota, *Okupowanej Warszawy dzień*, pp. 163–4.
233. Szymczak, 'Dni zgrozy i walki o wolność', pp. 34–40.
234. *Ibid.*, pp. 100–1.
235. GSHI, A.9.III.2a/37, Letters from Poland, Ldz.1898/42, 5.V.42.
236. Szymczak, 'Dni zgrozy i walki o wolność', pp. 39, 57, and 83.
237. Madajczyk, *Polityka III Rzeszy*, vol. II, p. 68.
238. IH PAN, 'Raporty Fischera', May 1942, p. 107.
239. Szymczak, 'Dni zgrozy i walki o wolność', p. 57.
240. *A Worker's Day under German Occupation*, p. 11.
241. GSHI, PRM.46a/1941/23, Special Report 16.I–15.III.43, Ldz.3281/43, and A.XII.3/89, Report on political basis of the community, Ldz.3211/43, May 1943.
242. GSHI, A.XII.3/90–2, Information given by Mr K., 20.I.44.
243. AZHP, Krahelska, 'Praca Publicystyczna', p. 6; Szarota, *Okupowanej Warszawy dzień*, pp. 140–9; Bartoszewski, *Warsaw Death Ring*, p. 77.
244. AZHP, Krahelska, 'Praca Publicystyczna', pp. 5–6.
245. See p. 62.
246. *Dziennik Hansa Franka*, p. 353.
247. GSHI, A.9.III.2a/32, Report from Poland, 1941, and A.XII.3/90–2, Information given by Mr K., 20.I.44.
248. Bartoszewski, *Warsaw Death Ring*, p. 351.
249. Cf. p. 61. A full description of these activities can be found in IH PAN, 'Raporty Fischera', October and November 1942, p. 199, February and March 1943, p. 251, December 1943, p. 381, February and March 1944, p. 417.
250. *Biuletyn Informacyjny*, 30.VIII.40 and 1.XI.40.
251. GSHI, A.9.III.2a/31, Warsaw after one year of German occupation, pp. 9–10; AMW, Dąbrowa-Sierzputowski, 'Wspomnienia wojenne Warszawa', pp. 26, 27, 32.
252. See Bartoszewski, W., 'Organizacja małego sabotażu "Wawer" w Warszawie 1940–1944', *NDP II Wojny*, no. 10, 1966.
253. *Przez walkę do zwycięstwa*, no. 80, 20.V.43.
254. IH PAN, 'Raporty Fischera', March 1942, p. 54.
255. *Ibid.*, December 1942 and January, February and March 1943, pp. 223, 224, 251.
256. *Ibid.*, December 1943 and January 1944, pp. 381–2.
257. Madajczyk, *Polityka III Rzeszy*, vol. II, pp. 247–8.
258. Szarota, *Okupowanej Warszawy dzień*, pp. 612–14.
259. GSHI, PRM.76/1/1942, Report on Poland's internal affairs, March

1942, Ldz.1782/42, and PRM.76/1/1942/14, Report 15.VIII–15.X.1942; AZHP, Krahelska, 'Praca Publicystyczna', pp. 23–7.

260. *Biuletyn Informacyjny*, no. 194, 30.IX.43; cf. also Madajczyk, *Polityka III Rzeszy*, vol. II, pp. 190–1.

261. *Cywilna obrona Warszawy we wrześniu 1939*, p. 18.

262. Polonsky, A., *The Great Powers and the Polish Question 1941–1945*, London, 1976, p. 71. For details see Leslie, R.F., *The History of Poland since 1863*, Cambridge, 1980, pp. 219ff.

263. Polonsky, *Great Powers*, pp. 15–16.

264. Conditions in Nazi occupied Warsaw and some aspects of the problem for the rest of the Generalgouvernement have been dealt with in the preceding sections of this chapter.

265. AZHP, Krahelska, 'Praca Publicystyczna', p. 31.

266. *Ibid.*, pp. 4–5. *Sanacja* in the Polish language refers to a purge or reform of an administration in the sense of being a purification. The *Sanacja* government refers to the system of government of Gen. Piłsudski and his followers after 1926, which was aimed at removing the negative features of the pre-1926 political system.

267. Jacobmeyer, *Heimat und Exil*, pp. 144–5.

268. GSHI, A.9.III.2a/32, Report from Poland, 1941, Report on attitudes towards Gen. Sikorski's government, 3.II.41, and Report from Poland on morale of the community, 1941.

269. *Ibid.*, Report from Poland on morale of the community, 1941; Terej, J., *Na rozstajach dróg*, Wrocław, 1978, pp. 21–3.

270. For a description of these events see Pobóg-Malinowski, W., *Najnowsza historia polityczna Polski*, vol. III, London, 1960, pp. 53–82 and Duraczyński, E., *Wojna i okupacja*, pp. 107–16.

271. GSHI, PRM.46a/1941, Report on a three week stay in Poland, November 1941, no. 2733/11/41, and A.9.III.2a/32, Report from Poland on the morale of the community, 1941; Nowak, *Kurier z Warszawy*, London, 1978, p. 94.

272. GSHI, A.9.III.2a/32, Report from Poland on the morale of the community, 1941; Nowak, *Kurier z Warszawy*, pp. 94–5.

273. GSHI, A.9.III.2a/32, Interview with two foreigners in Stockholm who had been in Warsaw, 12.IX.41.

274. GSHI, PRM.46a/1941/2, Report on a three week stay in Poland, November 1941, no. 2733/11/41.

275. GSHI, A.9.III.2a/32, Report from Poland on the morale of the community, 1941.

276. *Documents on Polish–Soviet Relations 1939–1945*, vol. I, London, 1961, pp. 141–2.

277. *Ibid.*

278. GSHI, PRM.46a/1941/23, Delegate's Report, no. 3126/11/43 and PRM.46/1941/12, Report on situation in Poland, no. 2748/II/41, 1.VIII.44.

279. *Ibid.*

280. Polonsky, *Great Powers*, pp. 90–1.
281. *Ibid.*, p. 20.
282. *Biuletyn Informacyjny*, 26.VI.41; GSHI, PRM.46a/1941/12, Report on situation in Poland, no. 2748/II/41, I.VIII.44.
283. GSHI, *Ibid.*; cf. PRM.46a/1941/23, Delegate's Report, no. 3126/11/43.
284. Ciechanowski, *The Warsaw Rising*, p. 87.
285. *Ibid.*; Mastny, V., *Russia's Road to the Cold War*, New York, 1979, p. 87. Mastny quotes figures of 4,000 members by mid 1942 and a doubling of membership by early 1943.
286. Ciechanowski, *The Warsaw Rising*, pp. 114–15.
287. GSHI, PRM.L.9, Despatch from Poland, Ldz.549/44, 22.V.44; Rzepecki, J., *Wspomnienia i przyczynki historyczne*, Warsaw, 1956, p. 268.
288. Ciechanowski, *The Warsaw Rising*, p. 114
289. AZHP, Krahelska, 'Praca Publicystyczna', pp. 31–2; Ciechanowski, *The Warsaw Rising*, pp. 114–15; Mastny, *Russia's Road to the Cold War*, p. 172.
290. PRO, FO.371/39424 C5334/61/55, 22.IV.44; AZHP, Krahelska, 'Praca Publicystyczna', p. 41.
291. Cf. GSHI, A.XII.3/89, Report on the political basis of the community, May 1943, Ldz.3211/43.
292. *Biuletyn Informacyjny*, no. 193, 23.IX.43.
293. AZHP, Krahelska, 'Praca Publicystyczna', pp. 31–2 and 41.
294. GSHI, A.9.III.2a/32, Report from Poland, 1941.
295. GSHI, A.X.III.3/90, Information of Mr K., 20.I.44. A similar attitude can be found during the Uprising, see p. 155.
296. GSHI, A.XII.1/63, Nowak Report, 21.II.44; Nowak, *Kurier z Warszawy*, pp. 94–5.
297. Polonsky, *Great Powers*, p. 114; Lukas, R.C., *The Strange Allies*, Knoxville, 1978, p. 26.
298. For full details of the Katyn discovery see Zawodny, J.K., *Death in the Forest*, London, 1971.
299. AZHP, Krahelska, 'Praca Publicystyczna', p. 29.
300. PAN, Srokowski, 'Zapiski', p. 237.
301. GSHI, A.XII.3/89, Report on the political basis of the community, May 1943, Ldz.3211/43.
302. Polonsky, *Great Powers*, p. 26.
303. PAN, Srokowski, 'Zapiski', p. 245.
304. Verbal information.
305. PRO, FO.371/39426 C7860/61/55, 29.V.44.
306. Polonsky, *Great Powers*, pp. 28–9.
307. Lukas, *The Strange Allies*, pp. 46–7; Ciechanowski, *The Warsaw Rising*, pp. 13–17.
308. Ciechanowski, *The Warsaw Rising*, pp. 52–4.
309. PRO, FO.371/39500 C13218/1077/55, 21.IX.44.
310. APUST, Teczka 15 pz. 8, 'Sytuacja w Polsce', 23.III.43; Zaremba, Z., *Wojna i konspiracja*, London, 1957, p. 230; Polonsky, *Great Powers*,

pp. 163–8.

311. PRO, FO.371/39424 C5224/61/55, 22.IV.44; GSHI, A.XII.3/90–2, Information of Mr K., 20.I.44.

312. GSHI, *ibid.*

313. GSHI, PRK.L.9, Despatch from Poland, Ldz.549/GNW/44, 22.V.44. Churchill in his speech made reference to the Polish border question in the following manner: 'I may remind the House that we ourselves have never in the past guaranteed, on behalf of His Majesty's Government, any particular frontier line to Poland. We did not approve of the Polish occupation of Wilno in 1920. The British view in 1919 stands expressed in the so-called Curzon line which attempted to deal, at any rate partially, with the problem … I cannot feel that the Russian demand for a reassurance about her Western frontiers goes beyond the limits of that which is reasonable or just. Marshal Stalin and I also spoke and agreed upon the need for Poland to obtain compensation at the expense of Germany both in the North and West.' Jędrzejewicz, W., *Poland in the British Parliament*, vol. II, New York, 1959, p. 341.

314. GSHI, A.9.III.4/24, Reaction to speech of Churchill, 362/1P nr 10/IP/44, 18.IV.44.

315. *Ibid.*

316. PRO, FO.371/39424 C5334/61/55, 22.IV.44; Nowak, *Kurier z Warszawy*, p. 311. Nowak also states that as Poland was fed selective information by the BBC, Polish society was not well acquainted with the situation, and so idealised the Allies and overestimated the importance of Poland to them; p. 149.

317. GSHI, PRM.L.5., Despatch from Poland, Ldz.K.3670/44, 29.VI.44 and A.XII.3/89, Ldz.3281/43; cf. also IH PAN, 'Raporty Fischera', August and September 1943, p. 326, December 1943 and January 1944, p. 382, February and March 1944, p. 417, April and May 1944, p. 445.

318. GSHI, PRM.76/1/1942.7, Report on situation in Poland, 23.III.43.

319. *Ibid.*, Report on internal Polish affairs, Ldz.1782/42.

320. AZHP, Krahelska, 'Praca Publicystyczna', p. 6.

321. GSHI, A.XII.3/89, Despatch from Poland, Ldz.2574/43, 26.V.43.

322. PRO, FO.371/39500 C13218/1077/55, 21.IX.44.

323. Valcini, A., *Golgota Warszawy* (first published 1945), Warsaw, 1973, pp. 317–18.

2 The outbreak of the Uprising and the implications of the first days

2.1 The Polish Underground State

1. *PSZ*, p. 50.

2. Ciechanowski, *The Warsaw Rising*, p. 69; See also *Armia Krajowa w Dokumentach*, vol. I, London, 1970, pp. 1–4.

3. *PSZ*, p. 50.

4. As quoted in Ciechanowski, *The Warsaw Rising*, p. 78. For full text see *Armia Krajowa w Dokumentach*, vol. I, pp. 31–7.
5. *PSZ*, pp. 50–1; Korboński, S., 'Polskie państwo podziemne z lat 1939–45', *Orzeł Biały*, July–August 1969, p. 13.
6. Korboński, *ibid.*, p. 13. Poland was divided into six districts: Warsaw, Kraków, Poznań, Toruń, Białystok, and Lwów, which were further sub-divided into *województwa* (voivodeships) and *powiaty* (districts).
7. *PSZ*, p. 51.
8. *Ibid.* See also *Armia Krajowa w Dokumentach*, vol. I, pp. 10–21.
9. *Armia Krajowa w Dokumentach*, vol. II, London, 1973, p. 199.
10. *Ibid.*, vol. I, p. 11.
11. *PSZ*, pp. 52–3.
12. Garliński, J., 'Polskie państwo podziemne 1939–45', *ZH*, no. 29, 1974, pp. 9–10.
13. Korboński, 'Polskie państwo podziemne z lat 1939–45', p. 13.
14. *PSZ*, p. 53.
15. *Ibid.*, p. 54. See also *Armia Krajowa w Dokumentach*, vol. I, pp. 270–1.
16. Korboński, 'Polskie państwo podziemne z lat 1939–45', p. 14.
17. *Armia Krajowa w Dokumentach*, vol. I, pp. 271–3.
18. Michalewski, J., 'Relacja Delegatury Rządu', *ZH*, no. 26, 1973 pp. 70–1.
19. *Ibid.*; Korboński, 'Polskie państwo podziemne z lat 1939–45', p. 14.
20. *Armia Krajowa w Dokumentach*, vol. I, pp. 368–9. The three Government Delegates were: C. Ratajski, December 1940–August 1942; J. Piekałkiewicz, September 1942–February 1943; J.S. Jankowski, May 1943–March 1945.
21. For further discussion on this problem see *Armia Krajowa w Dokumentach*, vol. I, pp. 404–5, 436–7 and 446–7; Michalewski, 'Relacja', pp. 73–4.
22. Michalewski, 'Relacja', pp. 73–4; Zaremba, *Wojna i konspiracja*, pp. 158–61.
23. *PSZ*, pp. 59–60.
24. *Armia Krajowa w Dokumentach*, vol. I, pp. 219–22 and 508–11.
25. Michalewski, 'Relacja', p. 76.
26. *Ibid.*, p. 74; Garliński, 'Polskie państwo podziemne 1939–45', p. 10.
27. Michalewski, 'Relacja', pp. 76–9; *PSZ*, p. 60. Later a Department of Foreign Affairs was created. See also Korboński, S., *The Polish Underground State: A Guide to the Underground, 1939–1945*, New York, 1978, pp. 41–55.
28. *Documents on Polish–Soviet Relations 1939–1945*, vol. II, London, 1969, Polish Government Memorandum to Mr Eden, 19.XII.43, p. 108.
29. *PSZ*, p. 54.
30. Michalewski, 'Relacja', p. 109. This problem is extremely complex and not within the scope of this study. See Terej, *Na rozstajach dróg*, pp. 62–4 and 145–8.
31. Korboński, 'Polskie państwo podziemne z lat 1939–45', p. 17.

32. Zaremba, *Wojna i konspiracja*, pp. 162ff.
33. For a full discussion see Michalewski, 'Relacja', pp. 109–15.
34. *Ibid.*, p. 112.
35. Korboński, 'Polskie państwo podziemne z lat 1939–45', p. 17.
36. *Ibid.*; Michalewski, 'Relacja', p. 113; See also Korboński, S., *Fighting Warsaw*, London, 1956, pp. 288–9.
37. Korboński, 'Polskie państwo podziemne z lat 1939–45', p. 17.
38. Verbal information of S. Korboński.
39. See pp. 207–8.
40. *PSZ*, p. 58; Garliński, 'Polskie państwo podziemne 1939–45', p. 32.
41. *PSZ*, p. 59–61.
42. *Ibid.*, p. 50. It was published on 20 August 1944.
43. *Ibid.*, p. 60; Zaremba, *Wojna i konspiracja*, pp. 202–3.
44. *PSZ*, p. 60.
45. Ciechanowski, *The Warsaw Rising*, p. 122.
46. *Rzeczpospolita Polska*, no. 15, 20.VIII.43.
47. *PSZ*, pp. 65–74.
48. Hochfeld, J., 'The Social Aspects of the Warsaw Uprising', *Journal of Central European Affairs*, no. 1, 1945, p. 39.
49. Garliński, 'Polskie państwo podziemne 1939–45', p. 18. For a full description of the work of the KWC see Korboński, *Fighting Warsaw*, pp. 114–20 and *The Polish Underground State*, pp. 71–82.
50. *Documents on Polish–Soviet Relations 1939–1945*, vol. II, Polish Government Memorandum to Mr Eden, 19.XII.43, p. 108; Korboński, 'Polskie państwo podziemne z lat 1939–45', p. 17.
51. Garliński, 'Polskie państwo podziemne 1939–45', p. 19; Korboński, *Fighting Warsaw*, p. 287.
52. Garliński, 'Polskie państwo podziemne 1939–45', p. 19.
53. Korboński, *Fighting Warsaw*, pp. 287–8.
54. See pp. 36–7.
55. APUST, SPP.B.I, Więckowski, J., 'Tajne nauczanie w zakresie Gimnazjum Ogólnokształcącego'.
56. Garliński, 'Polskie państwo podziemne 1939–45', p. 25.
57. *Ibid.*; Konarski, S., 'Z dziejów tajnego szkolnictwa wyższego w Warszawie w latach okupacji', *Rocz. Warsz.*, no. 7, 1966, pp. 446–9.
58. Bartelski, L., 'Warszawa jako ośrodek ruchu oporu w kulturze', *Rocz. Warsz.*, no. 7, 1966, p. 434.
59. Sieroszewski, W., 'Z działalności Wojskowego Sądu Specjalnego Okręgu a następnie Obszaru Warszawskiego', *NDP II Wojny*, no. 8, 1964, p. 121.
60. *Armia Krajowa w Dokumentach*, vol. II, pp. 149–53.
61. Garliński, 'Polskie państwo podziemne 1939–45', pp. 28–9.
62. Sieroszewski, 'Z działalności Wojskowego Sądu Specjalnego', p. 122.
63. Korboński, 'Polskie państwo podziemne z lat 1939–45', p. 17.
64. *Ibid.*, pp. 17–18.
65. *Ibid.*

66. *Ibid.*
67. *Ibid.*

2.2 The staging of the Warsaw Uprising

1. Borkiewicz, *Powstanie Warszawskie 1944*, pp. 25–6. For a full description of the evolution of the plans for an uprising and the events leading to the outbreak of the Uprising in Warsaw see Ciechanowski, *The Warsaw Rising*, pp. 129–281 and *PSZ*, pp. 541–666.
2. Borkiewicz, *Powstanie Warszawskie 1944*, pp. 24–6.
3. See Ciechanowski, *The Warsaw Rising*, pp. 149–71 for development of plan.
4. Ciechanowski, *The Warsaw Rising*, p. 167.
5. *Ibid.*
6. *Ibid.*, p. 166.
7. *Ibid.*, p. 156–66.
8. *Ibid.*, pp. 169–70; Bór-Komorowski, T., *The Secret Army*, London, 1950, p. 202.
9. *PSZ*, p. 651.
10. Ciechanowski, *The Warsaw Rising*, p. 143.
11. *Ibid.*, pp. 162–3.
12. *Ibid.*, pp. 212, 214ff.
13. *Ibid.*, p. 269.
14. *Ibid.*, p. 163.
15. *Ibid.*, pp. 269–72.
16. *Ibid.*, pp. 190–211; *PSZ*, pp. 580–649.
17. Ciechanowski, *The Warsaw Rising*, pp. 268–9.
18. Quoted in *ibid.*, p. 211.
19. *Ibid.*, pp. 212–18.
20. *Ibid.*, p. 249.
21. *Ibid.*, pp. 212–13.
22. Czajkowski, Z., and Taborski, B., 'O polskiej technice powstań', *Kultura* (Paris), no. 5/127, 1958, p. 142.
23. *Ibid.*
24. Ciechanowski, *The Warsaw Rising*, pp. 234–5; Nowak, *Kurier z Warszawy*, p. 317–18.
25. Ciechanowski, *The Warsaw Rising*, p. 234.
26. *Ibid.*, p. 213.
27. *Ibid.*, p. 259; Bór-Komorowski, *The Secret Army*, p. 216.
28. Ciechanowski, *The Warsaw Rising*, pp. 258–9. See pp. 69–70.
29. *Ibid.*, pp. 272–3.
30. *Ibid.*, p. 259 and p. 267.
31. *Ibid.*, pp. 247–8.
32. *Biuletyn Informacyjny*, nos. 65, 91 and 93, 28.VIII.44, 23 and 25.IX.44.
33. Ciechanowski, J.M., 'Gdy ważyły się losy stolicy: Notatka z rozmowy z Gen. Tadeuszem Borem Komorowskim, odbytej w maju 1965 w

Londynie w obecności Prof. J.K. Zawodny', *Wiadomości*, no. 39, 1971, p. 2; Ciechanowski, *The Warsaw Rising*, p. 247.
34. Verbal information of S. Korboński.
35. AAN, RGO 518, Reports on PKO activity in Warsaw, June 1944, pp. 83 and 87; cf. 'Sprawozdanie Zarządu RGO', 18.IX.44 in *LCPW II*, pp. 414–16.
36. Józef Piłsudski Institute of America, New York, 'Badacz' (Mjr T. Dołęga Kamienski), 'Powstanie Warszawskie – Kwatermistrzostwo', p. 7; Małecki, J. Sęk, *Armia Ludowa w Powstaniu Warszawskim*, Warsaw, 1962, p. 38.
37. *Ibid.*; Bór-Komorowski, *The Secret Army*, p. 205.

2.3 Warsaw in the last days of July 1944

1. Wilmot, C., *The Struggle for Europe*, London, 1952, p. 436.
2. Kirchmayer, *Powstanie Warszawskie*, p. 60.
3. Bartoszewski, W., *1859 dni Warszawy*, Kraków, 1974, pp. 567 and 569; Szarota, T., 'Warszawa przed godziną "W"', *Życie Warszawy*, no. 185, 1973, p. 5.
4. *Ibid.*
5. *Głos Warszawy*, no. 136, 2.VI.44.
6. GSHI, PRM.L.5, Despatch from the Government Delegate, Ldz.k.3670/44, 29.IV.44.
7. Bartelski, L., *Powstanie Warszawskie*, Warsaw, 1967, pp. 12–13; Bartoszewski, W., 'Sierpień i wrzesień Warszawy 1944', *TP*, no. 30, 1957, p. 1; Korboński, *Fighting Warsaw*, p. 346; Valcini, *Golgota Warszawy*, p. 330.
8. Korboński, *Fighting Warsaw*, p. 345.
9. BN, Rkps. akc. 7165, Sarnecki, T., 'Heroiczna Warszawa – memoire o powstaniu', pp. 6–7.
10. Bartoszewski, 'Sierpień i wrzesień', p. 1.
11. AMW, Dąbrowa-Sierzputowski, 'Wspomnienia wojenne', pp. 50–1.
12. *Głos Warszawy*, no. 144, 4.VII.44.
13. *Ibid.*, nos. 144, 145, 147, 150 and 151, 4, 7, 14, 20, and 25.VII.44.
14. Bartoszewski, *1859 dni Warszawy*, p. 562. Cf. Pełczyński's statement quoted in Ciechanowski, *The Warsaw Rising*, p. 245.
15. Ciechanowski, *The Warsaw Rising*, pp. 223–4.
16. Bartoszewski, *Warsaw Death Ring*, pp. 326–7.
17. *Ibid.*
18. Szarota, 'Warszawa przed godziną "W"', p. 8.
19. Bartoszewski, 'Sierpień i wrzesień', p. 1.
20. *PSZ*, p. 697; Letter from Julian Kulski in *TP*, no. 33, 1974. Julian Kulski was the Deputy Mayor of Warsaw and Director of the Zarząd Miejski during the occupation.
21. Bartoszewski, *Warsaw Death Ring*, p. 327.
22. AMW, Dąbrowa-Sierzputowski, 'Wspomnienia wojenne', p. 51.

23. Bartelski, *Powstanie Warszawskie*, p. 27.
24. *PSZ*, p. 697; Bartoszewski, 'Sierpień i wrzesień', p. 1.
25. *Ibid.*
26. Bartoszewski, *Warsaw Death Ring*, p. 327.
27. Skarżyński, *Polityczne przyczyny*, p. 222; Szarota, 'Warszawa przed godziną "W"', p. 8.
28. Skarżyński, *Polityczne przyczyny*, p. 222.
29. Ciechanowski, *The Warsaw Rising*, p. 229.
30. Serwański, *Życie w powstańczej Warszawie*, p. 63.
31. Ciechanowski, *The Warsaw Rising*, p. 229.
32. *Ibid.*, p. 63.
33. *Biuletyn Informacyjny*, no. 238, 27.VII.44.
34. 'Wewnętrzny meldunek sytuacyjny (nr 5) Wydział Informacji ... BIP KG AK', *LCPW II*, pp. 26–7; Kliszko, Z., *Powstanie Warszawskie*, Warsaw, 1967, p. 159.
35. Bartoszewski, 'Sierpień i wrzesień', p. 1.
36. Ciechanowski, *The Warsaw Rising*, p. 230.
37. *PSZ*, p. 698; Bartoszewski, 'Sierpień i wrzesień', p. 1.
38. Bartoszewski, 'Sierpień i wrzesień', p. 1; Kulski, *Zarząd Miejski Warszawy*, p. 89; AMW, Dąbrowa-Sierzputowski, 'Wspomnienia wojenne', p. 52.
39. Bartoszewski, 'Sierpień i wrzesień', p. 1.
40. Ciechanowski, *The Warsaw Rising*, p. 230.
41. *Ibid.*, p. 235.
42. *PSZ*, p. 698.
43. Skarżyński, *Polityczne przyczyny*, p. 236.
44. Ostrowska, E., *W Alejach spacerują 'Tygrysy'*, Warsaw, 1973, p. 36; verbal information of W. Bartoszewski.
45. GSHI, PRM.L.5, Despatch from Warsaw to London, Ldz.4282/44, 30.VII.44.
46. *Rzeczpospolita*, no. 85, 31.VII.44; Bień, *Wspomnienia*, p. 97; Czugajewski, R., *Na barykadach, w kanałach i gruzach Czerniakowa*, Warsaw, 1970, p. 8.
47. IZ, Dok. II.130, Przykucka, W., 'Moje przeżycie w czasie wojny i okupacji', p. 13; Bień, *Wspomnienia*, p. 97.
48. Bartoszewski, *1859 dni Warszawy*, p. 572.
49. GSHI, PRM.L.5., Despatch from Warsaw to London, Ldz.4282/44, 30.VII.44.; *Dzień Warszawy*, no. 997, 31.VII.44; *Rzeczpospolita*, no. 85, 31.VII.44; Bartoszewski, 'Sierpień i wrzesień', p. 2.
50. IZ, Dok. II.130, Przykucka, 'Moje przeżycie w czasie wojny i okupacji', p. 13; *Rzeczpospolita*, no. 85, 31.VII.44.
51. Bartoszewski, *Warsaw Death Ring*, p. 328.
52. Bór-Komorowski, *The Secret Army*, pp. 212–13; Bartoszewski, *1859 dni Warszawy*, pp. 570–1.
53. 'Wewnętrzny meldunek sytuacyjny (nr 5) Wydział Informacji ... BIP KG AK', *LCPW II*, pp. 26–7.
54. *Ibid.*; such a feeling had also been supported by articles in *Biuletyn*

Informacyjny, no. 67, 30.VIII.44 and *Rzeczpospolita*, no. 42, 31.VIII.44.
55. Ciechanowski, *The Warsaw Rising*, p. 242.
56. Bartelski, *Powstanie Warszawskie*, p. 34; Bór-Komorowski, *The Secret Army*, p. 215; Kozłowski, S. Lis, 'Fragmenty wspomnień spod okupacji i z powstania', *Kurier Polski* (Buenos Aires), no. 37, 1969, p. 3.
57. 'Meldunek nr 9 – D. 3', 1.VIII.44; cf. Borkiewicz, *Powstanie Warszawskie 1944*, p. 47.
58. This point will be expanded in Chapter 4.
59. 'Meldunek nr. 9 – D. 3', 1.VIII.44.
60. Czugajewski, *Na barykadach*, p. 8.
61. Ossol., 52/60, Lasocka, J., 'Powstanie Warszawskie', p. 229.

2.4 'W' hour

1. Ciechanowski, *The Warsaw Rising*, p. 232.
2. Verbal information of Korboński.
3. Report of S. Talikowski in *LCPW I.i*, p. 297.
4. Borkiewicz, *Powstanie Warszawskie 1944*, pp. 32–3 and 47ff; Kirchmayer, *Powstanie Warszawskie*, p. 188.
5. Bień, *Wspomnienia*, p. 99.
6. Dzendel, H., 'Powstańczy dziennik ludowy' in *Wspomnienia dziennikarzy z okresu okupacji hitlerowskiej*, Warsaw, 1970, p. 18.
7. Woźniewski, Z., *Pierwsze dni powstania warszawskiego w szpitalach na Woli*, Warsaw, 1947, p. 24.
8. Skarżyński, A., *Powstańcza Warszawa w dniach walki*, Warsaw, 1965, p. 22.
9. Report of Zofia Turska in *LCPW I.ii*, p. 96.
10. Verbal information of anonymous witness from Żoliborz; Report of Maria Gieysztor in *LCPW I.ii*, p. 308.
11. Gieysztor in *LCPW I.ii*, p. 308; Turska in *LCPW I.ii*, p. 96; Report of Jolanta Wadecka (in author's possession), pp. 5–6.
12. BN, Rkps. sygn. III.6402, Chomicki, A., '63 dni w płonącej Warszawie', p. 1.
13. BN, Rkps. akc. 6682, Anonymous, 'Powstanie Polskie z sierpnia 1944 widziane z odcinka Mokotów w Warszawie', p. 2.
14. Szymczak, 'Dni zgrozy i walki o wolność', p. 140.
15. Ossol., 134/64, Krobicka-Modzelewska, L., 'Wrzesień 1939, Pawiak, Powstanie Warszawskie', p. 77.
16. Borkiewicz, *Powstanie Warszawskie 1944*, p. 58.
17. Ossol., 134/64, Krobicka-Modzelewska, 'Wrzesień 1939', p. 77.
18. *Ibid.*
19. Bór-Komorowski, *The Secret Army*, p. 233.
20. Borkiewicz, *Powstanie Warszawskie 1944*, p. 58.
21. Bór-Komorowski, *The Secret Army*, p. 221.
22. Map no. 32 in *PSZ*; Borkiewicz, *Powstanie Warszawskie 1944*, p. 65.
23. Fajer, L., *Żołnierze Starówki*, Warsaw, 1957, p. 25.

24. Florczak, Z., 'O dozorcy domu Józefie Decu (Wspomnienia)', *TP*, no. 31, 1973, p. 5.
25. Serwański, *Życie w powstańczej Warszawie*, p. 97.
26. Florczak, 'O dozorcy domu Józefie Decu' p. 6.
27. Report of Irena Zgrychowa in *LCPW I.i*, p. 516.
28. Hoppe, *Wspomnienia, przyczynki, refleksje*, p. 365.
29. *Ibid*; Serwański, *Życie w powstańczej Warsawie*, p. 104.
30. Ossol., 134/64, Krobicka-Modzelewska, 'Wrzesień 1939', p. 77.
31. 'Wewnętrzny meldunek sytuacyjny placówki informacyjno-radiowej BIP KG AK', 2.VIII.44, *LCPW II*, p. 33; Report of M. Porowski in *LCPW I.i*, p. 112; Report of W. Bartoszewski and S. Kulesiński in *LCPW I.ii*, pp. 354 and 387; Filipowicz, J., *Miałem wtedy 14 lat*, Warsaw, 1972, p. 34.
32. Bór-Komorowski, *The Secret Army*, p. 237.
33. Report of M. Manteufflowa in *LCPW I.ii*, p. 60.

2.5 *The first days of the Uprising*

1. GSHI, A.XII.3/88, Despatch from Poland, Ldz.6314/44, 3.VIII.44.
2. *Ibid.*, Despatch from Poland, Ldz.6366/44, 4.VIII.44.
3. 'Fragment wewnętrznego meldunku sytuacyjnego', 3.VIII.44, *LCPW II*, p. 34; 'Powstanie warszawskie w świetle meldunków BIP', ed. A. Przygoński, *Gazeta Krakowska*, no. 187, 1957, report no. 18.
4. *Robotnik*, no. 10, 3.VIII.44.
5. Report of Z. Namitkiewicz in *LCPW I.i*, p. 212; Report of M. Gajewska in *LCPW I.ii*, pp. 230 and 233.
6. Kulesiński in *LCPW I.ii*, pp. 388–9; Serwański, *Życie w powstańczej Warszawie*, p. 244.
7. Kulesiński in *LCPW I.ii*, p. 389.
8. Article in *Warszawa Twierdza*, 2.VIII.44 as quoted in *LCPW III*, p. 26–7.
9. 'Fragment wewnętrznego meldunku sytuacyjnego', 3.VIII.44. *LCPW II*, p. 34.
10. Troński, B. *Tędy przeszła śmierć*, Warsaw, 1970, pp. 30–1.
11. Czugajewski, *Na barykadach*, p. 27; BN, Rkps. akc. 293, Rafałowski, J., 'Szlakiem "Zośki"', p. 11.
12. Czajkowski-Dębczyński, Z., *Dziennik Powstańca*, Kraków, 1969, p. 17.
13. Pluta-Czachowski, K., 'W sztabie operacyjnym KG AK na Woli', *Za i Przeciw*, no. 36, 1968, p. 15; Borkiewicz, *Powstanie Warszawskie 1944*, p. 83.
14. 'Fragment wewnętrznego meldunku sytuacyjnego', 3.VIII.44, *LCPW II*, p. 34; 'Powstanie w świetle meldunków BIP', report no. 18; Talikowski in *LCPW I.i*, p. 298.
15. 'Meldunki sytuacyjne "Montera" z powstania warszawskiego', *NDP II Wojny*, no. 3, 1959, p. 101.
16. Borkiewicz, *Powstanie Warszawskie 1944*, p. 113n.

17. Czajkowski-Dębczyński, *Dziennik Powstańca*, p. 20.
18. Cf. Report of Jan Rosner in *LCPW I.i*, pp. 344–5; Jasinkowicz, M., 'Młodzi i najmłodsi w powstaniu warszawskim', *Wiadomości*, no. 1479, 1974, p. 4.
19. Polak, T., *63 dni powstania warszawskiego*, Warsaw, 1946, p. 11.
20. Skarżyński, *Powstańcza Warszawa w dniach walki*, p. 20.
21. AMW, Dąbrowa-Sierzputowski, 'Wspomnienia wojenne', p. 54.
22. Talikowski in *LCPW I.i*, p. 299.
23. AMW, Dąbrowa-Sierzputowski, 'Wspomnienia wojenne', p. 55; 'Fragment wewnętrznego meldunku sytuacyjnego' 3.VIII.44, *LCPW II*, p. 36. The Soviet advance on the east of Warsaw had been halted by the German Army.
24. *Biuletyn Informacyjny*, no. 243, 2.VIII.44.
25. *Armia Ludowa*, 15.VIII.44.
26. Pluta-Czachowski, 'W sztabie operacyjnym KG AK na Woli', p. 15.
27. GSHI, A.XIII.3/88, Despatch from Poland, Ldz.6416/44, 5.VIII.44; Borkiewicz, *Powstanie Warszawskie 1944*, p. 119.
28. Skarżyński, *Powstańcza Warszawa w dniach walki*, p. 19; Borkiewicz, *Powstanie Warszawskie 1944*, p. 94.
29. Bór-Komorowski, *The Secret Army*, p. 233.
30. Borkiewicz, *Powstanie Warszawskie 1944*, p. 119.
31. *Ibid.*, p. 93; Skarżyński, *Polityczne przyczyny*, pp. 387ff.
32. Borkiewicz, *Powstanie Warszawskie 1944*, p. 93.
33. Skarżyński, *Polityczne przyczyny*, pp. 390–1.
34. 'Meldunki sytuacyjne "Montera"', p. 101.
35. Pluta-Czachowski, 'W sztabie operacyjnym KG AK na Woli', p. 15; Borkiewicz, *Powstanie Warszawskie 1944*, p. 112; Kirchmayer, *Powstanie Warszawskie*, p. 239.
36. GSHI, A.XII.3/88, Despatch from Poland, Ldz.6314/44, 3.VIII.44.
37. *Walka*, no. 40, 14.VIII.44; Bartoszewski, *1859 dni Warszawy*, p. 600.
38. Bór-Komorowski, *The Secret Army*, p. 238. The Germans throughout the Uprising dropped leaflets which tried to undermine the community's support for the Uprising, as well as calling on people to leave the city. These usually brought no results (see Chapter 3).
39. Żeromska, M., 'Notatki z powstania warszawskiego' (1944).
40. See Chapter 4.
41. 'Meldunek do Borodzicza od Rafała', 2.VIII.44, *LCPW II*, p. 32.
42. *Biuletyn Informacyjny*, no. 242, 2.VIII.44.
43. *W Walce*, no. 3, 4.VIII.44.
44. *Biuletyn Informacyjny*, no. 255, 10.VIII.44; *Rzeczpospolita*, no. 22, 11.VIII.44.
45. Wnuk, W., 'W powstaniu z piórem w ręku', *Życie i Myśl*, no. 7/8, 1971, pp. 175–6.
46. 'Wewnętrzny meldunek sytuacyjny placówki informacyjno-radiowej BIP KG AK "Anna"', 5.VIII.44 in *LCPW II*, p. 56.

2.6 *The German reaction to the outbreak of the Uprising and their treatment of the civilian population*

1. Krannhals, H. von, *Der Warschauer Aufstand 1944*, Frankfurt am Main, 1964, pp. 117ff.
2. Dunin-Wąsowicz, K., 'Władze hitlerowskie wobec powstania warszawskiego' *Prze. Hum.*, no. 1, 1975, p. 53.
3. Krannhals, *Der Warschauer Aufstand*, p. 214.
4. *Ibid.*, pp. 308–9.
5. *Ibid.*, p. 283.
6. Borkiewicz, *Powstanie Warszawskie 1944*, p. 85.
7. *Zburzenie Warszawy, Zeznania generałów niemieckich przed polskim prokuratorem członkiem polskiej delegacji przy międzynarodowym trybunale wojennym w Norymberdze*, Warsaw, 1946, Evidence of Gen. von dem Bach, p. 33.
8. Borkiewicz, *Powstanie Warszawskie 1944*, p. 85.
9. *Zburzenie Warszawy*, pp. 125–7.
10. Krannhals, *Der Warschauer Aufstand*, pp. 124 and 465.
11. *Ibid.*, pp. 125–7.
12. *Ibid.*, pp. 127 and 319; cf. Lewickij, B., 'Ukraińcy i likwidacja powstania warszawskiego', *Kultura* (Paris), no. 6/56, 1952, pp. 74–87 and Ortynskyi, L., 'Prawda o ukraińskiej dywizji', *Kultura* (Paris), no. 11/61, 1952, pp. 109–16.
13. Krannhals, *Der Warschauer Aufstand*, p. 245.
14. Drescher, G., *Warsaw Rising*, New York, 1972, p. 62.
15. *Zburzenie Warszawy*, Evidence of Ernest Rode, p. 90.
16. Drescher, *Warsaw Rising*, p. 62. Cf. Lewickij, 'Ukraińcy i likwidacja': 'The RONA group was for the most part made up of young soldiers, at the oldest eighteen, but they already had two years of hard fighting behind them', p. 78.
17. Statement of von dem Bach in Krannhals, *Der Warschauer Aufstand*, p. 246.
18. IZ, Dok.v.223, 'Protokóły do powstania warszawskiego (Zbrodnia i życie)', protocol no. 502.
19. 'Dziennik działań Niemieckiej 9 Armii', ed. J. Matecki, *ZH*, no. 15, 1969, p. 85.
20. Bartoszewski, W., *Erich von dem Bach: War Crimes in Poland*, Warsaw, 1961 and 'Sierpień i wrzesień', p. 1; Przygoński, A., *Powstanie Warszawskie w sierpniu 1944*, Warsaw, 1980, vol. I, p. 254.
21. Kirchmayer, *Powstanie Warszawskie*, p. 281.
22. *Zburzenie Warszawy*, Evidence of Gen. von dem Bach, p. 34.
23. Przygoński, *Powstanie Warszawskie*, vol. I, pp. 232ff.
24. Krannhals, *Der Warschauer Aufstand*, p. 315.
25. See Klimaszewski, T., *Verbrennungskommando Warschau*, Warsaw, 1960.
26. Moczulski, L., 'Kościół św. Wojciecha', *Stolica*, no. 31, 1968, p. 13; Drescher, K., 'Komisja lekarska obozu przejściowego w Pruszkowie w

czasie powstania warszawskiego', *Arch. Hist. Med.*, no. 2, 1968, pp. 271ff; Krzyczkowski, H., 'Obóz przejściowy "Dulag 121" – Pruszków', *TP*, no. 31, 1972, pp. 1–2. For a full description of conditions in the Pruszków transit camp see Serwański, E., *Dulag 121 – Pruszków*, Poznań, 1946.

27. 'Wewnętrzne sprawozdanie delegata władz naczelnych RGO', 25.VIII.44, *LCPW II*, p. 176; Borkiewicz, *Powstanie Warszawskie 1944*, p. 545; Ossol., 13482/11, Tyrankiewiczowa, H., 'W rękach hitlerowców: wspomnienia obozowe', 1947, pp. 162–4.

2.7 German crimes in Warsaw, 1–6 August 1944

1. Pluta-Czachowski, K., 'Godzina "W" na Woli', *Stolica*, no. 39, 1969, p. 6. For the most complete documented account of the German crimes against the Polish population during the Uprising see *Documenta Occupationis Teutonicae*, vol. II, *Zbrodnia niemiecka w Warszawie 1944*, ed. Serwański, E. and Trawińska, I., Poznań, 1946 (hereafter quoted as *DOT*), and *Zbrodnie okupanta hitlerowskiego na ludności cywilnej w czasie powstania warszawskiego*, Główna Komisja Badania Zbrodni Hitlerowskich w Polsce, ed. Datner, S. and Leszczyński, K., Warsaw, 1962, (hereafter quoted as *GKBZH*).
2. *GKBZH*, Statement of W. Bomber and S. Mielczarek, pp. 19–21.
3. *Ibid.*, Statement of K. Szajewski, pp. 30–1.
4. *Ibid.*, Statement of B. Filipiuk, pp. 38–44.
5. *Ibid.*, Statement of W. Pec, pp. 36–8. The approximate figure given by Pec in his statement is 4,000; the figure of 2,000 was that given by F. Zasada who worked in the *Verbrennungskommando* which cleared the area, see pp. 244–8. The figure of 3,000 was given by Janina Mamontowicz in her statement, pp. 44–6.
6. *Ibid.*, Statement of B. Filipiuk, pp. 38–44; *DOT*, pp. 33–4 and 36–8; Woźniewski, *Pierwsze dni powstania warszawskiego* p. 8; Misiewicz, J., 'Zapiski z dni powstania warszawskiego w Szpitalu Wolskim, *Prze. Lek.*, no. 2/1, 1967, p. 152.
7. *GKBZH*, Statement of B. Filipiuk, pp. 38–44.
8. W.M., 'Czego nie powiedział Generał Reinefarth: Piekło Woli', *Stolica*, no. 31, 1973, p. 6.
9. *DOT*, p. 51; Woźniewski, *Pierwsze dni powstania warszawskiego*, p. 21.
10. Woźniewski, *Pierwsze dni powstania warszawskiego*, p. 25; *DOT*, p. 15.
11. Woźniewski, *Pierwsze dni powstania warszawskiego*, p. 28; Manteuffel, L., 'Rozstrzelany szpital', *Kultura*, no. 530, 1973, p. 5.
12. Woźniewski, *Pierwsze dni powstania warszawskiego*, p. 29.
13. *DOT*, pp. 43–6. The witness quotes 5–7,000; *GKBZH*, Statement of F. Zasada, pp. 244–8.
14. *DOT*, pp. 43–6.
15. Bartoszewski, 'Sierpień i wrzesień', p. 1.
16. Krannhals, *Der Warschauer Aufstand*, pp. 214 and 308.

17. Turlejska, M., 'Nieznane dokumenty o powstaniu warszawskim', *Polityka*, no. 37, 1974, p. 27.
18. Borkiewicz, *Powstanie warszawskie 1944*, p. 127.
19. Pobóg-Malinowski, *Najnowsza historia polityczna Polski*, p. 679.
20. These figures calculated on the basis of witnesses' statements.
21. 'Dziennik Iwana Waszenko', *Dzieje Najnowsze*, 1947, pp. 326–67.
22. *GKBZH*, Statement of J. Laskowski, pp. 96–9 and B. Mazurkiewicz, pp. 97–102; *DOT*, pp. 80–1.
23. *GKBZH*, Statement of B. Mazurkiewicz, pp. 97–102.
24. *Ibid.*, Statement of J. Laskowski, pp. 96–9.
25. *Ibid.*, Statement of J. Górski, pp. 86–8.
26. Wroniszewski, J., *Ochota 1944*, Warsaw, 1970, pp. 145–6 (no source given).
27. *GKBZH*, Statement of L.E. Majchrzak, pp. 88–9.
28. Report of S. Trojanowski in *LCPW I.i*, p. 239; Wroniszewski, *Ochota 1944*, p. 150.
29. *GKBZH*, Statement of E. Barcz, pp. 84–6.
30. *Ibid.*, Statement of S. Andrzejewski, pp. 93–4.
31. *Ibid.*, Statement of I. Rzepecka, pp. 79–82; *DOT*, pp. 86–7.
32. *GKBZH*, Statement of W. Michalski, pp. 89–90.
33. *DOT*, pp. 86–7.
34. See statements in *GKBZH* and *DOT* dealing with Ochota.
35. Turlejska, 'Nieznane dokumenty o powstaniu warszawskim', p. 27.
36. *GKBZH*, Statement of A. Kisiel, pp. 124–7; *DOT*, p. 124.
37. IZ, Dok.v.223, 'Protokóły do powstania warszawskiego (Zbrodnia i Życie)', protocol no. 239.
38. *GKBZH*, Statement of A.J. Porzgoński, pp. 128–30; *DOT*, pp. 124–5.
39. *Ibid.*, p. 126.
40. See statements in *GKBZH* and *DOT*.
41. IZ, Dok.v.220, 'Protokóły i materiały do pracy pt. "Życie w powstaniu warszawskim"', vol. III, protocol no. 227; *Biuletyn Informacyjny*, no. 253, 8.VIII.44; Bór-Komorowski, *The Secret Army*, p. 247.

2.8 Results of the German action

1. Krannhals, *Der Warschauer Aufstand*, p. 130.
2. Borkiewicz, *Powstanie Warszawskie 1944*, p. 119.
3. IZ, Dok.v.223, 'Protokóły do powstania warszawskiego (Zbrodnia i Życie)', protocol no. 265.
4. *Biuletyn Informacyjny*, nos. 250 and 251, 6 and 7.VIII.44, *Rzeczpospolita*, no. 17, 7.VIII.44.
5. Krannhals, *Der Warschauer Aufstand*, p. 134.
6. Report of J. Rossman in *LCPW I.i*, p. 150.
7. 'Fragment meldunku patrolu Wojskowej Służby Społecznej', 7.VIII.44 (AWIH, Sygn.III.24/22 k. 5).
8. Bór-Komorowski, *The Secret Army*, p. 251. This figure was probably too

high.

9. AZHP, ADR.202/XX-20, k. 1–2, 10.VIII.44. See p. 139 for an explanation of these regional districts.
10. *Biuletyn Informacyjny*, no. 264, 19.VIII.44.
11. *PSZ*, p. 713.
12. Krannhals, *Der Warschauer Aufstand*, p. 372. Gollert, F., 'Powstanie Warszawskie 1944', *ZH*, no. 43, 1978, p. 193.
13. APUST, 3.9.2.8, Radio messages received from John Ward, 22.VIII.44.
14. Kirchmayer, *Powstanie Warszawskie*, p. 270.

3 The course of the Uprising

3.1 Wola

1. Paszkowski, Z., 'GL i AL na Woli', *Dzieje Woli*, Warsaw, 1974, p. 410; Puchalski, Z., 'Wola w powstaniu warszawskim', *Z lat wojny i okupacji*, vol. III, p. 171.
2. Bór-Komorowski, *The Secret Army*, pp. 233–4.
3. Paszkowski, 'GL i AL na Woli', p. 410.
4. *DOT*, pp. 30–2 and 40–1.
5. Kamiński, A., *Zośka i Parasol*, Warsaw, 1970, p. 217.
6. *DOT*, pp. 30–2; Bartelski, L. 'Walki powstańcze na Woli', *Dzieje Woli*, Warsaw, 1974, p. 403; Misiewicz, 'Zapiski z dni powstania', p. 149; Kamiński, *Zośka i Parasol*, pp. 220ff.
7. Woźniewski, *Pierwsze dni powstania warszawskiego*, p. 27; Manteuffel, 'Rozstrzelany szpital', p. 4.
8. Misiewicz, 'Zapiski z dni powstania', p. 149.
9. Woźniewski, *Pierwsze dni powstania warszawskiego*, pp. 24–6; Manteuffel, 'Rozstrzelany szpital', p. 4; Misiewicz, 'Zapiski z dni powstania', p. 151.
10. Misiewicz, 'Zapiski z dni powstania', p. 149; Woźniewski, *Pierwsze dni powstania warszawskiego*, p. 4.
11. Manteuffel, 'Rozstrzelany szpital', p. 4.
12. Misiewicz, 'Zapiski z dni powstania', p. 149.
13. *Ibid.*, p. 152.
14. Bór-Komorowski, *The Secret Army*, p. 240.
15. Verbal information of W. Bartoszewski; Report of J. Rossman in *LCPW I.i*, p. 149.
16. Bartoszewski, W., 'Prasa powstania warszawskiego. Zarys Historyczno-bibliograficzny', *Rocznik Warszawski*, vol. XI, Warsaw, 1972, p. 38.
17. Misiewicz, 'Zapiski z dni powstania', p. 149.
18. 'Powstanie w świetle meldunków BIP', report no. 8.
19. Kamiński, *Zośka i Parasol*, p. 220.
20. Paszkowski, 'GL i AL na Woli', p. 36; Kamiński, *Zośka i Parasol*, pp. 271ff.
21. 'Wewnętrzny meldunek sytuacyjny', 5.VIII.44, *LCPW II*, p. 56.

22. Bartelski, 'Walki powstańcze na Woli', p. 405.
23. Kamiński, *Zośka i Parasol*, p. 271.

3.2 Ochota

1. Kirchmayer, *Powstanie Warszawskie*, p. 135.
2. Report of S. Mirowski in *LCPW I.i*, p. 205; Borkiewicz, *Powstanie Warszawskie 1944*, p. 69.
3. Kirchmayer, *Powstanie Warszawskie*, p. 196; *LCPW I.i*, p. 198.
4. Borkiewicz, *Powstanie Warszawskie 1944*, pp. 69 and 80; Chyczewski, J., 'Godzina "W" na Ochocie', *TP*, no. 33, 1964, p. 6.
5. Chyczewski, *ibid.*; Wroniszewski, *Ochota 1944*, p. 105.
6. Wroniszewski, *Ochota 1944*, p. 89; Borkiewicz, *Powstanie Warszawskie 1944*, p. 70. ZUS was the 'Zakład Ubezpieczeń Społecznych' – the Institute of Social Insurance.
7. Borkiewicz, *ibid.*; Wroniszewski, *Ochota 1944*, p. 109.
8. Borkiewicz, *Powstanie Warszawskie 1944*, pp. 100 and 136.
9. Report of Z. Namitkiewicz in *LCPW I.i*, p. 212; Borkiewicz, *Powstanie Warszawskie 1944*, p. 100; Wroniszewski, *Ochota 1944*, p. 103.
10. Borkiewicz, *Powstanie Warszawskie 1944*, p. 100.
11. *DOT*, pp. 103 and 113; Serwański, *Życie w powstańczej Warszawie*, p. 73; Wroniszewski, *Ochota 1944*, p. 116.
12. *Ibid.*, pp. 87–8; Chyczewski, 'Godzina "W" na Ochocie', p. 6.
13. Wroniszewski, *Ochota 1944*, p. 206.
14. Mirowski in *LCPW I.i*, p. 206.
15. Wroniszewski, *Ochota 1944*, p. 206.
16. *Ibid.*; Mirowski in *LCPW I.i*, p. 206.
17. Mirowski in *LCPW I.i*, p. 206; Wroniszewski, *Ochota 1944*, pp. 206–7.
18. Wroniszewski, *Ochota 1944*, p. 43; Namitkiewicz in *LCPW I.i*, pp. 209–10.
19. Wroniszewski, *Ochota 1944*, p. 206.
20. Memoir of A. Bagieńska in *LCPW I.i*, p. 202.
21. *Ibid.*
22. *Ibid.*, p. 201; Wroniszewski, *Ochota 1944*, p. 207.
23. Wroniszewski, *Ochota 1944*, p. 208.
24. *DOT*, p. 114.
25. Report of J. Rużyłło-Stasiakowa in *LCPW I.i*, p. 217.
26. Namitkiewicz in *LCPW I.i*, p. 212.
27. Rużyłło-Stasiakowa in *LCPW I.i*, p. 221.
28. Serwański, *Życie w powstańczej Warszawie*, pp. 90–1.
29. Wroniszewski, *Ochota 1944*, p. 158.
30. Rużyłło-Stasiakowa, in *LCPW I.i*, pp. 217 and 221.
31. Wroniszewski, *Ochota 1944*, p. 43.
32. Namitkiewicz in *LCPW I.i*, p. 218.
33. Wroniszewski, *Ochota 1944*, p. 161.
34. Rużyłło-Stasiakowa in *LCPW I.i*, p. 218.

35. Serwański, *Życie w powstańczej Warszawie*, p. 89.
36. *Ibid.*, pp. 82–3; Rużyłło-Stasiakowa in *LCPW I.i*, pp. 218–19.
37. Report of Namitkiewicz in *LCPW I.i*, p. 212.
38. Wroniszewski, *Ochota 1944*, pp. 74–5; *DOT*, pp. 114 and 115; Rużyłło-Stasiakowa in *LCPW I.i*, pp. 223.
39. Namitkiewicz in *LCPW I.i*, p. 212.
40. Serwański, *Życie w powstańczej Warszawie*, pp. 82–3; cf. APUST, wpł. z sztabu B.I., Sieroszewski, W., 'Sprawozdanie z odcinka "Wawelska" 1.VIII–11.VIII', p. 6. He wrote that on the whole the attitude of the civilians was very good with the exception of a few malcontents on ul. Mianowskiego 24, who asked the unit to leave.
41. *Ibid.*, pp. 86 ff.
42. Borkiewicz, *Powstanie Warszawskie 1944*, p. 137.
43. Rużyłło-Stasiakowa in *LCPW I.i*, pp. 222–3.
44. *Ibid.*, p. 224.
45. Borkiewicz, *Powstanie Warszawskie 1944*, p. 137.
46. Rużyłło-Stasiakowa in *LCPW I.i*, p. 225; Borkiewicz, *Powstanie Warszawskie 1944*, p. 138.
47. Borkiewicz, *ibid.*; Rużyłło-Stasiakowa in *LCPW I.i*, p. 226.
48. Rużyłło-Stasiakowa, *ibid.*; Wroniszewski, *Ochota 1944*, p. 226.
49. Rużyłło-Stasiakowa in *LCPW I.i*, p. 227; *DOT*, pp. 114–15; Borkiewicz, *Powstanie Warszawskie 1944*, p. 138.
50. Wroniszewski, *Ochota 1944*, p. 108.
51. Borkiewicz, *Powstanie Warszawskie 1944*, p. 136; Chyczewski, A., 'Samotna walka Ochoty', *TP*, no. 34, 1964, pp. 2–3.
52. Bartoszewski, 'Prasa powstania warszawskiego', pp. 334 and 355.
53. Chyczewski, 'Samotna walka Ochoty', p. 2.
54. Wroniszewski, *Ochota 1944*, p. 201; Borkiewicz, *Powstanie Warszawskie 1944*, pp. 136–7.
55. Borkiewicz, *Powstanie Warszawskie 1944*, p. 110; Kirchmayer, *Powstanie Warszawskie*, p. 232.
56. *DOT*, p. 113; Serwański, *Życie w powstańczej Warszawie*, p. 73.
57. *DOT*, p. 113.
58. Wroniszewski, *Ochota 1944*, pp. 227ff.

3.3 The Old Town

1. Report of G. Dąbrowska in *LCPW I.i*, p. 375.
2. Borkiewicz, *Powstanie Warszawskie 1944*, p. 192.
3. Podlewski, S., *Przemarsz przez piekło*, Warsaw, 1971, p. 113; Czajkowski-Dębczyński, *Dziennik Powstańca*, pp. 30, 35 and 38; Dobraczyński, J., 'Pierwsze dni', *WTK*, no. 32, 1962, pp. 6–7; PAN, III-7/130, Dzwonkowski, W., 'Pamiętnik: Okres Powstania Warszawskiego 1944', p. 29; BN, Rkps. akc. 7165, Sarnecki, 'Heroiczna Warszawa', p. 32; IZ, Dok.v.220, 'Protokóły i materiały do pracy pt. "Życie w powstaniu warszawskim"', vol. III, protocol no. 160.

4. See Bartoszewski, 'Prasa powstania warszawskiego', p. 321.
5. *W Walce*, 5.VIII.44; Podlewski, *Przemarsz przez piekło*, p. 113; Serwański, *Życie w powstańczej Warszawie*, p. 137.
6. AMW, Dąbrowa-Sierzputowski, 'Wspomnienia wojenne Warszawa', p. 57.
7. *Ibid.*; *PSZ*, p. 789.
8. AMW, Dąbrowa-Sierzputowski, 'Wspomnienia wojenne Warszawa', p. 58.
9. Dobraczyński, 'Pierwsze dni', pp. 6–7.
10. *Ibid.*; Komornicki, S., *Na barykadach Warszawy*, Warsaw, 1972, p. 76; AMW, Dąbrowa-Sierzputowski, 'Wspomnienia wojenne Warszawa', p. 59; Rossman in *LCPW I.i*, p. 151; Troński, *Tędy przeszła śmierć*, p. 130.
11. 'Wewnętrzny meldunek płk. Wachnowskiego, dowódcy Grupy AK "Północ" do Okręgowego Delegata Rządu na m.st. Warszawę' in *LCPW II*, pp. 107–8.
12. Report of S. Tarnawski in *LCPW I.i*, p. 465.
13. Dobraczyński, 'Pierwsze dni', pp. 6–7.
14. BN, Rkps. akc. 7165, Sarnecki, 'Heroiczna Warszawa', p. 90.
15. *PSZ*, p. 798.
16. APUST, 3.9.2.8, Radio messages received from John Ward, 14.VIII.44.
17. *PSZ*, p. 798.
18. See p. 51.
19. AMW, Dąbrowa-Sierzputowski, 'Wspomnienia wojenne Warszawa', p. 62.
20. Fajer, *Żołnierze Starówki*, p. 197; 'Powstanie warszawskie w świetle meldunków BIP', report no. 32, 17.VIII.44.
21. *Ibid.*, report no. 31, 17.VIII.44.
22. *Ibid.*, report no. 32, 17.VIII.44.
23. Bór-Komorowski, *The Secret Army*, p. 285; Borkiewicz, *Powstanie Warszawskie 1944*, p. 180.
24. 'Sprawozdanie Okręgowego Delegata Rządu z 19.VIII.44' in Przygoński, *Powstanie Warszawskie*, vol. II, p. 124.
25. IH PAN, Report of W. Świdowski, pp. 13–14, 22, and 27–8; Laryssa, W., *Wspomnienie i uwagi uczestnika powstania warszawskiego*, London, 1947, p. 17; Podlewski, *Przemarsz przez piekło*, p. 380.
26. Report of M. Porowski in *LCPW I.i*, p. 118.
27. Cf. Stawski, T., 'Wrześniowy kryzys powstania warszawskiego', *Kultura* (Paris), no. 9/35, 1950, p. 122.
28. IH PAN, Report of Świdowski, pp. 30–4; Fajer, *Żołnierze Starówki*, p. 78.
29. IH PAN, Report of Świdowski, pp. 12–34; Report of S. Sobolewski in *LCPW I.i*, pp. 449ff.
30. *Dzień Warszawy*, no. 1037, 27.VIII.44; *Nowy Swiat*, no. 5, 27.VIII.44;

Rzeczpospolita, no. 39, 28.VIII.44.

31. *Warszawianka*, no. 4, 11.VIII.44.
32. Sobolewski in *LCPW I.i*, p. 454 (cf. original recording in IH PAN, p. 25).
33. *Warszawianka*, no. 1, 7.VIII.44.
34. Sobolewski in *LCPW I.i*, pp. 454–5.
35. Fajer, *Żołnierze Starówki*, p. 67.
36. Podlewski, *Przemarsz przez piekło*, p. 16.
37. Stawski, 'Wrześniowy kryzys powstania warszawskiego', p. 122.
38. IZ, Dok.v.220 p. 3., protocol no. 160.
39. PAN, Dzwonkowski, 'Pamiętnik', p. 21; AMW, Dąbrowa-Sierzputowski, 'Wspomnienia wojenne Warszawa', p. 62.
40. PAN, Dzwonkowski, 'Pamiętnik', p. 80.
41. Stawski, 'Wrześniowy kryzys powstania warszawskiego', p. 122.
42. Report of Rosner in *LCPW I.i*, p. 341.
43. *Ibid.*; Report of O. Benwenuty Kwiatkowski in *LCPW I.i*, p. 414.
44. AMW, Dąbrowa-Sierzputowski, 'Wspomnienia wojenne Warszawa', p. 62.
45. Report of S. Tarnawski in *LCPW I.i*, p. 462.
46. *Ibid.*, pp. 458–66; Bayer, S., 'Służba Zdrowia w czasie powstania warszawskiego', PhD thesis, Warsaw, 1968, p. 31; Fajer, *Żołnierze Starówki*, p. 73.
47. Podlewski, *Przemarsz przez piekło*, p. 113.
48. Tarnawski in *LCPW I.i*, pp. 460–1.
49. *Ibid.*, pp. 460–1 and 465.
50. Bayer, 'Służba Zdrowia', p. 39.
51. *Warszawianka*, no. 19, 26.VIII.44.
52. 'Wewnętrzny meldunek płk. Wachnowskiego' in *LCPW II*, pp. 107–8.
53. 'Powstanie warszawskie w świetle meldunków BIP', report no. 42, 26.VIII.44.
54. Report on the situation in the Old Town, 21.VIII.44 (AWIH Sygn. III/40/30 k. 23).
55. Serwański, *Życie w powstańczej Warszawie*, p. 145.
56. APUST, 3.9.2.8, Radio messages received from John Ward, 22.VIII.44.
57. Report on the situation in the Old Town, 21.VIII.44.
58. Troński, *Tędy przeszła śmierć*, p. 167.
59. Dąbrowska in *LCPW I.i*, p. 376.
60. GSHI, A.x.3/88, Despatch from Warsaw, Ldz.6309/44, 4.VIII.44.
61. This poem, written by a young insurgent at the end of August, summarises well the attitude of Warsaw to the Soviets.

> We are waiting for you, you red pest,
> To deliver us from the black death.
> It would be a salvation welcomed with loathing
> For our nation, quartered and plundered.

We are waiting for you, power of the masses
Dehumanised under the fist of your governors.
We are waiting for you to come and crush us underfoot
With the deluge and roar of slogans.

We are waiting for you our age long enemy,
Murderer of thousands of our brothers –
We wait – not in revenge
But to welcome you with bread on homeground.

If you knew, hated redeemer,
The kind of death we wish on you in thanks,
And how feebly we wring our hands
Asking for help from you, insidious slaughterer!

If only you knew how painful
For us, children of the Free, Independent and Sacred
Poland, manacled in irons, your slanderous favour is,
Reeking of the yoke of ages of servitude.

If you knew our Grandfathers' hangman,
The Siberian prisons of gloomy legend,
How your kindness will be cursed by everyone here –
All of them Slavs, all of them your brothers.

Your army, victorious and red, has halted
At the edge of the glow of burning Warsaw
And your foul carcasslike soul devours itself with the
Bloody pain of a handful of madmen dying in the rubble.

We are waiting for you – not for our soldiers,
But for our injured, there are thousands here,
And there are children and nursing mothers as well,
And the plague is spreading through the cellars.

A month has already passed since we started the fight,
You deceive us sometimes by the din of action
Knowing how difficult it would be for us
To tell ourselves again, that once more you have tricked us.

We are waiting for you, who procrastinate and delay,
You are afraid of us, we know that,
You would like us all to fall here side by side,
Whilst outside Warsaw you await our extinction.

It does not matter to us, you have the right to choose,
You may help us, you may save us –
Or carry on waiting and leave us to die,
Death is not to be feared, we know how to die.

But you know that on our graves
A new victorious Poland will be born
And on this earth you will not tread,
You red lord of savage strength.

62. Dąbrowska in *LCPW I.i*, p. 377.
63. GSHI, PRM.L.9, Despatch from Warsaw, Ldz.4810/44, 23.VIII.44.
64. *Ibid.*, and PRM.L.26, Ldz.7172/44, 22.VIII.44.
65. Serwański, *Życie w powstańczej Warszawie*, p. 146; Dąbrowska in *LCPW I.i*, p. 378.
66. Troński, *Tędy przeszła śmierć*, p. 145.
67. Dąbrowska in *LCPW I.i*, p. 378. A. Pomian has written the following about the playing of 'Z dymem pożarów' during the Uprising. It was 'broadcast daily at the end of the "Radio Polskie" programme from London. It caused general irritation in Warsaw – "instead of help they send us lamentation, weakening our spirit" – Warsaw complained. The insurgents were not always aware, however, that although the "chorale" was put into the programmes it did not have any connection with the situation in Warsaw: it was decided on beforehand and proposed by the Poles in Poland as a signal for the provincial AK commanders to start the "Burza" plan. Because it was feared that its removal might lead to misunderstanding and confusion, the signal was not changed, although it was realised how inappropriate it was during the Uprising.' (Pomian, A., *Wiersze i pieśni Powstania Warszawskiego*, Tonbridge, 1952, p. 46.)
68. Ossol., 52/60, Lasocka, 'Powstanie Warszawskie', p. 231; Kamiński, *Zośka i Parasol*, pp. 444–5; Słomczyński, A., *W Warszawskim Arsenale*, Warsaw, 1971, p. 265.
69. PAN, Dzwonkowski, 'Pamiętnik', p. 77.
70. Dąbrowska in *LCPW I.i*, pp. 378–80; Report of O. Medarda Parysz in *LCPW I.i*, p. 429; Kamiński, *Zośka i Parasol*, p. 444; Podlewski, *Przemarsz przez piekło*, pp. 380–1; Słomczyński, *W Warszawskim Arsenale*, pp. 266–7.
71. Despatch from Warsaw, 25.VIII.44 in Majorkiewicz, F., *Dane nam było przeżyć*, Warsaw, 1972, p. 202; Borkiewicz, *Powstanie Warszawskie 1944*, p. 212.
72. Majorkiewicz, *Dane nam było przeżyć*, p. 296.
73. 'Meldunek Gromskiego do Borodzicza', 26.VIII.44 (AWIH Sygn. III/40/30 k. 128, 129).
74. *PSZ*, p. 759; Majorkiewicz, *Dane nam było przeżyć*, pp. 233–4.
75. Podlewski, *Przemarsz przez piekło*, p. 353.
76. Borkiewicz, *Powstanie Warszawskie 1944*, p. 221.
77. Podlewski, *Przemarsz przez piekło*, p. 380.
78. Majorkiewicz, *Dane nam było przeżyć*, p. 235.
79. IH PAN, *ŻHP*. Organizacja Harcerek. Warszawska Chorągiew Harcerek 1939–1945. Dokumenty, relacje, wspomnienia, compiled by

Zawadzka, Z., 'Dziennik Wiesławy Kempera', pp. 1026–112.
80. Kamiński, *Ṕośka i Parasol*, p. 444; Podlewski, *Przemarsz przez piekło*, p. 383.
81. Rosner in *LCPW I.i*, p. 348; Serwański, *Życie w powstańczej Warszawie*, p. 161.
82. 'Powstanie warszawskie w świetle meldunków BIP', report no. 42, 26.VIII.44.
83. *Ibid.*, report no. 44, 27.VIII.44.
84. BN, Rkps. akc. 7852, Rewska, H., 'Pamiętnik z Powstania Warszawskiego, 1944', p. 138.
85. Borkiewicz, *Powstanie Warszawskie 1944*, p. 221.
86. 'Pismo Okręgowego Delegata Rządu na m. st. Warszawę do dowódcy AK Grupy "Północ"', 29.VIII.44 in *LCPW II*, pp. 205–6.
87. Bogusławska, A., *Ludzie walczącej Warszawy*, West Germany, 1947, p. 131.
88. *Warszawianka*, no. 22, 28.VIII.44.
89. Sobolewski in *LCPW I.i*, p. 456.
90. Fajer, *Żołnierze Starówki*, pp. 340–1.
91. Borkiewicz, *Powstanie Warszawskie 1944*, pp. 229 and 238; Podlewski, *Przemarsz przez piekło*, p. 382; Słomczyński, *W Warszawskim Arsenale*, p. 267.
92. 'Meldunek sytuacyjny nr 23 z 29.VIII.44' quoted in Przygoński, *Powstanie Warszawskie*, vol. II, p. 414.
93. Słomczyński, *W Warszawskim Arsenale*, p. 267; Grunwald, H., 'Świerszcz na kościele Kapucynów', *Prze. Kul.*, no. 33–4, 1959, p. 4.
94. Komornicki, *Na barykadach Warszawy*, pp. 173–5.
95. Borkiewicz, *Powstanie Warszawskie 1944*, p. 237.
96. *Warszawianka*, no. 23, 30.VIII.44.
97. Borkiewicz, *Powstanie Warszawskie 1944*, p. 239.
98. Czajkowski-Dębczyński, *Dziennik Powstańca*, p. 159; *ŻHP*, 'Dziennik Wiesławy Kempera', pp. 1026–112.
99. Rosner in *LCPW I.i*, pp. 348–9.
100. Borkiewicz, *Powstanie Warszawskie 1944*, p. 246.
101. Sobolewski in *LCPW I.i*, p. 457.
102. 'Dziennik działań Niemieckiej 9 Armii', p. 104.
103. Przygoński, *Powstanie Warszawskie*, vol. II, p. 505.
104. Kirchmayer, *Powstanie Warszawskie*, p. 329; cf. *GKBZH*, p. 193.

3.4 Powiśle

1. Kirchmayer, *Powstanie Warszawskie*, p. 135 – see map no. 14.
2. Report of B. Hac in *LCPW I.i*, p. 481.
3. Laryssa, *Wspomnienie i uwagi*, p. 16.
4. 'Meldunek, Dział Polowy PSW Nienaski', 11.VIII.44 (AWIH, III/40/30, k. 3); 'Fragment meldunku (nr 78) placówki informacyjno-radiowej BIP KG AK', 20.VIII.44 in *LCPW II*, pp. 141–2; *Biuletyn*

Informacyjny, no. 254, 9.VIII.44; *Rzeczpospolita*, no. 18, 8.VIII.44; *Polityka* competition, 'Byli wówczas dziećmi', entry by R. Hładko, p. 24; Orska, I., *Silent is the Vistula*, London, 1946, pp. 96 and 108.

5. Report of Maria Majewska in *LCPW I.i*, p. 492.
6. 'Fragment meldunku (nr 78) placówki informacyjno-radiowej BIP KG AK', 20.VIII.44 in *LCPW II*, p. 141–2.
7. AZHP, ADR 202/XX-20 k. 1–2, 16.VIII.44; *Serwis Krajowy*, no. 10, 12.VIII.44; 'Polskie Radio Warszawa', 12.VIII.44; Laryssa, *Wspomnienie i uwagi*, p. 16; 'Meldunek płk. 'Łaszcza' do KG AK', 31.VIII.44 in *LCPW II*, pp. 232–33.
8. Laryssa, *Wspomnienie i uwagi*, p. 16.
9. AZHP, ADR 202/XX-22, k. 1–7, 25.VIII.44 and ADR 202/XX-25, k. 4–5, 9.VIII.44. See also p. 208.
10. AZHP, ADR 202/XX-24, k. 4, 10.VIII.44.
11. Laryssa, *Wspomnienie i uwagi*, pp. 17–18.
12. AZHP, ADR 202/XX-20, k. 1–2, 16.VIII.44.
13. *Ibid.*, ADR 202/XX-22, k. 1–7, 25.VIII.44.
14. *Ibid.*
15. Laryssa, *Wspomnienie i uwagi*, pp. 18–19.
16. AZHP, ADR 202/XX-22, k. 1–7, 25.VIII.44.
17. Laryssa, *Wspomnienie i uwagi*, p. 18.
18. AZHP, ADR 202/XX-22, k. 1–7, 25.VIII.44.
19. *Ibid.*
20. *Ibid.*
21. AZHP, ADR 202/XX-20, k. 1–2, 16.VIII.44.
22. *Ibid.*
23. 'Fragment meldunku (nr 78) placówki informacyjno-radiowej BIP KG AK', 20.VIII.44 in *LCPW II*, pp. 141–2.
24. 'Wspomnienia – Szare Urszulanki na Powiślu' in *LCPW I.i*, p. 512; Report of I. Zgrychowa in *LCPW I.i*, p. 516.
25. AZHP, ADR 202/XX-22, k. 1–7, 25.VIII.44.
26. *Serwis Krajowy*, no. 10, 12.VIII.44; *Rzeczpospolita*, no. 46, 3.IX.44.
27. *Rzeczpospolita*, no. 46, 3.IX.44.
28. Article in *Na szlaku kresowej* (Rome), no. 9, 1946, p. 16.
29. 'Wspomnienia – Szare Urszulanki' in *LCPW I.i*, p. 512.
30. 'Fragment meldunku (nr 78) placówki informacyjno-radiowej BIP KG AK', 20.VIII.44 in *LCPW II*, p. 141–2.
31. 'Wspomnienia – Szare Urszulanki', *LCPW I.i*, p. 512.
32. AZHP, ADR 202/XX-22, k. 1–7, 25.VIII.44.
33. *Ibid.*
34. *Ibid.*
35. *Ibid.*
36. *Ibid.*
37. 'Polskie Radio Warszawa', 23.VIII.44.
38. 'Wspomnienia – Szare Urszulanki', *LCPW I.i*, p. 505.
39. Laryssa, *Wspomnienie i uwagi*, p. 20.

40. 'Fragment meldunku wewnętrznego Wydziału Informacji BIP KG AK', 30.VIII.44 in *LCPW II*, p. 216.
41. *Ibid.*
42. Borkiewicz, *Powstanie Warszawskie 1944*, pp. 345–5.
43. Zgrychowa in *LCPW I.i*, p. 523.
44. Majewska in *LCPW I.i*, pp. 492–3 and 513.
45. 'Sprawozdanie sytuacyjne nr 23, Okręgowy Delegat Rządu m. st Warszawy, Wydział Bezpieczeństwa', 5.IX.44.
46. *Ibid.* It is interesting to note that the knowledge and implications of this fact are virtually never mentioned either in contemporary reports and memoirs, or in those written after the war.
47. 'Meldunek, Rejonowy Delegat Rządu; Warszawa Południe', 7.IX.44; cf. Orska, *Silent is the Vistula*, p. 198.
48. 'Sprawozdanie sytuacyjne nr 23', 5.IX.44; cf. 'Meldunki sytuacyjne "Montera"', pp. 132–3.
49. 'Sprawozdanie sytuacyjne nr 23', 5.IX.44.
50. Borkiewicz, *Powstanie Warszawskie 1944*, p. 368; Komornicki, *Na barykadach Warszawy*, p. 229.
51. Bogusławska, *Ludzie walczącej Warszawy*, p. 144.
52. 'Meldunek, Rejonowy Delegat Rządu: Warszawa Południe', 7.IX.44; Borkiewicz, *Powstanie Warszawskie 1944*, pp. 370–2.
53. *Ibid.*

3.5 The Uprising in Śródmieście (1 August – 1 September)

1. Kamiński, *Zośka i Parasol*, p. 524.
2. BN, Rkps. akc. 7165, Sarnecki, 'Heroiczna Warszawa', p. 156; Czajkowski-Dębczyński, *Dziennik Powstania*, p. 162; Troński, *Tędy przeszła śmierć*, p. 223.
3. Komornicki, *Na barykadach Warszawy*, pp. 205–7.
4. Rosner, J., 'Wspomnienie Redaktora "Warszawianki"', *Warszawa lat wojny i okupacji*, vol. II, p. 298.
5. Borkiewicz, *Powstanie Warszawskie 1944*, p. 24.
6. APUST, 1785/III 3.(5).B.I, Zarzycki, T., 'Relacja', p. 14; 'Meldunek sytuacyjny (nr 71) Wydziału Informacyjnego BIP KG AK', 8.VIII.44 in *LCPW II*, pp. 81–4; 'Meldunek sytuacyjny nr 13', 10.VIII.44 in 'Meldunki sytuacyjne "Montera"', pp. 111–12; Ochman, B., 'Szpital powstańczy na Chmielnej', *NDP II Wojny*, no. 7, 1963, p. 107; Report of 15.VIII.44 in 'Nastroje w powstaniu, Dokumenty 1944', ed. J. Białek, *Polityka*, no. 40, 1964, p. 8; Rudziński, A., *Dziennik z powstania warszawskiego*, London, 1974, p. 24.
7. 'Raport Borysa Mykita', 8.VIII.44 (AWIH III/40/25 k. 3); 'Wewnętrzny meldunek sytuacyjny placówki informacyjno-radiowej BIP KG AK', 10.VIII.44 in *LCPW II*, p. 95.
8. 'Wewnętrzny meldunek sytuacyjny placówki informacyjno-radiowej BIP KG AK', 5.VIII.44 in *LCPW II*, p. 56.

9. 'Meldunek sytuacyjny (nr 71) Wydziału Informacyjnego BIP KG AK', 8.VIII.44 and 'Meldunek wewnętrzny dowódcy patrolu Wojsk. Służ. Info. ppor. Bończewskiego do BIP', 9.VIII.44 in *LCPW II*, pp. 81–4 and pp. 92–3.
10. 'Wewnętrzny meldunek sytuacyjny placówki informacyjno-radiowej BIP KG AK', 10.VIII.44 in *LCPW II*, p. 95.
11. 'Meldunek 74', 8.VIII.44 (AWIH III/42/24 k. 105–8).
12. 'Meldunek sytuacyjny (nr 71) Wydziału Informacyjnego BIP KG AK', 8.VIII.44 in *LCPW II*, pp. 81–4; 'Meldunek nr 41, Kowal do Rafała', 10.VIII.44 (AWIH III/42/24 k. 137–8); Report of 15.VIII.44 in 'Nastroje w powstaniu, Dokumenty 1944', p. 8.
13. 'Wewnętrzny meldunek sytuacyjny placówki informacyjno-radiowej BIP KG AK', 5.VIII.44 in *LCPW II*, p. 56; Rudziński, *Dziennik z powstania warszawskiego*, p. 11.
14. 'Wewnętrzny meldunek sytuacyjny (nr 71) Wydziału Informacyjnego BIP KG AK', 8.VIII.44 (AWIH III/42/24 k. 118–19).
15. 'Meldunek wewnętrzny dowódcy patrolu Wojsk. Służ. Info. ppor. Bończewskiego do BIP', 9.VIII.44 in *LCPW II*, pp. 92–3.
16. 'Wewnętrzny meldunek sytuacyjny placówki informacyjno-radiowej BIP KG AK', 10.VIII.44 in *LCPW II*, p. 95.
17. 'Meldunek nr 41, Kowal do Rafała', 10.VIII.44 (AWIH III/42/24 k. 137–8).
18. *Ibid.*; see pp. 60–1.
19. *Ibid.*
20. 'Meldunek wewnętrzny nr 3', 12.VIII.44 in *LCPW II*, pp. 103–5.
21. 'Meldunek nr 41, Kowal do Rafała', 10.VIII.44 (AWIH III/42/24 k. 137–8).
22. GSHI, PRM.L.26, Despatch from Warsaw, Ldz.807/GNW/44, 10.VIII.44.
23. AZHP, ADR 202/XX-24, k. 25, 14.VIII.44; 'Wewnętrzny meldunek sytuacyjny BIP KG AK', 21.VIII.44 in *LCPW II*, pp. 145–6.
24. GSHI, PRM.L.5, Ldz.4609/44, 15.VIII.44; 'Wewnętrzny meldunek sytuacyjny BIP KG AK', 21.VIII.44 in *LCPW II*, pp. 145–6.
25. Report of J. Lis Błońska in *LCPW I.ii*, pp. 300–1.
26. 'Raport wewnętrzny placówki informacyjno-radiowej BIP KG AK', 12.VIII.44 in *LCPW II*, pp. 108–9.
27. 'Meldunek wewnętrzny nr 3', 12.VIII.44 in *LCPW II*, pp. 103–5.
28. Report of 12.VIII.44 in 'Nastroje w powstaniu warszawskim', ed. Turlejska, M., *Polityka*, no. 42, 1958, p. 5.
29. Skarżyński, *Powstańcza Warszawa w dniach walki*, pp. 27–8.
30. *Ibid.*, p. 30.
31. AZHP, ADR 202/XX-24, k. 26, 17.VIII.44 and k. 106, 20.VIII.44; 'Pisma por. "Borodzicza"', 17.VIII.44 in *LCPW II*, pp. 126–7.
32. Report of 17.VIII.44 in 'Nastroje w powstaniu, Dokumenty 1944', p. 8.
33. 'Wewnętrzny meldunek sytuacyjny placówki informacyjno-radiowej BIP KG AK', 20.VIII.44 in *LCPW II*, pp. 139–41.
34. Cf. GSHI, PRM.L.9, Ldz.4761/44, 21.VIII.44.

35. It is interesting to compare this to the attitude of the British War Cabinet at the time. See p. 168 n. 29.
36. AZHP, ADR 202/XX-24, k. 117, 21.VIII.44.
37. 'Meldunek wewnętrzny (nr 82)', 22.VIII.44 (AWIH, III/40/26 k. 36).
38. AZHP, ADR 202/XX-24, k. 145, k. 180–1, 24 and 27.VIII.44.
39. *Ibid.*, k. 145, 24.VIII.44.
40. *Ibid.*, k. 152, 25.VIIII.44.
41. *Ibid.*, k. 247 and k. 278–9, 1 and 5.IX.44.
42. *Ibid.*, k. 218, 29.VIII.44.
43. 'Meldunek BIP (Bończewski)', 22.VIII.44 (AWIH III/43/16 k. 4); AZHP, ADR 202/XX-24, k. 223 and 278–9, 30.VIII.44 and 5.IX.44; 'Wewnętrzny meldunek sytuacyjny placówki informacyjno-radiowej BIP KG AK', 22.VIII.44 in *LCPW II*, pp. 151–2.
44. 'Meldunek BIP, Wojsk. Służ. Info. Społ', 22.VIII.44 (AWIH III/43/16 k. 2–3).
45. AZHP, ADR/XX-24, k. 180–1, 27.VIII.44.
46. *Ibid.*; 'Meldunek BIP (Bończewski)', 22.VIII.44 (AWIH III/40/26 k. 26).
47. AZHP, ADR 202/XX-24, k. 186, 28.VIII.44. The 'Konwent' was formed in 1942 by a group of Piłsudski supporters.
48. 'Meldunek wewnętrzny patrolu Wojsk. Służ. Info. Społ', 23.VIII.44, and 'Meldunek sytuacyjny placówki informacyjno-radiowej BIP KG AK', 24.VIII.44 in *LCPW II*, pp. 165–6 and 168–9; 'Meldunek nr 88', 24.VIII.44 (AWIH III/40/26 k. 46).
49. 'Meldunek nr 88', 24.VIII.44; AZHP, ADR 202/XX-11, k. 1–2, 29.VIII.44.
50. 'Fragmenty meldunku wewnętrznego Oddziału Informacyjno-wywiadczowego Komendy Okręgu Warszawskiego AK', 31.VIII.44 in *LCPW II*, pp. 224–7; Gieysztor, M.K., 'Dziennik z powstania warszawskiego', *Polityka*, no. 30, 1967, p. 6.
51. Gieysztor, 'Dziennik z powstania warszawskiego', p. 6.
52. 'Meldunek z dnia 23.VIII.44, Śniady' (AWIH III/42/19 k. 25); AZHP, ADR 202/XX-11, k. 1–2, 29.VIII.44.
53. 'Mełdunek z dnia 23.VIII.44, Śniady' (AWIH III/42/19 k. 25).
54. 'Raport D3', 23.VIII.44 (AWIH III/42/19 k. 21–2).
55. 'Wewnętrzny meldunek sytuacyjny (nr 99)', 28.VIII.44 in *LCPW II*, pp. 195–6.
56. 'Fragmenty meldunku wewnętrznego Oddziału Informacyjno-wywiadczowego Komendy Okręgu Warszawskiego AK', 31.VIII.44 in *LCPW II*, pp. 224–7.
57. *Ibid.*; AZHP, ADR 202/XX-11, k. 1–2, 29.VIII.44; 'Fragment meldunku ogólnego', 31.VIII.44 and 'Wewnętrzny meldunek sytuacyjny placówki informacyjno-radiowej BIP KG AK', 30.VIII.44 in *LCPW II*, pp. 233–5 and 210–11.
58. 'Fragment meldunku ogólnego', 31.VIII.44 in *LCPW II*, pp. 233–5.
59. *Ibid.*, and 'Fragmenty meldunku wewnętrznego Komendy Okręgu

Warszawskiego', 31.VIII.44 in *LCPW II*, pp. 224–7.

60. *LCPW II*, pp. 210–11.
61. *Ibid.*; this part has been omitted in the published part of the original.
62. *Ibid.*, pp. 224–7.
63. *Ibid.*, pp. 210–11.
64. *Ibid.*, pp. 224–7.
65. *Ibid.*; 'Fragment meldunku wewnętrznego Wydziału Informacji BIP KG AK', 30.VIII.44 and 'Fragmenty meldunku wewnętrznego' 4.IX.44 in *LCPW II*, pp. 215–16 and 272–5.
66. 'Wewnętrzny meldunek specjalny placówki informacyjno-radiowej BIP KG AK', 26.VIII.44, 'Fragmenty meldunku wewnętrznego Oddziału informacyjno-wywiadczowego Komendy Okręgu Warszawskiego AK', 31.VIII.44 and 'Fragment meldunku ogólno-sytuacyjnego', 31.VIII.44, all in *LCPW II*, pp. 186–7, 224–7 and 233–5.
67. *Biuletyn Informacyjny*, no. 273, 28.VIII.44.
68. APUST, 1785/III 3.(5).B.I., Zarzycki, 'Relacja', p. 14.
69. 'Meldunek BIP, Rejon III, Patrol I'; 'Meldunek Patrolu Wojsk. Służ. Info. Społ., Obwód I, odc. II'; 'Meldunek BIP, Rejon III, Obwód V'; 'Meldunek BIP, Rejon III, Obwód I'; 'Meldunek BIP, Rejon III, Obwód II'; 'Meldunek BIP, Rejon III, Patrol IV'; 'Meldunek Patrol Wojsk. Służ. Info. Społ. ... odc. II (?)'; 'Meldunek Patrol Wojsk. Służ. Info. Społ., Rejon II'; 'Meldunek Patrolu Wojsk. Służ. Info. Społ., Obwód I, odc. II', 31.VIII.44.
70. AZHP, ADR 202/XX-24, k. 4, 10.VIII.44; *Biuletyn Informacyjny*, no. 256, 11.VIII.44.
71. AZHP, ADR 202/XX-24, k. 4, 10.VIII.44; Sendlak, S., 'W powstaniu bez broni', *TP*, no. 37, 1964, p. 2.
72. Bartoszewski, W., 'Na ulicy Wspólnej', *Więź*, no. 10, 1974, p. 104; *Biuletyn Informacyjny*, no. 262, 17.VIII.44. Region IV was often referred to simply as Warsaw South.
73. AZHP, ADR 202/XX-20, k. 1–2, 16.VIII.44.
74. *Ibid.*, ADR 202/XX-6, k. 41, 28.VIII.44.
75. *Ibid.* and k. 57–8, 4.IX.44 and ADR 202/XX-9, k. 10, 4.IX.44; *PSZ*, p. 804.
76. Sendlak, 'W powstaniu bez broni', p. 2.
77. *Biuletyn Informacyjny*, no. 258, 13.VIII.44.
78. AZHP, ADR 202/XX-13, k. 111–16, 17.VIII.44.
79. *Ibid.*
80. AZHP, ADR 202/XX-9, k. 10, 4.IX.44.
81. *Ibid.*, k. 1–8, 30.IX.44.
82. Sendlak, 'W powstaniu bez broni', p. 2.
83. *Robotnik*, no. 19, 12.VIII.44 and no. 27, 20.VIII.44.
84. Bayer, 'Służba Zdrowia', p. 113.
85. AZHP, ADR 202/XX-6, k. 41, 28.VIII.44.
86. *Ibid.*, 202/XX-23, k. 3, 202/XX-25, k. 26, and 202/XX-26, k. 30 11.VIII.44; *Robotnik*, no. 30, 23.VIII.44 and no. 32, 25.VIII.44;

Rzeczpospolita, no. 29, 18.VIII.44; *Dziennik Obwieszczeń Rejonowego Delegata Rządu Warszawa Południe*, no. 1, 20.VIII.44; Ochman, 'Szpital powstańczy na Chmielnej', *NDP II Wojny*, no. 7, 1963, p. 113; 'Polskie Radio Warszawa', 25.VIII.44; APUST, B.II. 3861/1.2, Jasiukowicz, M., 'Sanitariat Okręgu Warszawskiego'.

87. Bukowski, S., 'Apteki południowego Śródmieścia Warszawy w czasie powstania 1944', *Arch. Hist. Med.*, no. 4, 1964, pp. 463–80; 'Zarządzenie Rejonowego Delegata Rządu Warszawa Południe', 14.VIII.44 in *LCPW II*, pp. 112–14.
88. *Dziennik Obwieszczeń Rejonowego Delegata Rządu Warszawa Południe*, no. 1, 20.VIII.44.
89. *Ibid.*
90. AZHP, ADR 202/XX-11, k. 1, 29.VIII.44.
91. See p. 136.
92. Ochman, 'Szpital powstańczy na Chmielnej', p. 119.
93. *Biuletyn Informacyjny*, no. 277, 1.IX.44; 'Zarządzenie Komendy Okręgu Warszawskiego AK', 31.VIII.44 in *LCPW II*, pp. 228–9.
94. Cf. pp. 214–15.
95. AZHP, ADR 202/XX-15, k. 2, 24.VIII.44.
96. Cf. p. 215.
97. Korboński, *Fighting Warsaw*, pp. 371–2.
98. AZHP, ADR 202/XX-17, k. 4, 30.VIII.44. Cf. pp. 213–14.

3.6 The September crisis and the civilian evacuation (1–10 September)

1. 'Meldunek BIP, Rejon III, Patrol nr 2', 4.IX.44; 'Meldunek BIP, Rejon III, Patrol nr 5', 5.IX.44; 'Meldunek Wojsk. Patrolu Służ. Info. Społ. na odc. II + III, Obwód I Południe BIP', 5. and 7.IX.44; 'Meldunek BIP, Rejon III, Patrol nr 3', 6.IX.44; 'Meldunek BIP, Rejon III, Patrol nr 4', 6.IX.44. These are just a few examples.
2. 'Meldunek BIP, Obwód I, odc. II', 5.IX.44; 'Meldunek BIP, Rejon III, Patrol nr 3', 6.IX.44; 'Meldunek BIP, Rejon III, Patrol nr 4', 6.IX.44; 'Meldunek BIP, Rejon III, Patrol nr 1', 6.IX.44; AZHP, ADR 202/XX-6, k. 77, and 202/XX-24, k. 287, 6.IX.44; 'Wewnętrzny meldunek sytuacyjny placówki informacyjno-radiowej BIP KG AK', 2.IX.44 and 'Fragment meldunku wewnętrznego Oddziału Informacyjno-wywiadowczego Komendy Okręgu Warszawskiego AK', 4.IX.44 in *LCPW II*, pp. 251–2 and 272–5. (In this report it is also stated that no one feared the coming of the Russians any longer if it meant an end to the fighting and bombings.)
3. 'Meldunek Wojsk. Patrolu Służ. Info. Społ. na odc. II i IV, Obwód I, Południe,' 7.IX.44; 'Meldunek BIP, Rejon III, Patrol nr 2', 6.IX.44.
4. *Ibid.*
5. 'Meldunek wewnętrzny Wojsk. Patrolu Służ. Info. Społ., BIP Obwód I, odc. 2 i 3', 4.IX.44 in *LCPW II*, pp. 294–5.
6. Majorkiewicz, *Dane nam było przeżyć*, p. 210.

7. 'Meldunek BIP, Rejon III, Patrol nr 2', 6.IX.44; 'Polskie Radio Warszawa', 8.IX.44.
8. Bór-Komorowski, *The Secret Army*, p. 310.
9. 'Meldunek BIP, Rejon III, Patrol nr 2', 6.IX.44.
10. 'Sprawozdanie sytuacji: Okręgowa Delegatura Rządu na m. st. Warszawę, Wydział Bezpieczeństwa, nr 23', 5.IX.44.
11. *Ibid.*; 'Meldunek BIP, Obwód I, odc. II', 5.IX.44; 'Meldunek Wojsk. Patrolu Służ. Info. Społ.', 5.IX.44.
12. 'Meldunek BIP, Obwód I, odc. II', 4 and 5.IX.44.
13. 'Meldunek Wojsk. Patrolu Służ. Info. Społ., BIP Obwód I, Południe na odc. II i III', 7.IX.44.
14. 'Meldunek BIP, Rejon III, Patrol nr 2', 6.IX.44.
15. 'Meldunek wewnętrzny Wojsk. Patrolu Służ. Info. Społ., Obwód I, odc. II i III', 4.IX.44 in *LCPW II*, pp. 294–5.
16. 'Meldunek BIP, Rejon III, Patrol nr 2', 6.IX.44.
17. 'Meldunek płk. "Sulimy"', 3.IX.44 in *LCPW II*, pp. 262–3.
18. Bień, *Wspomnienia*, p. 183, and his report in *LCPW II*, p. 65; Stawski, 'Wrześniowy kryzys powstania Warszawskiego', p. 124; Korboński, *Fighting Warsaw*, p. 335 and verbal information of the same.
19. Report of J. Stopnicki in *LCPW I.i*, p. 435.
20. GSHI, A.XII.3/88, Despatch from Poland, Ldz.7494/44, 29.VIII.44. For a full discussion of these plans see Pobóg-Malinowski, *Najnowsza historia*, pp. 752–9 and Przygoński, *Powstanie Warszawskie*, vol. II, pp. 331–8.
21. GSHI, A.XII.3/88, Despatch from Poland, Ldz.7730/44, 3.IX.44.
22. Skarżyński, *Powstańcza Warszawa w dniach walki*, p. 40.
23. *Biuletyn Informacyjny*, no. 281, 5.IX.44.
24. *Rzeczpospolita*, no. 51, 5.IX.44.
25. Bartoszewski, W., 'Kronika ważniejszych wydarzeń powstania warszawskiego' in *LCPW III*, p. 473 and copy of the pamphlet printed between pp. 368 and 369.
26. AZHP, ADR 202/XX-24, k. 288, 6.IX.44; 'Raport Sytuacyjny Ekspozytury Departmentu Informacji Delegatury Rządu' 6.IX.44 in *LCPW II*, pp. 301–2; Serwański, *Życie w powstańczej Warszawie*, p. 297.
27. 'Meldunek wewnętrznego Oddziału Informacyjno-wywiadowczego Komendy Okręgu Warszawskiego o nastrojach ludności na terenie Śródmieścia', 7.IX.44 in *LCPW II*, pp. 309–10.
28. Bartoszewski, W., 'Kryzys kapitulacyjny 8–11 września w świetle nieznanych dokumentów', *Stolica*, no. 39, 1956, p. 2.
29. 'Apel Okręgowego Delegata Rządu na m. st. Warszawę', 6.IX.44 in *LCPW II*, pp. 355–6.
30. GSHI, A.XII.3/88, Despatch from Poland, Ldz.8025/44, 6.IX.44. See also n. 75 below.
31. *Ibid.*, Despatch from Poland, Ldz.7991/44, 6.IX.44. My italics. Cf. p. 168 n. 29.
32. Majorkiewicz, *Dane nam było przeżyć*, p. 245.

33. 'Wezwanie do ludności o zachowanie spokoju', 7.IX.44 in *LCPW III*, p. 362.
34. 'Specjalny meldunek wewnętrzny Wydziału Informacji BIP KG AK o postawie społeczeństwa, stronnictw i grup politycznych' in *LCPW II*, p. 385.
35. 'Apel Okręgowego Delegata Rządu na m. st. Warszawę do ludności w sprawie niemieckich ulotek dywersyjnych,' 6.IX.44 in *LCPW II*, pp. 355–6.
36. *Biuletyn Informacyjny*, no. 284, 8.IX.44.
37. *Robotnik*, no. 46, 9.IX.44.
38. *Armia Ludowa*, no. 32, 8.IX.44.
39. *Rzeczpospolita*, no. 51, 8.IX.44.
40. AZHP, ADR 202/XX-18, k. 12, 9.IX.44.
41. Verbal information of S. Korboński.
42. Majorkiewicz, *Dane nam było przeżyć*, p. 316. Majorkiewicz's figures are nearly the same as those published in *Biuletyn Informacyjny*, no. 287, 11.IX.44. According to the paper about 6,000 people left on 9.IX.44 and 940 on 10.IX.44; Borkiewicz, *Powstanie Warszawskie 1944*, pp. 382, 385, quotes a figure of 6,000 for the first day and 2,000 for the second; Bartoszewski in *LCPW III*, p. 476, gives a figure of about 8,000, whereas Rosner in *LCPW I*.; p. 362, quotes 10,000; 'Dziennik działań Niemieckiej', p. 107.
43. GSHI, PRM.L.5, Despatch from Poland, Ldz.652, 12.IX.44.
44. *Ibid.*, Despatch from Poland, Ldz.5521/44, 22.IX.44.
45. Majorkiewicz, *Dane nam było przeżyć*, p. 316.
46. 'Fragment z meldunku', 8.IX.44 (AWIH III/42/22, k. 141).
47. 'Meldunek wewnętrzny Oddziału Informacyjno-wywiadowczego Komendy Okręgu Warszawskiego AK', 10.IX.44 in *LCPW II*, pp. 342–4; Ostrowska, *W Alejach spacerują 'Tygrysy'*, p. 199.
48. 'Meldunek wewnętrzny Oddziału Informacyjno-wywiadczowego Komendy Okręgu Warszawskiego AK', 10.IX.44 (?), in *LCPW II*, p. 343; Ossol., 13482/11, Tyrankiewiczowa, 'W rękach hitlerowców', pp. 162–4.
49. Ostrowska, *W Alejach spacerują 'Tygrysy'*, pp. 198–9.
50. Verbal information; 'Meldunek wewnętrzny (L.p.209) Oddziału Informacyjno-wywiadczowego Komendy Okręgu Warszawskiego AK', 8.IX.44 in *LCPW II*, p. 324.
51. Report of Jolanta Wadecka, p. 1.
52. 'Wewnętrzny meldunek informacyjny Prasowego Sprawozdawcy Wojennego "Alfreda"', 8.IX.44 in *LCPW II*, p. 327; verbal information.
53. 'Polskie Radio Warszawa'. 10.IX.44; Rosner in *LCPW I.i*, p. 356.
54. Rosner in *LCPW I.i*, p. 356; 'Meldunek BIP, Obwód I, odc. II', 10.IX.44; Żeromska, M., 'Notatki z powstania warszawskiego'; 'Meldunek wewnętrzny Prasowego Sprawozdawcy Wojennego "Wojnicza"', 8.IX.44 in *LCPW II*, p. 328.

55. *LCPW II*, pp. 327–8; Troński, *Tędy przeszła śmierć*, pp. 255–6; Prorok, L., 'Przed końcem', *Literatura*, no. 30, 1973, p. 4.
56. 'Wewnętrzny meldunek informacyjny Prasowego Sprawozdawcy Wojennego "Alfreda"', 8.IX.44 in *LCPW II*, p. 327. The author of this report also wrote that several AK soldiers from Powiśle left in the crowd.
57. *Ibid.*; cf. APUST, Wpl. ze sztabu, Bucza, M., 'Ankieta w sprawie uczestnictwie w AK', May 1946. Bucza also writes that the September evacuation had a significant influence on the morale of soldiers with families in the city. Some had to decide whether to go with them or make them stay and risk their lives.
58. 'Raport Rejonowego Delegata Rządu Warszawa-Południe. Dział Informacji i Prasy', 17.IX.44.
59. Report of J. Nalazek in *LCPW I. ii*, p. 425; 'Meldunek wewnętrzny Prasowego Sprawozdawcy Wojennego "Wojnicza"', 8.IX.44 in *LCPW II*, p. 328.
60. *LCPW II*, p. 328; Ostrowska, *W Alejach spacerują 'Tygrysy'*, p. 199.
61. Ossol., 13482/11, Tyrankiewiczowa, 'W rękach hitlerowców' pp. 161–4.
62. Borkiewicz, *Powstanie Warszawskie 1944*, p. 401; According to Kazimierz Bagiński, the Director of the Department of Internal Affairs, the RJN recommended on 7 September that the battle in Warsaw be ended (see Zawodny, J.K., *Nothing but Honour*, London, 1978).
63. Borkiewicz, *Powstanie Warszawskie 1944*, p. 403; Kirchmayer, *Powstanie Warszawskie*, p. 378.
64. Kirchmayer, *ibid.*; Majorkiewicz, *Dane nam było przeżyć*, p. 255.
65. Borkiewicz, *Powstanie Warszawskie 1944*, pp. 397–403; Kirchmayer, *Powstanie Warszawskie*, pp. 373–9; Majorkiewicz, *Dane nam było przeżyć*, pp. 243–59; Bartoszewski, 'Kryzys kapitulacyjny' pp. 2–3 and 13.
66. Cf. p. 155; GSHI, PRM.L.7 Despatch from Poland, Ldz.7991/44, 7.IX.44.
67. Quoted in Borkiewicz, *Powstanie Warszawskie 1944*, p. 400.
68. Rosner – unpublished section of memoirs.
69. Rosner in *LCPW I.i*, p. 362.
70. 'Meldunek BIP, Rejon III, Patrol I', 12.IX.44.
71. 'Meldunek wewnętrzny Oddziału Informacyjno-wywiadowczego Komendy Okręgu Warszawskiego AK', 11.IX.44 in *LCPW II*, pp. 361–2.
72. 'Meldunek Patrolu Wojsk. Służ. Info. Społ., Obwód I', 10.IX.44; Report of S. Sendlak in *LCPW I.ii*, p. 264.
73. 'Meldunek wewnętrzny Prasowego Sprawozdawcy Wojennego "Wojnicza"' 8.IX.44 in *LCPW II*, p. 328.
74. 'Meldunek Patrolu Wojsk. Służ. Info. Społ., Obwód I, odc. II', 11.IX.44; 'Meldunek wewnętrzny Oddziału Informacyjno-wywiadczego Komendy Okręgu AK', 10.IX.44 in *LCPW II*, pp. 344–5.

75. On 1 September Mikołajczyk broadcast to Warsaw, encouraging the city to carry on the battle. In part of his broadcast he said:
Fight on! I know you will continue your battle. You have no choice. Any doubts or hesitations will not bring victory but death. You have and desire to have the right to exist – be victorious and live! You have every right to be helped. No one for either political or opportunistic reasons should underestimate the value of your efforts, undertaken with the highest intentions. You have not received the help due to you, in spite of the sacrifice of British, South African and Polish pilots, who alone have recently brought you help. We are doing everything we can, so that help will be sent to Warsaw in the right amount and quickly. I have not lost hope that it will be sent. If this help does not come I shall once again publicly appeal to Marshal Stalin, President Roosevelt and Premier Churchill. Leaders of great powers! Commanders of powerful and victorious air and sea forces – Warsaw is waiting! The whole Polish nation is waiting. World public opinion is waiting.' (Mikołajczyk, S., *La viol de la Pologne*, Paris, 1948, pp. 103–4.)

3.7 The Uprising in Śródmieście (10–30 September)

1. For a full description of the fighting in the area during the first ten days of September, see Borkiewicz, *Powstanie Warszawskie 1944*, pp. 354–93.
2. GSHI, PRM.L.7, Despatch from Poland, Ldz.8235/44, 12.IX.44; 'Meldunek BIP, Rejon III, Patrol nr 3', 12.IX.44; 'Referat Informacji i Prasy, Rejonowa Delegatura Rządu Warszawa Południe', 12.IX.44; 'Meldunek wewnętrzny Oddziału Informacyjno-wywiadowczego Komendy Okręgu Warszawskiego AK', 11.IX.44 in *LCPW II*, pp. 361–2.
3. 'Meldunek Wojsk. Patrolu Służ. Info. Społ., Obwód I, odc. II', 10.IX.44.
4. 'Meldunek BIP, Rejon III, Patrol nr 5', 12.IX.44.
5. *PSZ*, p. 799.
6. Polak, *63 dni powstania warszawskiego*, p. 108.
7. 'Referat Informacji i Prasy, Rejonowa Delegatura Rządu Warszawa Południe', 13.IX.44. The announcement of Gen. 'Monter' referred to was that of 7 September in which he spoke of help coming in four to five days.
8. 'Specjalny meldunek wewnętrzny Wydziału Informacji BIP KG AK', 15.IX.44 in *LCPW II*, pp. 384–9.
9. 'Meldunek Wojsk. Patrolu Służ. Info. Społ., Obwód I, odc. II i III', 14.IX.44; AZHP, ADR 202/XX-6, k. 97; Prorok, 'Przed końcem', p. 4.
10. 'Referat Informacji i Prasy, Rejonowa Delegatura Rządu Warszawa Południe', 12.IX.44.
11. 'Meldunek Wojsk. Patrolu Służ. Info. Społ., Obwód I, odc. II i III', 14.IX.44.
12. Kulesiński, in *LCPW I.ii*, pp. 393–4.

13. AZHP, ADR 202/XX-9, k. 15, 14.IX.44.
14. Serwański, *Życie w powstańczej Warszawie*, p. 299; *Biuletyn Informacyjny*, no. 290, 14.IX.44. The word hunger in all these references is used in a rather loose sense and does not necessarily mean starvation, but rather that there was never enough to eat and that people were going hungry.
15. 'Meldunek Wojsk. Patrolu Służ. Info. Społ., Obwód I, odc. II i III', 14.IX.44.
16. GSHI, A.12/73/7, Part of text from Radio 'Błyskawica', 15.IX.44.
17. *Ibid.*, Message from the RJN and KRM to the Polish government in London, 15.IX.44.
18. AZHP, ADR 202/XX-9, k. 17, 18.IX.44.
19. 'Wewnętrzne sprawozdanie sytuacyjne Wydziału Bezpieczeństwa Okręgowej Delegatury Rządu', 22.IX.44 in *LCPW II*, p. 435.
20. Rozwadowska, H., *Wspomnienia ważne i nieważne*, Warsaw, 1966, p. 350.
21. Polak, *63 dni powstania warszawskiego*, p. 103.
22. Gieysztor, 'Dziennik z powstania warszawskiego', p. 7.
23. GSHI, PRM.L.26, Despatch from Poland, Ldz.8598/44, 20.IX.44.
24. 'Referat Informacji i Prasy, Rejonowa Delegatura Rządu Warszawa Południe, Raport nr 5', 16.IX.44.
25. *Ibid.*, 'Raport nr 7', 18.IX.44.
26. Borkiewicz, *Powstanie Warszawskie 1944*, p. 425.
27. GSHI, PRM.L.7, Despatch from Poland, Ldz.8463/44, 16.IX.44.
28. Bór-Komorowski, *The Secret Army*, p. 350.
29. *PSZ*, p. 789. At a British government Cabinet meeting on 5 September 1944, the Vice-Chief of Staff stated that it was estimated that during an American daylight raid from a height of over 10,000 feet, not more than 10% of the materials dropped would be received by the Poles – 'In other words the operation would be a gesture the military value of which would be small' (PRO, Secretaries Standard File of the War Cabinet CAB.65.47 W.M.(44) 117th. Conclusion. Minute 1 Confidential Annex, 5.IX.44, pp. 57–9).
30. 'Depesza Dowódcy AK do Władz Naczelnych w Londynie', 19.IX.44 in Majorkiewicz, *Dane nam było przeżyć*, pp. 320–1.
31. Kulesiński in *LCPW I.ii*, p. 393.
32. APUST, 2940/1–I.B.I., Skrzyńska-Pierre, J., 'Powstanie I.VIII–5.X.44', p. 28.
33. See n. 29 above.
34. For a full description see Borkiewicz, *Powstanie Warszawskie 1944*, pp. 422–30.
35. GSHI, PRM.L.5, Despatch from Poland, Ldz.5505/44, 20.IX.44; 'Meldunek wewnętrzny Oddziału Informacyjno-wywiadowczego Komendy Okręgu Warszawskiego AK', 19.IX.44 in *LCPW II*, pp. 417–18.
36. AZHP, ADR 202/XX-6, k. 117, 22.IX.44.
37. 'Referat Informacji i Prasy, Rejonowa Delegatura Rządu Warszawa Południe, Raport nr 7', 18.IX.44.

38. BN, Chomicki, '63 dni w płonącej Warszawie', pp. 29–30.
39. *PSZ*, p. 799.
40. *Barykada Wolności*, no. 147, 16.IX.44.
41. *Biuletyn Informacyjny*, no. 262, 17.IX.44.
42. *Nowy Świat*, no. 11, 22.IX.44.
43. *Barykada Wolności*, no. 152, 25.IX.44.
44. *Głos Warszawy*, (Śródmieście-South), no. 177, 26.IX.44.
45. *Armia Ludowa* (Śródmieście-South), nos. 31–7, 15.IX.44 until 21.IX.44.
    According to one Eastern European specialist PKWN members were
    pleading with Stalin to help save Warsaw (Mastny, *Russia's Road to the
    Cold War*, p. 189.)
46. Ochman, 'Szpital powstańczy na Chmielnej', p. 139.
47. Ossol., 134/64, Krobicka-Modzelewska, L., 'Wrzesień 1939', p. 110.
48. BN, Rps. syn. IV.6400, Kirkor-Kiedroniowa, 'Wspomnienia i notatki
    pisane w czasie powstania warszawskiego', p. 56.
49. *Ibid.*
50. Prorok, 'Przed końcem', p. 4.
51. 'Bezpiecznik nr 30', 21.IX.44.
52. Bór-Komorowski, *The Secret Army*, p. 358.
53. GSHI, PRM.L.5, Despatch from Poland, Ldz.714/2, 22.IX.44 and
    Ldz.5521/44, 23.IX.44.
54. *Ibid*, Ldz. 5521/44; 'Bezpiecznik nr 30', 21.IX.44.
55. 'Meldunek sytuacyjny D-cy Baonu Panc.', 22.IX.44 (AWIH, III/43/49,
    k. 25); 'Wewnętrzne sprawozdanie sytuacyjne Wydziału Bezpiecz-
    eństwa Okręgowej Delegatury Rządu na m. st. Warszawę', 22.IX.44 in
    LCPW II, p. 435.
56. Serwański, *Życie w powstańczej Warszawie*, p. 300.
57. 'Bezpiecznik nr 30', 21.IX.44.
58. Gieysztor, 'Dziennik z powstania warszawskiego', p. 8.
59. AZHP, ADR 202/XX-18, k. 14, 21.IX.44.
60. *Ibid.*, ADR 202/XX-11, k. 19, 21.IX.44.
61. APUST, 3.9.2.8, Radio messages received from John Ward, 23.IX.44.
62. AZHP, ADR 202/XX-2, k. 3, 24.IX.44.
63. 'Bezpiecznik nr 30', 21.IX.44.
64. *Ibid.*
65. 'Bezpiecznik nr 32', 23.IX.44.
66. *Ibid.*
67. AZHP, ADR 202/XX-2, k. 3, 24.IX.44.
68. *Ibid.*, ADR 202/XX-6, k. 161, 26.IX.44.
69. 'Meldunek wewnętrzny Oddziału Informacyjno-wywiadowczego
    Komendy Okręgu Warszawskiego', 24.IX.44 in *LCPW II*, p. 451.
70. AZHP, ADR 202/XX-17, k. 21. 24.IX.44.
71. *Ibid.*, ADR 202/XX-17. k. 30 and 31, 26 and 27.IX.44.
72. *Ibid.*, ADR 202/XX-6, k. 160 and 162, 26.IX.44; 'Meldunek wewnętrzny
    patrolu Wojsk. Służ. Info. Społ, BIP (Obwód I, odc. 2 i 3)', 25.IX.44
    and 'Meldunek wewnętrzny patrolu (nr 4) Wojsk. Służ. Info. Społ.

BIP (Obwód I, Rejon III)', 26.IX.44 in *LCPW II*, pp. 461–3 and p. 474.

73. 'Meldunek wewnętrzny patrolu Wojsk. Służ. Info. Społ. (Obwód I, odc. 2 i 3)', 26.IX.44 in *LCPW II*, p. 478.
74. Bór-Komorowski, *The Secret Army*, p. 358.
75. 'Polskie Radio Warszawa', 28.IX.44; Zagórski, W., *Seventy Days*, London, 1957, p. 231.
76. Ostrowska, *W Alejach spacerują 'Tygrysy'*, p. 261.
77. GSHI, A.XII.3/88, Despatch from Poland, Ldz.9107/44, 26.IX.44.
78. Zagórski, *Seventy Days*, p. 139.
79. 'Meldunek sytuacyjny Radwana nr 105', 25.IX.44 (AWIH III.43/4 k. 119).
80. APUST, 3.9.2.8, Radio messages received from John Ward, 29.IX.44.
81. GSHI, PRM.L.5, Despatch from Poland, Ldz.5609/44, 26.IX.44.
82. 'Depesza Dowódcy AK do Władz Naczelnych w Londynie', 29.IX.44 in Majorkiewicz, *Dane nam było przeżyć*, pp. 229–30.
83. AZHP, ADR 202/XX-9, k. 29, 30.IX.44.
84. *Ibid.*, k. 26, 27.IX.44.
85. *Ibid.*, k. 1–8, 30.IX.44.
86. 'Polskie Radio Warszawa', 28.IX.44.
87. AZHP, ADR 202/XX-11, k. 25, 29.IX.44; cf. 'Sprawozdanie sytuacyjne nr 7, Wydział Bezpieczeństwa', 26.IX.44.
88. AZHP, ADR 202/XX-11, k. 25, 29.IX.44.
89. Meldunek wewnętrzny patrolu Wojsk. Służ. Info. Społ. BIP (Obwód I, odc. 2 i 3)', 24.IX.44 in *LCPW II*, pp. 497–9.
90. GSHI, A.XII.3/88, Despatch from Poland, Ldz.9107/44, 26.IX.44.
91. 'Sprawozdanie ...', 25.IX.44. This was probably a report written by the Director of the Department of Social Care.
92. 'Sprawozdanie sytuacyjne nr 7, Wydział Bezpieczeństwa', 26.IX.44.
93. AZHP, ADR 202/XX-2, k. 5, 6, and 7, 26, 27, and 29.IX.44.
94. 'Raport sytuacyjny Komendy Obwodu I, Śródmieście, Szef II Oddział Sztabu', 27.IX.44 (AWIH III/43/11 k. 3).
95. AZHP, ADR 202/XX-2, k. 7, 29.IX.44.
96. *Ibid.*, ADR 202/XX-6, k. 160, 26.IX.44 and ADR 202/XX-2, k. 6, 27.IX.44.
97. *Ibid.*, k. 5, 26.IX.44.
98. *Ibid.*
99. *Ibid.*, ADR 202/XX-2, k. 6, 26.IX.44.

3.8 Mokotów

1. Kirchmayer, *Powstanie Warszawskie*, p. 199.
2. See map in *ibid.*, between pp. 251 and 252.
3. *Ibid.*, p. 199.
4. See p. 12.
5. Ostrowska, *W Alejach spacerują 'Tygrysy'*, p. 110. For a full description of the opening of the sewer routes see pp. 96–112.

6. Report of W. Sala in *LCPW I.ii*, pp. 84–5; Krawczyńska, J., 'Powstanie warszawskie na Mokotowie' in *Zapiski Dziennikarki Warszawskiej 1939–1947*, Warsaw, 1971, pp. 185–6; Report of 'Baszta' officer 'Wicher' in Kirchmayer, *Powstanie Warszawskie*, pp. 399–400.

7. Report of M. Manteufflowa in *LCPW I.ii*, p. 61.

8. Bartelski, L.M., *Mokotów 1944*, Warsaw, 1972, p. 382.

9. Dobraczyński, *Tylko w jednym życiu*, p. 201 and pp. 276–8.

10. *Komunikat Informacyjny*, no. 41, 16.IX.44.

11. Dobraczyński, *Tylko w jednym życiu*, p. 277–8.

12. APUST, B.I., Nieznany, 'Relacja o powstaniu sierpniowo-wrześniowym', pp. 4–5.

13. Krawczyńska, 'Powstanie warszawskie na Mokotowie', pp. 185–6.

14. APUST, B.I., Nieznany, 'Relacja o powstaniu sierpniowo-wrześniowym', p. 6.

15. Krawczyńska, 'Powstanie warszawskie na Mokotowie', p. 204; Woszczyk, A., *Baszta K3 walczy*, Łódź, 1973, pp. 191–2.

16. Krawczyńska, 'Powstanie warszawskie na Mokotowie', p. 204.

17. *Ibid.*

18. *Ibid.*; Report of 'Baszta' officer 'Wicher' in Kirchmayer, *Powstanie Warszawskie*, pp. 399–400.

19. Serwański, *Życie w powstańczej Warszawie*, p. 193.

20. 'Meldunek "Tura"', 29.IX.44 (AWIH III/40/19 cz. 2, k. 332–3).

21. See p. 12.

22. BN, Rkps. akc. 6682, Anonymous, 'Powstanie polskie z sierpnia 1944 widziane z odcinka Mokotowa w Warszawie', pp. 7, 8–14, 25, 31, 35, 42, 50, 54–5, and 60. *Gwardia*, which literally means 'guard', is used here in a negative sense and probably has some connotation with Gwardia Ludowa, the original name of the Communist Underground Army, Armia Ludowa.

23. *Komunikat Informacyjny*, no. 1, 7.VIII.44; Bartelski, *Mokotów 1944*, pp. 331 and 381.

24. Bartelski, *Mokotów 1944*, p. 380.

25. Sala in *LCPW I.ii*, pp. 81–90.

26. Bartelski, *Mokotów 1944*, p. 380.

27. *Ibid.*; Report of A. Boliński in *LCPW I.ii*, p. 47.

28. *LCPW I.ii*, pp. 47–9; Krawczyńska, *Zapiski Dziennikarki Warszawskiej*, pp. 191–2 and 196.

29. Bartelski, *Mokotów 1944*, p. 381.

30. Sala in *LCPW I.ii*, pp. 83–4.

31. Serwański, *Życie w powstańczej Warszawie*, p. 191.

32. *Komunikat Informacyjny*, no. 24, 27.VIII.44.

33. Serwański, *Życie w powstańczej Warszawie*, p. 191; Krawczyńska, *Zapiski Dziennikarki Warszawskiej*, p. 190.

34. Boliński, *LCPW I.ii*, p. 48.

35. BN, Rkps. akc. 6682, Anonymous, 'Powstanie polskie', pp. 6, 24, 25, 41, 54, 59 and 63; cf. Borkiewicz, *Powstanie Warszawskie 1944*, p. 490.

36. BN, *ibid.*; Report of 'Baszta' officer 'Wicher' in Kirchmayer, *Powstanie Warszawskie*, pp. 399–400.
37. Borkiewicz, *Powstanie Warszawskie 1944*, p. 490; Kroll, B., 'Opieka społeczna nad ludnością Warszawy w okresie powstania warszawskiego i po powstaniu', PhD thesis, Warsaw, p. 10.
38. Kroll, *ibid.*; Report of 'Baszta' officer 'Wicher' in Kirchmayer, *Powstanie Warszawskie*, pp. 399–400.
39. *Komunikat Informacyjny*, no. 21, 27.VII.44.
40. Boliński in *LCPW I.ii*, p. 48.
41. Bayer, 'Służba Zdrowia', pp. 66 and 68.
42. *Ibid.*; Bayer, S., 'Z historii warszawskich szpitali powstańczych', *Prze. Lek.*, no. 1, 1975, p. 151.
43. Bayer, 'Służba Zdrowia', pp. 6–8.
44. *Ibid.* Szukiewicz, H., 'Służba zdrowia na Mokotowie podczas powstania warszawskiego', *Arch. Hist. Med.*, no. 2, 1970, pp. 215–16.
45. Krawczyńska, *Zapiski Dziennikarki Warszawskiej*, p. 192.
46. Boliński in *LCPW I.ii*, p. 48.
47. Szukiewicz, 'Służba zdrowia na Mokotowie', p. 218; Bayer, 'Służba Zdrowia', p. 68.
48. Report of J. Ledóchowska in *LCPW I.ii*, p. 57.
49. BN Rkps. akc. 6682, Anonymous, 'Powstanie polskie', p. 8.
50. *Komunikat Informacyjny*, nos. 16 and 47, 22.VIII.44 and 22.IX.44.
51. *Ibid.*
52. Report of B. Szatyński in *LCPW I.ii*, pp. 94–5.
53. Gryżewski, T., *Harcerska poczta polowa powstania warszawskiego 1944*, Warsaw, 1966, pp. 18–19.
54. Szatyński in *LCPW I.ii*, p. 94.
55. *Komunikat Informacyjny*, no. 10, 19.VIII.44.
56. Bartoszewski, 'Prasa powstania warszawskiego', pp. 333, 339, 346, 350, 352 and 361.
57. 'Wewnętrzny meldunek sytuacyjny placówki informacyjno-radiowej BIP KG AK', 19.VIII.44 in *LCPW II*, p. 135.
58. *Ibid.*; Sala in *LCPW I.ii*, p. 85.
59. Bartelski, *Mokotów 1944*, pp. 512–17.
60. APUST, B.I., Nieznany, 'Relacja o powstaniu sierpniowo-wrześniowym', p. 9.
61. Borkiewicz, *Powstanie Warszawskie 1944*, p. 492.
62. 'Fragment meldunku sytuacyjnego Komendanta Obwodu Mokotów do Ko. Okręgu Warszawskiego AK', 25.IX.44 in *LCPW II*, p. 458.
63. *Ibid.*
64. APUST, 3.9.2.8, Teka II, Prom. no. 47, 26.9.godz.12.30, Karol, Ldz.9079.
65. Bartelski, *Mokotów 1944*, pp. 561–2.
66. Borkiewicz, *Powstanie Warszawskie 1944*, p. 501.
67. APUST, 3.9.2.8, Teka II, Prom. no. 47, 26.9.godz.12.30, Karol, Ldz.9124.

68. Bartelski, *Mokotów 1944*, p. 565; Kirchmayer, *Powstanie Warszawskie*, p. 408.
69. Borkiewicz, *Powstanie Warszawskie 1944*, p. 500; see also 'Pismo Gen. von dem Bacha, 26.IX.44 in *LCPW II*, pp. 467–8.
70. Bartelski, *Mokotów 1944*, p. 567.
71. APUST, 3.9.2.8, Teka II, Prom. no. 47, 26.9.godz.12.30, Karol, Ldz.9124; Bartelski, *Mokotów 1944*, p. 568.
72. Bartelski, *Mokotów 1944*, p. 572; Woszczyk, *Baszta K3 walczy*, p. 215; Ostrowska, *W Alejach spacerują*, p. 260. The sewers quickly became blocked and obstructed by panicking people, trying to escape, losing their way, collapsing, dying, and by the dead. Therefore, some of the units and civilians had to turn back. Furthermore the Germans, discovering that the sewers were being used as an escape route, threw hand grenades and gas into them. About 150 of the escaping insurgents were shot by the Germans after having been arrested at the manhole on ul. Dworkowa. About 600 people reached Śródmieście.
73. Kirchmayer, *Powstanie Warszawskie*, pp. 408–9.
74. Borkiewicz, *Powstanie Warszawskie 1944*, pp. 501–2; 'Dziennik działań Niemieckiej 9 Armii', p. 123.

3.9 Żoliborz

1. Borkiewicz, *Powstanie Warszawskie 1944*, p. 24; Kirchmayer, *Powstanie Warszawskie*, p. 189.
2. Kirchmayer, *ibid.*, pp. 189–91.
3. Podlewski, S., *Rapsodia Żoliborska*, Warsaw, 1957, pp. 38–9 and 44.
4. Kirchmayer, *Powstanie Warszawskie*, pp. 191 and 226–7.
5. Report of J. Dunin-Wąsowicz in *LCPW I.ii*, p. 151; Serwański, *Życie w powstańczej Warszawie*, p. 228; Podlewski, *Rapsodia Żoliborska*, p. 61.
6. Podlewski, *ibid.*, p. 70.
7. Dunin-Wąsowicz in *LCPW I.ii*, p. 147.
8. Report of Maria Müllerowa in *LCPW I.ii*, p. 134; Serwański, *Życie w powstańczej Warszawie*, p. 232.
9. Müllerowa in *LCPW I.ii*, p. 134; IZ, Dok.V.220, 'Protokóły i materiały do pracy pt. "Życie w powstańczej Warszawie"', protocol no. 33.
10. Müllerowa in *LCPW I ii*, p. 134.
11. Szymczak, 'Dni zgrozy i walki o wolność', p. 145.
12. Rossman in *LCPW I.i*, p. 152.
13. Kozłowska, H.B., *Mur miał dwie strony*, Warsaw, 1958, p. 108; cf. Szymczak, 'Dni zgrozy i walki o wolność', p. 145.
14. Podlewski, *Rapsodia Żoliborska*, p. 61.
15. *Dziennik Radiowy AK*, no. 51, 19.IX.44.
16. Report of S. Tołwiński in *LCPW I.ii*, p. 140; Podlewski, *Rapsodia Żoliborska*, p. 62; Dunin-Wąsowicz, J., 'Ludność cywilna i prasa powstańczego Zoliborza' in *Warszawa lat wojny i okupacji*, vol. II, p. 256.
17. Podlewski, *Rapsodia Żoliborska*, p. 62.

18. Tołwiński in *LCPW I.ii*, pp. 139–40. These divisions were based on the pre-war divisions formed by the housing co-operatives in Żoliborz.

19. 'Wytyczne organizacji Samorządu i Samopomocy Sąsiedzkiej Mieszkańców osiedli na Żoliborzu', (about 15.VIII.44) in *LCPW II*, pp. 122–3; cf. figures for the end of September as shown in 'Pismo Samorządu Osiedla na Skarpie do Prezydium Samorządu Dzielnicy Żoliborskiej o stanie liczebnym osiedla' in *LCPW II*, pp. 448–9, which are much lower.

20. *LCPW II*, pp. 122–3. For a full theoretical description of the functions of the settlement *Samorząd* see 'Pismo okólne nr 2 S. Tołwińskiego, przewodniczącego Samorządu Mieszkańców Dzielnicy Żoliborskiej do Samorządu Osiedla na Skarpie wraz z instrukcją organizacyjną dla Samorządu Mieszkańców Osiedla' in *LCPW II*, pp. 239–43.

21. Tołwiński and report of F. Zelcer in *LCPW I.ii*, pp. 140 and 175.

22. *Ibid.*, p. 143; Podlewski, *Rapsodia Żoliborska*, p. 62; AZHP, ADR 202/XX-26, k. 13, 13.VIII.44.

23. *Biuletyn Okręgu IV PPS Warszawa Północ*, no. 13, 16.VIII.44. WSM was the Warsaw housing co-operative; see p. 11.

24. Tołwiński in *LCPW I.ii*, p. 143.

25. Zelcer in *LCPW I.ii*, p. 175.

26. Tołwiński in *LCPW I.ii*, p. 140.

27. Podlewski, *Rapsodia Żoliborska*, p. 62.

28. AZHP, ADR 202/XX-26, k. 13, 13.VIII.44.

29. Podlewski, *Rapsodia Żoliborska*, p. 63.

30. 'Pismo "A. Górala", Kierownika Ekspozytury Starostwa Warszawa Północ do Samorządu na Skarpie (Żoliborskiej)' in *LCPW II*, p. 167; Podlewski, *Rapsodia Żoliborska*, p. 64, Cf. pp. 237–8.

31. *Robotnik*, no. 38, 31.VIII.44.

32. Serwański, *Życie w powstańczej Warszawie*, p. 231.

33. Dunin-Wąsowicz in *LCPW I.ii*, p. 150.

34. *Ibid.*; 'Pismo okólne (nr 10) S. Tołwińskiego ... w sprawie opieki społecznej i zaopatrzenia w żywność', in *LCPW II*, pp. 399–400; Müllerowa in *LCPW I.ii*, p. 133; Serwański, *Życie w powstańczej Warszawie*, p. 231.

35. Podlewski, *Rapsodia Żoliborska*, p. 272.

36. Serwański, *Życie w powstańczej Warszawie*, p. 231.

37. Borkiewicz, *Powstanie Warszawskie 1944*, p. 503.

38. APUST, 3.9.2.8., Teka II 'Depesze radiowe z okresu powstania warszawskiego od 1.IX.44–12.X.44', Prom. nr 81 od Żywiciela, 10.IX.44, Ldz.8187; Serwański, *Życie w powstańczej Warszawie*, p. 231; Borkiewicz, *Powstanie Warszawskie 1944*, p. 503.

39. Tołwiński in *LCPW II*, p. 141, and cf. p. 222.

40. Serwański, *Życie w powstańczej Warszawie*, p. 231.

41. *Ibid.*; AK *Dziennik Radiowy XXII*, no. 57, 25.IX.44; *Biuletyn Podokręgu nr 2 AL*, no. 38, 11.IX.44.

42. Podlewski, *Rapsodia Żoliborska*, p. 86; Bayer, 'Z historii warszawskich

308 *Notes to pp. 190–192*

szpitali powstańczych', p. 152.
43. Report of J. Żuchniewska in *LCPW I.ii*, p. 181; Podlewski, *Rapsodia Żoliborska*, p. 87.
44. Serwański, *Życie w powstańczej Warszawie*, p. 225.
45. *Ibid.*, p. 232.
46. Podlewski, *Rapsodia Żoliborska*, p. 86.
47. Serwański, *Życie w powstańczej Warszawie*, p. 225.
48. Podlewski, *Rapsodia Żoliborska*, p. 90.
49. Bayer, 'Służba Zdrowia', p. 91.
50. Serwański, *Życie w powstańczej Warszawie*, pp. 231–2.
51. Tołwiński in *LCPW I.ii*, p. 141.
52. Dunin-Wąsowicz, 'Ludność cywilna i prasa powstańczego Żoliborza', p. 256.
53. Serwański, *Życie w powstańczej Warszawie*, p. 232.
54. Tołwiński in *LCPW I.ii*, p. 142.
55. Bartoszewski, W., 'Prasa powstania warszawskiego', p. 322.
56. *Biuletyn Okręgu IV PPS i OW PPS Warszawa Północ*, no. 8, 11.VIII.44.
57. Tołwiński in *LCPW I.ii*, p. 142; Serwański, *Życie w powstańczej Warszawie*, p. 232; Podlewski, *Rapsodia Żoliborska*, p. 66.
58. Rossman in *LCPW I.i*, p. 153; Szymczak, 'Dni zgrozy i walki o wolność', p. 145.
59. Rossman in *LCPW I.i*, p. 153. Three unsuccessful landings were made by Polish soldiers of the 6th Infantry Regiment (from the Polish 2nd Infantry Division), from the eastern bank of the Vistula on 17, 19 and 20 September on the western bank in the area of Żoliborz. A radio operator also landed whose task it was to establish radio contact (Borkiewicz, *Powstanie Warszawskie 1944*, pp. 422–30).
60. APUST, 3.9.2.8, Prom no. 107, 18.IX.44, Sytuacja za 18.IX. od Żywiciela, Ldz.9683; 'Dokumenty do kapitulacji powstania warszawskiego', *NDP II Wojny*, no. 4, 1960, p. 108.
61. *Biuletyn Okręgu IV PPS i OW PPS Warszawa Północ*, no. 52, 24.IX.44. The forts referred to in the article are the Sokolnicki Forts in the Żeromski Park. They belonged to the original group of forts built by the Russians after the November Uprising of 1830 in order to help maintain law and order in the city and defend the Russian garrison. The Sokolnicki Forts were built between 1849 and 1850.
62. Dunin-Wąsowicz in *LCPW I.ii*, pp. 148–9. The word *Barakowcy* is taken from the word *barak* which means barrack. The *Barakowcy* were the people, the unemployed, who lived in these barracks.
63. Kliszko, *Powstanie Warszawskie*, p. 200.
64. Podlewski, *Rapsodia Żoliborska*, pp. 218–19.
65. Borkiewicz, *Powstanie Warszawskie 1944*, pp. 508–9; Kirchmayer, *Powstanie Warszawskie*, p. 413.
66. Borkiewicz, *Powstanie Warszawskie 1944*, p. 251.
67. 'Dokumenty do kapitulacji powstania warszawskiego', pp. 135–8. For

a full discussion of the capitulation see pp. 193ff.
68. Serwański, *Życie w powstańczej Warszawie*, p. 226.
69. Report of W. Marczuk in *LCPW I.ii*, p. 131.

3.10 The capitulation of Warsaw

1. Ossol., 134/64, Krobicka-Modzelewska, 'Wrzesień 1939', p. 11.
2. Polak, *63 dni powstania warszawskiego*, p. 126.
3. 'Dokumenty do kapitulacji powstania warszawskiego', p. 141.
4. GSHI, PRM.L.7, Despatch from Poland, Ldz.9383/44, 1.x.44.
5. 'Dokumenty do kapitulacji powstania warszawskiego', p. 114.
6. *Ibid.*, pp. 114–20.
7. *Ibid.*
8. *Ibid.*, pp. 120–4.
9. *Ibid.*
10. *Ibid.*
11. *Ibid.*; cf. p. 152.
12. *Ibid.*
13. *Ibid.*
14. *Ibid.*
15. *Ibid.*
16. *Ibid.*, pp. 125–30.
17. *Ibid.*, pp. 130–1.
18. *Ibid.*, pp. 109–10.
19. *Ibid.*, p. 139.
20. *Ibid.*, p. 140; *Biuletyn Informacyjny*, no. 307, 1.x.44.
21. Bartoszewski in *LCPW III*, p. 13.
22. *Głos Warszawy*, no. 181, 1.x.44; *Wojsko Polskie Organ Połączonych Sił Zbrojnych AL, PAL i KB*, no. 9, 1.x.44.
23. *Biuletyn Informacyjny*, no. 308, 2.x.44.
24. Polak, *63 dni powstania warszawskiego*, p. 126.
25. Serwański, *Życie w powstańczej Warszawie*, p. 302; Ochman, 'Szpital powstańczy na Chmielnej', p. 143; Report of J. Wadecka, p. 9.
26. Polak, *63 dni powstania warszawskiego*, p. 127; Bartoszewski in *LCPW I.ii*, p. 366.
27. Ostrowska, *W Alejach spacerują 'Tyrgrysy'*, p. 299.
28. BN, Chomicki, '63 dni', p. 32.
29. Serwański, *Życie w powstańczej Warszawie*, p. 282; BN, Chomicki, '63 dni', p. 32.
30. IH PAN, ZHP, 'Dziennik Wiesławy Kempera', pp. 1026–112; BN, Chomicki, '63 dni', p. 32; Zagórski, *Seventy Days*, p. 243.
31. Serwański, *Życie w powstańczej Warszawie*, p. 302.
32. *Ibid.*; cf. Ostrowska, *W Alejach spacerują 'Tygrysy'*, p. 303.
33. Bień in *LCPW I.i*, p. 68.
34. Majorkiewicz, *Dane nam było przeżyć*, p. 231; Iranek-Osmecki, K.,

'Kapitulacja Warszawy', *Kultura* (Paris), no. 12, 1948, p. 79.

35. *Ibid.*; Bartoszewski in *LCPW I.ii*, pp. 366–7.
36. Korboński, *Fighting Warsaw*, pp. 397–8.
37. 'Dokumenty do kapitulacji powstania warszawskiego', pp. 144–7.
38. GSHI, PRM.L.7, Despatch from Poland, Ldz.9383/44, 1.X.44.
39. 'Dokumenty do kapitulacji powstania warszawskiego', pp. 148–50.
40. *Ibid.*, pp. 150–1.
41. *Rzeczpospolita*, no. 77, 4.X.44.
42. Bartoszewski in *LCPW I.ii*, p. 367.
43. Rozwadowska, *Wspomnienia ważne i nieważne*, p. 300.
44. Report of A. Twardowska, London, July 1974, p. 3.
45. Serwański, *Życie w powstańczej Warszawie*, p. 69.
46. APUST, 1785/III 3.(5).B.I., Zarzycki, 'Relacja', p. 14. and Wojsłomska, J., 'Odpowiedź na ankietę w sprawie AK', p. 3.
47. Gieysztor, 'Dziennik z powstania warszawskiego', pp. 9–10.
48. Verbal information of S. Korboński; Report of J. Wadecka, p. 2; Rudziński, *Dziennik z powstania warszawskiego*, p. 96.
49. Verbal information of Korboński.
50. Ciechanowski, J., 'Notatki z rozmowy z płk. dypl. J. Bokszczaninem', *ŻH*, no. 27, 1974, p. 145.
51. *Ibid.*; Report of J. Wadecka, p. 5.
52. Ziemba, S., 'Opowiadam o powstaniu', *Życie Literackie*, no. 32, 1972, p. 3.
53. APUST, Letter from Mjr Gen. L. Okulicki to the President of the Republic, Ldz.1780/I, 9.XII.44.
54. GSHI, A.12/73/7, 3.X.44.
55. 'Dokumenty do kapitulacji powstania warszawskiego', pp. 125–30.
56. Krannhals, *Der Warschauer Aufstand*, p. 293.
57. 'Dziennik działań Niemieckiej 9 Armii', pp. 127–9. It is not stipulated whether or not this figure included the Army. It must also be remembered that quite a few insurgents, especially women, left as civilians.
58. AZHP, ADR 202/XX-6, k. 57–58 and 202/XX-9, k. 10, 4.IX.44.
59. Borkiewicz, *Powstanie Warszawskie 1944*, p. 547.
60. Krannhals, *Der Warschauer Aufstand*, p. 214.
61. Podlewski, S., 'Próba bilansu strat powstania warszawskiego', *Dziś i Jutro*, no. 31, 1947, pp. 6–7.
62. GSHI, A.12/73/7, 3.X.44. About 500,000 Varsovians passed through Pruszków and 50,000 through other camps, e.g. Ursus (Borkiewicz, *Powstanie Warszawskie 1944*, pp. 544–5).
63. Kirchmayer, *Powstanie Warszawskie*, p. 423; Borkiewicz, *Powstanie Warszawskie 1944*, p. 549; Podlewski, 'Próba bilansu strat powstania warszawskiego', p. 6. It is interesting to compare figures for the Slovakian Uprising of 1944, where sixty villages were destroyed and 7,000 people killed (Madajczyk, *Polityka III Rzeszy*, vol. II, p. 392) and during the liberation of Paris, where 2,000 were killed and about the same number injured.

4. Life in insurgent Warsaw

4.1 The administration of insurgent Warsaw

1. Sendlak, 'W powstaniu bez broni', p. 2.
2. Korboński, *Fighting Warsaw*, p. 368; *63 Days: The Story of the Warsaw Rising*, Newton, Montgomeryshire, 1947, p. 50.
3. Ciechanowski, *The Warsaw Rising*, p. 238; Pluta-Czachowski, K., 'Wspomnienia o "odcinku cywilnym"' (Delegackim) w powstaniu warszawskim' (Warsaw, 1970), p. 5.
4. Pluta-Czachowski, *ibid.*; Ciechanowski, *The Warsaw Rising*, p. 240; Bór-Komorowski, *The Secret Army*, p. 214.
5. Bień, *Wspomnienia*, p. 99.
6. *Ibid.*; Ciechanowski, *The Warsaw Rising*, p. 240.
7. Bień, *Wspomnienia*, p. 99.
8. Pluta-Czachowski, 'Wspomnienia o "odcinku cywilnym"', p. 7.
9. *Ibid.*, p. 3.
10. Cf. Ciechanowski, *The Warsaw Rising*, p. 240.
11. Pluta-Czachowski, 'Wspomnienia o "odcinku cywilnym"', pp. 5–6; Ciechanowski, *The Warsaw Rising*, p. 238.
12. Nowak, *Kurier z Warszawy*, p. 377.
13. Hoppe, *Wspomnienia, przyczynki, refleksje*, pp. 362–3.
14. Korboński, *Fighting Warsaw*, pp. 350–1.
15. *Ibid.*, pp. 355–7.
16. Dzendzel, H., 'Powstańczy dziennik ludowy' in *Wspomnienia dziennikarzy z okresu okupacji hitlerowskiej*, pp. 17–18.
17. Bień in *LCPW I.i*, p. 48.
18. Verbal information of S. Korboński; Pluta-Czachowski, 'Wspomnienia o "odcinku cywilnym"', pp. 7–8.
19. 'Powstanie w świetle meldunkow BIP', report no. 6.
20. Bień, *Wspomnienia*, p. 103.
21. Bień in *LCPW I.i*, p. 50.
22. *Ibid.*, p. 51; Bień, *Wspomnienia*, p. 107.
23. Pluta-Czachowski, 'Wspomnienia o "odcinku cywilnym"', p. 7.
24. Porowski in *LCPW I.i*, p. 119.
25. *Ibid.*, p. 113; See p. 59.
26. Bień in *LCPW I.i*, p. 52.
27. *PSZ*, p. 802.
28. Verbal information of S. Korboński; *LCPW I.i*, p. 113n.
29. *Biuletyn Informacyjny*, no. 249, 5.VIII.44.
30. Ziemba, S., 'Opowiadam o powstaniu', p. 3.
31. Wnuk, 'W powstaniu z piórem w ręku', pp. 175–6.
32. AZHP, ADR 202/XX-14, k. 6–7, 2.IX.44; *Rzeczpospolita*, no. 23, 12.VIII.44.
33. AZHP, ADR 202/XX-25, k. 4–5, 9.VIII.44.
34. 'Zarządzenie Komendanta Okręgu Stołecznego AK "Montera"',

9.VIII.44 in *LCPW II*, p. 90; 'Polskie Radio Warszawa', 11.VIII.44; *Biuletyn Informacyjny*, no. 255, 10.VIII.44; *Rzeczpospolita*, no. 22, 11.VIII.44.

35. *Rzeczpospolita*, no. 22, 11.VII.44.
36. See pp. 108–11.
37. See pp. 181–2 and 188–9.
38. Sendlak, 'W powstaniu bez broni', p. 3.
39. *Robotnik*, no. 21, 14.VIII.44; *Dzień Warszawy*, no. 1019, 14.VIII.44.
40. Korboński, *Fighting Warsaw*, p. 368.
41. *Rzeczpospolita*, no. 16, 6.VIII.44; *Warszawianka*, no. 1, 7.VIII.44; *Iskra*, no. 16, 10.VIII.44; 'Polskie Radio Warszawa', 13.VIII.44.
42. 'Zarządzenie Okręgowego Delegata Rządu', 17.VIII.44 in *LCPW II*, pp. 148–50; *Robotnik*, no. 39, 1.IX.44; *Dziennik Obwieszczeń Rejonowego Delegata Rządu Warszawa Południe*, no. 7, 6.IX.44.
43. AZHP, ADR 202/XX-1, k. 10, 12.IX.44 and 202/XX-25, k. 4–5, 9.VIII.44; Report of J. Dusza in *LCPW I.i*, pp. 88; Sendlak, 'W powstaniu bez broni', p. 3; Nałęcz, W., 'Społeczne oblicze powstania', *Na Szlaku Kresowej*, no. 9/39, 1946, p. 15.
44. AZHP, ADR 202/XX-24, k. 225, 30.VIII.44.
45. *Ibid.*, 202/XX-14, k. 6–7, 2.IX.44.
46. *Ibid.*
47. Ossol., 5/65, Skierski, Z., 'Polskie Radio w czasie powstania warszawskiego', 1961, p. 11.
48. 'Polskie Radio Warszawa', 16.VIII.44; Kroll, 'Opieka społeczna nad ludnością Warszawy w okresie powstania warszawskiego', pp. 40–1. See pp. 232–3.
49. Kroll, *ibid.*, p. 31; See p. 109.
50. See pp. 224–5.

4.2 The infrastructure and internal trade of insurgent Warsaw

1. Reports of Z. Borowy, Z. Kwieciński and S. Ruskowski in *LCPW I.i*, pp. 73, 104 and 156.
2. *Ibid.*, pp. 104–5.
3. *Ibid.*, pp. 109–10; Korboński, *Fighting Warsaw*, pp. 371–2.
4. AZHP, ADR 202/XX-17, k. 4, 30.VIII.44.
5. Korboński, *Fighting Warsaw*, p. 370; see n. 1 in *LCPW II*, p. 127.
6. Ruskowski in *LCPW I.i*, pp. 156–7.
7. Report of Z. Budzyński in *LCPW I.i*, p. 85.
8. *Ibid.*, p. 86 and Ruskowski, p. 158; Korboński, *Fighting Warsaw*, p. 370.
9. AZHP, ADR 202/XX-14, k. 6 and 7, 2.IX.44; Meldunek wew. (nr 5/A) Wydział Informacji BIP KG AK', 28.VIII.44 in *LCPW II*, pp. 196–9.
10. AZHP, ADR 202/XX-6, k. 57–58, 4.IX.44 and 202/XX-15, k. 1, 20.VIII.44; Ruskowski in *LCPW I.i*, p. 158.
11. AZHP, ADR 202/XX-20, k. 5, 24.VIII.44.
12. *Ibid.*, ADR 202/XX-15, k. 1 and 4, 20.VIII and 11.IX.44, and ADR 202/XX-

16, k. 3, 25.IX.44.
13. Korboński, *Fighting Warsaw*, p. 370.
14. AZHP, ADR 202/XX-15, k. 4, 11.IX.44 and k. 3, 12.IX.44.
15. *Ibid.*, ADR 202/XX-16, k. 3, 25.IX.44.
16. Bień in *LCPW I.i*, p. 67.
17. AZHP, ADR 202/XX-16, k. 13, 22.IX.44.
18. Budzyński and Ruskowski in *LCPW I.i*, pp. 86 and 159.
19. *Encyklopedia Warszawy*, Warsaw, 1975, p. 169.
20. Gieysztor in *LCPW I.ii*, p. 309.
21. *LCPW III*, p. 481.
22. GSHI, PRM.L.5, Despatch from Poland, 22.IX.44.
23. Report of S. Broniewski in *LCPW I.i*, p. 81; *Polska Agencja Telegraficzna: Serwis Krajowy*, no. 7, 9.VIII.44; *Z Pierwszej Linii Frontu*, 15.VIII.44.
24. *Dziennik Obwieszczeń Rejonowego Delegata Rządu Warszawa Południe*, no. 1, 20.VIII.44.
25. 'Rozkaz nr 14 Pkt. 10/VI- Poczta Polowa' in Gryżewski, *Harcerska poczta polowa*, p. 9.
26. Broniewski in *LCPW I.i*, pp. 82–4.
27. *Ibid.* By 27 August 5,000 books had been collected (*Walka*, no. 74, 27.VIII.44).
28. *Dzień Warszawy*, no. 1010, 9.VIII.44.
29. *Robotnik*, no. 31, 3.IX.44.
30. Gryżewski, *Harcerska poczta polowa*, p. 13.
31. *Biuletyn Informacyjny*, no. 258, 13.VIII.44.
32. Gryżewski, *Harcerska poczta polowa*, p. 30.
33. *Robotnik*, no. 41, 3.IX.44.
34. *Biuletyn Informacyjny*, no. 259, 14.VIII.44.
35. Wojewódzki, M., 'Jak drukowaliśmy powstańcze znaczki pocztowe', *Stolica*, no. 30, 1969, p. 7.
36. *Robotnik*, no. 41, 3.IX.44; *Walka*, no. 76, 3.IX.44.
37. Gryżewski, *Harcerska poczta polowa*, p. 61.
38. *Ibid.*, p. 33.
39. 'Poczta polowa', *WTK*, no. 34, 1964, p. 5.
40. *Ibid.*; Gryżewski, *Harcerska poczta polowa*, p. 29.
41. *Biuletyn Informacyjny*, no. 247, 4.VIII.44.
42. Gieysztor in *LCPW I.ii*, p. 268.
43. Borowy in *LCPW I.i*, pp. 72–5.
44. Report of J. Gradowski in *LCPW I.i*, p. 393.
45. Borowy in *LCPW I.i*, p. 72; *63 Days: The Story of the Warsaw Rising*, p. 51.
46. AZHP, ADR 202/XX-25, k. 4–5, 9.VIII.44.
47. Serwański, *Życie w powstańczej Warszawie*, pp. 314–15.
48. Report of S. Sendlak in *LCPW I.ii*, p. 260.
49. 'Meldunek BIP, Rej. III, Patrol IV', 31.VIII.44.
50. AZHP, ADR 202/XX-26, k. 5, 4.VIII.44. The poster was signed by the District Government Delegate for Warsaw.

51. *Dziennik Obwieszczeń Rejonowego Delegata Rządu Warszawa Południe*, nos. 4 and 5, 23 and 27.VIII.44; *Warszawa Walczy*, no. 35, 15.VIII.44.

52. 'Wewnętrzny meldunek sytuacyjny (nr 9/A) Wydziału Informacji BIP KG AK', 2.IX.44 in *LCPW II*, pp. 253–4.

53. Polak, *63 dni powstania warszawskiego*, p. 55; Serwański, *Życie w powstańczej Warszawie*, p. 275; Report of W. Sala in *LCPW I.ii*, p. 88.

54. Serwański, *Życie w powstańczej Warszawie*, p. 275; Polak, *63 dni powstania warszawskiego*, p. 55.

55. BN, Rkps. akc. 6682, Anonymous, 'Powstanie polskie', p. 62.

56. AZHP, ADR 202/XX-11, k. 25, 16.IX.44.

57. Zagórski, *Seventy Days*, p. 178.

58. AZHP, ADR 202/XX-2, k. 6, 27.IX.44; 'Bezpiecznik nr 30', 21.IX.44; *Barykada Powiśla*, no. 8, 14.VIII.44.

59. Serwański, *Życie w powstańczej Warszawie*, p. 275; Rudziński, *Dziennik z powstania warszawskiego*, p. 93; *Barykada – Warszawa Walczy*, no. 47, 27.IX.44; 'Zarządzenie Rejonowego Delegata Rządu Warszawa-Południe', 14.VIII.44 in *LCPW III*, pp. 112–14.

60. *Ibid.*, *LCPW III*, AZHP, ADR 202/XX-2, k. 6, 27.IX.44.

61. Ossol., (no. ref), Rodziewiczówna, M., 'Ostatni Kalendarzyk'; *Barykada Powiśla*, no. 8, 14.VIII.44; *Wiadomość Powstańcza*, no. 95, 27.IX.44 in *LCPW III*, pp. 389–99; *Wojsko Polskie, Organ połączonych Sił Zbrojnych, AL, PAL i KB*, no. 6, 28.IX.44; Polak, *63 dni powstania warszawskiego*, p. 122; cf. official prices on 1.VIII.44 in *LCPW II*, p. 457.

62. AZHP, ADR 202/XX-5, k. 7, 2.IX.44.

63. Szarota, *Okupowanej Warszawy dzień*, p. 329.

64. *Ibid.*, p. 335.

65. *Z Pierwszej Linii Frontu*, 11.VIII.44.

66. *Dziennik Obwieszczeń Rejonowego Delegata Rządu Warszawa Południe*, no. 2, 21.VIII.44.

67. Zaremba, *Wojna i konspiracja*, p. 250.

68. AZHP, ADR 202/XX-14, k. 1–7, 2.IX.44.

69. Tołwiński and Zelcer in *LCPW I.ii*, pp. 141 and 177.

70. *Komunikat Informacyjny*, no. 8, 8.VIII.44 in *LCPW III*, pp. 55–6.

71. AZHP, ADR 202/XX-18, k. 5, 16.VIII.44.

72. *Ibid.*, k. 10, 25.VIII.44; 'Polskie Radio Warszawa', 29.VIII.44.

73. *Biuletyn Informacyjny*, no. 287, 11.IX.44.

74. AZHP, ADR 202/XX-13, k. 17, 4.IX.44.

75. *Ibid.*, ADR 202/XX-17, k. 30–1, 26–27.IX.44.

76. 'Polskie Radio Warszawa', 24.VIII.44.

77. *Biuletyn Informacyjny*, no. 302, 26.IX.44; *Barykada – Warszawa Walczy*, no. 45, 25.IX.44; *Wiadomości z Miasta i Wiadomości Radiowe*, no. 23, 14.VIII.44.

78. *Dzień Warszawy*, no. 1028, 23.VIII.44.

79. *Warszawianka*, no. 19, 26.VIII.44.

80. *Komunikat Informacyjny*, no. 13, 13.VIII.44.

81. AZHP, ADR 202/XX-17, k. 30, 27.IX.44.

82. *Ibid.*, ADR 202/XX-18, k. 13, 19.IX.44.
83. Report to the Regional Government Delegate, 28.IX.44.
84. Report of L. Marszałek in *LCPW I.ii*, pp. 242–4; *Harcerki 1939–1945*, Warsaw, 1973, p. 346.
85. *Harcerki*, p. 346; Marszałek in *LCPW I.ii*, pp. 244–6; *Biuletyn Informacyjny*, no. 262, 17.VIII.44; *Serwis Krajowy*, no. 39, 30.VIII.44; *Dziennik Obwieszczeń Rejonowego Delegata Rządu Warszawa Południe*, no. 5, 27.VIII.44; IH PAN, *ZHP*, T. Cieszewska, pp. 976–7.
86. *PSZ*, p. 682.
87. Verbal information.
88. Serwański, *Życie w powstańczej Warszawie*, pp. 191 and 231; Sendlak, 'W powstaniu bez broni', p. 2; Korboński, *Fighting Warsaw*, p. 370; Boliński in *LCPW I.ii*, p. 48.
89. Stawski, 'Wrześniowy kryzys', p. 123.
90. *Biuletyn Informacyjny*, no. 258, 13.VIII.44; *Serwis Krajowy*, no. 10, 12.VIII.44.
91. *Ibid.*; 'Polskie Radio Warszawa', 12.VIII.44. See example on p. 146.
92. AZHP, ADR 202/XX-25, k. 134, 9.VIII.44.
93. Polak, *63 dni powstania warszawskiego*, p. 15.
94. Kulesiński in *LCPW I.ii*, p. 388.
95. See p. 110.
96. Müllerowa in *LCPW I.ii*, pp. 133–4.
97. *Warszawianka*, no. 4, 11.VIII.44.
98. *Biuletyn Informacyjny*, no. 262, 17.VIII.44.
99. *Robotnik*, no. 19, 12.VIII.44.
100. *Ibid.* and no. 27, 20.VIII.44.
101. AZHP, ADR 202/XX-22, k. 1–7, 9.VIII.44; *Rzeczpospolita*, no. 46, 3.IX.44.
102. Kulesiński in *LCPW I.ii*, pp. 393–4.
103. AZHP, ADR 202/XX-9, k. 1–8, 1.X.44.
104. *Ibid.*, ADR 202/XX-9, k. 15 and 17, 14 and 18.IX.44.
105. *Ibid.*, ADR 202/XX-24, k. 1, 20 and 180–1.
106. *Ibid.*, ADR 202/XX-6, k. 67, 5.IX.44.
107. Zelcer in *LCPW I.ii*, pp. 176–7.
108. Boliński in *LCPW I.ii*, p. 47.
109. *Biuletyn Informacyjny*, no. 266, 21.VIII.44.
110. *Barykada*, no. 12, 28.VIII.44; AZHP, ADR 202/XX-9, k. 10, 4.IX.44.
111. *Rzeczpospolita*, no. 51, 3.IX.44; *Serwis Krajowy*, no. 10, 12.VIII.44.
112. *Nowy Świat*, no. 5, 27.VIII.44.
113. *Serwis Krajowy*, no. 10, 12.VIII.44.
114. IZ, Dok.V.220 t. 3, 'Protokóły i materiały do pracy pt. "Życie w Powstaniu Warszawskim"', protocol no. 6; *Biuletyn Informacyjny*, no. 258, 13.VIII.44; *Serwis Krajowy*, no. 10, 12.VIII.44.
115. Kwiatkowski in *LCPW I.i*, p. 414.
116. AZHP, ADR 202/XX-24, k. 39, 15.VIII.44.
117. *Robotnik*, no. 19, 12.VIII.44.
118. Bukowski, 'Apteki południowego Śródmieścia Warszawy', p. 475.

119. 'Raport z dnia 16 września do Pana Delegata Rządu Warszawa Południe', 17.IX.44; GSHI, PRM.L.5, Despatch from Poland, Ldz.5519/44/K and Ldz.5521/44/K, 21 and 23.IX.44.

120. IH PAN, A.67/59, Domosławski, B., 'Przeżycia cywila w powstaniu warszawskim', p. 95; Bór-Komorowski, *The Secret Army*, p. 358.

121. AZHP, ADR 202/XX-9, k. 15 and 17, 14 and 18.IX.44.

122. *Ibid.*, ADR 202/XX-18, k. 15, 21.IX.44; *Nowiny Żoliborskie*, no. 34, 5.IX.44.

123. AZHP, ADR 202/XX-9, k. 18, 18.IX.44.

124. *Ibid.*, k. 10, 4.IX.44.

125. *Ibid.*, k. 19, 19.IX.44.

126. GSHI, A.XII.3/88, Despatch from Poland, Ldz.9107/44, 26.IX.44; AZHP, ADR 202/XX-9, k. 15, 14.IX.44.

127. GSHI, PRM.L.5, Despatch from Poland, Ldz.5521/44/1, 23.IX.44.

128. 'Raport nr 15 do Pana Delegata Rządu Warszawa Południe', 27.IX.44.

129. AZHP, ADR 202/XX-18, k. 15, 21.IX.44.

130. Cf. pp. 94–5.

131. AZHP, ADR 202/XX-22, k. 1–7, 25.VIII.44.

132. *Rzeczpospolita*, no. 37, 26.VIII.44.

133. AZHP, ADR 202/XX-20, k. 2, 16.VIII.44.

134. 'Fragment meldunku wewnętrznego (nr 7/A) Wydziału Informacji BIP KG AK', 31.VIII.44 in *LCPW II*, pp. 235–6.

135. *Dziennik Obwieszczeń Rejonowego Delegata Rządu Warszawa Południe*, no. 6, 29.VIII.44.

136. *Ibid.*

137. AZHP, ADR 202/XX-14, k. 8–9, 4.IX.44.

138. *Ibid.*, k. 15, 14.IX.44.

139. *Komunikat Informacyjny*, no. 9, 9.VIII.44 in *LCPW III*, p. 63.

140. See p. 232.

141. Sala in *LCPW I.ii*, p. 87.

142. *W Walce*, no. 28, 19.VIII.44.

143. *Biuletyn Informacyjny*, no. 263, 18.VIII.44.

144. 'Polskie Radio Warszawa', 13.VIII.44.

145. *Warszawa Walczy*, no. 36, 15.VIII.44; *Biuletyn Informacyjny*, no. 259, 14.VIII.44.

146. 'Polskie Radio Warszawa', 16.VIII.44.

147. *Rzeczpospolita*, no. 27, 16.VIII.44.

148. *Barykada*, no. 8, 18.VIII.44.

149. Tołwiński in *LCPW I.ii*, pp. 141 and 147.

150. *Komunikat Informacyjny*, no. 9 and 28, 15 and 30.VIII.44.

151. 'Polskie Radio Warszawa', 16.VIII.44.

152. AZHP, ADR 202/XX-14, k. 8–9, 4.IX.44.

153. APUST, 3.9.2.8, Radio messages received from John Ward, 6.IX.44.

154. AZHP, ADR 202/XX-9, k. 10 and 13, 4.IX.44; *Biuletyn Informacyjny*, no. 277, 30.VIII.44; *Czerniaków w Walce*, no. 17, 8.IX.44; *Rzeczpospolita*, no. 46, 3.IX.44; *Robotnik*, no. 29, 22.VIII.44; *Serwis Krajowy*, no. 10, 12.VIII.44; Sendlak in *LCPW I.ii*, p. 257.

155. *Harcerki*, p. 343.
156. *Biuletyn Informacyjny*, no. 265, 20.VIII.44; *Czerniaków w Walce*, no. 17, 8.IX.44.
157. GSHI, PRM.L.5, Despatch from Poland, Ldz.4972/44, 29.VIII.44.
158. *Harcerki*, pp. 343 and 354.
159. *Dziennik Obwieszczeń Rejonowego Delegata Rządu Warszawa Południe*, no. 6, 29.IX.44.
160. Boliński in *LCPW I.ii*, p. 48.
161. Tołwiński in *LCPW I.ii*, p. 141 and Zelcer, p. 177.
162. IH PAN, *ŻHP*, Straszewska, M., 'Mleko', p. 380; Bór-Komorowski, *The Secret Army*, p. 310.
163. *Komunikat Informacyjny*, nos. 8 and 9, 8 and 9.VIII.44 in *LCPW III*, pp. 55 and 61–3; *Czerniaków w Walce*, no. 6, 28.VIII.44; *Dziennik Obwieszczeń Rejonowego Delegata Rządu Warszawa Południe*, no. 1, 20.VIII.44; 'Zarządzenie sanitarne dla ludności', 9.VIII.44 in *LCPW I.ii*, pp. 65–6.
164. *Biuletyn Okręgu IV PPS*, no. 33, 5.IX.44.
165. AZHP, ADR 202/XX-18, k. 3, 14.VIII.44; *Dziennik Obwieszczeń Rejonowego Delegata Rządu Warszawa Południe*, no. 1, 20.VIII.44; 'Zarządzenie sanitarne dla ludności', 9.VIII.44 in *LCPW III*, pp. 65–6.
166. *Ibid.*, *LCPW III*; *Komunikat Informacyjny*, no. 8, 8.VIII.44 in *LCPW III*, p. 55.
167. *Czerniaków w Walce*, no. 6, 28.VIII.44; *Dziennik Obwieszczeń Rejonowego Delegata Rządu Warszawa Południe*, no. 1, 20.VIII.44.
168. 'Zarządzenie sanitarne dla ludności', 9.VIII.44 in *LCPW III*, pp. 65–6.
169. AZHP, ADR 202/XX-6, k. 41, 28.VIII.44; *Dziennik Obwieszczeń Rejonowego Delegata Rządu Warszawa Południe*, no. 1, 20.VIII.44.
170. *Ibid.*, no. 5, 27.VIII.44; AZHP, ADR 202/XX-11, k. 1–2 and 202/XX-24, k. 106 and 223, 20 and 30.VIII.44; GSHI, PRM.L.5, Despatch from Poland, Ldz.4972/44, 29.VIII.44; 'Bezpiecznik nr 30', 21.IX.44.
171. 'Sprawozdanie wewnętrzne dla "Koryckiego" terenowej komórki BIP KG AK', 22.VIII.44 in *LCPW II*, pp. 155–6.
172. AZHP, ADR 202/XX-20, k. 1–2, 16.VIII.44 and ADR 202/XX-22, k. 1–7, 9.VIII.44.
173. IZ, Dok.V.22, 'Protokóły i materiały do pracy pt. "Życie w powstańczej Warszawie"'.
174. Report of H. Bielska-Poręda in *LCPW I.ii*, pp. 207–9 and J. Zachwatowicz, p. 442.
175. 'Wykaz artystów występujących w imprezach dla jednostek wojskowych AK', 22.VIII.44 in *LCPW II*, pp. 157–9; *Robotnik*, no. 26, 13.VIII.44.
176. *Robotnik*, no. 19, 13.VIII.44; *Baszta*, no. 3, 15.VIII.44.
177. *Komunikat Informacyjny*, no. 14, 20.VIII.44.
178. *Rzeczpospolita*, no. 27, 16.VIII.44.
179. *Barykada*, no. 18, 3.IX.44. For a lengthy description of a concert see Radzymińska, J., 'Koncert' in *Milion Walecznych*, Warsaw, 1971, pp. 240–4.

180. Sala in *LCPW I.ii*, p. 85.
181. *Serwis Krajowy*, no. 13, 15.VIII.44; Zachwatowicz in *LCPW I.ii*, p. 447.
182. Anonymous, 'Przyczynek do Historii Wojskowych Sądów Specjalnych', Warsaw, 1974, pp. 89ff and p. 101. See also p. 62.
183. *Ibid.*; the districts were Śródmieście, the Old Town, Żoliborz and Mokotów.
184. Sieroszewski, W., 'Służba sprawiedliwości w powstaniu warszawskim' *Prawo i Życie*, no. 7, 1956, p. 5.
185. 'Przyczynek do Historii WSS', p. 99.
186. Sieroszewski, "Służba sprawiedliwości w powstaniu warszawskim', p. 5.
187. Verbal information.
188. Podlewski, *Rapsodia Żoliborska*, p. 64.
189. 'Przyczynek do Historii WSS', p. 99.
190. Sieroszewski, 'Służba sprawiedliwości w powstaniu warszawskim', p. 5.
191. 'Przyczynek do Historii WSS', p. 99.
192. *Dziennik Obwieszczeń Rejonowego Delegata Rządu Warszawa Południe*, no. 2, 21.VIII.44.
193. 'Przyczynek do Historii WSS', p. 102.
194. *Ibid.*, p. 104.
195. Verbal information.
196. *Komunikat Informacyjny*, no. 2, 8.VIII.44; *Biuletyn Informacyjny*, nos. 261 and 277, 16.VIII and 1.IX.44; (AWIH, III/42/39 k. 9); 'Przyczynek do Historii WSS', pp. 105–6. SA and SD were Nazi security organisations.
197. *LCPW II*, pp. 64–5.

4.3 The press during the Warsaw Uprising

1. *LCPW III*, p. 13. For a full catalogue of newspapers printed during the Uprising see Bartoszewski, 'Prasa powstania warszawskiego', pp. 329–79.
2. Out of the 134 papers listed in Bartoszewski, 'Prasa powstania warszawskiego', about 39% were published by the AK or Delegatura Rządu, 13.5% by parties in the PKWN, 25% by other parties and 22% privately.
3. *LCPW III*, p. 13.
4. AZHP, ADR 202/XX-5, k. 2–4, 22.VIII.44 and ADR 202/XX-20, k. 9, 19.VIII.44; IZ, Dok.V.223, 'Protokóły i materiały do pracy pt. "Życie w powstańczej Warszawie"', protocol no. 19.
5. *LCPW III*, p. 13; cf. Bartoszewski, 'Prasa powstania warszawskiego', p. 318.
6. See p. 104.
7. See p. 102.
8. Bartoszewski, 'Prasa powstania warszawskiego', p. 304.

9. *LCPW III*, p. 10.
10. Bartoszewski, W., 'Prasa powstańczej Warszawy', *TP*, no. 34, 1961, p. 5.
11. Bartoszewski, W., 'Prasa powstańcza', *TP*, no. 30, 1957, p. 6; Dunin-Wąsowiczowa, J., '"Nowiny Żoliborskie" podczas powstania warszawskiego', *Rocz. Hist. Czas.*, no. 8, 1969, p. 272, and 'Ludność cywilna i prasa powstańczego Żoliborza', p. 266.
12. Bartoszewski, 'Prasa powstańczej Warszawy', p. 5.
13. *Ibid.* and author's own impressions.
14. *Ibid.*; Bartoszewski, 'Prasa powstania warszawskiego', pp. 324–5.
15. *LCPW III*, p. 7; Kitzner, R., '"Błyskawica" w akcji', *Radioamat*, no. 7, 1967, pp. 176–7. Struś, E., 'Życie kulturalne w czasie powstania warszawskiego', *Chrześcijanin w Świecie*, no. 93, 1980, pp. 32–3.
16. Ossol., 5/65, Skierski, Z., 'Polskie Radio w czasie powstania warszawskiego', p. 40; *Rzeczpospolita*, no. 37, 26.VIII.44; Ziółek, Z., 'Powstańcze radio', *Kalendarz Katolicki*, 1970, pp. 121–9.
17. *LCPW III*, p. 7.
18. *Głos Starego Miasta*, no. 6. 17.VIII.44.
19. AZHP, ADR 203/VII-24, k. 58 and 69, 24.VIII.44.
20. *Ibid.*
21. *Ibid.*; 'Meldunek BIP Obwód I, Odc. II, Patrol Wojsk. Służ. Info. Społ', 31.VIII.44; 'Meldunek BIP Rej. III, Patrol I', 31.VIII.44; 'Meldunek BIP Rej. III, Obwód 2', 31.VIII.44; 'Meldunek BIP Rej. III, Patrol nr 2', 4.IX.44; 'Meldunek BIP Obwód I, Odc. II, Patrol Wojsk. Służ. Info. Społ.', 4.IX.44; 'Meldunek BIP Obwód I, Odc. II', 5.IX.44.
22. BN, Chomicki, '63 dni w płonącej Warszawie', p. 7; 'Wewnętrzny meldunek sytuacyjny placówki informacyjno-radiowej BIP KG AK', 10.VIII.44 in *LCPW II*, pp. 95–7.
23. 'Meldunek BIP Rej. III, Patrol 1', 31.VIII.44; 'Meldunek BIP Patrol Wojsk. Służ. Info. Społ. na Rej. II i III', 1.IX.44; Serwański, *Życie w powstańczej Warszawie*, p. 271.
24. 'Meldunek BIP Rej. III, Patrol IV', 31.VIII.44; 'Meldunek BIP Rej. II', 31.VIII.44; 'Meldunek BIP Rej. III, Patrol nr 4', 4.IX.44; 'Meldunek BIP Rej. III, Patrol I', 12.IX.44.
25. BN, Chomicki, '63 dni', p. 9.
26. 'Meldunek BIP Rej. III, Patrol IV', 31.VIII.44; AZHP, ADR 202/XX-24, k. 25, 14.VIII.44.
27. Bartoszewski in *LCPW I.ii*, pp. 356–7.
28. 'Raport z patrolu', 7.VIII.44 (AWIH III/42/24 k. 60).
29. Bartoszewski, 'Prasa powstania warszawskiego', p. 338.
30. See pp. 190–1.
31. See pp. 102–4.
32. *Biuletyn Informacyjny*, no. 242, 2.VIII.44.
33. *Armia Ludowa* (Old Town), no. 15, 15.VIII.44.
34. *Robotnik*, no. 17, 7.VIII.44.
35. *Biuletyn Informacyjny*, no. 255, 10.VIII.44.

36. *Ibid.*, no. 257, 12.VIII.44.
37. *Ibid.*, nos. 288–302, 22–6.IX.44.
38. *Barykada Wolności*, no. 152, 25.IX.44.
39. *Ibid.*, no. 149, 22.IX.44.
40. *Biuletyn CKL*, no. 3, 25.VIII.44.
41. *Głos Warszawy*, no. 177, 26.IX.44.
42. Dunin-Wąsowicz, 'Ludność cywilna i prasa powstańczego Żoliborza' in *Warszawa lat wojny i okupacji*, vol. II, p. 276.
43. *Ibid.*
44. Rosner, 'Wspomnienie Redaktora "Warszawianki"' in *Warszawa lat wojny i okupacji*, vol. II, pp. 295 and 298.
45. AZHP, ADR 202/-24, k. 59, 60 and 109, 24, 25 and 26.VIII.44; 'Bezpiecznik nr 32', 23.IX.44.
46. 'Powstanie w świetle meldunków BIP', report no. 19, 4.VIII.44.
47. Misiewicz, 'Zapiski z dni powstania warszawskiego', p. 149.
48. 'Wewnętrzny meldunek sytuacyjny placówki informacyjno-radiowej BIP KG AK', 25.VIII.44 in *LCPW II*, pp. 178–9.
49. 'Meldunek wewnętrzny (nr 3)', 12.VIII.44 and 'Wewnętrzny meldunek sytuacyjny placówki informacyjno-radiowej BIP KG AK', 30.VIII.44 in *LCPW II*, pp. 103–5 and 210–11.
50. AZHP, ADR 202/XX-11, k. 25, 29.IX.44.
51. *Ibid.*, 202/XX-20, k. 12–13, 21.VIII.44.
52. 'Sprawozdanie sytuacyjne nr 7', 26.IX.44.
53. Dąbrowska in *LCPW I.i*, p. 378.
54. Polak, *63 dni powstania warszawskiego*, p. 51.
55. Krawczyńska, *Zapiski Dziennikarki Warszawskiej*, p. 186.
56. BN, Anonymous, 'Powstanie polskie', p. 35.
57. Cf. p. 112.

4.4 Religion

1. BN, Rafałowski, 'Szlakiem "Zośki"', p. 20.
2. Bartoszewski, W., 'Życie religijne powstania warszawskiego', *TP*, no. 36, 1957, p. 10.
3. *W Walce*, no. 3, 4.VIII.44.
4. Dunin-Wąsowicz, 'Ludność cywilna i prasa powstańczego Żoliborza' in *Warszawa lat wojny i okupacji*, vol. II, p. 261.
5. BN, Chomicki, '63 dni', p. 23; Serwański, *Życie w powstańczej Warszawie*, pp. 289, 295, 296ff.
6. AZHP, ADR 202/XX-20, k. 15, 24.VIII.44.
7. *Biuletyn Informacyjny*, no. 263, 18.VIII.44.
8. AZHP, ADR 202/XX-24, k. 20, 13.VIII.44; BN, Anonymous, 'Powstanie polskie', p. 14 and Chomicki, '63 dni', p. 16; IH PAN, Masz. III, 1944, 'Pamiętnik Hanki – fragmenty', 6.VIII.44; Dąbrowska in *LCPW I.i*, p. 379; Białoszewski, M., *Pamiętniki z Powstania Warszawskiego*, 2nd edn, Warsaw, 1971, p. 34; Ostrowska, *W Alejach spacerują 'Tygrysy'*, p. 116;

Słomczyński, *W warszawskim Arsenale*, pp. 266–7.

9. IH PAN, A 67/59, Domosławski, B., 'Przeżycia cywila w Powstaniu Warszawskim', p. 67.
10. IZ, Dok.V.220, 'Protokóły i materiały do pracy pt. "Życie w powstańczej Warszawie"'.
11. *Biuletyn Informacyjny*, nos. 255 and 280, 10.VIII and 4.IX.44; Zgrychowa in *LCPW I.i*, p. 516.
12. IH PAN, 228, Grajewska, M., 'Fragmenty przeżyć i myśli z Powstania'.
13. 'Wewnętrzny meldunek sytuacyjny placówki informacyjno-radiowej BIP KG AK', 30.VIII.44 in *LCPW II*, pp. 210–11.
14. Bień in *LCPW I.i*, p. 58.
15. Zgrychowa in *LCPW I.i*, p. 516; Serwański, *Życie w powstańczej Warszawie*, pp. 295–6.
16. Prorok, L., 'Plac Napoleona', *Życie Warszawy*, no. 186, 1973, p. 7; Rudziński, *Dziennik z powstania warszawskiego*, p. 18.
17. Report of J. Wadecka, p. 9.
18. BN, Kirkor-Kiedroniowa, 'Wspomnienia i notatki pisane w czasie powstania warszawskiego', p. 46.
19. IH PAN, *ZHP*, Cichotka-Chojnicka, D., 'Dziennik', vol. V, pp. 1181–284.
20. Bogusławska, *Ludzie walczącej Warszawy*, p. 120.
21. Białoszewski, *Pamiętniki z Powstania Warszawskiego*, p. 55.
22. IZ, Dok.V.220, 'Protokóły i materiały do pracy pt. "Życie w Powstańczej Warszawie"'; Kwiatkowski in *LCPW I.i*, pp. 414–16 and Parysz, pp. 427–9; See also p. 110.
23. 'Szare Urszulanki na Powiślu – Wspomnienie' in *LCPW I.i*, pp. 501–11. See pp. 125–6.
24. Ledóchowska in *LCPW I.ii*, pp. 55–9. See p. 183.
25. Podlewski, *Rapsodia Żoliborska*, pp. 86–8.
26. Report of M. Chorembalska in *LCPW I.ii*, pp. 381–3.

Conclusion

1. See pp. 63–7.
2. See Stypułkowski, Z., *Invitation to Moscow*, New York, 1962.
3. Mikołajczyk, S., *The Rape of Poland; The Pattern of Soviet Domination*, New York, 1948, pp. 221–2.
4. Dziewanowski, M., *The Communist Party of Poland*, Cambridge, Mass., 1959, pp. 279–80.
5. *Time*, 8 November 1976, p. 69.

Bibliography

Primary sources

Unpublished documents and personal accounts.

Archiwum Akt Nowych, Warsaw (AAN)

Records of Rada Główna Opiekuńcza

Archiwum Państwowe m. st. Warszawy i woj. warszawskiego (AMW)

The following sources were used:

Records from 'Szef Dystryktu' File no. 5
Broniewski, S., 'Całym Życiem'
Dąbrowa-Sierzputowski, J., 'Wspomnienia wojenne Warszawa 1939–1944'

Archives of the Polish Underground Movement Study Trust, London (APUST)

Records of the following were used:

The Commander in Chief's Office
The Ministry of Internal Affairs
Other personal accounts, brochures and pamphlets

Archiwum Komitetu Centralnego PZPR, Warsaw (AZHP)

Records of the following were used:

Files of the Delegatura Rządu from the period of the Uprising
Underground and insurgent newspapers
Krahelska, H., 'Pamiętniki z okresu okupacji'

Biblioteka Narodowa, Dział Rękopisów, Warsaw (BN)

The following personal memoirs and diaries were used:

Anonymous, 'Powstanie polskie z sierpnia 1944r. widziane z odcinka
    Mokotów w Warszawie'

Chomicki, A., '63 dni w płonącej Warszawie – Zapiski z powstania'
Dobiecki, Z., 'Pamiętnik z 1944r.'
Kirkor-Kiedroniowa, Zofia z Grabskich, 'Wspomnienia i notatki pisane w czasie powstania warszawskiego'
Kulczycki, 'Zapiski z powstania warszawskiego'
'Pieśni i poezje z okresu powstania warszawskiego'
Podhorska-Okołów, S., 'Notatki z powstania warszawskiego 1944r.'
Rafałowski, J., 'Szlakiem "Zośki"'. 1945
Rewska, H., 'Pamiętnik z Powstania Warszawskiego, 1944'
Rzepecka, W., 'Droga krzyżowa'
Sarnecki, T., 'Heroiczna Warszawa – memoire o powstaniu'
'Sonety i opowieści powstańcze'
'Urywek ze wspomnień – humoreska z Woli'
Więckowska, H., 'Łączność z tamtą stroną Wisły nawiązana'
Wyszyński, F., 'Dziennik 1.XII.1941–28.II.1944'

The Archives of the General Sikorski Historical Institute, London (GSHI)

Records of the following were used:

The Prime Minister's Office
The Polish High Command – the Commander-in-Chief, the General Chief and the Ministry of National Defence
The Ministry of Foreign Affairs
The Ministry of Internal Affairs
The collected documents of Gen. W. Anders

Archiwum Polskiej Akademii Nauk, Warsaw (PAN)

The following memoirs were used:

Srokowski, S., 'Zapiski, wrzesień 1939–sierpień 1944
Dzwonkowski, W. 'Pamiętnik: Okres Powstania Warszawskiego 1944'

Instytut Historii PAN, Warsaw (IH PAN)

The following sources were used:

Raporty Fischera
ZHP. Organizacja Harcerek. Warszawska Chorągiew Harcerek 1939–1945. Dokumenty, relacje, wspomnienia, compiled by Z. Zawadzka
Other memoirs

Instytut Zachodni, Poznań (IZ)

'Iskra Dog' documents consulted

Biblioteka Zakładu Naukowego im. Ossolińskich, Wrocław (Ossol.)

The following memoirs were used:

Bobrzyńska, M. z Paygertów, 'Życie zmiennym jest: Pamiętnik z lat 1900–1958'
Gawiecki, B., 'Wspomnienia'
Gracki, W., 'Powstanie Warszawskie'
Kornecki, H., 'Wrzesień 1939 w Warszawie, okupacja w Warszawie, Powstanie Warszawskie'
Krobicka-Modzelewska, L., 'Wrzesień 1939, Pawiak, Powstanie Warszawskie'
Lasocka, J., 'Powstanie Warszawskie'
Młynarski, F., 'Za kulisami wielkich wydarzeń'
Rodziewiczówna, M., 'Ostatni Kalendarzyk'
Skierski, Z., 'Polskie Radio w czasie powstania warszawskiego'. 1961
Tyrankiewiczowa, H., 'W rękach hitlerowców: wspomnienia obozowe'. 1947
Wilczyński, S., 'Wspomnienia'

Printed documentary sources

Armia Krajowa w Dokumentach 1939–1945, vols. I, II, III and IV, London, 1970, 1973, 1975, 1977
Bach, E. von dem, 'Relacja von dem Bacha o Powstaniu Warszawskim', ed. S. Płoski, *NDP II Wojny*, no. 1, 1947
Ciechanowski, J., 'Pierwsza relacja Gen. Bora-Komorowskiego o AK i Powstaniu Warszawskim', *ZH*, no. 49, 1979
Conditions in Occupied Territories. A series of reports issued by the Inter-Allied Information Committee, 1942
Cywilna obrona Warszawy we wrześniu 1939, Warsaw, 1964
Documenta Occupationis Teutonicae, vol. II, *Zbrodnia niemiecka w Warszawie 1944*, ed. E. Serwański and I. Trawińska, Poznań, 1946
Documents on Polish–Soviet Relations 1939–1945, vols. I–II, London, 1961–9
'Dokumenty do kapitulacji powstania warszawskiego', ed. S. Płoski, *NDP II Wojny*, no. 4, 1960
'Dziennik działań Niemieckiej 9 Armii', ed. J. Matecki, *ZH*, no. 15, 1969
Dziennik Hansa Franka, ed. S. Piotrowski, Warsaw, 1970
Fischer, A., 'Grundsätzliche Bemerkungen über die Gestattung Warschau während des Krieges und nach dem Kriege', *Rocz. Warsz.*, 1960
Gollert, F., 'Powstanie Warszawskie 1944', *ZH*, no. 43, 1978
Jędrzejewicz, W., *Poland in the British Parliament 1939–1945*, vols. I and II, 1946 and 1959
Ludność Cywilna w Powstaniu Warszawskim, vols. I–III, Warsaw, 1974
'Meldunki sytuacyjne "Montera" z powstania warszawskiego', ed. J. Kirchmayer, *NDP II Wojny*, no. 3, 1959
'Nastroje w powstaniu, Dokumenty 1944', ed. J. Białek, *Polityka*, no. 40, 1964
'Nastroje w powstaniu warszawskim', ed. M. Turlejska, *Polityka*, no. 42, 1958
'Niemieckie materiały do historii powstania warszawskiego', ed. S. Płoski,

NDP II Wojny, no. 1, 1957

Polonsky, A., *The Great Powers and the Polish Question 1941–1945*, London, 1976

'Pomoc Anglosasów dla Powstania Warszawskiego', ed. S. Zabiełło, *NDP II Wojny*, no. 8, 1964

'Powstanie warszawskie w świetle meldunków BIP', ed. A. Przygoński, *Gazeta Krakowska*, nos. 187 and 190, 1957

Serwański, E., *Życie w powstańczej Warszawie*, Warsaw, 1965

Zbrodnie okupanta hitlerowskiego na ludności cywilnej w czasie powstania warszawskiego w 1944r, GKBZH, ed. S. Datner and K. Leszczyński, Warsaw, 1962

Zburzenie Warszawy, Zeznania generałów niemieckich przed polskim prokuratorem członkiem polskiej delegacji przy międzynarodowym trybunale wojennym w Norymberdze, Warsaw, 1946.

Newspapers

All published in Warsaw.

Underground newspapers

Armia Ludowa, Biuletyn Informacyjny, Dzień Warszawy, Głos Warszawy, Przez Walkę do Zwycięstwa, Robotnik, Rzeczpospolita Polska

Insurgent newspapers

Armia Ludowa (Old Town), *Armia Ludowa* (Śródmieście South), *Armia Ludowa* (Śródmieście North), *Barykada* (Śródmieście South), *Barykada Powiśla* (Powiśle), *Barykada – Warszawa Walczy* (Śródmieście South), *Barykada Wolności* (Śródmieście), *Baszta* (Mokotów), *Bądź Gotów* (Śródmieście), *Biuletyn Centralnego Komitetu Ludowego* (Śródmieście), *Biuletyn Informacyjny* (Śródmieście), *Biuletyn Okręgu IV PPS i OW PPS Warszawa Północ* (Żoliborz), *Biuletyn Podokręgu nr 2 Armii Ludowej* (Żoliborz), *Biuletyn Radiowy* (Śródmieście North), *Czerniaków w Walce* (Czerniaków), *Demokrata* (Śródmieście), *Dziennik Obwieszczeń Rejonowego Delegata Rządu Warszawa Południe* (Śródmieście South), *Dziennik Radiowy AK XXII Obwodu* (Żoliborz), *Dziennik Ustaw Rzeczypospolitej Polskiej* (Śródmieście), *Dzień Warszawy* (Śródmieście North), *Dzień Warszawy* (Śródmieście South), *Głos Demokracji* (Śródmieście South), *Głos Warszawy* (Old Town), *Głos Warszawy* (Śródmieście North), *Głos Warszawy* (Śródmieście South), *Granat* (Mokotów), *Iskra* (Śródmieście), *KB Ład* (Śródmieście North), *Kobieta na Barykadach* (Śródmieście North), *Komunikat Informacyjny* (Powiśle), *Komunikat Informacyjny* (Mokotów), *Komunikat Informacyjny Zgrupowania III Warszawa – Powiśle* (Powiśle), *Kronika Polska* (Old Town), *Kurier Mokotowski* (Mokotów), *Kurier Stołeczny* (Old Town), *Kurier Stołeczny* (Śródmieście South), *Naród Walczy* (Śródmieście), *Nowiny Żoliborskie* (Żoliborz), *Nowy Świat* (Śródmieście North), *Polska Agencja*

Telegraficzna (Śródmieście), *Polska Ilustrowana* (Śródmieście North), *Powstaniec* (Old Town), *Prawda* (Śródmieście North), *Przegląd Prasy* (Śródmieście North), *Rejonówka* (Śródmieście North), *Robotnik* (Śródmieście), *Robotnik* (Śródmieście South), *Robotnik Mokotowski* (Mokotów), *Rzeczpospolita Polska* (Śródmieście), *Serwis dla Prasy* (Śródmieście), *Serwis dla Radia* (Śródmieście), *Sprawa* (Old Town and Śródmieście South), *Syndykalista* (Śródmieście), *Szaniec* (Śródmieście), *Tygodnik Katolicki* (Sródmieście South), *W Walce* (Old Town), *Walka* (Śródmieście) *Walka – Warszawski Głos Narodowy* (Śródmieście South), *Walka o Wolność* (Śródmieście South), *Warszawa Walczy* (Śródmieście North), *Warszawa Walczy* (Wola), *Warszawianka* (Old Town), *Wiadomości z Miasta i Wiadomości Radiowe* (Śródmieście South), *Wiadomości Radiowe* (*PPS–WRN*) (Śródmieście North), *Wiadomości Radiowe* (Śródmieście), *Wiadomości Radiowe* (Delegatura III Rejonu) (Śródmieście North), *Wiadomości Radiowe* (Żoliborz), *Wiadomości z Radia, Prasy i Ulic Warszawy Walczącej* (?), *Wojsko Polskie* (Śródmieście North), *Z Pierwszej Linii Frontu* (Śródmieście North), *Żywią i Bronią* (Żoliborz).

Memoirs

Adamski, J., 'Stary notatnik Akowca', *Prze. Kul.*, no. 31, 1956

Akcja 'N': Wspomnienia 1941–1944, Warsaw, 1972

Balicka-Kozłowska, H., 'Powstańcze szpitale', *Walka Młodych*, no. 36, 1968
'Była "Moja Ulica"', *Życie Lit.*, no. 31, 1969

Białoszewski, M., *Pamiętniki z Powstania Warszawskiego*, 2nd edn, Warsaw, 1971

Blätter, F., *Warschau 1942: Tatsachenbericht eines Motorfahres der zweiten schweizerischen Ärtzenmission 1942 in Polen*, Zurich, 1945

Bogdanowicz, W., 'Powstanie oczami 8-letniego chłopca', *Stolica*, no. 32, 1968

Bogusławska, A., *Ludzie walczącej Warszawy*, West Germany, 1947
Food for the Children, London, 1975

Bokszczanin, W., 'W oczach dziecka', *Polityka*, no. 31, 1972

Borg, G., 'Działo się w Warszawie', *Wiadomości*, no. 44, 1950

Born, R., 'W zgrupowaniu "Chrobry II"', *TP*, no. 31, 1968.

Borowy, W., *Okres powstania 1944r w Bibliotece Uniwersyteckiej w Warszawie*, Warsaw, 1965

Borzykowski, T., *Between Tumbling Walls*, Tel Aviv, 1972

Bożena, K., 'Ostatnia noc Starego Miasta', *Tyg. Warsz.*, no. 34, 1948

Bór-Komorowski, T., *The Secret Army*, London, 1950

Brzozowska, H., 'Trzy msze', *Tyg. Warsz.*, no. 32, 1947

Bukowski, S., 'Apteki południowego Śródmieścia Warszawy w czasie powstania 1944', *Arch. Hist. Med.*, no. 4, 1964

Bykowski, L., 'Polskie powstanie w Warszawie', *ZH*, no. 5, 1964

Chocimski, J., 'Szpital Maltański w dniach powstania', *WTK*, no. 50, 1969

Chruściel, A., *Powstanie Warszawskie*, London, 1948

Churchill, W., *The Second World War*, vols. I–VI, London, 1948–54
Chybczyńska-Lewandowska, J., 'Nie tylko drzewo było świadkiem', *Stolica*, nos. 46–7, 1961
Chyczewski, A., 'Samotna walka Ochoty', *TP*, no. 34, 1964
Chyczewski, J., 'Godzina "W" na Ochocie', *TP*, no. 33, 1964
Ciechanowski, J., *Defeat in Victory*, London, 1948
Czajkowski-Dębczyński, Z., *Dziennik Powstańca*, Kraków, 1969
Czapska, M., 'Kartki z pamiętnika', *Orzeł Biały*, no. 37, 1946
Czugajewski, R., *Na barykadach, w kanałach i gruzach Czerniakowa*, Warsaw, 1970
Diok, 'Ulica Bielańska', *Tyg.warsz.*, no. 35, 1947
Dobraczyński, J., 'Ze wspomnień kapelana', *WTK*, no. 37, 1966
'Pierwsze dni', *WTK*, no. 32, 1962
Tylko w jednym życiu, Warsaw, 1970
Drescher, E., 'Szpital powstańczy przy ulicy Poznańskiej 11 w Warszawie w 1944', *Wojsk. Prz. Hist.*, no. 2, 1967
Drescher, K., 'Komisja lekarska obozu przejściowego w Pruszkowie w czasie powstania warszawskiego', *Arch. Hist. Med.*, no. 2, 1968
Dunin-Wąsowiczowa, J., '"Nowiny Żoliborskie" podczas powstania warszawskiego', *Rocz. Hist. Czas.*, no. 8, 1969
'Dziennik Iwana Waszenko', *Dzieje Najnowsze*, 1947
Fajer, L., *Żołnierze Starówki*, Warsaw, 1957
Ficowski, J., 'Katolicyzm powstańców', *TP*, no. 26, 1947
Filipowicz, J., *Miałem wtedy 14 lat*, Warsaw, 1972
Fiszgrund, S., 'Nasz udział w powstaniu warszawskim', *Biuletyn Bundu*, no. 3, 1945
Florczak, Z., 'O dozorcy domu Józefie Decu', *TP*, no. 31, 1973
Gawrońska, J., 'Droga przez mękę', *Stolica*, no. 38, 1969
Gieysztor, M., 'Dziennik z powstania warszawskiego', *Polityka*, no. 30, 1967
Ginter, M., *Life in Both Hands*, London, 1969
Gizella, Z., *Niemiecki Nalot*, Poznań, 1946
Gosieniecki, W., *Warszawa: sierpień–wrzesień 1944*, Poznań, 1945
Gotesman, S., 'Nasz udział w powstaniu warszawskim', *Ichud*, no. 3, 1946
Grunwald, H., 'Świerszcz na kościele Kapucynów', *Prze. Kul.*, no. 33–4, 1959
Guderian, H., *Erinnerungen eines Soldaten*, Heidelberg, 1951. English translation: *Panzer Leader*, London, 1952
Harcerki 1939–1945, Warsaw, 1973
Herbst, S., 'Z przeżyć na Mokotowie', *TP*, no. 31, 1973
Hirszfeld, L., *Historia jednego Życia*, Warsaw, 1969
Hoppe, J., *Wspomnienia, przyczynki, refleksje*, London, 1972
J.P., 'W szpitalu u Sióstr Zmartwychwstania', *Tyg. Warsz.*, no. 39, 1947
'Jak to było na kompletach', *TP*, no. 12, 1945
Janiec, J.K., 'Ksiądz żołnierz', *TP*, no. 5, 1957
Jankowski, S., 'Pomidory na Żoliborzu', *Świat*, no. 32, 1957
'W kanałach', *Świat*, no. 30, 1957

Kalisz, M., Kalkowski, J., '63 dni powstania – diariusz i fragmenty dokumentów', *Przekrój*, no. 1529, 1974
Kalski, J., 'Z czasów walki', *TP*, no. 33, 1945
Kann, M., *Niebo nieznane*, Warsaw, 1968
Karski, J., *Story of a Secret State*, London, 1945
Kitzner, R., ' "Błyskawica" w akcji', *Radioamat*, no. 7, 1967
Klimaszewski, T., *Verbrennungskommando Warschau*, Warsaw, 1960
Kliszko, Z., *Powstanie Warszawskie*, Warsaw, 1967
Koliński, K., 'Niezwykły dziennik na powstańczym Żoliborzu', *Stolica*, no. 32, 1969
Komornicki, S., *Na barykadach Warszawy*, Warsaw, 1972
Kopański, S., *Wspomnienia 1939–1945*, London, 1962
Korboński, S., *Fighting Warsaw*, London, 1956
Kotowicz, J., 'Twierdza Mokotowa', *TP*, no. 31, 1947
Kozłowska, H., *Mur miał dwie strony*, Warsaw, 1958
Kozłowski, S. Lis, 'Fragmenty wspomnień spod okupacji i z powstania', *Kurier Polski* (Buenos Aires), nos. 36–9, 45, 1969
Krawczyńska, J., *Zapiski Dziennikarki Warszawskiej 1939–1947*, Warsaw, 1971
Krzyczkowski, H., 'Obóz przejściowy "Dulag 121" Pruszków', *TP*, no. 31, 1972
Krzyczkowski, J., *Konspiracja i powstanie w Kampinosie*, Warsaw, 1961
Kulski, J., *Zarząd Miejski Warszawy 1939–1944*, Warsaw, 1964
Kummant, S., 'Przed niemieckimi czołgami', *Stolica*, no. 34, 1957
Kumor, E., *Wycinek z historii jednego życia*, Warsaw, 1967
Landau, L., *Kronika lat wojny i okupacji*, vols. I–III, Warsaw, 1962–3.
Laryssa, W., *Wspomnienie i uwagi uczestnika powstania warszawskiego*, London, 1947
Lasocka, J., 'Zagłada biblioteki', *Stolica*, no. 29, 1967
Leszczyński, H., 'Barykady i ołtarze', *Krol Apóst.*, no. 8, 1948
Lis, W., 'W dniu wybuchu powstania', *Tyg. Warsz.*, no. 39, 1947
Lis-Błońska, J., 'Pierwsze dni na Starówce', *Nowa Epoka*, nos. 29–30, 1946
   'Blisko 4 miesiące pod ziemią', *Nowa Epoka*, no. 8, 1946
Lorentz, S., 'Muzeum Narodowe podczas powstania warszawskiego', *Muzealnictwo*, no. 13, 1966
Łopalewski, T., *Obok Zagłady*, Warsaw, 1957
M., 'Przeżycia, ktorych nic nie zatrze', *Gaz. Lud.*, no. 192, 1946
(M.W.), 'Kartki z powstania warszawskiego', *Nasze Słowo*, no. 12, 1948
Majorkiewicz, F., 'Ostatnie dni Starówki', *TP*, no. 35, 1960
Malewska, H., 'Sierpień i wrzesień', *Twórczość*, no. 1, 1945
Małecki, J. Sęk, *Armia Ludowa w Powstaniu Warszawskim*, Warsaw, 1962
Manteuffel, L., 'Rozstrzelany szpital', *Kultura*, no. 530, 1973
Mikołajczyk, S., *La viol de la Pologne*, Paris, 1948
Milion walecznych, Warsaw, 1971
Misiewicz, J., 'Zapiski z dni powstania warszawskiego w Szpitalu Wolskim', *Prze. Lek.*, no. 2/1, 1967

Mitkiewicz, L., 'Powstanie Warszawskie (z mojego notatnika w Waszyngtonie)' *ZH*, no. 1, 1962

W najwyższym sztabie zachodnich aliantów 1943–1945, London, 1971

Moczarski, K., 'Hallo "Ciotka" – tu mowi "Rafał", *Tyg. Dem.*, no. 30, 1958

Moczulski, L., 'Kościół Św. Wojciecha – miejsce martyrologii mieszkańców Warszawy', *Stolica*, no. 31, 1968

'800,000', *Stolica*, no. 3, 1968

Morawski, K., 'Po powstaniu', *TP*, no. 45, 1965

Morawski, T., 'Konkurs poetycki w czasie powstania warszawskiego', *Stolica*, no. 28, 1967

Mrożewski, S., 'Byłem rozstrzelany', *Stolica*, no. 32, 1969

My z głodujących miast, Warsaw, 1961

Nowak, J., *Kurier z Warszawy*, London, 1978

Nowakowski, W., 'Początek', *Stolica*, no. 31, 1966

Ochman, B., 'Szpital powstańczy na Chmielnej', *NDP II Wojny*, no. 7, 1963

Olbrycht, J., 'Przeżycia medyka sądowego w czasie okupacji hitlerowskiej oraz po wyzwoleniu w sprawach z nią związanych', *Prze. Lek.*, no. 1, 1968

Orkieszewski, E., 'Przy końcu pierwszego miesiąca', *Ziem. Pom.*, no. 246, 1946

Orska, I., *Silent is the Vistula*, London, 1946

Ostaszewski, J., *Powstanie Warszawskie*, Rome, 1945

Ostrowska, E., 'Upadek Mokotowa', *Stolica*, no. 6, 1969

W Alejach spacerują 'Tygrysy', sierpień–wrzesień 1944, Warsaw, 1973

Ozimek, S., 'Kamery na powstańczych barykadach', *Kino*, no. 5, 1969

Stare Miasto, Warsaw, 1971

Pamiętniki lekarzy, Warsaw, 1964

Pamiętniki robotników z czasów okupacji, Warsaw, 1948

Pamiętniki żołnierzy baonu 'Zośka', ed. T. Sumiński, Warsaw, 1957

Pawłowicz, H., 'Komisariat cywilny przy Dowództwie Obrony Warszawy we wrześniu 1939', *NDP II Wojny*, no. 5, 1961

Pawłowska-Wilde, B., 'Utracone dzieciństwo', *TP*, nos. 32 and 33, 1960

Pełczyński, W., 'Rozgłośnia walczącej Warszawy', *Tydzień Polski*, no. 292, 1964

Pluta-Czachowski, K., 'Godzina "W" na Woli', *Stolica*, no. 39, 1969

'Na posterunku dowodzenia KG', *Za i Przeciw*, no. 38, 1969

'W sztabie operacyjnym Komendy Głównej AK na Woli', *Za i Przeciw*, nos. 34, 35, 36, 37, 1968

'Z Woli na Starówkę', *Za i Przeciw*, no. 16, 1969

Polak, T., *63 dni powstania warszawskiego*, Warsaw, 1946

Prorok, L., 'Plac Napoleona', *Życie Warszawy*, no. 186, 1973

'Przed końcem', *Literatura*, no. 30, 1973

Przelaskowski, R., 'Warszawska Biblioteka Publiczna w okresie okupacji', *NDP II Wojny*, no. 5, 1960

Przybylska, W., *Cząstka mojego serca*, Warsaw, 1964

Pużak, K., 'Wspomnienia', *ZH*, no. 41, 1977

Rachymińska, J., *Dwa razy popiół*, Kraków, 1970
Raczyński, E., *In Allied London*, London, 1962
Ropelewski, *Wspomnienia z AK*, Warsaw, 1957
Roztworowski, T., 'Przygoda', *TP*, no. 41, 1948
Rozwadowska, H., *Wspomnienia ważne i nieważne*, Warsaw, 1966
Rudziński, A., *Dziennik z powstania warszawskiego*, London, 1974
Rusinek, M., *Z barykady w dolinę głodu*, Kraków, 1946
Rzepecki, J., *Wspomnienia i przyczynki historyczne*, Warsaw, 1956
'Sanitariuszki', *WTK*, no. 35, 1956
Sendlak, S., 'W powstaniu bez broni', *TP*, no. 37, 1964
Seweryńska, J., 'W opuszczonej piwnicy', *Mowią Wieki*, no. 8, 1958
Sieroszewski, W., 'Służba sprawiedliwości w powstaniu warszawskim', *Prawo i Życie*, no. 7, 1956
'Z działalności Wojskowego Sądu Specjalnego Okręgu a następnie Obszaru Warszawskiego (1940–1944)', *NDP II Wojny*, no. 8, 1964
Siostra, Maria, 'W szpitalu', *TP*, no. 39, 1958
Skibniewski, S., 'Robotnicy Powiśla w akcji bojowej powstania', *Stolica*, no. 31, 1960
Skwarnicki, M., 'Ulica niczyja', *TP*, no. 32, 1967
Słomczyński, A., *W Warszawskim Arsenale*, Warsaw, 1971
Smólski, W., *Zaklęte Lata*, Warsaw, 1966
Sroczyńska, K.Z., '"Zofia": przez ruiny i kanały', *Więź*, no. 10, 1974
Straszewska, M., 'Biuletyn Informacyjny 1939–1944', *NDP II Wojny*, no. 11, 1967
Stypułkowski, Z., *Invitation to Moscow*, New York, 1962
Szostak, J., 'Dziesięć dni przed powstaniem w Warszawie 1944', *Stolica*, no. 31, 1969
Szpilman, W., *Śmierć miasta*, Warsaw, 1946
Szukiewicz, H., 'Służba Zdrowia na Mokotowie podczas Powstania Warszawskiego', *Arch. Hist. Med.*, no. 2, 1970
Szymanowski, A., 'Długa 7', *Nowa Epoka*, nos. 27–8, 1946
Tarajkowicz, L., 'Kapelan ojciec Paweł', *Za i Przeciw*, no. 31, 1958
Troński, B., *Tędy przeszła śmierć*, Warsaw, 1970
Valcini, A., *Golgota Warszawy* (first published 1945), Warsaw, 1973
W.M., 'Czego nie powiedział Generał Reinefarth: Piekło Woli', *Stolica*, no. 31, 1973
Wacek, S., 'W Szpitalu Ujazdowskim podczas okupacji hitlerowskiej', *Prze. Lek.*, no. 1, 1970
Wańkowicz, Z., 'Kombatanki (Powstania Warszawskiego)', *Kultura*, nos. 10/84 and 10/86, 1954
Wasilewski, M., 'Katolicyzm powstania warszawskiego', *TP*, no. 31, 1947
Wasilewski, Z., 'Powstanie na Pradze', *TP*, no. 31, 1946
Waszenko, I., 'Dziennik Iwana Waszenko', *Dzieje Najnow.*, no. 1, 1947
Wilczur, J., 'Droga wojenna Madziarów', *WTK*, no. 7, 1967
Wnuk, W., 'W powstaniu z piórem w ręku', *Życie i Myśl*, no. 7/8, 1971
Wojas, P., 'Moje wspomnienia z powstania warszawskiego', *Z Pola Walki*,

no. 4, 1961
Wojewódzki, M., *W tajnych drukarniach Warszawy 1939–1944*, Warsaw, 1976
Woszczyk, A., *Baszta K3 walczy*, Łódz, 1973
Woźniewski, Z., *Pierwsze dni powstania warszawskiego w szpitalach na Woli*, Warsaw, 1947
Wspomnienia dziennikarzy z okresu okupacji hitlerowskiej, Warsaw, 1970
Zadrożny, S., *Tu Warszawa – Dzieje radiostacji powstańczej 'Błyskawica'*, London, 1964
Zagórski, W., *Seventy Days*, London, 1957
Wicher Wolności, London, 1972
Zambrzycki, W., *Kwatera bożych pomyleńców*, Warsaw, 1959
Zaremba, Z., *Wojna i konspiracja*, London, 1957
Zieman, J., *The Cigarette Sellers of Three Crosses Square*, London, 1971
Ziemba, S., 'Opowiadam o powstaniu', *Życie Literackie*, no. 32, 1972
'Z Powstania Warszawskiego do Krakowa', *Życie Literackie*, no. 41, 1972
(Ziołek, Z.,) Sawa Józef, 'Pierwsze 48 godzin walki', *Kalendarz Katolicki*, 1968
'Powstańcze radio', *Kalendarz Katolicki*, 1970
'Radiostacja "Błyskawica"', *Antena*, nos. 8, 9, 10, 1957
'Z piosenką na barykady', *Robotnik*, no. 210, 1946
Żdżarski, W., 'Służba filmowa i fotograficzna Armii Krajowej', *Życie i Myśl*, no. 7/8, 1966
Żuławski, B., *Powstanie Warszawskie*, Łódź, 1946
Żurowski, A., 'Powstanie na Pradze', *WTK*, no. 35, 1967

Books and special studies

Bartelski, L., *Powstanie Warszawskie*, Warsaw, 1967
Mokotów 1944, Warsaw, 1972
'Warszawa jako ośrodek ruchu oporu w kulturze', *Rocz. Warsz.*, no. 7, 1966
Bartoszewski, W., *The Warsaw Death Ring 1939–1945*, Warsaw, 1968
'Życie wśród barykad', *TP*, nos. 34, 38, 39, 1966
'"Anna" w służbie powstania', *TP*, no. 32, 1958
'Kryzys kapitulacyjny 8–11 września w świetle nieznanych dokumentów', *Stolica*, no. 39, 1956
'Prasa powstańczej Warszawy', *TP*, no. 34, 1961
'Prasa powstańcza', *TP*, no. 30, 1957
'Sierpień i wrzesień Warszawy 1944', *TP*, no. 30, 1957
'Zburzona barykada', *TP*, no. 40, 1965
'Życie religijne powstania warszawskiego', *TP*, no. 36, 1957
Prawda o von dem Bach, Poznań, 1961
Erich von dem Bach: War crimes in Poland, Warsaw, 1961
1859 dni Warszawy, Kraków, 1974
'Na ulicy Wspólnej. Z dokumentów życia ludności w czasie powstania warszawskiego', *Więź*, no. 10, 1974

Dayer, S., 'Służba Zdrowia w czasie powstania warszawskiego', PhD thesis, Warsaw, 1968
'Z historii warszawskich szpitali powstańczych', *Prze. Lek.*, no. 1, 1975
'Służba Zdrowia Obwodu Żoliborza w.powstaniu warszawskim', *Prze. Lek.*, no. 1, 1975
Białokosz, M., 'Z historii Służby Zdrowia Warszawy – Śródmieście w powstaniu warszawskim', *Prze. Lek.*, no. 1, 1970
Bieńkowski, W., *Powstanie Warszawskie. Geneza i tło*, Warsaw, 1945
Borkiewicz, A., *Powstanie Warszawskie 1944. Zarys działań natury wojskowej*, 3rd edn, Warsaw, 1969
'W sprawie buntu na Starym Mieście', *Kierunki*, no. 27, 1956
Borzykowski, T., 'Żydzi w powstaniu warszawskim', *Pol. Zbroj.*, no. 182, 1946
Braütigam, O., *Überblick über die besetzten Ostgebiete während des zweiten Weltkrieges*, Tübingen, 1954
Bregman, A., *Bój o Warszawę, 1 sierpnia – 2 października 1944*, 1945
Broniewski, S., 'O harcerskiej poczcie polowej', *TP*, no. 31, 1973
Broszat, M., *Die nationalsozialistische Polenpolitik*, Stuttgart, 1961
Bruce, M., *The Warsaw Uprising 1944*, London, 1972
Ciechanowski, J., *The Warsaw Rising of 1944*, Cambridge, 1974
'Notatki z rozmowy z płk. dypl. J. Bokszczaninem', *ZH*, no. 27, 1974
'Notatki z rozmowy z płk. dypl. J. Rzepeckim', *ZH*, no. 27, 1974
'Gdy ważyły się losy stolicy: Notatka z rozmowy z Gen. Tadeuszem Borem Komorowskim, odbytej w maju 1965 w Londynie w obecności Prof. J.K. Zawodny', *Wiadomości*, no. 39, 1971
Czajkowski, Z., and Taborski, B., 'O polskiej technice powstań', *Kultura*, no. 5/127, 1958
'Polska technika po raz drugi', *Kultura*, no. 1/2, 1960
Ostatnie dni: Wspomnienia o K.K. Baczyńskim, Krakow, 1967
Czapski, J., 'Powstanie Warszawskie, Homo Guigam i von Krannhals', *Kultura*, no. 204, 1964
Czarski, A., *Najmłodsi żolnierze walczącej Warszawy*, Warsaw, 1971
Dobroszycki, L., *Centralny Katalog Polskiej Prasy Konspiracyjnej 1939–1945*, Warsaw, 1962
'Studies of the underground press in Poland 1939–1945', *Acta Poloniae Historica*, no. 8, 1962
Dobrowolski, L., 'Służba Zdrowia w powstaniu warszawskim' in *Pamiętniki II Krajowego Zjazdu Lekarzy ZBOWiD*, Warsaw, 1949
Drescher, G., *Warsaw Rising*, New York, 1972
Drozdowski, M., *Alarm dla Warszawy. Obrona cywilna stolicy we wrześniu 1939*, Warsaw, 1964
'Struktura społeczno-zawodowa ludności Warszawy w latach 1918–1939', *NDP 1914–1939*, no. 5, 1962
Dunin-Wąsowicz, K., 'Władze hitlerowskie wobec powstania warszawskiego', *Prze. Hum.*, no. 1, 1975
Duraczyński, E., *Stosunki w kierownictwie podziemia londyńskiego 1939–1945*,

Warsaw, 1966
Wojna i okupacja wrzesień 1939 – kwiecień 1943, Warsaw, 1974
Kontrowersje i Konflikty 1939–1945, Warsaw, 1977
Dzieje Mokotowa, ed. J. Kazimierski, Warsaw, 1972
Dzieje Ochoty, ed. J. Kazimierski, Warsaw, 1973
Dzieje Śródmieścia, ed. J. Kazimierski, Warsaw, 1975
Dzieje Żoliborza, ed. J. Kazimierski, Warsaw, 1971
Dzieje Woli, ed. J. Kazimierski, Warsaw, 1974
Dziewanowski, M., *The Communist Party of Poland: An Outline of History*, Cambridge, Mass., 1959
Ehrman, J., *Grand Strategy*, vol. v, London, 1956
European Resistance Movements, vols. I and II, London, 1960 and 1964
Forbert, J., *O Powstaniu Warszawskim*, Lublin, 1944
Galast, S., 'Działalność społeczno charytatywna Ks. Władysława Łysika w latach 1939–1945', M.A. Thesis, Lublin, 1972
Garliński, J., 'Polskie państwo podziemne 1939–45', *ZH*, no. 29, 1974
Gawlin, J., 'Pius XII a Powstanie Warszawskie', *Kultura*, no. 87/8, 1955
German Crimes in Poland, Warsaw, 1946
Gołubiew, A., 'Myśli o powstaniu warszawskim', *TP*, no. 31, 1946
Gross, J., *Polish Society under German Occupation. The Generalgouvernement 1939–1944*, Princeton, 1979
Grumkowski, J., *Młodzież polska podczas okupacji*, Warsaw, 1966
Grünbaum, D., 'Żydzi w powstaniu warszawskim', *Opinia*, nos. 23–4, 1974
Gryżewski, T., *Harcerska poczta polowa powstania warszawskiego 1944*, Warsaw, 1966
Hochfeld, J., 'The Social Aspects of the 1944 Warsaw Uprising', *Journal of Central European Affairs*, no. 1, 1945
Iranek-Osmecki, K., 'Przyczynki do powstania warszawskiego', *Kultura*, 1953
'"Ptaszki", "Zrzutki"', *Kultura*, no. 1/27, 1950
'Problemy powstania warszawskiego', *Tydzień Polski*, 1960
'Kapitulacja Warszawy', *Kultura*, no. 12, 1948
'Postawa Warszawy', *Tydzień Polski*, no. 3, 1963
Jacobmeyer, W., *Heimat und Exil*, Hamburg, 1973
Jasinkowicz, M., 'Młodzi i najmłodsi w Powstaniu Warszawskim', *Wiadomości*, no. 1479, 1974
'Październik 1944', *Wiadomości*, no. 1492, 1974
Jasiński, Z., 'Pieśń o Powstaniu', *Kultura*, no. 1/2, 1955
Jastrzębowski, W., *Gospodarka niemiecka w Polsce*, Warsaw, 1946
Kaczyński, Z., 'Londyn wobec Powstania Warszawskiego', *Tyg. Warsz.*, no. 34, 1946
Kamiński, A., *Zośka i Parasol*, Warsaw, 1970
Kirchmayer, J., *Powstanie Warszawskie*, 4th edn, Warsaw, 1970
Klessmann, C., *Die Selbstbehaltung einer Nation: Kulturpolitik und polnische Widerstandbewegung*, Hamburg, 1972
Komisja Historyczna Polskiego Sztabu Głównego w Londynie, *Polskie Siły*

Zbrojne w Drugiej Wojnie Światowej: Armia Krajowa, vol. III, London, 1950

Konarski, S., 'Z dziejów tajnego szkolnictwa wyższego w Warszawie w latach okupacji', *Rocz. Warsz.*, no. 7, 1966

Korboński, A., 'The Warsaw Rising Revisited', *Survey*, no. 76, 1970

Korboński, S., 'Polskie państwo podziemne z lat 1939–45', *Orzeł Biały*, July/August 1969

   The Polish Underground State: A Guide to the Underground, 1939–1945, New York, 1978

Krannhals, H. von, *Der Warschauer Aufstand 1944*, Frankfurt am Main, 1964

Krasuski, J., *Tajne szkolnictwo polskie w okresie okupacji hitlerowskiej 1939–1945*, Warsaw, 1971

Kroll, B., *Opieka i Samopomoc społeczna w Warszawie 1939–1945*, Warsaw, 1977

Kuropieska, J., 'Gen. "Monter" – Chruściel a Powstanie Warszawskie', *Życie Lit.*, no. 31, 1974

Lewickij, B., 'Ukraińcy i likwidacja powstania warszawskiego', *Kultura*, nos. 6/56 and 7/87, 1952

Leslie, R.F., *The History of Poland since 1863*, Cambridge, 1980

Luczak, C., 'Aktion Warschau', *Polish Western Affairs*, no. 1, 1968

Lukas, R.C., *The Strange Allies. The United States and Poland 1941–1945*, Knoxville, 1978

M.S., 'Duchowieństwo w walce z okupantem', *Za i Przeciw*, no. 39, 1958

Machalski, T., 'Cztery aspekty powstania warszawskiego', *Horyzonty* (Paris), no. 119, 1966

Madajczyk, C., *Generalna Gubernia w planach hitlerowskich*, Warsaw, 1961

   Polityka III Rzeszy w okupowanej Polsce, vols. I and II, Warsaw, 1970

   'Miejsce Warszawy w walce z najeźdźcą i okupantem', *Rocz. Warsz.*, no. 7, 1966

Majorkiewicz, F., *Dane nam było przeżyć*, Warsaw, 1972

Malinowski, K., 'Organizacja łączności w powstaniu warszawskim 1944', *NDP II Wojny*, no. 7, 1963

Małcużyński, K., *Zanim zapłonęła Warszawa*, Warsaw, 1955

Manteuffel, E., 'Zapiski na temat pracy społecznej w Warszawie podczas okupacji i w latach poprzedzających II wojnę światową', *NDP II Wojny*, no. 8, 1964

Marczak-Oborski, S., *Teatr czasu wojny 1939–1945*, Warsaw, 1967

Mastny, V., *Russia's Road to the Cold War*, New York, 1979

Mazurkiewicz, J., 'Myśli i rozwiązania o Powstaniu Warszawskim', *TP*, nos. 6 and 7, 1957

Michalewski, J., 'Relacja Delegatury Rządu', *ZH*, no. 26, 1973

Nałęcz, W., 'Społeczne oblicze powstania', *Na Szlaku Kresowej*, no. 9/39, 1946

Orłowski, L., 'The Insurrection of Warsaw', *Journal of Central European Affairs*, no. 8, 1957

Ortynskyi, L., 'Prawda o ukraińskiej dywizji', *Kultura*, no. 11/61, 1952

Parcent, D., *La drame de Varsovie*, Paris, 1946

Pobóg-Malinowski, W., *Najnowsza historia polityczna Polski*, vol. III, London,

1960
'Poczta polowa', *WTK*, no. 34, 1964
Podlewski, S., *Przemarsz przez piekło*, Warsaw, 1971
  Rapsodia Żoliborska, Warsaw, 1957
  Wierni Bogu i Ojczyźnie, Warsaw, 1971
  'Próba bilansu strat powstania warszawskiego', *Dziś i Jutro*, no. 31, 1947
  'Książka w Powstaniu Warszawskim', *Za i Przeciw*, nos. 31 and 32, 1965
  'Klasztor S. Wizytek – reduta powstańcza Warszawy', *Za i Przeciw*, no. 32, 1973
Pomian, A., *Powstanie Warszawskie*, London, 1946
  Jozef Retinger: Memoirs of an eminence grise, Sussex, 1972
  Wiersze i pieśni Powstania Warszawskiego, Tonbridge, 1952
Poterański, W., 'Położenie i walka Warszawskiej Klasy Robotniczej w okresie okupacji hitlerowskiej', *Rocz. Warsz.*, no. 7, 1966
  'Powstanie 1944 – rozmowa z prof. dr. Stefanem Kieniewiczem', *Życie Warszawy*, no. 181, 1974
Przygoński, A., *Udział PPR i AL w Powstaniu Warszawskim*, Warsaw, 1970
  Z Problematyki Powstania Warszawskiego, Warsaw, 1970
  Powstanie Warszawskie w sierpniu 1944, Warsaw, 1980
Rosiak, J., 'Report on Massacre of Jesuit Priests', *Kronika*, nos. 32 and 33, 1966
Rybicki, L., 'Tragedia warszawskich szpitali', *WTK*, no. 13, 1976
Serwański, E., *Dulag 121 – Pruszków sierpień–październik 1944*, Poznań, 1946
Siemaszko, Z.S., 'Powstanie Warszawskie', *Wiadomości*, no. 3/4, 1970
  'Odbiór warszawskiej "Błyskawicy"', *Tydzień Polski*, no. 28, 1965
63 Days: The Story of the Warsaw Rising, Newton, Montgomeryshire, 1947
Skarżyński, A., *Polityczne przyczyny powstania warszawskiego*, 3rd edn, Warsaw, 1969
  Powstańcza Warszawa w dniach walki, Warsaw, 1965
Sobczak, K., 'Warszawa w planach niemieckich po stłumieniu Powstania', *NDP II Wojny*, no. 6, 1962
Sołowij, K., 'Powstanie Warszawskie i problemy odpowiedzialności', *Kultura*, 1951
Sroczyński, K., 'Szpitale warszawskie w okresie okupacji hitlerowskiej', *Prze. Lek.*, no. 1, 1976
Stawski, T., *Straty kulturalne Warszawy*, Warsaw, 1948
  'Wrześniowy kryzys powstania warszawskiego', *Kultura*, no. 9/35, 1950
Strzembosz, T., *Akcje zbrojne podziemnej Warszawy 1939–1944*, Warsaw, 1978
Strzetelski, S., *Bitwa o Warszawę, 1 sierpnia–2 października 1944*, New York, 1945
Struś, E., 'Życie kulturalne w czasie powstania warszawskiego', *Chrześcijanin w Świecie*, no. 93, 1980
Szarota, T., *Okupowanej Warszawy dzień powszedni*, 2nd edn, Warsaw, 1978
  'Okupacyjna Warszawa w oczach cudzoziemców', *Kronika Warszawy*, no. 1/3, 1973
  'Warszawa przed godziną "W"', *Życie Warszawy*, no. 185, 1973

Szukiewicz, H., 'Służba zdrowia na Mokotowie podczas powstania warszawskiego', *Arch. Hist. Med.*, no. 2, 1970
Terej, J., *Na rozstajach dróg*, Wrocław, 1978
Turlejska, M., 'Nieznane dokumenty o powstaniu warszawskim', *Polityka*, no. 37, 1974
Warszawa II Rzeczypospolitej, ed. M. Drozdowski, vol. 1, Warsaw, 1968
Warszawa lat wojny i okupacji 1939–1944, ed. K. Dunin-Wąsowicz, 4 vols., Warsaw, 1971–5
Warszawa – Wola, Zbrodnie Hitlerowskie w Powstaniu, Warsaw, 1968
Wojewódzki, M., 'Jak drukowaliśmy powstańcze znaczki pocztowe', *Stolica*, no. 30, 1969
A Worker's Day under German Occupation, London, 1941
Wroniszewski, J., *Ochota 1944*, Warsaw, 1970
Załuski, Z., *Czterdziesty czwarty, wydarzenia obserwacje refleksje*, Warsaw, 1969
Zawodny, J., 'Wywiad z Gen. Bór Komorowskim', *Kultura*, no. 11/229, 1966
Nothing but Honour. The Story of the Warsaw Uprising 1944, London, 1978
Zych, J., *Rosja wobec Powstania Warszawskiego*, London, 1947
Żarnowski, J., *Struktura społeczna inteligencji w Polsce w latach 1918–1939*, Warsaw, 1964

Index

Polish alphabetical order has been adhered to in this index, so that accented letters follow unaccented ones.